WHICH? WAY TO

FIX IT

WHICH? WAY TO FIX IT

MIKE LAWRENCE

CONSUMERS' ASSOCIATION

Which? Books are commissioned and researched by Consumers' Association and published by Which? Ltd, 2 Marylebone Road, London NW1 4DF
Email address: books@which.net

Distributed by The Penguin Group:
Penguin Books Ltd, 27 Wrights Lane, London W8 5TZ

Which? Way to Fix It was written by Mike Lawrence with additional chapters by Dave Attwood and Peter Burgess. Contributors to second edition: Roy Brooker, Philip Dickins and Simon Leach

Original idea by John Reynolds

First edition November 1992
Reprinted December 1993
Reprinted March 1997
Second edition February 1999

British Library Cataloguing-in-Publication Data

A catalogue record for this book is available from the British Library

ISBN 0-85202-766-4

For a full list of Which? books, please write to Which? Books, Castlemead, Gascoyne Way, Hertford X, SG14 1LH
or access our web site at www.which.net

Typographic design by Eve White

Text illustrations
by John Baxter and Peter Harper

Cover design by Paul Saunders
Cover photograph by Zscharnack/BRITSTOCK-IFA

Typeset by Delta Print, Watford, Hertfordshire
Printed and bound in Great Britain by Bath Press Colourbooks, Glasgow

CONTENTS

When something needs fixing, all you need to know is which way to fix it

INTRODUCTION

How often have you felt powerless when faced with a non-functioning electrical appliance, a blocked sink or a car that refuses to start? And how often have you felt embarrassed by the ease with which the professional you have called in to fix it has put it right, outraged at how much he has charged you, or left with a sneaking suspicion that you have been well and truly ripped off? If any of this sounds familiar, then *Which? Way to Fix It* is for you.

All of us, no matter how non-materialistic we may think we are, rely heavily on a wide range of household services, fixtures, fittings, appliances and gadgets to be in working order day in and day out. We invest a lot of money in such goods and begrudge paying what can be a high proportion of the initial outlay in order to get them functioning again if they break down. High labour charges mean that for some items a professional repair is just not cost-effective, but for many of us throwing anything away goes against the grain; doing the job yourself may enable you to save the situation. On the other hand, if you are one of those people who tend to believe that something has reached the end of its days the moment it malfunctions, this book will open your eyes to how little is involved in much repair work, and reduce your chances of being a rogue repair man's victim.

Which? Way to Fix It is a different kind of d-i-y book, aimed at putting things right and keeping them that way, rather than teaching you how to build a house from scratch. It will spring to the rescue whether you quake at the mere prospect of wiring a plug or, at the other extreme, feel perfectly competent to tackle anything, but just need to be shown how it works. As well as repairs, this book includes 'fix-its' for all those household drips, squeaks, creaks, groans, flickers and wobbles that can irritate you for years if allowed to persist, and it will even help you get things working when nothing is broken except the English in the instruction manual.

INTRODUCTION

D-I-Y OR EXPERT HELP?

When something stops working, it needs fixing; what you have to decide is whether the job is within your capabilities or whether you need expert help. This book will extend your fixing skills, but will warn you when you would be better off calling in a professional at the outset. It covers most of the fixing jobs you are likely to encounter around the house, from mending a broken appliance to stopping a leak, and also deals with maintenance and repair work on cars and bicycles. It helps you to diagnose what has gone wrong and tells you how to put things right. Each repair job is explained step by step, with illustrations and checklists to help you do things in the right order and with the correct tools and materials. The majority of the jobs dealt with are well within the technical reach of most people: read through what is involved and decide whether or not you are up to tackling it.

When carrying out repairs you will sometimes need to exercise ingenuity and perseverance in obtaining spare parts and you will probably have to expand your tool kit to tackle certain jobs, but most of the time a basic selection of tools and materials will see you through. You will avoid expensive call-out charges and labour costs and have the knowledge that the job has been done carefully, plus the satisfaction of having sorted out the problem yourself.

However, there is one point to bear in mind as you set out to become a jack-of-all-repair-trades: the risk of making things worse. If you find that you are unable to fix whatever you are tackling and have to resort to calling in an expert after all, do not be surprised to be met with a combination of general unhelpfulness and a higher-than-ever bill. Most professional repairers hate having to rectify work bodged by enthusiastic but less-than-competent do-it-yourselfers. So if you are unsure about starting a particular job, at least get a range of estimates for the work from the appropriate professionals (which in itself should protect you from cowboy rip-offs) before deciding to go it alone.

HOUSEHOLD EMERGENCIES

- ELECTRICITY
- PLUMBING
- GAS
- DAMAGE

ELECTRICITY

We'd be lost without electricity. Treat it with respect and common sense and it won't let you down

LIGHTS

If something electrical stops working, don't panic. Just check things in a logical order until you pin-point the problem, which you can often put right yourself

THINGS YOU NEED

- **A torch**
- **An electrical screwdriver**
- **Wire strippers**
- **A card of fuse wire *or***
- **Replacement cartridge fuses**
- **Replacement plug fuses**
- **PVC insulating tape**

For some jobs:

- **Replacement flex**
- **Replacement cable**
- **Junction box**

The commonest causes of faults in lights and appliances are loose connections and accidental damage. You should investigate at the first sign of trouble.

1 If a ceiling or wall light doesn't work, switch off the mains supply and replace the bulb. If it still won't work, switch off again and go to step 2.

2 Check the main fuse box or consumer unit to see whether the lighting circuit fuse or miniature circuit breaker (MCB) has cut off the supply. If you have fuses, turn the main on-off switch to off and withdraw the fuse-holder. If the fuse wire has burnt out, replace it with new 5-amp fuse wire or 5-amp cartridge fuse and switch the power back on. If you have MCBs, simply switch the circuit MCB back on. Turn the affected light on again; if the fuse blows or the MCB trips again, go to step 3.

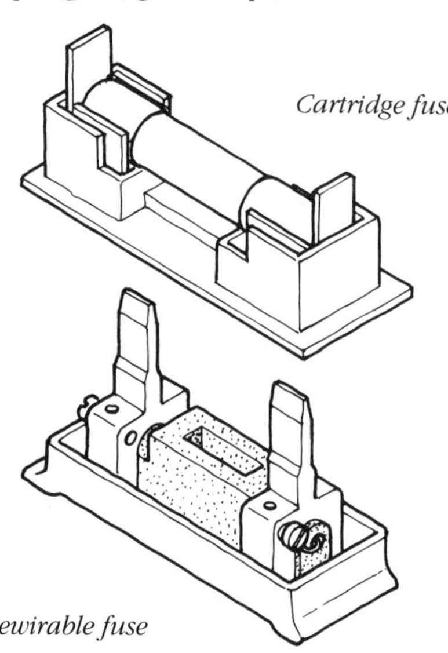

Cartridge fuse

Rewirable fuse

3 With the mains power switched off again, open up the ceiling rose or light fitting and look for loose connections or damaged insulation on flex cores which could cause a short circuit. Remake connections as necessary, and make a temporary repair to damaged insulation with PVC tape. Remove or replace the damaged section as soon as is practicable. Check that pendant flex cores in ceiling roses are hooked over their anchorages and replace the rose cover. Restore the power as in step 2 and operate the light; if the fuse blows or the MCB trips again, go to step 4.

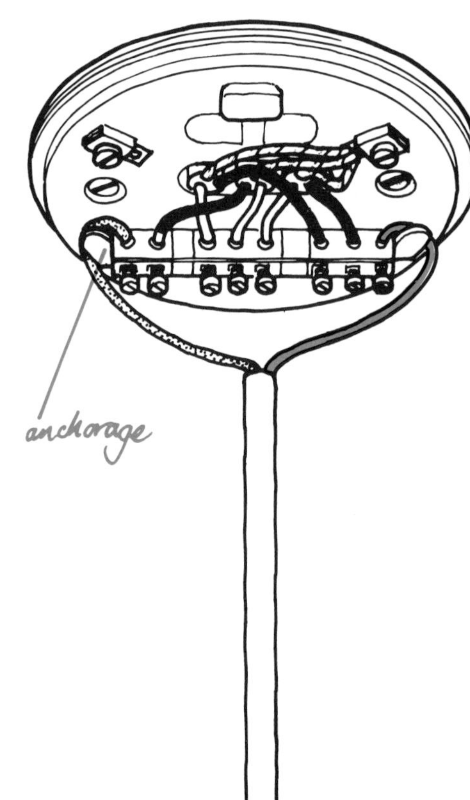

4 With the mains power off again, disconnect the flex from the rose and lampholder and test each core for breaks with a continuity tester. Replace the flex if any core fails, restore the power and operate the light. If the fuse blows or the MCB trips again, repeat steps 3 and 4 for other lights on the circuit, then go to Circuits.

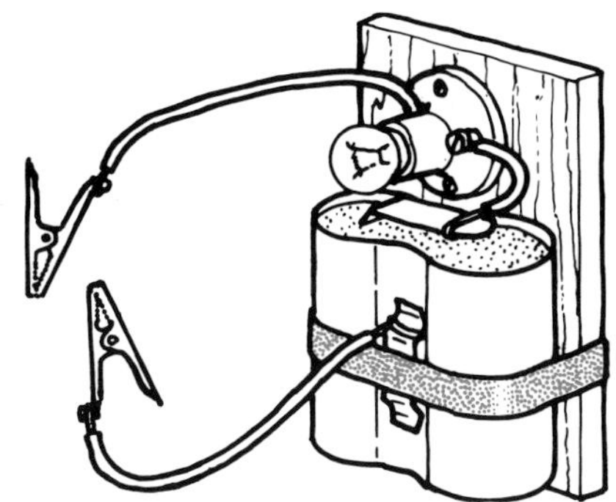

A typical continuity tester, which you could make yourself – if the clips are brought together or connected by an unbroken (closed) circuit, the lamp lights

APPLIANCES

1 If a plug-in light or appliance has simply stopped working and there is no smell of burning, plug another appliance into the same socket. If this works the original appliance is faulty: check the bulb if it is a light, then go to step 2. If other appliances won't work in the same socket, go to Circuits.

2 Unplug the appliance, undo its plug and check the flex core connections. Remake any that are loose, replace the plug top and test the appliance again. If it still doesn't work, go to step 3.

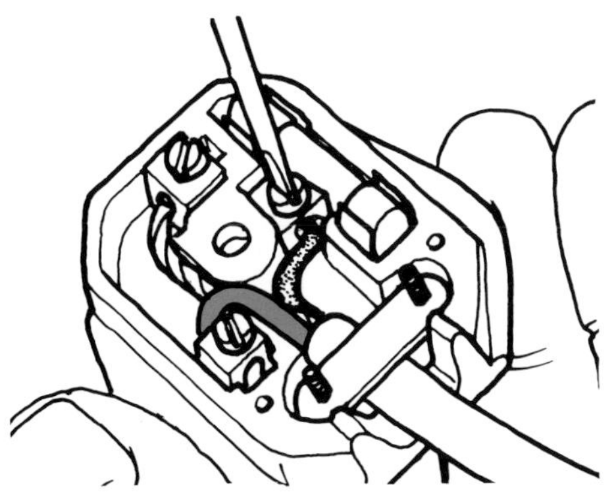

3 Open up the plug again and fit a new fuse of the correct rating for the appliance – a 3-amp one for appliances with a power rating below 720 watts, a 13-amp one otherwise – and test the appliance again. If it still doesn't work, go to step 4.

4 Unplug the appliance again and, if you can, open up its outer casing to reveal the terminal block to which the flex is connected and check the connections. Remake any that are loose, replace the casing and plug it in again. If it still fails to work, go to step 5.

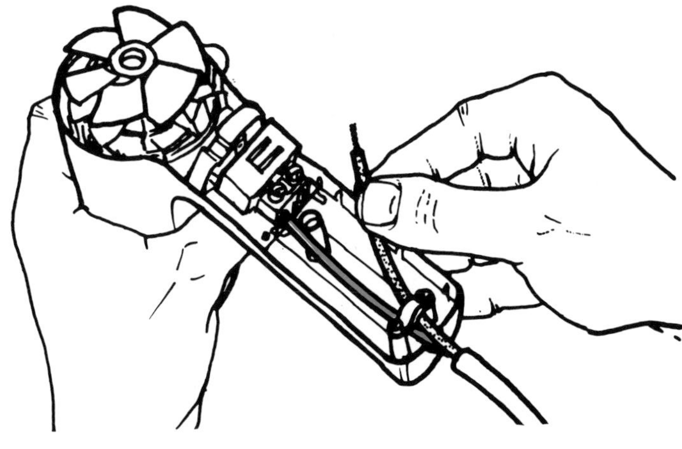

5 Repeat step 4 so you can test each flex core for breaks using a continuity tester. Replace the flex if any core fails, then reassemble the casing and test the appliance once more. If it still won't work, see chapter 2: Electrical Appliances.

CIRCUITS

1 If an entire lighting or power circuit is dead, switch off all lights and unplug all appliances supplied by it. Then check the circuit fuse or MCB as in Lights step 2, replacing the fuse or resetting the MCB as appropriate. Restore the power and go to step 2. If the fuse blows again or the MCB trips off and cannot be switched on, the fault is on the circuit wiring itself: go to step 3.

2 Switch lights on or plug in appliances one by one. If any one blows the circuit fuse or trips the MCB, check it as described in Lights and Appliances. Remember that an individual appliance may not be faulty, but may be overloading the circuit; don't connect too many high-wattage appliances (such as heaters) to any one circuit.

3 With the mains power off, open up switches and socket outlets and check for loose connections or physical damage to cable cores. Remake connections and repair damaged insulation with PVC tape, replace faceplates and restore the power. If the fuse blows or the MCB trips again, go to step 4.

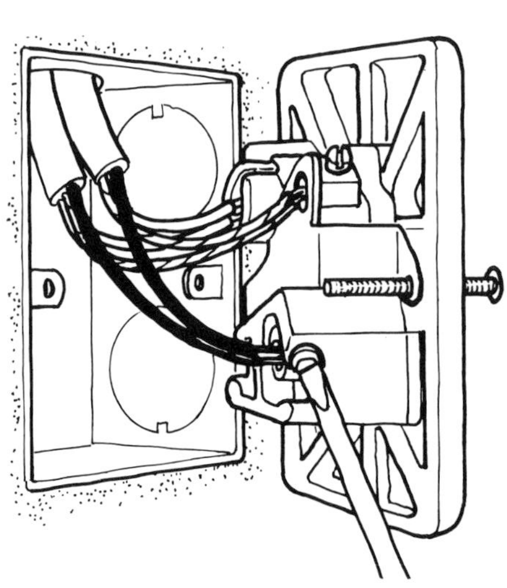

4 There is a fault somewhere else on the wiring. If you have damaged a cable by drilling through it or driving a nail into it, go to step 5. Otherwise call in a professional electrician to locate the fault.

5 If the damaged cable is buried in wall plaster, you will have to remove and replace the whole section between adjacent wiring accessories. If it is under the floor, lift the boards, cut through the cable where it is damaged and connect the stripped cable ends using a three-terminal junction box.

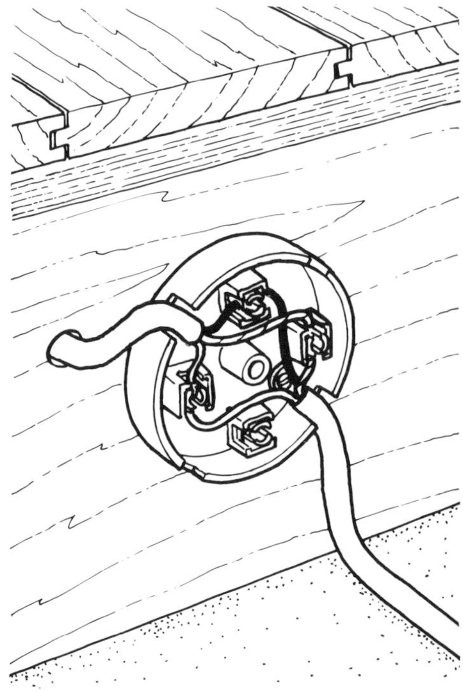

THINGS YOU NEED

- **A torch**
- **An electrical screwdriver**
- **Wire strippers**
- **A card of fuse wire *or***
- **Replacement cartridge fuses**
- **Replacement plug fuses**
- **PVC insulating tape**

For some jobs:

- **Replacement flex**
- **Replacement cable**
- **Junction box**

WHOLE SYSTEM

1 If nothing except the lights works or you seem to have a complete power failure, and your house wiring system is protected by a residual current device (RCD), check first whether this has tripped off.

If it has, try to reset it to on; it may have been tripped by a momentary fault in the electricity supply. If it has tripped and you cannot switch it on again, the fault is still present. Run through the checks under the other headings to find a possible appliance or circuit fault, or call in a professional electrician. If your RCD suffers regular nuisance tripping, notify your electricity distribution company.

2 If your system does not have RCD protection or if the RCD has not tripped, check with neighbours in case there is a local power cut. If so, notify your distribution company's 24-hour emergency number (see Electricity in your phone directory); they will confirm the fault and tell you when you can expect power supplies to be restored.

3 If there is no local power cut, you either have a fault in your house supply cable or the distribution company's fuse in the supply cable has blown, possibly due to serious overloading of the system. Call the emergency phone number and ask for an engineer to come as soon as possible to repair the fault.

SHOCK TREATMENT

- If an appliance, switch or socket gives you a minor shock, stop using it at once. Have the appliance checked by an engineer for earth safety, and replace damaged wiring accessories.

- If someone receives a major shock, try to turn off the source of the current as fast as you can. If you cannot, grab clothing (NOT bare flesh, or you too will get a shock if the power is still on) and drag the victim away from the power source.

- Conscious but visibly shocked: lay the victim flat on the back with legs slightly raised; turn the head to the side to keep the airway clear and cover with a blanket. Do not give anything to drink or smoke. Flood burns with cold water, then cover them with a clean sterile dressing; don't apply ointments or remove loose skin. Then call an ambulance.

- Unconscious: lay the victim in the recovery position. Keep the airway clear by tilting the head back and bringing the jaw forward. Cover with a blanket and call an ambulance immediately. If breathing or heartbeat stop, give artificial ventilation or external chest compression as necessary until the ambulance arrives.

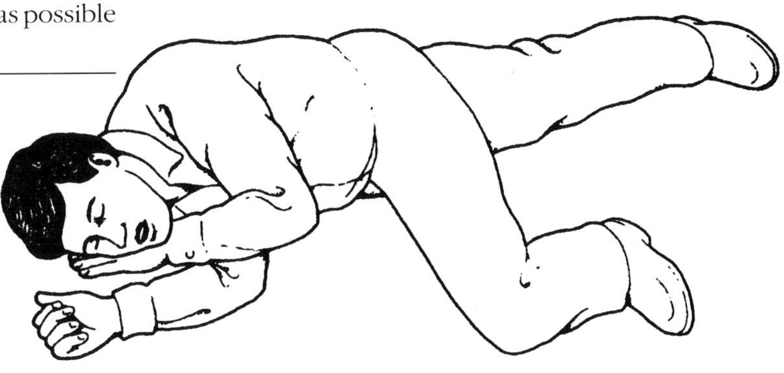

EMERGENCY ACTION

PLUMBING

We often take an efficient water supply and disposal system for granted... until an unexpected flood occurs

BURST PIPES

If you are faced with a leaking plumbing fitting, a burst pipe or a flood caused by a blocked drain, prompt action is essential to stem the flow and minimise the damage

THINGS YOU NEED

- **A pipe repair kit *or***
- **Two compression fittings and some spare pipe *or***
- **PVC tape, hose and wire**
- **PTFE plumber's tape**
- **Two adjustable spanners**
- **A pair of pliers**
- **A junior hacksaw**
- **A metal file**
- **A sink plunger**
- **Drain rods**
- **Waterproof repair tape *or***
- **Silicone sealant**

Find out where all the stoptaps, gate valves and draincocks are, so you can shut off and empty the system quickly.

The two commonest causes of burst pipes are winter freeze-ups and corrosion in the heating system. Both can cause serious damage, yet both are easily preventable.

1 If you discover a burst water pipe, turn off the water supply to the affected pipe as quickly as possible. Use the rising main stoptap for bursts on any mains-pressure pipes – in the kitchen, to tanks in the loft or to an outside tap, for example. For bursts on low-pressure pipes (fed from the tank in the loft), first turn off gate valves if they are fitted; if they are not, tie up the ballvalve to a piece of wood spanning the tank or turn off the rising main stoptap to stop the tank refilling. Then open hot and cold taps to empty the affected pipes.

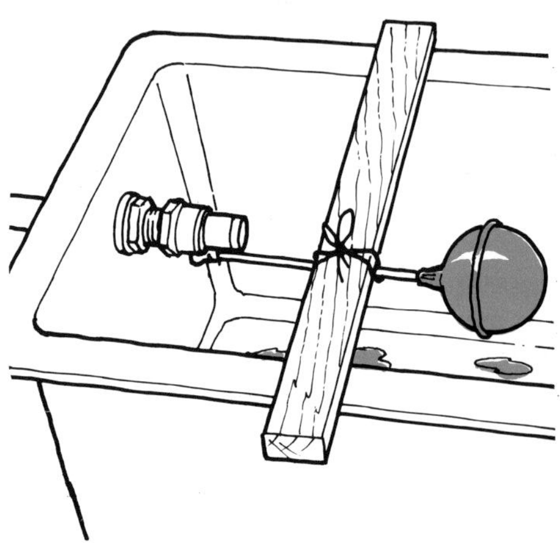

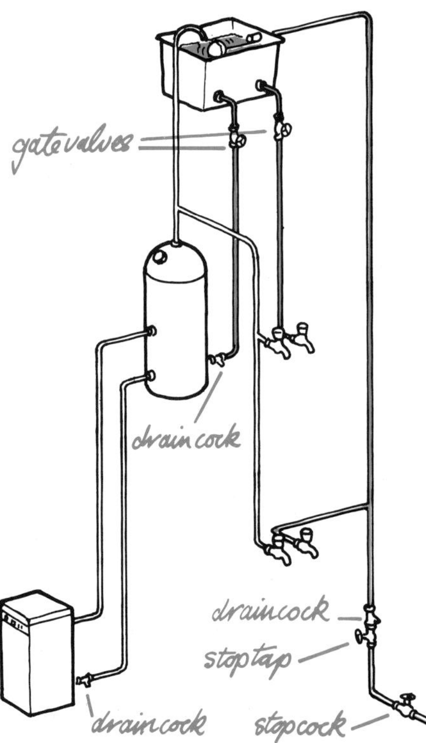

Control valves and draincocks in a typical plumbing system

2 If the burst is on the heating pipework, switch off the boiler and turn off the stoptap on the supply to the feed-and-expansion tank (if there is one) to stop it refilling. Then attach a length of garden hose to the lowest draincock on the system and take the other end to a gully or drain outside. Open the draincock valve to empty the system.

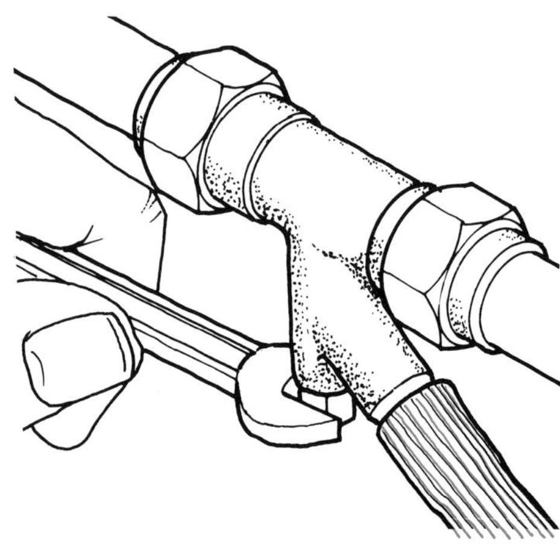

3 With the water flow stemmed, you can set about repairing the damage. If the burst is small and accessible – a pinhole in the pipe, for example – cut out about 20mm of pipe with a hacksaw and reconnect the cut ends with a compression fitting for a permanent repair. For a temporary one, use a burst-pipe clamp or repair putty. If the split is more extensive – such as one caused by ice – cut out the damaged section and join in a new length of pipe. If you don't have a repair kit of fittings available, use PVC tape, a split length of garden hose and some strong wire to make a temporary repair to the pipe.

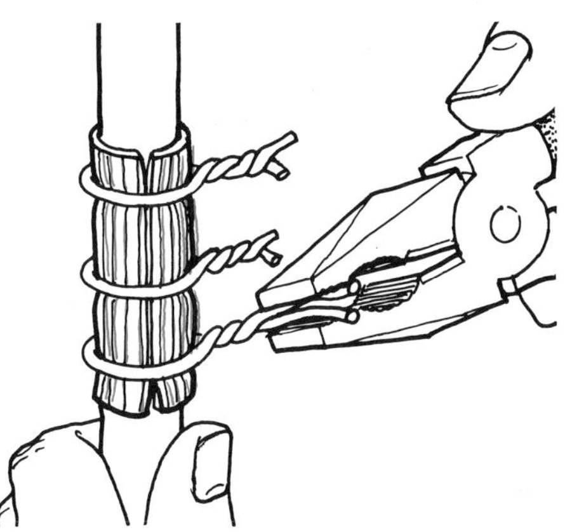

Emergency repair with tape, hose and wire

PLUMBING LEAKS

Even small leaks from plumbing fittings can create a great deal of mess, not to mention rot in structural timbers and dampness in walls and floors. To make matters more difficult, the source of the leak is often awkwardly inaccessible.

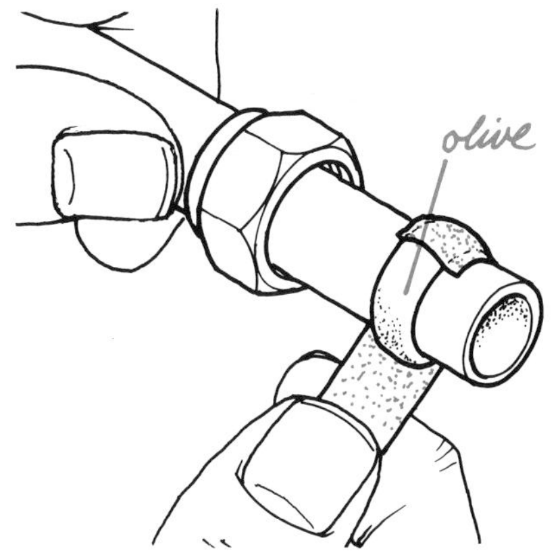

Using PTFE tape to repair a compression fitting

EXPOSED FITTINGS

Once the presence of a leak becomes apparent, how you tackle it depends on where it is. Leaks on exposed runs of copper pipework, which usually occur at pipe fittings, are relatively easy to deal with. Cure leaky compression fittings either by tightening up the cap nuts, or by draining the pipe, dismantling the fitting and remaking the joints after winding some PTFE tape over the sealing ring, or 'olive', on the pipe. Dismantle leaky capillary fittings with a blowlamp or hot air gun after draining the pipework, and replace them with a compression fitting. On plastic waste pipework assembled with push-fit fittings, open up leaky fittings and replace the sealing washer inside.

CONCEALED PIPES

If the leak is in concealed pipework, expose the source by lifting floorcoverings and floorboards, removing pipe boxing or chiselling away plaster or hard floor surfaces. Tackle leaks from compression or capillary fittings as described above, and leave the pipe exposed to allow its surroundings to dry out before replacing the materials you removed. If a buried pipe has been leaking for some time it may be worth hiring a dehumidifier to speed up the drying-out process.

If you drive a nail or screw through a pipe, leave it where it is while you drain the affected pipe to help staunch the flow. Similarly, if you drill through a pipe, quickly drive a screw into the hole.

LEAKING WC

If the leak is occurring at the joint between a WC pan and the soil pipe branch behind it, make a temporary repair with waterproof repair tape or silicone sealant. For a permanent cure, use a flexible plastic WC connector. In older homes a mortar or putty fillet usually fills the joint to a cast-iron or earthenware pipe, concealing a tarred hemp fibre sealing ring. Chip out the old mortar or putty, unscrew the pan from the floor and disconnect the cistern or flush pipe. Clean out the soil-pipe socket, insert the new connector and push the WC waste outlet into it. Resecure the pan and reconnect the cistern.

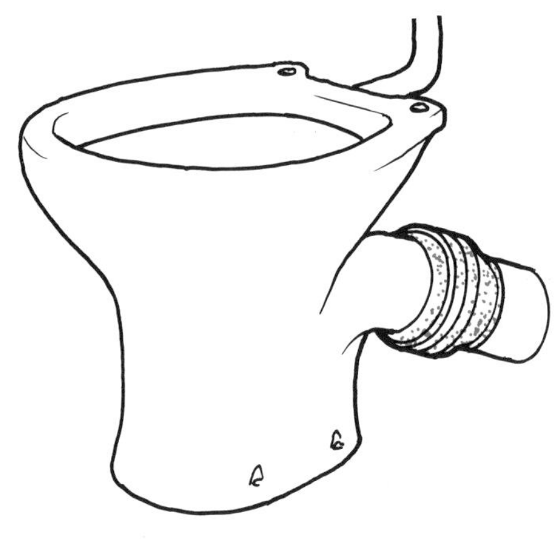

LEAKING RADIATOR

If a leak occurs along a radiator seam, you will need to replace the radiator. Turn off the valves at each end of the radiator; you will need pliers or a small spanner to close the lockshield valve (the one with a cover shroud). Note how many turns this takes so you can open it by the same amount when the leak has been repaired to maintain the balance of the heating system. Then place shallow containers beneath each end of the radiator and undo one of the coupling nuts connecting the valves to the radiator. Open the air vent at the top to speed up the draining process. Then undo the other coupling nut, lift the radiator off its brackets, drain off the last of the sludge into your container and carry it outdoors. Reverse the process to fit the replacement radiator.

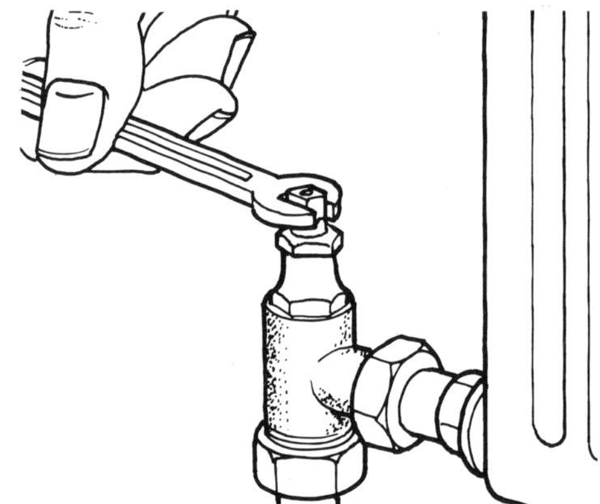

THINGS YOU NEED

- **A pipe repair kit *or***
- **Two compression fittings and some spare pipe *or***
- **PVC tape, hose and wire**
- **PTFE plumber's tape**
- **Two adjustable spanners**
- **A pair of pliers**
- **A junior hacksaw**
- **A metal file**
- **A sink plunger**
- **Drain rods**
- **Waterproof repair tape *or***
- **Silicone sealant**

BLOCKAGES

Blocked waste pipes – especially in kitchens – are a relatively common problem. Blockages in WC outlets, gullies and drains occur less frequently, but they can create a highly unpleasant mess.

1 If a sink, bath or basin waste pipe becomes blocked, first try to shift the problem with a plunger. Cover the overflow with a wet rag, run some water in and then pump the plunger cup up and down vigorously over the plug hole. If this doesn't clear the blockage, go to step 2.

2 Waste pipes are always fitted with some sort of trap beneath the outlet from the appliance. Place a bucket or bowl under the trap, put the plug in and undo the trap. Clean it out, remove any visible waste material from the underside of the plug hole and use coat-hanger wire to poke along the waste pipe leading away from the appliance. If the pipe clears, wash it through with boiling water and washing-up liquid. If not, go to step 3.

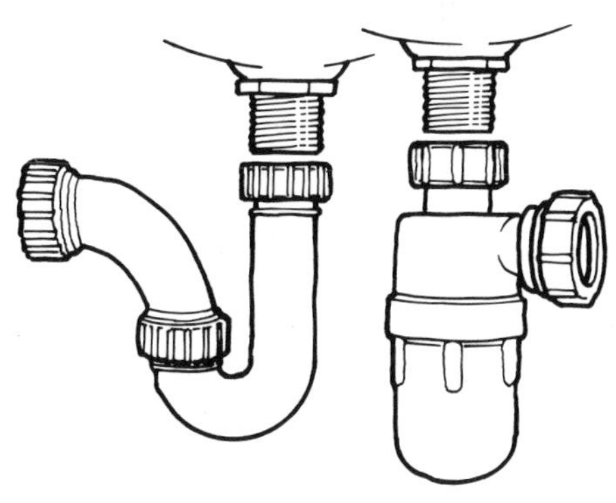

3 If the trap is clear, the blockage must be further along the waste pipe (or possibly in the drains). With push-fit fittings you can dismantle the pipe run as far as it remains visible; with the more permanent solvent-welded joints you will have to work from the pipe end next to the trap. Hire a plumber's snake and feed it into the pipe to clear the blockage.

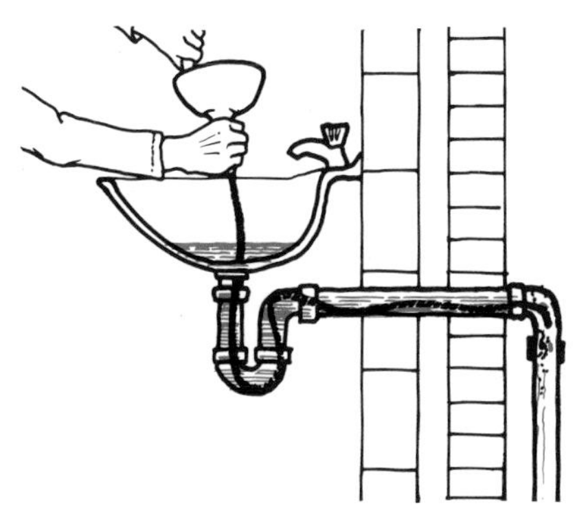

BLOCKED TOILETS

Blocked toilets are usually caused by excessive use of toilet paper or attempts to flush away larger objects like disposable nappies. The best way of clearing the blockage is with a plunger (you need a larger size than for sinks and basins) or with a drain rod fitted with a disc plunger.

BLOCKED DRAINS

1 Blockages further down the system may occur in gullies or in the drains themselves, and may result in waste water overflowing at gullies and manholes or backing up into the house's soil stack. Start by locating the source of the blockage. For example, if a gully is overflowing but the first manhole further down the drain run is clear, the blockage is either in the gully trap or in the pipe between it and the manhole.

2 If the first manhole is full but the next is empty, the blockage lies between the two. Use drain rods to clear blocked drains, feeding them down the drain towards the blockage if possible. Always turn the assembled rods clockwise to avoid sections unscrewing and becoming lost in the drain. Once the blockage is cleared, flush the drain through with lots of water.

3 Clear blocked gully traps by plunging a rod fitted with a disc plunger up and down in the gully, or by scooping out waste matter if the trap is shallow enough to be accessible. Flush it through with plenty of hot soapy water once the blockage is cleared.

4 As with waste-pipe blockages, call in a plumber or drain cleaner if you cannot clear a blocked drain or gully yourself, but be prepared for a relatively large bill if a high-pressure water jet is needed to clear the blockage.

EMERGENCY ACTION

GAS

Mains gas won't poison you, but it can explode if it leaks and can kill if it isn't burnt properly

GAS LEAKS

DO NOT attempt any d-i-y repairs to gas pipes, fittings or appliances

If there is a strong gas smell in the house:

- turn off the gas tap next to the meter
- open doors and windows to disperse the gas as quickly as possible.
- put out all naked lights and cigarettes, and turn off electric fires. DO NOT operate any other electric switches.

If the smell is slight, proceed as above and:

- check pilot lights on cookers and boilers
- check whether controls on cookers or gas fires have been left on without the burners being lit
- relight pilot lights when the smell has disappeared.

If the smell persists, call your local gas emergency telephone number immediately. The gas company must by law make a leak safe within 12 hours of being informed.

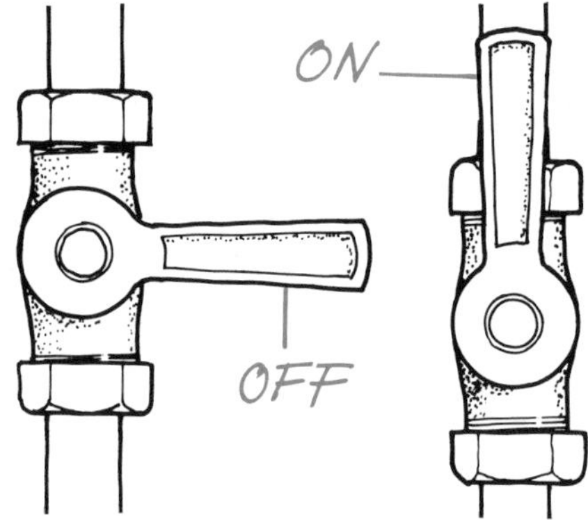

Gas supply isolating valve

GAS SAFETY

Gas is a perfectly safe fuel, so long as it is used correctly. Following these safety guidelines will ensure that no one in your home is put at any risk.

- Always buy appliances that comply with either British or European Standards. Gas showrooms sell only approved appliances.

- Have appliances installed by a qualified fitter - either a gas company employee or a member of CORGI (the Council for Registered Gas Installers).

- Have appliances serviced regularly - at least annually - either under a gas company service contract or by a CORGI-registered firm, to ensure that they are working safely and efficiently.

- Call the gas emergency number if you suspect that any gas appliance is faulty, and stop using it until you have had it checked over by an expert.

- Ensure that rooms containing gas-burning appliances are properly ventilated (except for balanced-flue appliances such as gas boilers, which take their air supply from outside). If you get headaches or nausea when an appliance is on, it may be that it is not burning properly and is giving off potentially lethal carbon monoxide gas. The room should have trickle ventilators above the window and an airbrick in an outside wall or a floor grille if the floor is suspended, and these should not be closed or covered up at any time. Carbon monoxide could still build up if these are too small for the gas-burning appliance being used in the room. Have conventional flues checked regularly for partial blockages - ideally when appliances are serviced.

- Consider having an electric gas detector installed - ideally a mains-powered type. There are different types for natural and bottled gas, and each must be installed correctly - high on a wall to detect the lighter-than-air methane in natural gas and low down for the heavier-than-air propane and butane in bottled gas. However, they do not detect a build-up of carbon monoxide. Buy one which displays the British Standard Kitemark symbol.

DAMAGE

Fires, floods, storms and intruders can make a mess of your home, but you can guard against them all

FIRE

If something suddenly catches fire or starts smouldering in the home, don't panic. What you do depends on what is ablaze

● For **chip pans** and **frying pans**, turn off the heat. Then cover the pan with its lid, a damp towel or a fire blanket if you have one, and leave it to cool down for at least 30 minutes. Don't try to move the pan, and NEVER throw water on to it.

● For **foam-filled furniture**, don't try to put the fire out; the fumes can kill within a minute or so. Get out of the room, close the door and call the fire brigade immediately.

● For **electrical fittings** and **appliances** (except TV sets and computers) unplug the appliance if possible or turn off the power at the fusebox. Then douse the flames with water or a fire extinguisher. Unplug **TVs** or **computers** and cover them with a damp blanket or a fire blanket to smother the fire; DON'T USE WATER.

● For **oil heaters**, use a fire blanket or a dry powder, foam or CO_2 fire extinguisher to smother the flames.

● If **clothes** catch fire, lay the victim down so the flames cannot reach the face and douse them with water or any non-flammable liquid such as milk. Alternatively, smother the flames with a blanket or rug as you lay the victim down. Depending on the extent of the burns, take the victim to a hospital casualty department, call a doctor or ring for an ambulance.

● If you smell smoke at night, wake everyone immediately and try to establish where the seat of the fire is. Close the door to the room if possible, but do not open any door that feels warm to the touch. Use the stairs if visibility permits and they are safe to use, get everyone out of the house and wake a neighbour to call the fire brigade. Do not try to go back inside to save possessions. If escape via the stairs is blocked, use an upstairs window as an escape route if possible. Otherwise go to a front bedroom, close the door and seal round it with bedding or clothes. Then open the window and call for help. Jump only as a last resort, lowering yourself feet first from the window sill to reduce the drop.

FIRE SAFETY

● Fit at least two smoke alarms - one in the hall and one on the landing. Buy models with the British Standard Kitemark symbol, test them regularly and replace the battery annually. Add one in the kitchen if you regularly run washing machines or dishwashers unattended overnight.

● Close all room doors last thing at night to improve your chances of escape if a fire starts. Make sure open fires are guarded, and that all smokers' materials are safely extinguished.

● Never leave chip pans unattended, and do not fill them more than one-third full. Use a thermostatically-controlled chip fryer rather than a chip pan if possible.

● Never dry clothes in front of an open fire or radiant heater, where they could fall or be blown on to the fire.

● Never store combustible materials under the stairs. They could fuel a fire and make your escape more difficult.

● Make sure that keys for window locks are kept close to the window, and that all rooms have at least one opening window for use as an escape route or rescue point.

● Make sure all new foam-filled furniture you buy is made from fire-resistant materials. Aim to replace all old foam-filled furniture as soon as finances allow.

FLOODING

Flooding is, after fire, the most destructive disaster that can hit your home. However, unlike the latter you do at least generally get some advance warning and can take action to reduce the damage

1 If you live in an area that is prone to flooding, be prepared. Keep a stock of plastic bags filled with sand or soil to block off outside doors and airbricks, and make sure you know how local flood alerts operate. It may be worth investing in purpose-built flood barriers.

2 If you are threatened by sudden flooding, turn off the gas and electricity supplies. Move valuables (including personal papers) and furniture upstairs, and lift downstairs carpets too if time permits. Then block off outside doors and airbricks to try to keep water out of the house; plastic shopping bags filled with soil are ideal, and should be placed against the outside faces of doors and airbricks.

3 If the water seems likely to rise well above ground-floor level, take food and a plentiful supply of drinking water upstairs, plus a torch and a battery-operated radio; add candles, matches or a lighter if you have them. Wrap up well: the house will be cold with no heating. Keep an eye open for rescue services, making your presence known to them as soon as they appear.

4 If the upper storey is also threatened, do not attempt to get on to the roof unless your house has a flat roof and there is some means of access to it from inside the house. Improvise a raft instead. Test that it floats and will support your weight, then take some sort of paddle with you, plus signalling equipment if it is dark. Wear as much warm clothing as you can to conserve your body's heat even if you are immersed in water.

AFTER THE FLOOD

If you return home to find your property flooded, don't try to gain entry until the flood waters subside. Once the water level drops, open doors if they are not too swollen to move or gain entry by breaking a window and start mopping up.

Turn gas and electricity supplies off first. Then remove furniture and lift floorcoverings so you can hose walls and floors down. Follow this by scrubbing all affected surfaces thoroughly with strong disinfectant; the flood water will probably have been contaminated with sewage.

Take doors off their hinges and stack them flat so they can dry out without warping. Lift some floorboards so the underfloor area can dry out (or be pumped out if necessary), and make sure airbricks are clear of debris. Open up flooded powerpoints. Lastly, when it is safe to use power supplies again, use space heaters or dehumidifiers to dry out the building as quickly as possible.

STORMS

The biggest threat of damage comes from strong winds; gales of 50mph are likely to cause some structural damage and may also interrupt power supplies.

1 Move under cover anything outside the house that might blow about – garden furniture, dustbins, bikes and toys, for example. Close greenhouse windows and secure doors to outbuildings. Move cars away from the house, where they might be hit by falling debris. Cut back any tree branches that could flail against windows and break the glass.

2 Close house windows. If the storm is likely to be severe, draw curtains and secure their hems to the window sill to contain the glass should the window be broken.

3 Make sure you have candles, matches and a torch to hand in case power supplies are interrupted. If you have a gas camping stove or lamp, check that you have some spare gas cylinders.

4 Have repair materials ready indoors to cope with any structural damage that may occur, especially buckets to catch leaks through damaged roofs and heavy-duty polythene sheeting to cover broken windows. If possible, fix the sheeting to the outside of the window frame, securing it with battens nailed round the edge.

AFTER THE STORM

● Once the storm has eased, go outside so you can assess the extent of any damage to the house. Look in particular at chimney stacks and roof slopes; the wind may have lifted flashings, dislodged tiles (which may be caught in gutters) and ripped down rooftop aerials. Check flat roofs too; the wind may have torn and lifted areas of felt, causing leaks to develop.

● Make temporary repairs as best you can, using polythene sheeting or tarpaulins to patch leaking roofs or cover broken windows. Notify your insurance company of any damage that is likely to result in an insurance claim.

BURGLARY

If you come home to find you have been burgled or wake to hear someone prowling around, it's vital to know what action to take

● If you return to your home and find it has been burgled, telephone the police immediately. Do not touch anything except to minimise any damage, but check whether known valuables have been stolen so you can give the police precise details when they arrive.

● If you arrive home and see signs of a break-in – an open door or window, for example – do not approach or enter the house. Go to a neighbour's house and telephone the police, then keep a discreet watch so you can give the police a description of anyone leaving the building.

● If you get indoors and then find an intruder in the house, ask calmly what he wants: getting angry may provoke a violent reaction. Do not attempt to restrain the burglar and do not fight over any of your stolen property. Try to memorise his appearance in as much detail as possible, and call the police as soon as he has left.

● If you suspect a night-time prowler is downstairs or you hear the sound of someone trying to break in, switch the lights on and make plenty of noise; most burglars will flee immediately. Stay upstairs, call the police if you have a bedroom phone extension and select something you can use as a weapon to defend yourself if you are attacked. As soon as you hear the intruder leave, try to see what he looks like and what he is wearing, which way he goes and whether he uses a vehicle. Then telephone the police.

● If you can get a good look at an intruder, try to memorise details to help police: age, sex, height, build, skin colour, hair style and colour, facial characteristics, clothing. For vehicles note the type, model, colour and registration number.

PREVENTING BURGLARY

Make your house as burglar-proof as you can without making your own life unbearable. Have a five-lever mortise lock and hinge bolts fitted to your front and back doors and install locks to all windows. Use them every time you leave the house. Add a burglar alarm to put amateur thieves off. Install outside security lighting to deter anyone from approaching the building at night, and use indoor security lighting to make the building look occupied if you're out in the evening. Have a safe installed to protect small valuables.

BROKEN WINDOW

Burglars and storms can both break windows, but it's fairly simple to replace a single pane

THINGS YOU NEED

- **Hammer and chisel**
  or
- **Glazier's hacking knife**
- **Wood or metal primer**
- **Replacement pane**
- **Putty**
- **Glazing sprigs or clips**
- **Putty knife**
- **Panel pins for beading**
- **Paint and paintbrush**

1 Start by lifting out as much of the broken glass as you can, wearing stout leather or PVC gloves to protect your hands. If the window is only cracked, stick tape over it in a criss-cross pattern to contain fragments and then tap out the pieces from the inside with a hammer. Wrap the pieces in newspaper, break them up to reduce them to a more manageable size if necessary and bag them up ready for safe disposal.

2 Working from outside, use a hammer and an old chisel (or a glazier's hacking knife if you have one) to chop out the old putty, any remaining bits of broken glass and the nails (called sprigs) that held the glass in place in the rebate. In metal frames, the glass will have been held in by small clips. Take these out as you uncover them, mark the hole positions on the frame and save them for later.

3 Apply primer to any bare wood or metal in the rebate, then measure up for the new glass. Check that the rebate is square by measuring all four sides, and use the smaller measurements in each case. Subtract 3mm (1/8in) from each measurement to allow for clearance. Then order the pane (plus the appropriate putty) from your glass merchant.

4 Apply the bedding putty in a thinnish bead all round the rebate, rest the bottom edge of the pane in the rebate and push it gently but firmly into place, pressing round the edge rather than in the centre of the pane to compress the putty evenly. Secure the pane with glazing sprigs about 300mm (12in) apart in a wooden frame, or with glazing clips in a metal one.

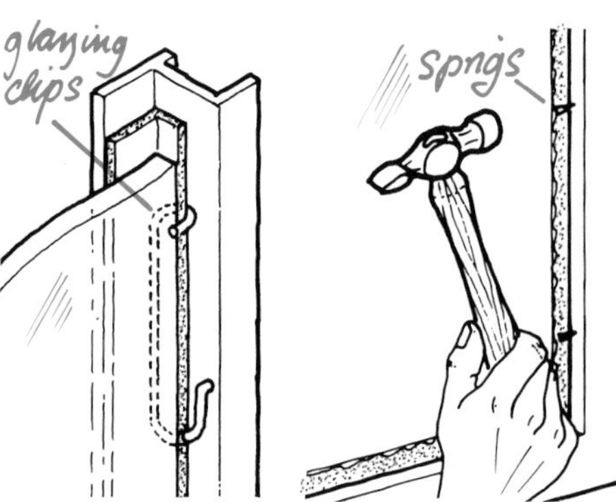

5 Add the facing putty all round, smoothing it to a 45° angle with a putty knife and leaving neat mitres at the corners. The top edge of the facing putty should be level with the inside of the rebate. Seal the join with the glass by drawing a moistened finger along the junction. Finish off by trimming away the bedding putty where it has squeezed out on the inside of the pane, and clean off putty marks with methylated spirits. Paint the putty after about 14 days.

ELECTRICAL APPLIANCES

- REPAIR GUIDELINES
- BASIC REPAIRS
- BASIC COMPONENTS
- A-Z FAULTFINDER

GUIDELINES

An introduction to the tools, techniques and basic jobs that keep all electrical equipment up and running

ESSENTIAL TOOLS

If you are going to tackle even simple repairs to your electrical appliances, you will need a range of tools and equipment. They aren't particularly expensive and you may own many of them already

1 Perhaps the most important group of tools you will need for carrying out appliance repairs are screwdrivers. You will find screws and bolts with slotted heads and several types of cross heads, such as Phillips and Pozidriv. Many appliance manufacturers also use recessed-head screws which are easier to drive on assembly lines than other types. The recesses may be square, hexagonal or the increasingly popular Torx pattern (a six-pointed star shape). Each type needs its own special screwdriver.

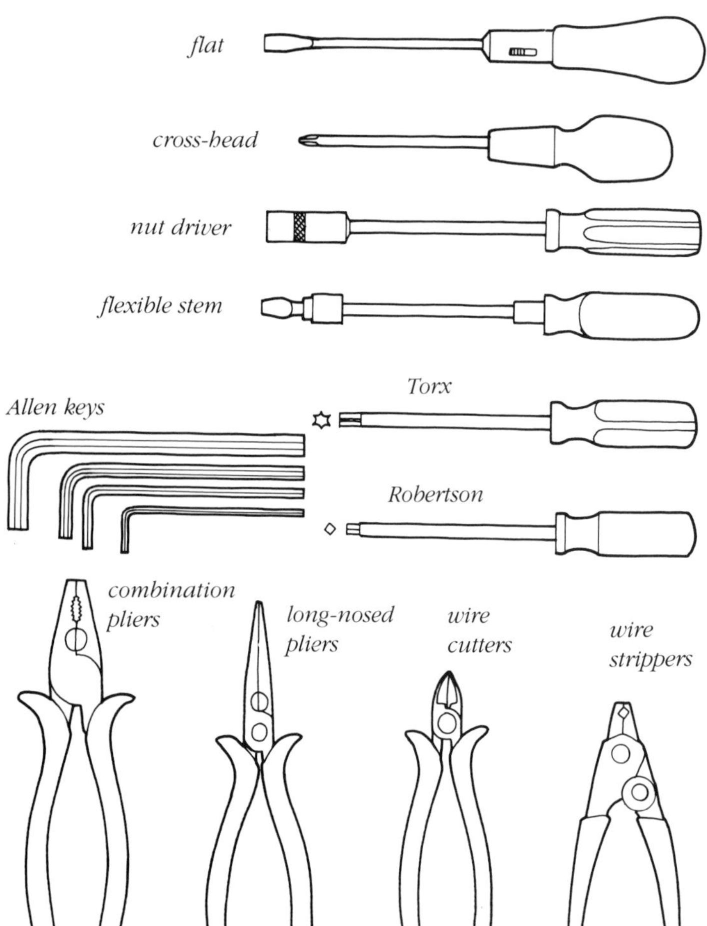

2 On the grounds that you cannot have too many different screwdrivers, you have two options: to buy separate types of driver in a range of different sizes, or to purchase a screwdriver bit set containing a drive handle and bit holder plus 20 or 30 different bits in a range of sizes and patterns. These sets often also include a nut driver, useful when screw heads are difficult to get at. If you opt for separate tools, you will need electrical screwdrivers, slotted screwdrivers, Phillips screwdrivers, Pozidriv screwdrivers, Robertson screwdrivers for screws with square recesses, Allen keys for hexagonal recesses and Torx screwdrivers for Torx screws. You will find several sizes and blade lengths essential, since you will often be working with limited access or in confined spaces. Note that Phillips and Pozidriv screwdrivers come in four sizes; No 1 drives screw gauges 0 to 4, No 2 gauges 5 to 10 and so on. Drivers for square-recess screws are numbered from 0 to 3, while Allen keys are sized in millimetres or fractions of an inch. Torx screwdrivers come in six common sizes – T10, T15, T20, T25, T30 and T40. You need a separate driver for each size of screw. Lastly, you may find an offset or flexible screwdriver useful for reaching otherwise inaccessible screws; different versions are available for driving slotted and cross-point screws.

3 The next essential group of tools is pliers, used for gripping and retrieving things, crimping wires together and a multitude of other unofficial uses. You can probably get by with just a pair of combination pliers, but a small pair of long-nosed pliers will be extremely useful for gripping small components in confined spaces. In the same tool family come wire strippers, essential for stripping flex core insulation without damaging the flex cores, and a pair of side cutters for cutting flex and trimming connections.

4 Nuts and bolts are used instead of machine screws to secure certain components on larger appliances, so you may need spanners to undo them and do them up again. Two or three sizes of adjustable crescent-pattern spanners may be enough; otherwise go for 12-point ring spanners which need be turned through only 30° to allow a new set of flats to be engaged – useful when working in confined spaces. The nuts and bolts you are working on are most likely to be metric; spanners for them are sized in millimetres to match the width of the bolt head. If you have a socket set for car maintenance work, its components may be useful for appliance repairs too.

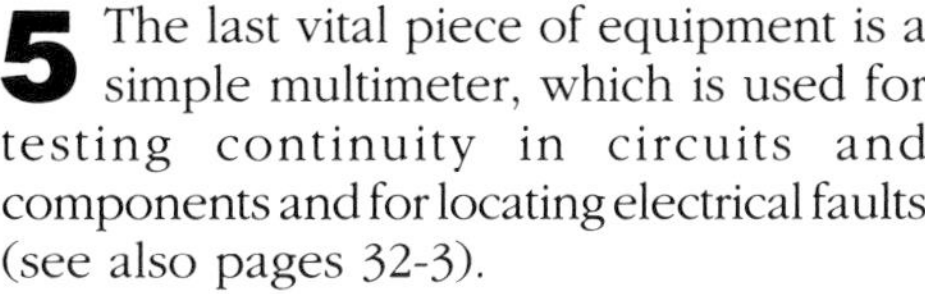

5 The last vital piece of equipment is a simple multimeter, which is used for testing continuity in circuits and components and for locating electrical faults (see also pages 32-3).

6 You may also need other general-purpose tools such as a Stanley or other craft knife, a hammer and a spirit level for checking that floor-standing appliances such as freezers and dishwashers are standing level, plus fine abrasive paper (useful for removing rust and cleaning contacts).

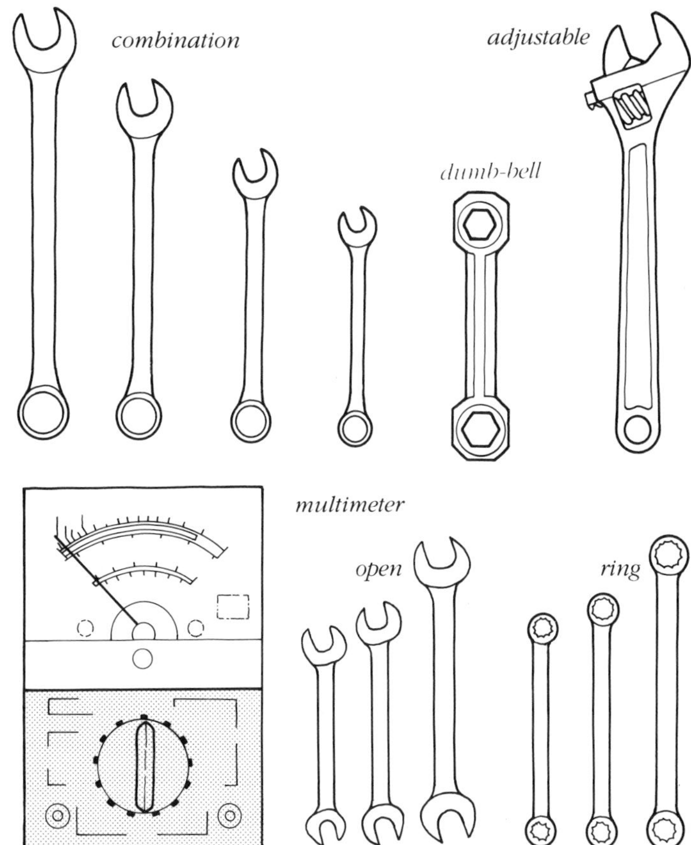

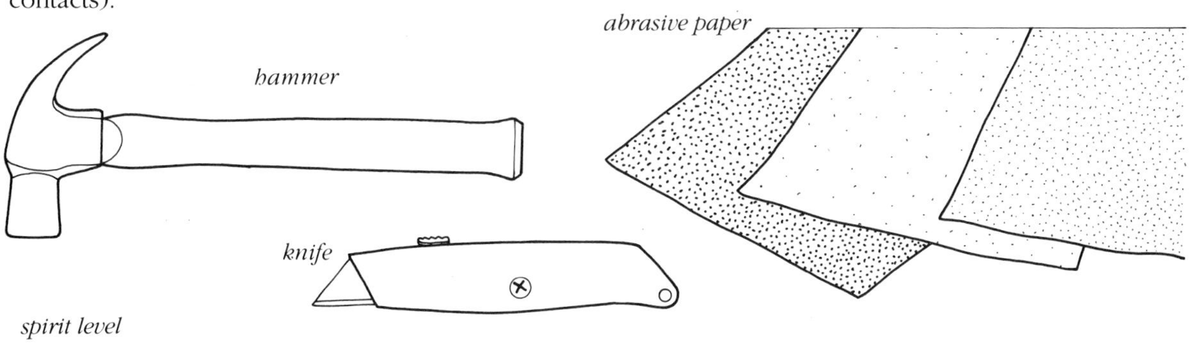

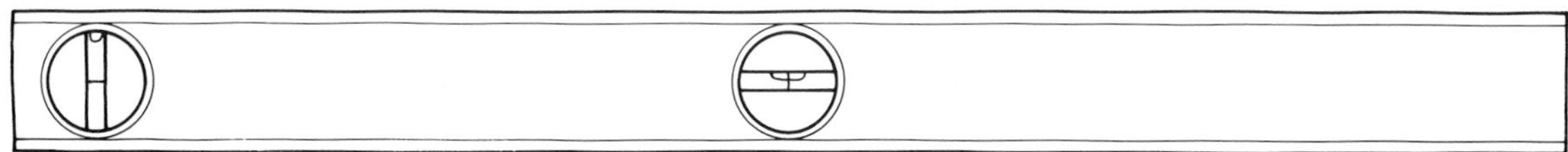

REGULAR CHECKS

Many appliances work less efficiently than they should because of a lack of basic care and maintenance

THINGS YOU NEED

- **Soft brush and cloth**
- **Descaling liquid**
- **Replacement indicator lamps**
- **Replacement control knobs**
- **Replacement handles**
- **Replacement machine screws**
- **Screwdrivers**
- **PVC insulating tape**

1 Many electrical appliances need cleaning from time to time. Appliances with motors invariably have an internal fan to keep the motor cool, and this will draw air into the appliance casing through grilles or vents. At the same time it will also suck in dust, fluff and anything else in the immediate vicinity (flour commonly clogs food mixers, for example). Check regularly that air vents are clear and wipe the casings after use to prevent a build-up of grease or other foreign matter. This also applies to products with heaters and fans – hair driers and convector heaters, for example – where dust and fluff on the element could cause a fire.

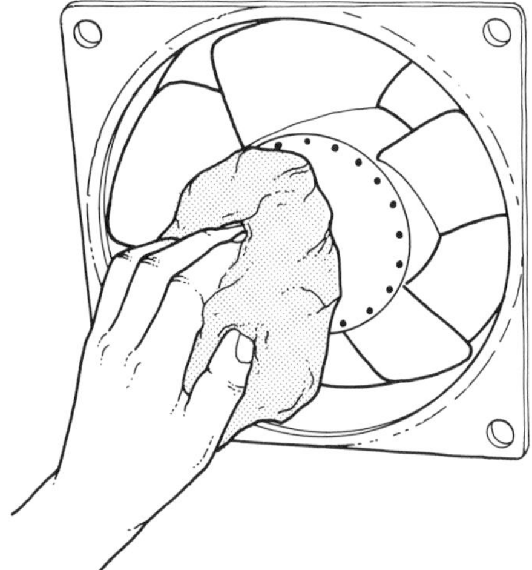

2 Small appliances that heat water – kettles and steam irons in particular – are prone to scaling up in areas of the country where the water is at all hard. Scale build-up in a kettle reduces the efficiency of the heating element and can eventually cause it to fail, while in an iron it clogs the steam outlets and can cause marks on clothes. Descale such appliances regularly to keep them working properly.

3 Many appliances with doors rely on flexible seals to keep heat or water in or out. Keep the seals clean, removing grease or hard water scale before it can affect the seal's flexibility. Check that seals are being properly compressed as the door closes; if they are misaligned or out of position they could be damaged, causing a washing machine to leak, for example.

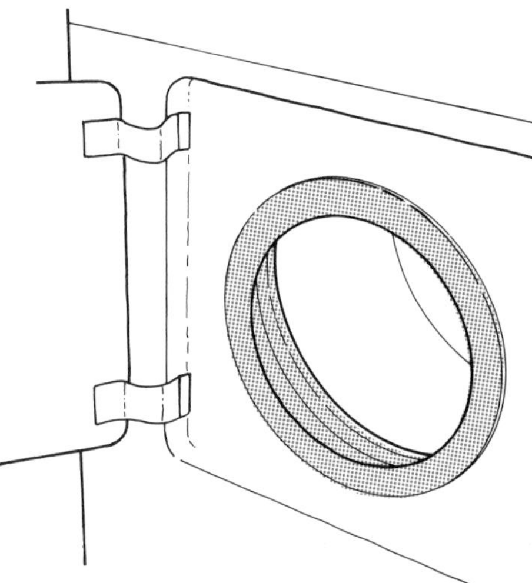

4 Many appliances contain indicator lamps which show whether the appliance is on or whether it is functioning correctly, such as lamps linked to a thermostat. Check regularly that these are working; a failed lamp could make the appliance a danger to the user.

5 Control knobs on both large free-standing and small portable appliances are prone to accidental damage, or may work loose and keep falling off. They may be the only feature that clearly indicates whether or not an appliance is on, so check them regularly. Replacements are generally extremely easy to fit, and will ensure that the appliance remains safe and easy to use.

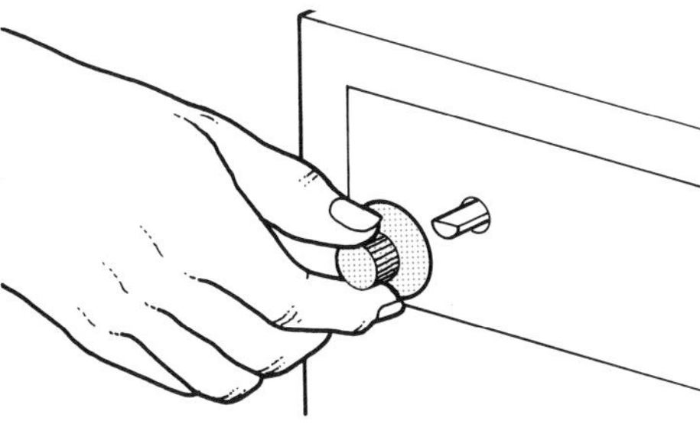

6 Handles on portable appliances can work loose or be damaged in use – if the appliance is dropped, for example. Check regularly that fixing screws are tight; again, replacements are readily available.

7 Portable appliances naturally undergo a lot of handling, and the vibration can cause fixing screws to work loose or even to drop out. Check regularly that all the screws are tight and if any are missing take one of the others with you when shopping for a replacement (specialist appliance repairers are the best source).

8 Vibration can also cause the casing fixing screws to work loose on large free-standing appliances such as washing machines, dishwashers and tumble driers, and it is a good idea to check these from time to time.

9 Use a box file or a kitchen drawer to file both instruction leaflets and guarantee cards for all appliances you buy or replace. The instructions will contain basic guidelines on the care and maintenance of the appliance, and you will need the guarantee card if the appliance breaks down during the guarantee period. If it does, there is little point in trying to repair the fault yourself, since you may find you cannot do so and by tampering with the appliance you will have invalidated the terms of the guarantee.

CRACKED CASING

1 Many small appliances have plastic outer casings which are easily cracked or broken by careless handling, exposing live internal parts that could be touched by the user. If you damage an appliance in this way, make a temporary repair immediately using PVC electrical insulating tape to shield any live parts.

2 Do not let this become a permanent repair; contact the manufacturer or service agent and ask whether a replacement casing can be ordered. If this is possible, fitting it is generally quite straightforward. Carefully remove the appliance's innards from the broken casing and reposition them in precisely the same way in the new one. Check that internal wiring is not stressed or trapped as you close the casing and make sure that protective grommets on the flex are correctly located.

INITIAL ASSESSMENT

When something stops working or appears to be malfunctioning, the first step is to assess your ability to repair it. You need to establish whether you will be able to find the fault and carry out any necessary repairs

Modern electrical appliances are very reliable; typically, 85-90 per cent need no repairs in their first three or four years of use, and many give much longer periods of trouble-free service. The main exceptions among major appliances are washing machines and dishwashers, where multiple functions and the presence of water seem to cause far more breakdowns – statistically there is roughly a 50:50 chance of a fault developing within three or four years. As for small appliances, irons and kettles seem the most prone to develop problems, although water (especially hard water) is often a contributing factor.

Faults can generally be divided into two categories: those that stop the machine from working properly, and those that stop it from working at all. The cause can range from simple (a loose electrical connection, for example) to catastrophic (such as a fire in the works). Trying to work out what has gone wrong must be your first priority.

1 With portable appliances, the plug and flex are the commonest cause of faults because of the wear and tear they suffer through regular handling. The plug may be cracked, exposing live parts. Inside it, terminal screws may work loose, allowing flex cores to pull away and touch each other, causing short circuits and blown plug fuses. Pulling on the flex may cause the cord grip to fail, leading to individual flex cores being stressed and broken. The flex itself may be damaged by careless handling, causing invisible breakage of one or more cores, or by heat or chemicals which damage the flex sheathing. Finally, the same problems that occur at the plug end of the flex can recur at the appliance end too. You need no specialist electrical knowledge to check the plug and flex for faults, and you will often save unnecessary repair bills by doing this first whenever a fault develops. See pages 30-9 for more details.

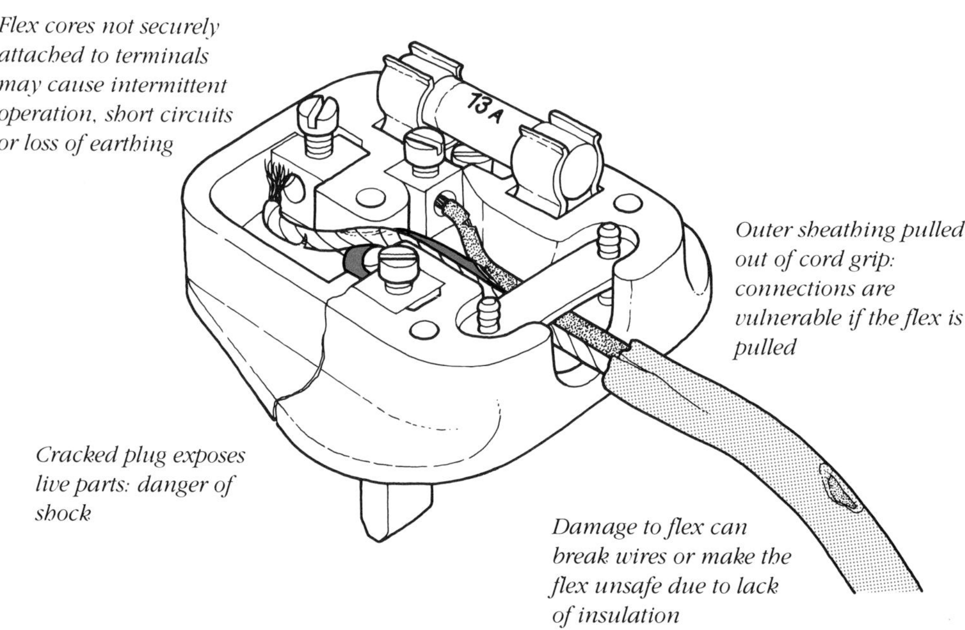
Flex cores not securely attached to terminals may cause intermittent operation, short circuits or loss of earthing
13A
Outer sheathing pulled out of cord grip: connections are vulnerable if the flex is pulled
Cracked plug exposes live parts: danger of shock
Damage to flex can break wires or make the flex unsafe due to lack of insulation

2 Many simple appliances contain just a small number of components – a switch, a motor or a heating element, for example – which may develop an obvious fault. Replacing failed components such as these is often quite straightforward, so long as the appliance casing can be opened easily, the faulty component identified and the spare parts obtained. Again, specialist knowledge is not necessary in the majority of cases, and a d-i-y repair can mean considerable savings. See pages 40-51 for more details on general repair techniques for common components, and pages 52-92 for faultfinding guidelines for individual appliances.

3 Larger appliances can pose bigger problems. For a start, there is generally more to go wrong because they contain more components and perform more complex tasks, especially since the introduction on some appliances of electronic or microchip control. For this reason you may prefer to leave any necessary repairs to a service engineer, especially if the appliance is under guarantee or you have a service contract. However, in many cases the problem is caused by one of a range of minor faults which can often be put right without the need to call in expert assistance. Often the main difficulty lies in gaining access to the faulty component, which can be almost impossible.

4 When assessing whether you can or should attempt to repair an appliance yourself, bear in mind that you may have difficulty in obtaining spares, especially for older appliances, and that you may take longer to complete the repair than a professional would – important if the appliance is used on a regular basis. On the other hand, you will have to wait for a professional engineer to come, and possibly for a return visit with the necessary parts. Check costs of parts and labour to see whether a d-i-y repair is going to be cost-effective; in some extreme cases it can be cheaper and more convenient to buy a replacement appliance than to attempt to carry out a repair.

5 Remember never to examine or dismantle any faulty appliance while it is still plugged into a power-point. Always unplug it first.

If a factory-fitted plug is damaged, cut it off and fit a new plug to the flex. Bend the old plug's pins out of alignment before discarding it, to ensure that an inquisitive child cannot insert it in a socket outlet and get a shock from the cut flex cores.

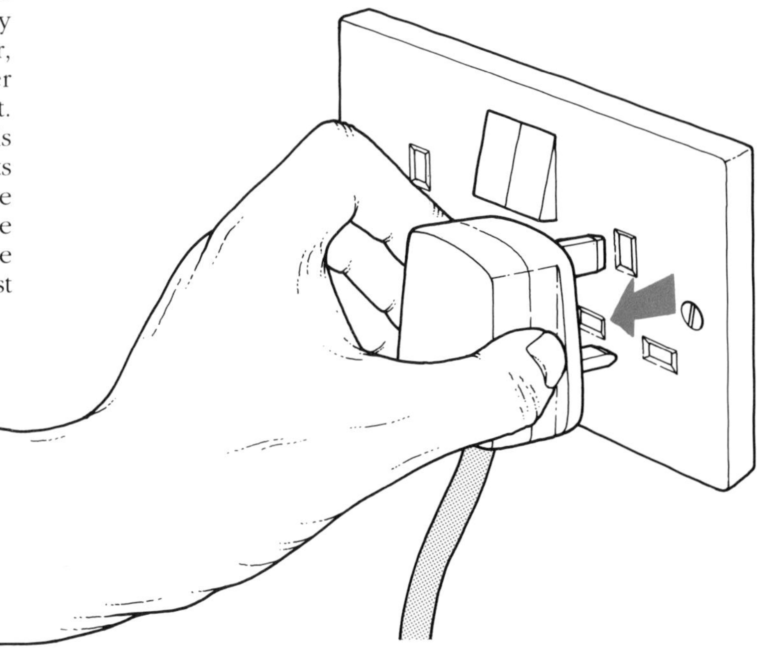

BASIC FAULTFINDING

Whenever an electrical appliance either malfunctions or stops working altogether, it pays to follow a logical sequence in tracking down what has gone wrong. The cause of the fault is often surprisingly obvious if you know where to look

Fault in cable: insulation may have failed on very old wiring or cable may have been damaged during d-i-y work

Consumer unit: fuse blown or MCB tripped due to fault in the circuit

Power cut

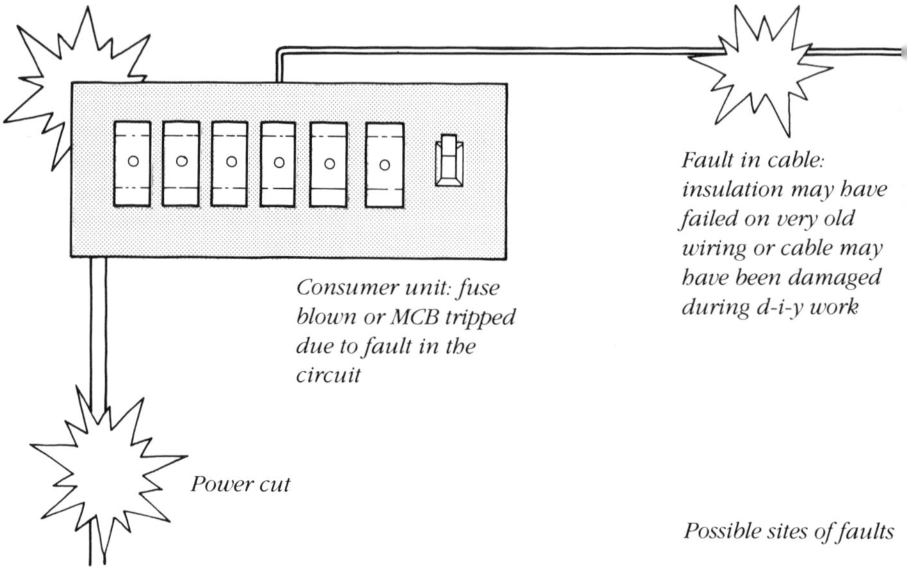

Possible sites of faults

THINGS YOU NEED

- **A working appliance**
- **Replacement fuse wire or fuses**

For rewirable fuses:

- **Electrical screwdriver**
- **Wire cutters or scissors**

1 When an appliance develops a fault, one of three things generally occurs. The appliance may simply stop working; it may continue to work, perhaps intermittently or below par; or lastly, it may overheat or catch fire. Whatever happens, the most important first step is to unplug it from the mains supply, especially if it is overheating, before making any attempt to track down what is wrong. Do not shake it, thump it or otherwise try to coax it back to life; you could cause even more damage.

2 Before rushing for your screwdrivers and starting to take the offending appliance apart, carry out a series of simple checks to see whether it is the appliance or the power supply that is at fault. First of all, plug another appliance in at the same socket outlet to check whether it still has a power supply. If the second appliance works, the first one is faulty. If it does not, two things may have happened: isolation of the power circuit concerned, due to the operation of its circuit fuse or miniature circuit breaker (MCB), or a power failure in the house supply.

3 Go to your main fuse box or consumer unit. If it contains rewirable or cartridge fuses, turn off the main isolating switch and remove the fuseholder for the power circuit concerned. You can generally see whether a rewirable fuse has blown (see pages 12-13 for how to replace one). However, you cannot tell whether a cartridge fuse has failed without using a continuity tester (see pages 32-3). If you do not have one, replace the suspect fuse with a new spare fuse of the same rating (20 or 30 amps: match what was originally fitted), and restore the power.

4 If your consumer unit contains MCBs, look to see whether the one protecting the power circuit concerned has tripped to the off position. Turn it back on if it has: being able to reset it indicates that using the appliance caused the fault. If you cannot reset it to on and you have unplugged the appliance, the indication is that there is a fault on the circuit wiring or within another appliance connected to the circuit. See pages 12-13 for more details of what to do next.

ALWAYS unplug an appliance before starting any work on it

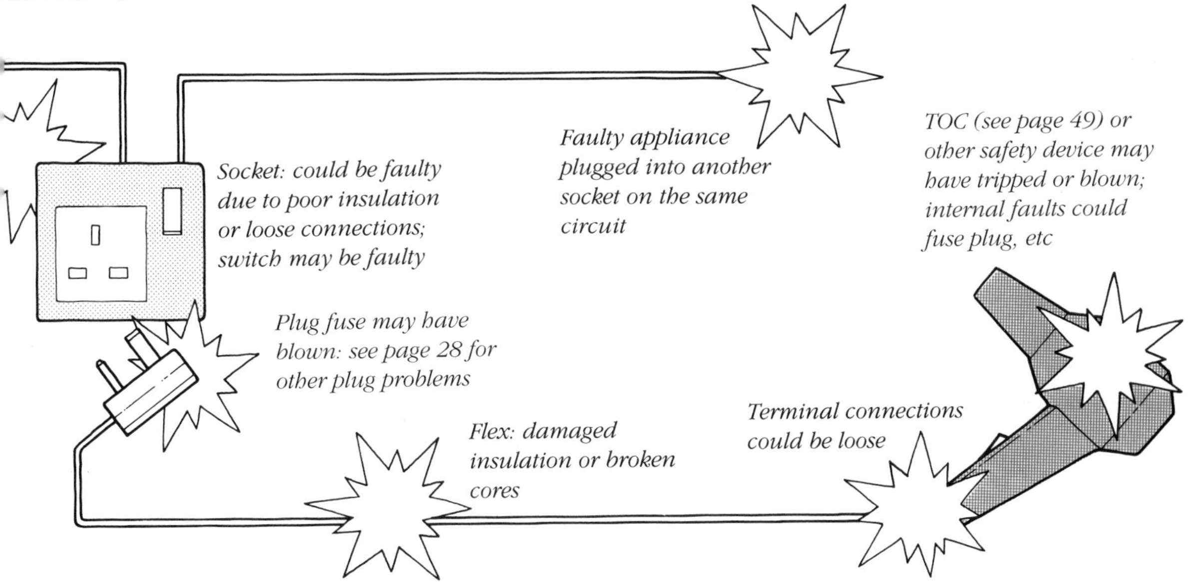
Socket: could be faulty due to poor insulation or loose connections; switch may be faulty
Faulty appliance plugged into another socket on the same circuit
TOC (see page 49) or other safety device may have tripped or blown; internal faults could fuse plug, etc
Plug fuse may have blown: see page 28 for other plug problems
Terminal connections could be loose
Flex: damaged insulation or broken cores

5 If your consumer unit also contains a residual current device (or one is fitted next to it to protect the house wiring), check to see whether this has tripped to the off position. As with MCBs, being able to reset the RCD switch to on indicates that the fault is no longer present, and was probably caused by the appliance. If you cannot switch the RCD back on, the fault is still present elsewhere on the system. Again, see pages 12-13.

6 Open the plug on the appliance you suspect to be faulty so you can inspect the flex connections. A loose connection could simply interrupt the power supply; if you find any, remake them by reattaching the bare end of the flex core concerned to its terminal. Also check that other cores are firmly anchored, and that they are not stressed due to misuse or failure of the cord grip (see pages 36-7). A loose connection could also lead to a short circuit within the plug if the bare core touches another terminal. This will generally blow the plug fuse, and may blow the circuit fuse or trip the MCB too. After remaking any faulty connections, fit a new plug fuse of the correct rating, reassemble the plug and test the appliance. If it now works, all well and good; if it does not, you must move on to the next stage in the investigation.

Never fit any other metallic object in place of fuse wire or a proper cartridge fuse; you may succeed in restoring the power supply, but its use will leave the circuit without fuse protection and this could kill someone. Always make sure you have a supply of replacement wire or cartridge fuses to hand next to the fuse box/consumer unit.

TESTING FOR FAULTS

If an appliance's plug and flex are sound and all the connections are properly made, its continued failure to work indicates that the fault lies within the appliance itself. You can often track the problem down by careful continuity testing

THINGS YOU NEED

- **Screwdrivers to open the appliance casing**
- **Continuity tester or test meter**

A simple bulb and battery continuity tester is a relatively inexpensive diagnostic tool, and will cope with the majority of wiring faultfinding. However, to test high-resistance components such as heating elements you will need a test meter. Do not waste money on an over-complex multimeter; you need one that simply indicates whether a circuit is closed (allowing current to flow) or open (no current flow) over a range of resistances.

1 To track down a faulty component or wiring link in an appliance, unplug it and open it up. Examine it so you can work out the sequence of current flow – for example from the terminal block via a switch to a motor or heating element and back again – and identify the individual components in the circuit. The manufacturer's literature may be helpful here, and often lists parts numbers too – invaluable if you have to order spares (see page 205); for this reason you should always keep instruction leaflets and wiring diagrams for any appliance you buy.

2 Check that the continuity tester or meter battery is sound by touching the probes together; if it is, the test bulb will light or the meter needle will register full-scale deflection.

3 Whenever possible, remove wiring links between components before starting to test them for continuity; otherwise you may get false readings from other components still in circuit. Then touch one test probe to one end of the wire or one terminal of the component you want to check, and the other probe to the other end or terminal. If the test bulb lights or the meter needle moves, there is a closed circuit through the wire or component and the fault lies elsewhere.

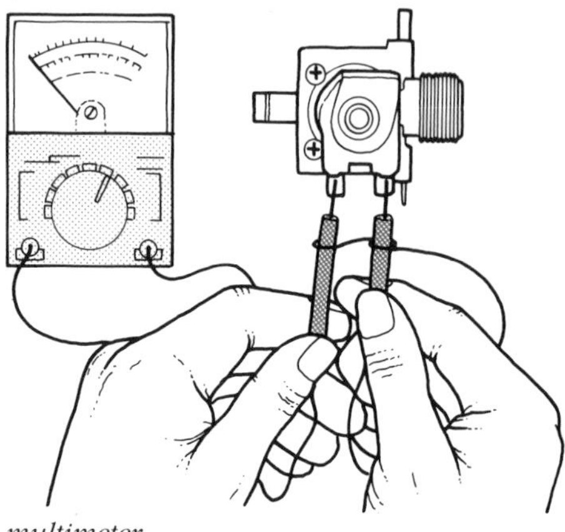

multimeter

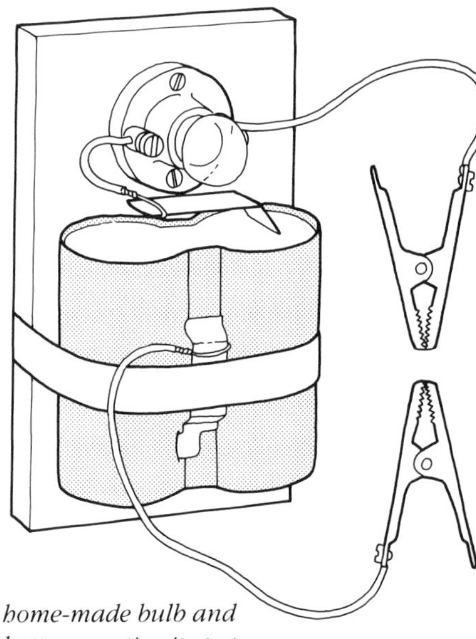

home-made bulb and battery continuity tester

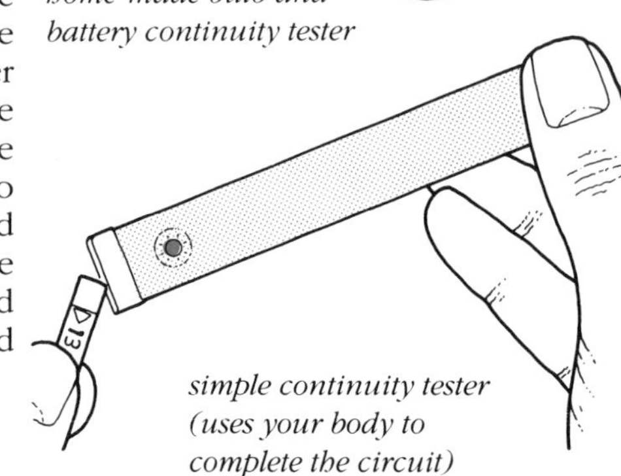

simple continuity tester (uses your body to complete the circuit)

TOC (see page 49)
motor
heating element
switch bank
terminal block
+
−

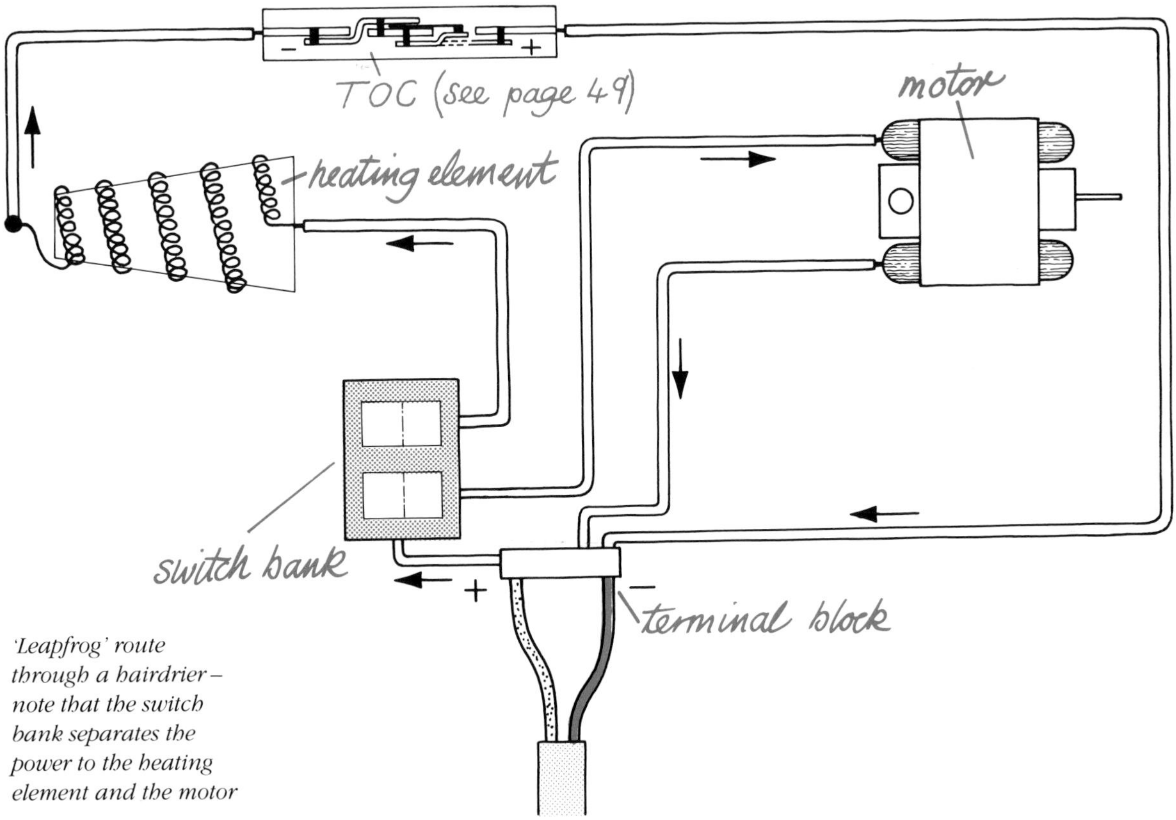

'Leapfrog' route through a hairdrier – note that the switch bank separates the power to the heating element and the motor

4 Use the 'leapfrog' technique to trace a fault in a circuit. For example, in a typical small appliance with a switch and motor, start testing at the terminal block. Check the flex link between it and the supply side of the switch first, then the switch itself (set in the ON position), the link to the motor terminals, the motor itself and back again to the switch. If an individual link or component shows an open circuit, go back and test the circuit continuity up to and beyond that point in the circuit to double-check that no other additional faults are present.

5 If you have a residual current device (RCD) protecting your house wiring, or you use a plug-in RCD with your portable garden appliances, you can use it to check whether an appliance is suffering from low internal insulation. This is a condition that results in a slight current leakage to earth (only in earthed appliances) and can eventually lead to component failure and possible risk to the user. If the RCD trips off when the power to the appliance is switched on, low insulation is indicated and the appliance should not be used until the fault has been located and put right.

DISMANTLING AND REASSEMBLY

As soon as it becomes apparent that the fault lies within the appliance itself rather that with its plug or its power supply, you have little option but to open up the appliance for further investigation

THINGS YOU NEED

- **Screwdrivers**
- **Specialist fixing tools**

1 Before you attempt to dismantle or repair any electrical appliance, always unplug it from the mains. It is suicidal to attempt any repairs without observing this elementary safety precaution, yet many ignore it. The time to check whether your repair works is when you have finished carrying it out and everything is reassembled.

2 Also check whether the appliance is still under guarantee. Domestic appliances are usually guaranteed for 12 months from the date of purchase, although many suppliers or manufacturers now offer extended warranty periods, especially on larger appliances, if the purchaser is prepared to pay for them. There are two reasons for checking. The first is that if you can get a fault repaired free of charge under a guarantee, it is silly to waste your own time and money on the job. The second is that guarantees are generally invalidated if the appliance has been tampered with, so if you fail to mend the fault yourself you will not then be able to invoke the manufacturer's guarantee to get it fixed for free.

3 If you decide to go ahead, your first task will be to discover how to gain access to the terminals to which the appliance flex is connected, so you can check for flex continuity and sound connections. Examine the appliance carefully before doing anything so you can work out how it has been assembled.

4 Look first of all for screw-on cover plates or control panels that are obviously designed for easy removal. Undo visible fixing screws to check your find, and note whether removing the cover plate reveals any other concealed fixings you may need to remove for further access to the appliance's works. Look too for control knobs which may have to be removed before the plate or panel beneath can be released; the vast majority simply pull off.

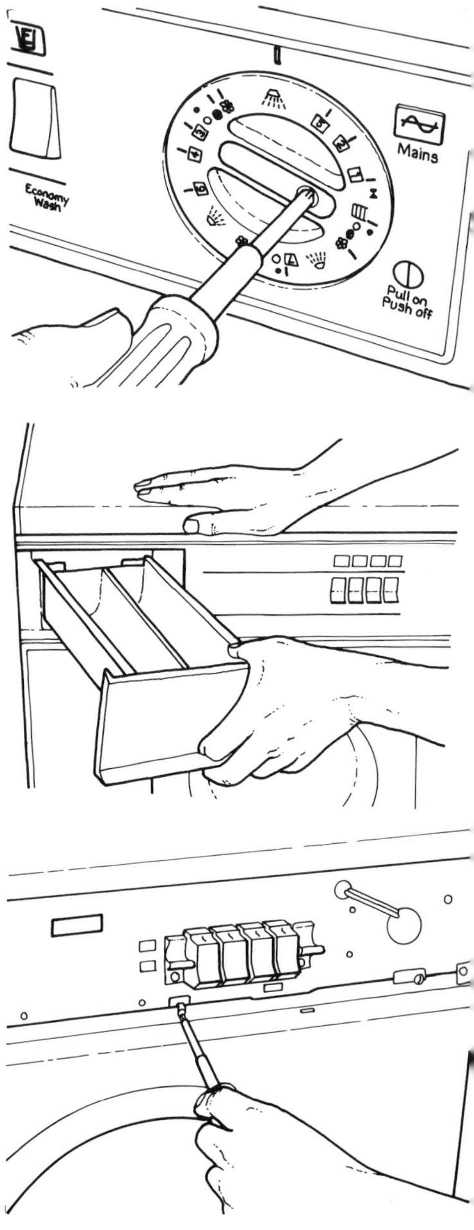

Removing cover plates to gain access to the works of a washing machine

ALWAYS unplug an appliance before starting any work on it

5 Many small appliances with moulded plastic bodies are designed on the clam-shell principle, with screws holding the two halves of the body together. Lay the appliance down with the screw heads facing upwards and remove each in turn. Because these are often of different sizes or lengths, lay each one on a sheet of paper and write alongside it where it came from, so you can replace it in the correct position when reassembling the appliance. Lift off the top half of the body so you can inspect the workings before proceeding further.

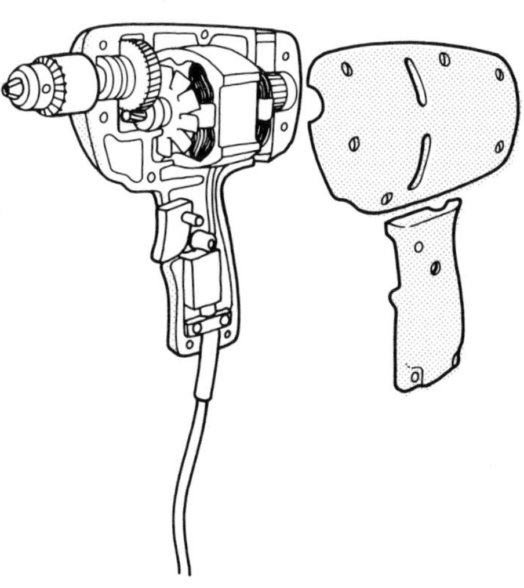

6 Other small appliances have either covers which can be removed or baseplates which can be unscrewed; again, careful investigation of the purpose of the various fixings that are visible will generally reveal the way in. Note the position of each screw as you remove it.

7 Larger appliances usually have an outer casing which is attached to a framework or chassis, often in sections. However, it may be necessary to remove these only for wholesale replacement of large components; for small-scale checks or repairs you may just need to remove smaller cover plates or control panels. The golden rule is to dismantle only as far as is necessary to further your investigations.

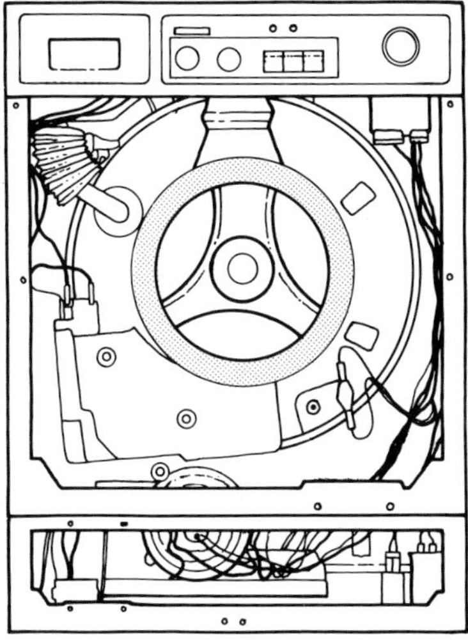

8 As you dismantle any appliance, do not be afraid to keep notes or make sketches. They often prove invaluable when it comes to reversing the procedure to put everything back together again.

9 You may have to buy specialist tools – or improvise your own – to gain access to many modern appliances. Manufacturers seem intent on making life difficult for the d-i-y repairer in this respect: most would clearly prefer you to throw away a small appliance and call in their own service engineers for larger ones than to attempt your own repairs, and the difficulty in obtaining many smaller spare parts (see page 205) seems to bear this out.

BASIC

REPAIRS

You often need to replace the plug or flex rather than repair an appliance; fitted well, they will be safe and long-lasting

FITTING A PLUG

The plug on any appliance is its link with life, enabling it to draw the power it needs from the house wiring. To work safely it must be fitted properly and used with care and respect

THINGS YOU NEED

- **A new plug**
- **The correct fuse**
- **Sharp Stanley knife**
- **Slotted screwdriver**
- **Electrical screwdriver**
- **Wire strippers**

All new electrical appliances must by law be sold with a fitted three-pin plug. This may be a one-piece moulded plug which cannot be opened, or a two-piece plug which can. This means you no longer have to fit a plug before you can use a new appliance. However, you will still need to know how to fit a replacement plug if the existing plug is damaged.

Modern wiring systems accept fused plugs with three rectangular pins. Make sure that any plug you buy is marked 'made to BS1363' and also carries the ASTA mark which indicates that it has been approved by the Association of Short Circuit Testing Authorities. The plug fuse should be marked 'made to BS1362' and should also carry the ASTA mark. Accept no others for safety's sake; there are many non-standard plugs on the market, even though they are illegal.

1 To fit a new plug, unscrew the plug top. Unless the screw is captive, place it in the plug top and set this aside. Then prise out the plug fuse with a screwdriver. Check that it is of the correct rating for the appliance – see Fuse ratings – and replace it if necessary.

2 Prepare the appliance flex by removing about 38mm ($1\frac{1}{2}$in) of the outer sheath. Use a sharp knife to nick the sheath and fold this back on itself to open up the slit. Repeat the process two or three times, working round the sheath until the cut is complete; this technique avoids the risk of nicking the insulation on the cores inside. If the flex cores are tinned (dipped in solder), cut them off flush with the end of the sheath first; they will not be cut to the correct length to fit the plug anyway.

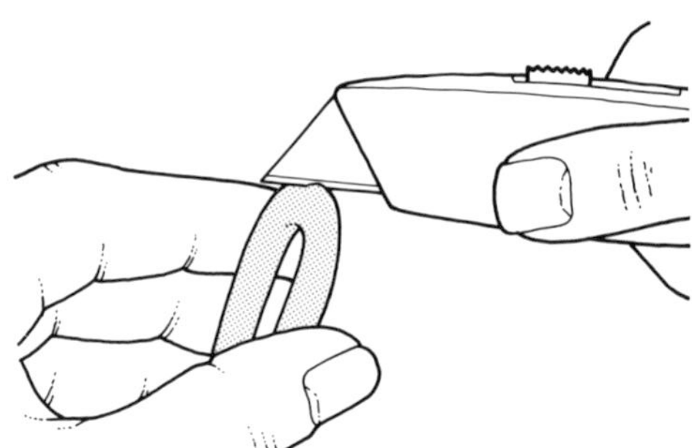

3 Lay the flex over the plug with the cut end of the sheath on top of the cord clamp, and cut each core so that it is about 13mm ($\frac{1}{2}$in) longer than it needs to be to reach its terminal. Remember that the live (brown) core goes to the terminal marked L – the one connected to the fuse – and the neutral (blue) core to the terminal marked N. The earth (green/yellow) core, if present, goes to the terminal marked E or ⏚ – the one with the longer plug pin.

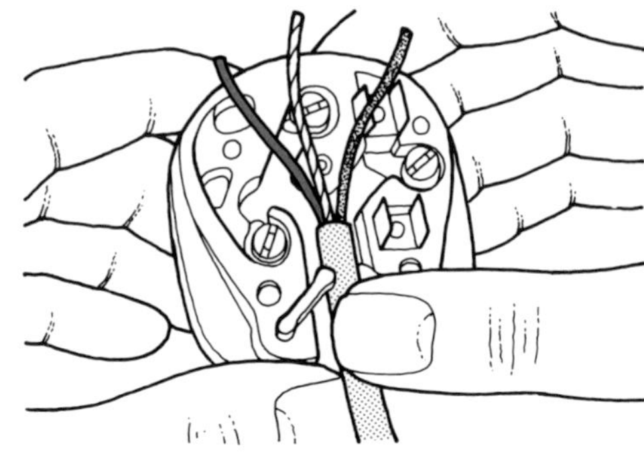

4 Use wire strippers to remove about 6mm (1/4in) of the insulation from each core, taking care not to cut through any of the core strands. Twist the cut strands neatly together so there are no loose ends.

5 If the plug has pillar terminals, loosen but do not remove the terminal screws with a small electrical screwdriver. Insert each bare core into the hole in the terminal so the core insulation reaches right up to it, and tighten the screw down securely. If it has stud terminals, remove the studs and wind each bare core round the stud in a clockwise direction. Then fit and tighten the stud, making sure not to trap the core insulation.

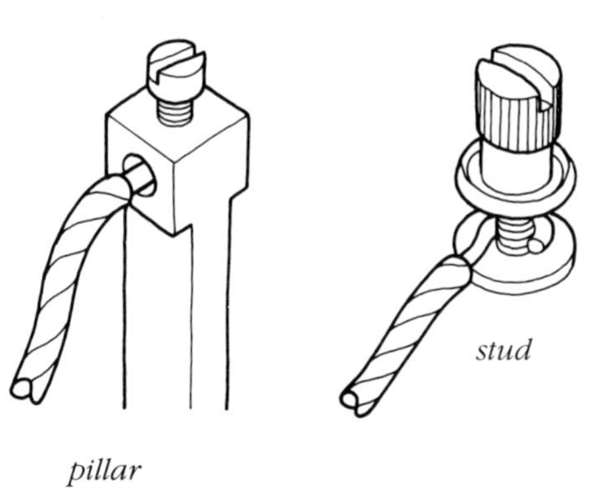

6 Next, insert the flex sheath in its clamp. With a bar-type clamp, loosen both screws and remove one so you can swing the clamp aside. Lay the flex sheath in position, and check that the flex cores lie neatly in their channels inside the plug. Then swing the clamp back over it and tighten the fixing screws so the clamp grips the sheath securely enough to resist a sharp tug. With jaw-type clamps, simply press the flex sheath down into the jaws.

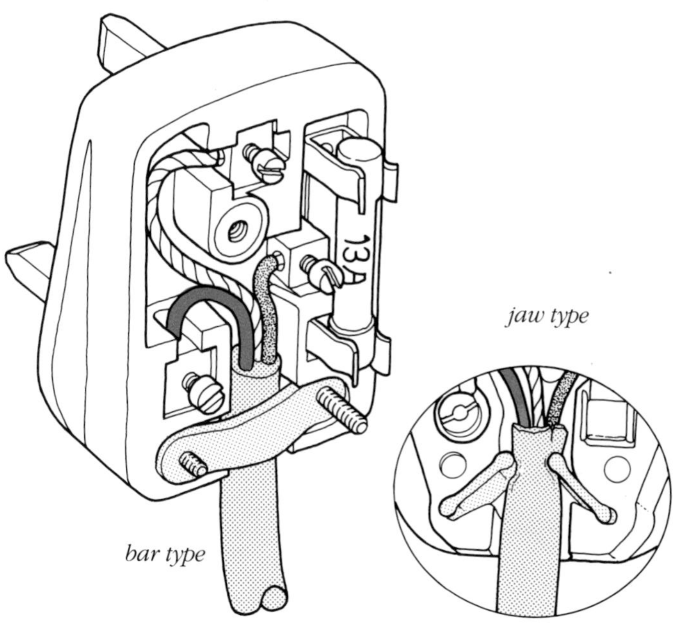

PLUG SAFETY

- **If your system still uses unfused round-pin plugs, at least have it checked regularly by a qualified electrician, and consider having it rewired to modern standards as soon as possible.**
- **New plugs all have sleeved live and neutral pins which are much safer than older ones with bare pins, especially if you have young children with inquisitive fingers.**
- **Before throwing away a damaged plug, bend the pins with hammer blows so it cannot be plugged into a socket by anyone finding it.**

7 Fit the plug fuse in its clips, check the cores and correctly positioned, replace the plug top and tighten the securing screw.

FUSE RATINGS

Use a 3-amp fuse (colour-coded red) for appliances rated at up to 720 watts, and a 13-amp fuse (colour-coded brown) for all higher-rated appliances. You will find the appliance wattage is stamped on its body or on a plate attached to the outer casing.

REPLACING FLEX

Flexible cord – flex for short – is by far the most vulnerable component of any electrical appliance, especially portable ones. Stretching or other damage can result in short circuits, overheating and the risk of electric shock

THINGS YOU NEED

- **Screwdrivers to open the appliance casing**
- **Electrical screwdriver**
- **Continuity tester**
- **Replacement flex**
- **Sharp Stanley knife**
- **Wire strippers**
- **Flex connector**

1 Get into the habit of checking the flex condition every time you use a portable appliance. Inspect the flex sheath carefully for signs of physical damage – splits, signs of stretching which could conceal a broken core inside, and heat or chemical damage. Check the points where the flex enters the plug and the appliance (or the plug-in connector) to make sure that the sheath is securely clamped and bare cores are not visible. Check the flex on larger appliances from time to time, in particular to ensure that it is not kinked or trapped underneath the appliance.

2 If the flex on an appliance is worn or damaged, or you suspect a core break is causing intermittent or permanent failure, unplug it so you can investigate further. Open the plug, and follow the guidelines on pages 34-5 to gain access to the terminal block within the appliance. Then use a continuity tester to check the continuity of each flex core in turn. If any core fails, you must replace the flex. Do this in any case if the appliance has old flex with cores colour-coded red, black and green.

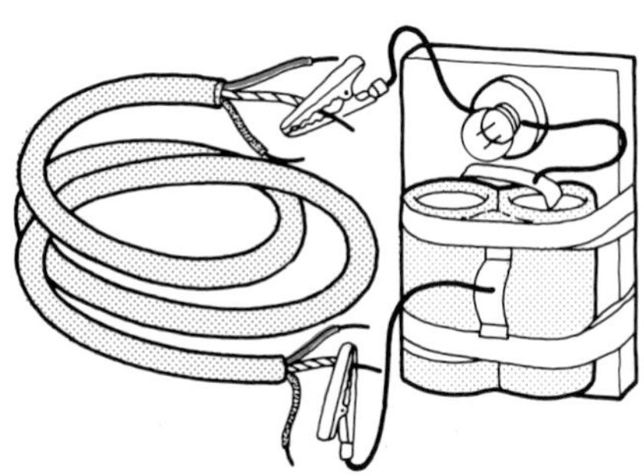

3 When replacing an appliance flex, you must ensure that you fit the correct type for the appliance concerned. If the flex is original, you can assume that the right type was fitted by the manufacturer, and copy it. Otherwise make sure that three-core flex is fitted unless the appliance is double-insulated (its body will carry the ⧈ symbol), in which case two-core flex with no earth core can be used. PVC-sheathed types are suitable for most appliances, but circular braided flex – especially the so-called unkinkable type – is often fitted on irons.

4 Next, check the wattage of the appliance; the figure is either stamped directly on the appliance body or printed on a small plate attached to it. Select flex with 0.75mm^2 cores for small appliances rated at up to 1500 watts; 1.0mm^2 up to 2000 watts; 1.25mm^2 up to 3000 watts; 1.5mm^2 up to 3500 watts. If the appliance uses a plug-in lead with a moulded-on connector, discard the old lead and buy a new one. If the plug is moulded on to the flex you are replacing, bend the pins and throw it away with the flex; do not try to re-use it.

PHILIPS
PHILIPS
TYPE HD 3240
240 V~ 50 Hz
2000W AT 240V
MADE IN GT. BRITAIN
BRITISH ELECTROTECHNICAL APPROVALS BOARD

5 When replacing flex, take this opportunity to fit a shorter or longer flex if this will make the appliance safer and easier to use or will avoid the use of adaptors or extension leads. Cut it to length, prepare the cores at one end and attach this to the plug (see pages 36-7). It is a good idea to replace the plug too if it is worn, cracked or has loose pins or a failed flex clamp.

ALWAYS unplug an appliance before starting any work on it

6 At the appliance, disconnect the old flex cores from the terminal block and draw the flex out through any protective sleeves or grommets, noting the path it followed. Then feed the new flex in along the same route until you reach the terminal block. Allow a little slack so there is no tension on the flex cores, and prepare these ready for connection. Take the live (brown) core to the terminal marked L, the neutral (blue) core to the terminal marked N and the earth core (if present) to the terminal marked E. Double-check that the connections are correct, that the terminal screws are tight and that there are no bare core strands visible. Then tighten the flex clamp if the appliance has one, and replace the cover plate or reassemble the appliance casing. Plug the appliance in to see if it now works, after checking that the plug fuse is of the correct rating.

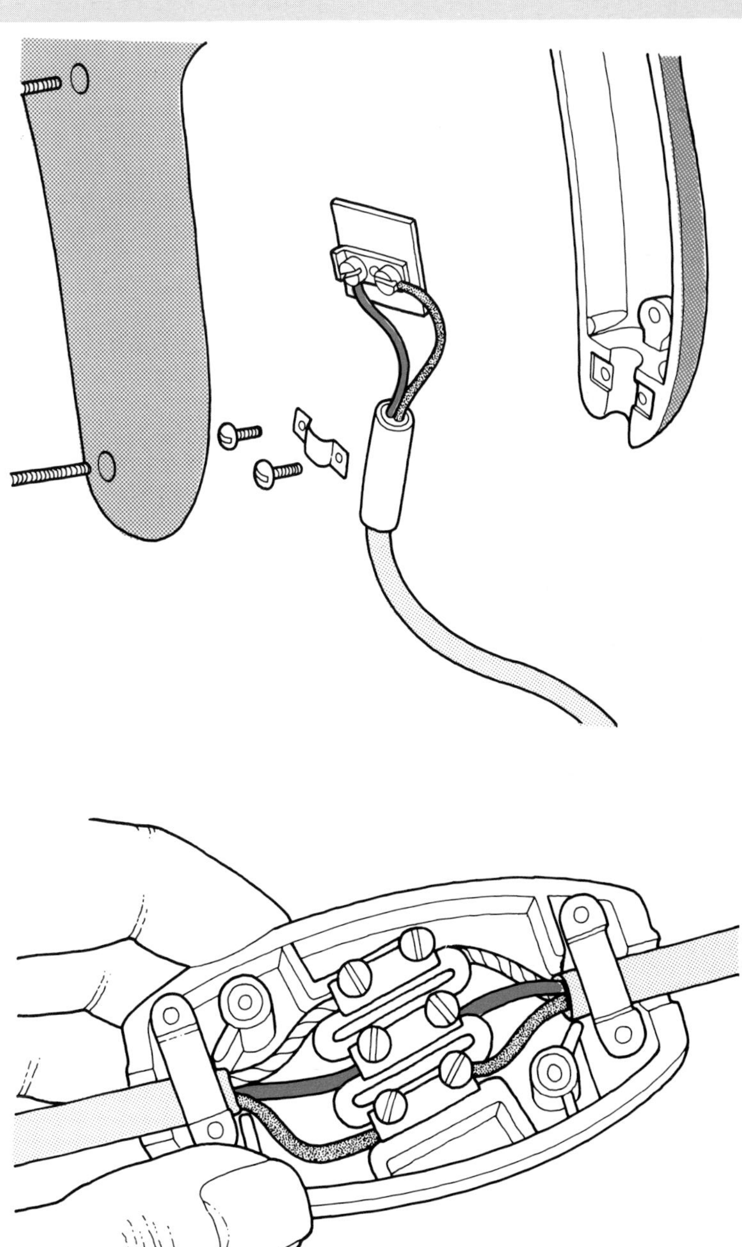

FLEX EXTENSION

If you want to extend a flex that is otherwise in good condition, always connect the extension piece with a proper flex connector. If the extension is to be permanent, use a one-piece connector; if you will want to unplug it (for use with a range of garden power tools, for example), choose a two-piece connector. Always ensure that the plug part of the connector is fitted to the flex leading to the appliance, and the socket part on the flex leading to the mains plug. If you fit them the other way round, the exposed connector plug pins will be live and potentially lethal. After connecting up the flex cores within the connector, make sure that the flex sheaths are securely anchored in their clamps before fitting the cover(s).

BASIC

COMPONENTS

Motors and heating elements are at the heart of many appliances; thermostats, switches and timers are added to control them

APPLIANCE GROUPS

Although many electrical appliances appear complicated, the majority are in fact surprisingly simple. They fall into three broad groups: appliances with motors, appliances with heating elements and those with both

APPLIANCES WITH MOTORS

Extractor fans, food mixers, sewing machines, shavers, vacuum cleaners and waste disposal units are the most common domestic electrical appliances with just a motor. Many d-i-y and garden power tools also fall into this category (see pages 156-7 and 160-1). The motor, generally the brush type, simply provides rotation, and is controlled by an on-off switch. The only other electrical component present will be a suppressor, which prevents the appliance from emitting radio waves that can interfere with radio or television reception and the performance of audio equipment.

APPLIANCES WITH HEATING ELEMENTS

1 Simple cookers, electric fires, irons, kettles and coffee makers, toasters and water heaters are among the many appliances featuring just a heating element. This may be an element that heats the air around it (and anything close to it, such as the ironing or the toast), or one that heats water (a kettle or immersion heater element, for example). The operation of the element is controlled by an on-off switch and also by a thermostat, which regulates the temperature at which the element operates. This may be pre-set to one temperature (as in a kettle) or may be fully adjustable (as in a cooker or iron).

2 These appliances often have an additional component called a thermal overload cut-out (TOC), which is an electromechanical device designed to prevent the element from exceeding its safe working temperature. If this occurs, the TOC cuts off the current; some then need manual resetting (by pushing a button) before the appliance can operate, while others reset themselves automatically when the temperature drops again. Some appliances use a safety device called a thermal fuse, microtemp or safety diode to guard against overheating instead of a TOC. It is much smaller than a TOC, and must be replaced if it trips.

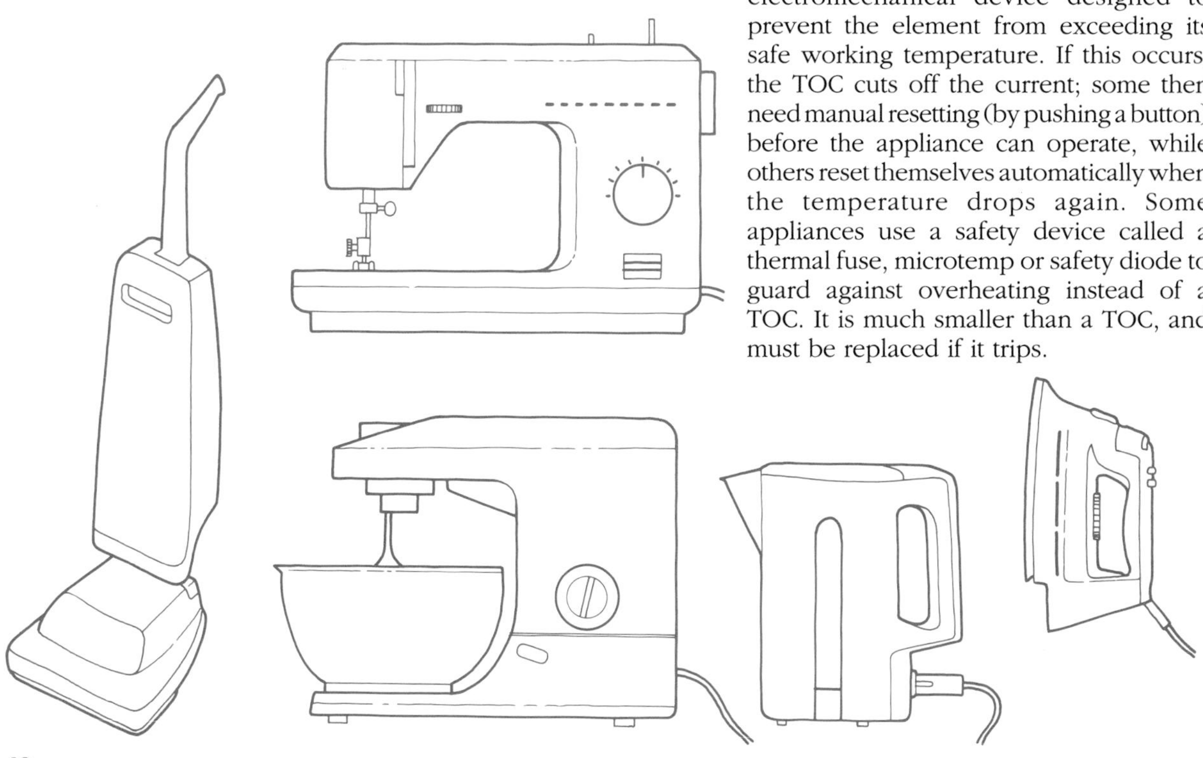

APPLIANCES WITH MOTORS AND HEATERS

Fan heaters, hair driers and tumble driers are the chief contenders in this group. All operate on broadly the same principle: the motor drives a fan which blows incoming cold air over a heating element and out again. The motor is commonly the induction type, and the on-off switching is arranged so that the elements cannot heat up unless the motor is running, to prevent overheating. The operating temperature is governed by a thermostat, and there will also be a TOC, usually self-resetting.

OTHER APPLIANCES

1 Two major groups of electrical appliances fall outside this simple classification – fridges and freezers, and washing machines and dishwashers. Fridges and freezers contain an induction motor which drives the compressor, and operating temperatures are governed by thermostats. There will also be a TOC protecting the motor, an internal light (usually only in fridges) operated by a door microswitch, and a defrost heater on fridges with automatic defrosting.

2 Dishwashers contain an induction motor which pumps water to the two spray arms, and to the outlet hose via a filter when the washing cycle is complete (some machines have a separate outlet pump). Inlet valves control the flow of water into the machine sump, where it is heated by a submerged element to the required temperature (governed by a thermostat), after it has passed through a built-in water softener. The operation of the machine is under the control of a programmer/timer.

3 Washing machines are the most complex of everyday electrical appliances, due to the addition of the drum rotation mechanism to the already complex array of inlet valves, circulating pumps, heating elements and controls. This explains why they break down more often than other appliances.

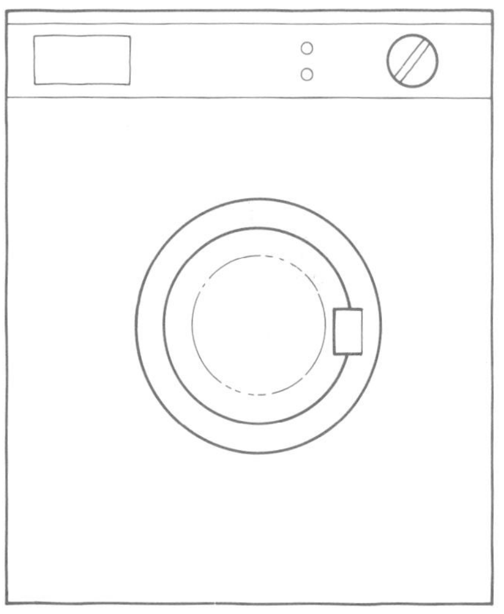

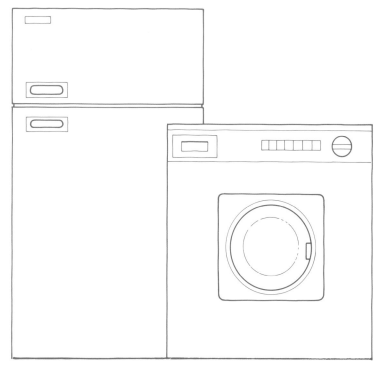

MOTORS

The majority of domestic appliances use an electric motor of some sort. Knowing how each type works makes tracking down faults a relatively simple matter

THINGS YOU NEED

- **Tools for gaining access**
- **Electrical screwdriver**
- **Methylated spirits**
- **Fine abrasive paper**
- **Small paintbrush**
- **Cotton buds**
- **Replacement armature bearings**
- **Replacement carbon brushes/ springs**
- **Replacement armature/stator/ motor**

At the heart of every electric motor are two sets of *electromagnets,* formed by winding coils of wire round an iron core. When an electric current is passed through the coils, the iron becomes a magnet with a north and a south pole. One set of coils, called the *armature,* is free to revolve inside the hollow centre of the other fixed set, called the *stator* or *field coil.* When the electricity supply to the coils is switched on, the north poles of the stator magnet attract the south poles of the armature and vice versa. This sets the armature in motion and turns the shaft to which it is attached; how it is then kept in motion depends on the type of motor.

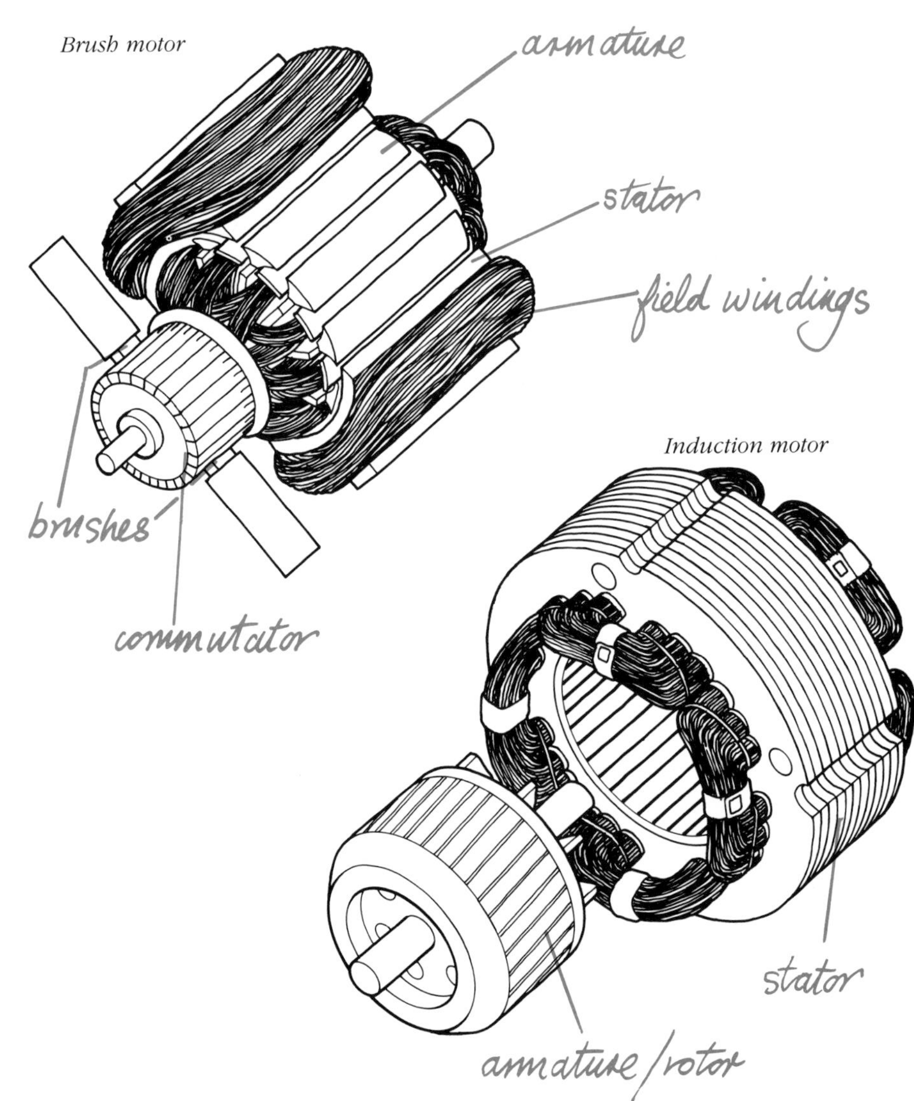

BRUSH MOTOR

This is the most common type of motor found in domestic appliances and d-i-y power tools. At one end of the armature is the *commutator* – a cylinder consisting of a number of slim parallel copper strips set in line with the motor shaft. Each diametrically opposite pair of these strips is connected to a separate winding in the armature itself. Current is supplied to the armature via two small graphite contacts called *brushes*, which are held against opposite sides of the commutator and are each in contact with just one copper strip at any moment.

The current flow through the winding to which these copper strips are connected magnetises the armature and causes it to rotate within the stator (also magnetised), so bringing the next sections of the commutator into contact with the brushes, repeating the magnetising process and keeping the armature spinning.

INDUCTION MOTOR

This type differs from the brush motor in that the current is supplied only to the fixed stator coils. This induces the armature or *rotor* to become magnetised too, since it is in the centre of the stator's magnetic field. Because alternating current oscillates 50 times a second, the direction of the magnetic field in the stator also reverses 50 times a second. However, the direction of magnetism induced in the rotor stays constant, so the stator attracts and then repels the rotor magnets in turn, causing continuous rotation. The rotor magnets are slightly skewed in relation to the motor shaft to create torque and start the rotor spinning when the current is switched on.

The stator has two sets of windings set at 90° to each other. The current flow to one set is delayed fractionally using either a *relay* or a *capacitor*, and since the two are therefore out of phase the resulting rotating magnetic field quickly accelerates the rotor to full working speed.

Shaded-pole induction motor (see over)

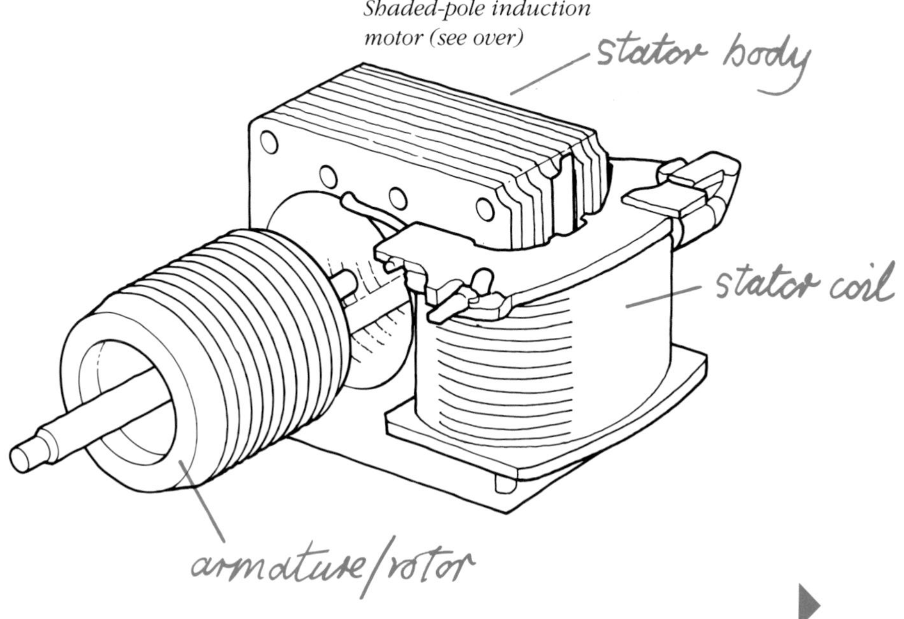

MOTORS continued

When investigating faults on induction motors, remember that the capacitor will still contain a charge even though the appliance has been isolated from the mains. Discharge the capacitor by bridging its two terminals with the shaft of an insulated electrical screwdriver, making sure you are touching only its handle as you do so.

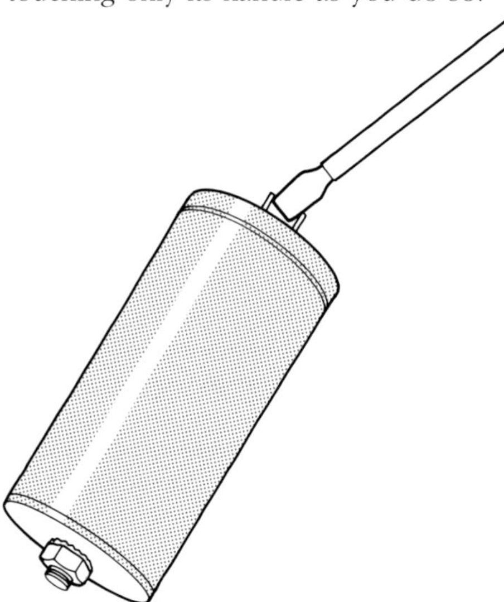

SHADED-POLE INDUCTION MOTOR

This is a simpler version of the capacitor-start motor, and has only one set of stator windings. To create the imbalance in the magnetic field necessary to start the rotor, copper bands are inserted in the poles of the stator. This imbalance also causes the stator to heat up in use, and to protect it from overheating the stator coils are usually protected by a thermal overload cut-out (TOC), generally the self-resetting type.

DC MOTOR

This type of motor is often used in portable hair driers because of its small size. Incoming alternating current is converted to direct current (DC) by a device called a *rectifier*, and is then supplied to the motor's armature via a commutator as in the brush motor. The stator coil is often a permanent magnet rather than an electromagnet, making the motor both smaller and lighter and reducing the power consumption.

ALWAYS unplug an appliance before starting any work on it

CURING MOTOR FAULTS

1 All motors suffer from dust and debris getting between the armature and the stator, and with brush motors dirt can also get between the brushes and the commutator. This occurs particularly with appliances such as food mixers, power tools and garden tools, which get clogged up with flour, sawdust and grass respectively. To clean the motor, open the appliance casing so you can gain access to the motor by removing any secondary casing covering it or a gearbox assembly attached to it. Undo any fixing screws and lift the motor out. Unscrew or unclip the carbon brushes from their holders after noting the brush positions, so they can be refitted the right way round.

2 Slide the armature out and check the commutator for signs of wear. Clean it with methylated spirits and fine abrasive paper if necessary. Use a small paintbrush to clean the surface of the armature and the inside of the stator. Clean out the brush holders with a cotton bud.

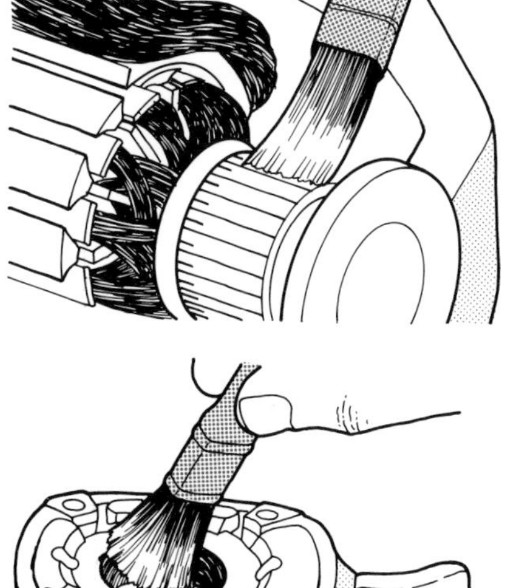

3 Inspect the armature and stator windings for any signs of discoloration or charring, which could indicate overheating or short-circuit faults. Such faults generally mean complete replacement, either of the affected components or of the entire motor.

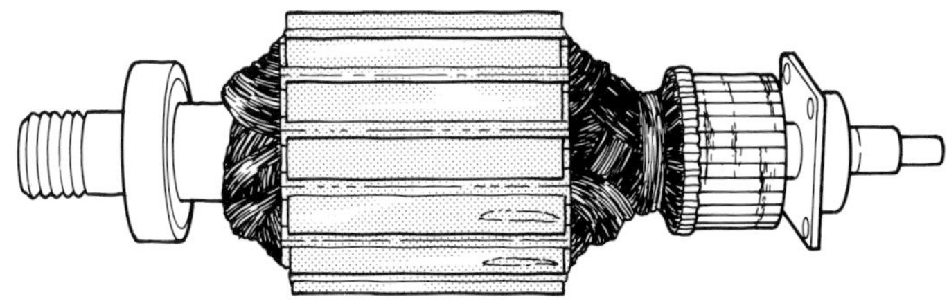

4 Check the armature bearings for excessive play, which can allow it to bind within the stator and will make the motor run sluggishly. Renew them if they are badly worn. Reassemble the motor and replace the carbon brushes, making sure they can move freely within their holders. Fit new brushes and springs if the old ones are badly worn, causing sparking and intermittent running of the motor.

HEATING ELEMENTS

Many domestic appliances contain heating elements, usually either the exposed single-wire type found in hair driers, toasters and so on, or the metal-sheathed, enclosed type found in cookers, immersion heaters and kettles

THINGS YOU NEED

- **Tools for gaining access**
- **Replacement element**
- **Replacement seals (for kettles, etc.)**

EXPOSED SINGLE-WIRE ELEMENTS

1 This element consists of a length of bare wire which heats up to red hot when a current is passed through it. In appliances such as toasters it is the radiant heat which does the appliance's job of browning the toast. In fan heaters and hair driers, the element is kept slightly cooler by a fan which blows a stream of cool air over it; the heat is transferred to the air stream ready to warm the room or dry your hair.

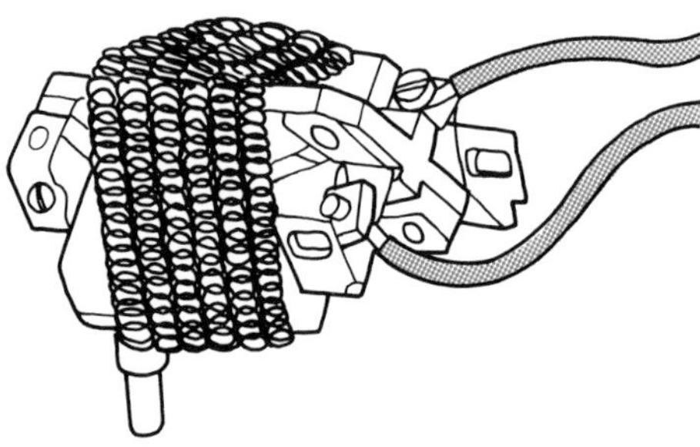

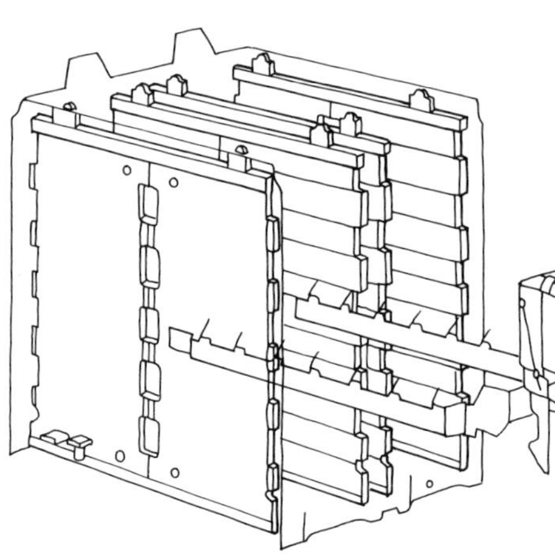

2 The element may be in the form of a semi-rigid coil held between terminals or may be wound on to a rigid fire-resistant material. In some fan heaters and hair driers it now often takes the form of a rigid finned component which is much less prone to accidental damage than bare coils. Spares are generally easy to get hold of, although with many modern toasters only complete units consisting of the latch mechanism and a set of elements are available, meaning that it is often cheaper to buy a new toaster than to repair one with a broken element.

3 Because the element is in the form of a bare live wire, care must be taken not to touch it while the appliance is in use, especially when trying to unjam a toaster, for example. Always unplug the appliance first.

IRON ELEMENTS

Old-fashioned dry irons had the heating element clamped against the sole plate, and replacement was a relatively simple job. However, modern irons have sole plates with integral heating elements, and failure of the element means fitting a complete new sole plate unit – often not worth the time and expense involved.

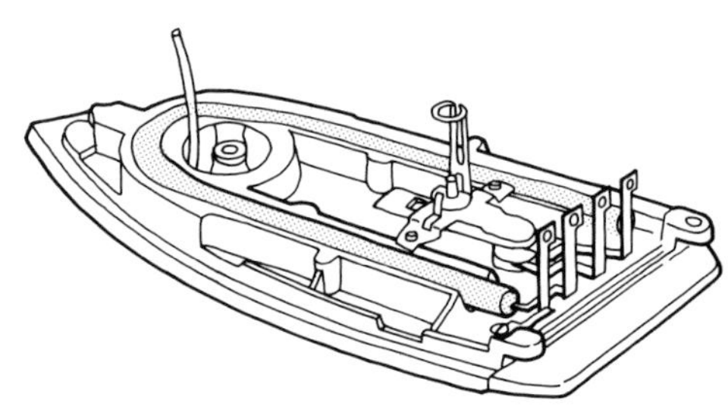

ALWAYS unplug an appliance before starting any work on it

METAL-SHEATHED, ENCLOSED ELEMENTS

1 This type of element consists of a metal outer sheath containing the current-carrying conductor. This is completely surrounded by magnesium oxide powder so that it is electrically insulated from the sheath. However, the oxide filling conducts heat very efficiently, allowing the element to heat up to a red glow in appliances such as grills, ovens and hobs, or to heat water in a kettle or immersion heater.

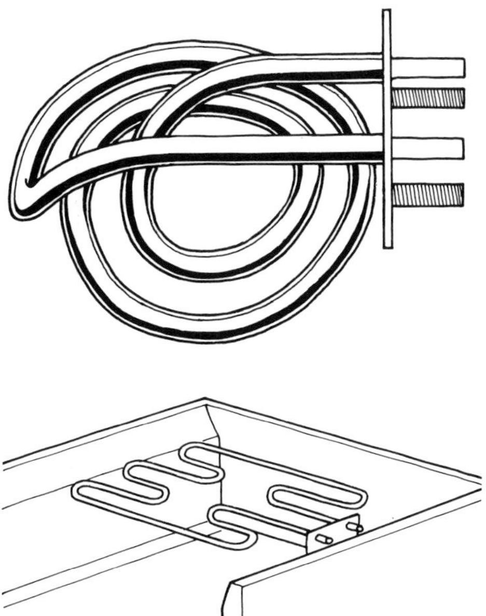

2 Because the element is manufactured in the form of a tube, it can be bent into a wide range of configurations, from the spiral of an electric hob to the shapely element in an electric kettle. Failure generally occurs either because of faulty connections to the terminals causing overheating or because of a short circuit between the conductor and the sheathing due to damage to the element. In the case of immersed elements, failure may be due to the sheathing being attacked by 'aggressive' water. Poor insulation (see page 33) can also be a problem. Whatever is wrong, complete replacement of the heating element is always the only solution.

FIRE ELEMENTS

Electric fires use a wide range of different elements, ranging from wire coils mounted on fireclay rods or in shaped fireclay formers to spirals enclosed in silica tubes. Those with bare live wires are obviously potentially dangerous if the coil is broken, because the wire remains live. Silica tubes, used in infra-red reflector fires, are by contrast completely safe, and are often used in bathrooms for this reason. Complete replacement is the only cure when an element fails.

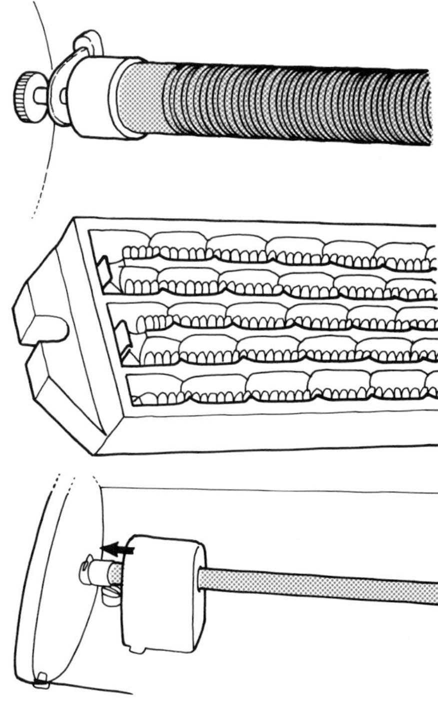

THERMOSTATS AND CUT-OUTS

Temperature control is a vital function for many electrical appliances, either to ensure that they operate at the right temperature or that they don't overheat

FIXED THERMOSTATS

1 This type of thermostat makes or breaks a circuit at a pre-set temperature which cannot be varied by the user. This is usually marked on the body of the thermostat, along with a coded marking which indicates how it works. NO means the thermostat is normally open, closing to make the circuit at the stated temperature, while NC means that it is normally closed, opening to break the circuit at the stated temperature. Some combine both functions, usually as a means of incorporating protection against overheating. In this case, one thermostat will be used to turn the appliance on at its working temperature, the other to turn it off at danger level.

2 At the heart of a fixed thermostat is a bi-metallic strip or disc. This consists of two pieces of different metals bonded together. Each expands at a different rate when heated, so the strip or disc deforms as the temperature changes, and this mechanical action can be used to open or close a switch. Different combinations of metals are used to give different operating temperatures.

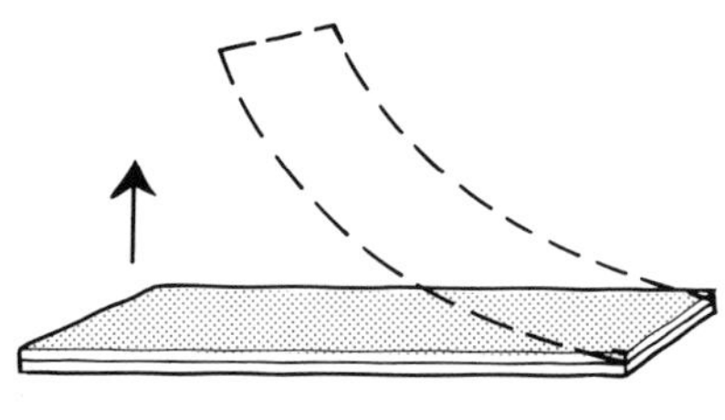

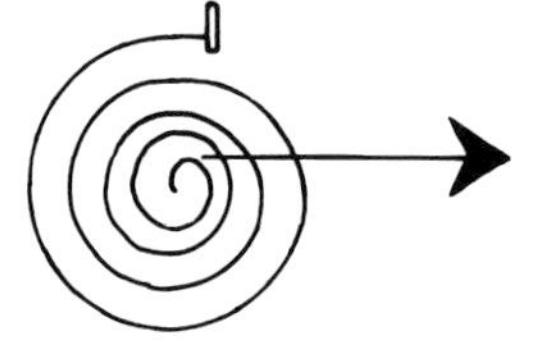

VARIABLE THERMOSTATS

1 As their name implies, variable thermostats allow the user to vary the temperature setting at which the thermostat operates. There are two common varieties: the bi-metallic plate type and the pod type. The former is often used on appliances such as electric irons. It has one contact point on the bi-metallic strip, and an opposing contact point on a movable threaded shaft which is turned by the temperature control knob. The temperature at which the two contacts meet is governed by the setting on the knob. In time, the constant flexing of the bi-metallic strip can lead to inaccurate temperature regulation, and replacement is generally the only cure.

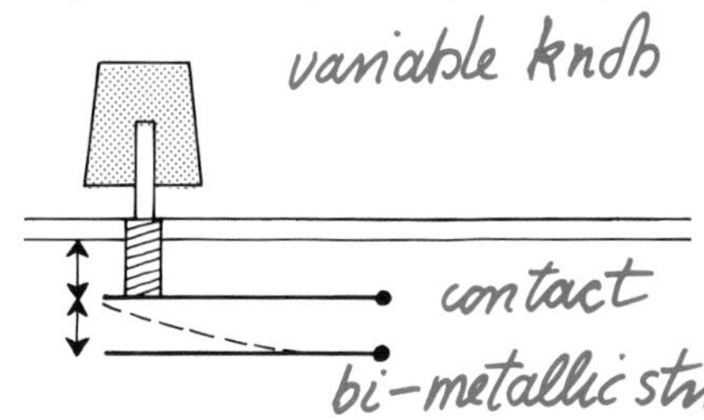

2 The pod type is widely used in cookers, fridges and freezers. It consists of an oil-filled pod or probe connected to the thermostat switch by a long capillary tube, allowing the switch to be kept away from extreme heat or cold. As the oil in the pod expands or contracts with changing temperatures, it operates a diaphragm which makes or breaks the switch. As with bi-metallic variable thermostats, the second contact is on the end of the shaft carrying the temperature control knob.

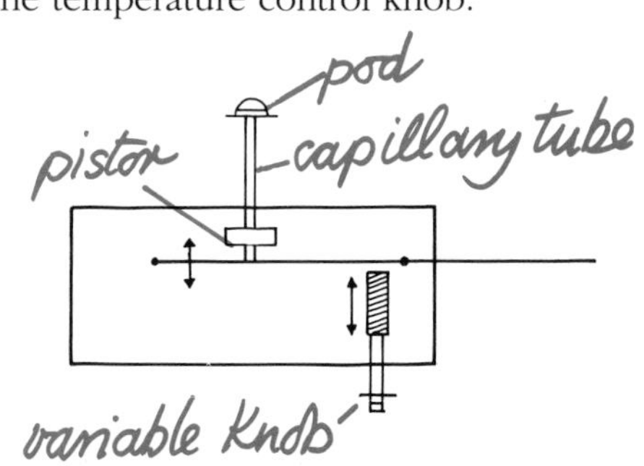

ALWAYS unplug an appliance before starting any work on it

THERMAL OVERLOAD CUT-OUTS

1 Many appliances incorporate a safety device called a thermal overload cut-out (TOC) designed to prevent overheating, which could cause a fire. It cuts off the power supply to the component it is protecting if its safe working temperature is exceeded. The simplest TOCs are similar in principle to fixed thermostats, and contain a bi-metallic strip that makes or breaks contact as the temperature varies. This type suffers from the drawback that it is self-resetting, so will restore the power supply as the operating temperature drops, causing cycling to occur which can eventually lead to failure of the TOC and the loss of the protection it provides. Types requiring manual resetting – usually by pressing a button – are better overheat protectors.

2 Some appliances now use non-mechanical overheat protection devices called thermal fuses, microtemps or safety diodes instead of TOCs. They are foolproof, in that once they trip they cannot be reset and must be replaced – a nuisance in a sense, but at least they provide guaranteed protection against overheating.

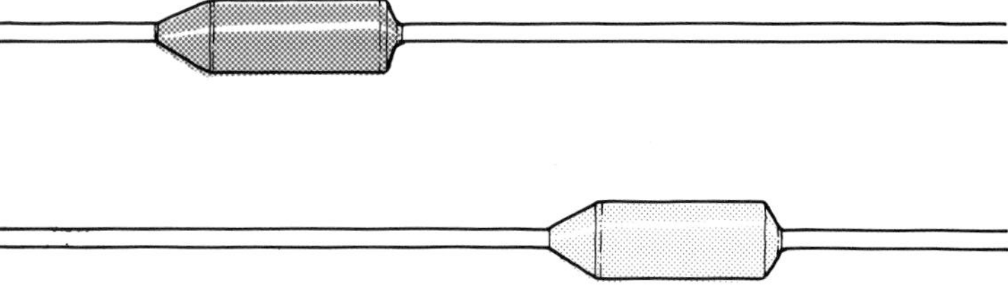

Thermal fuses

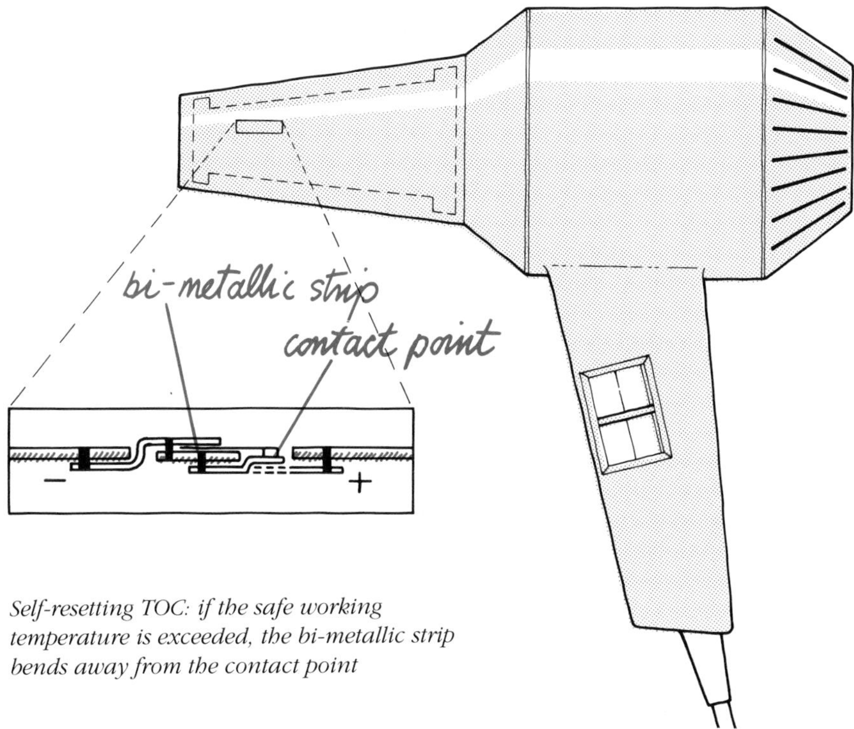

Self-resetting TOC: if the safe working temperature is exceeded, the bi-metallic strip bends away from the contact point

SWITCHES AND TIMERS

On many appliances a simple on-off switch provides control of the incoming power supply. On others you will find more complex switching arrangements, and function selection and timer control

THINGS YOU NEED

- **Tools for gaining access**
- **Continuity tester**
- **Replacement components**

ON-OFF SWITCHES

1 Many domestic appliances, especially small or portable types, have just a single-function switch that turns the appliance on and off. This is wired in line and is generally the first component in the circuit after the terminal block to which the appliance flex is connected. The switch itself may fail after extended use, but is generally simple to reach, remove and replace. Problems apparently due to switch failure are more often caused by faulty connections to the switch itself, especially in portable appliances where vibration may loosen the terminal screws.

2 On some appliances, such as fan heaters and hair driers, there may be a switch bank which controls options such as heat output and fan speed. It may be possible to replace these individually if one fails, but generally a complete new switch bank must be fitted.

3 On others, such as food mixers, there is a speed selector switch which varies the power supply to the field coils and so controls the motor speed. The switch is less likely to fail than the field coil, which will need complete replacement if a fault develops in its windings.

4 Non-automatic kettles have an on-off switch which must be operated manually, and a thermal overload cut-out (TOC) to protect the element from overheating. Some can be reset once the kettle has cooled down, but others cannot; once the TOC has been activated, complete element replacement is necessary. Automatic kettles combine an on switch with a fixed bi-metallic strip thermostat which turns the switch off when the water boils. There is again a separate TOC to protect the element from overheating.

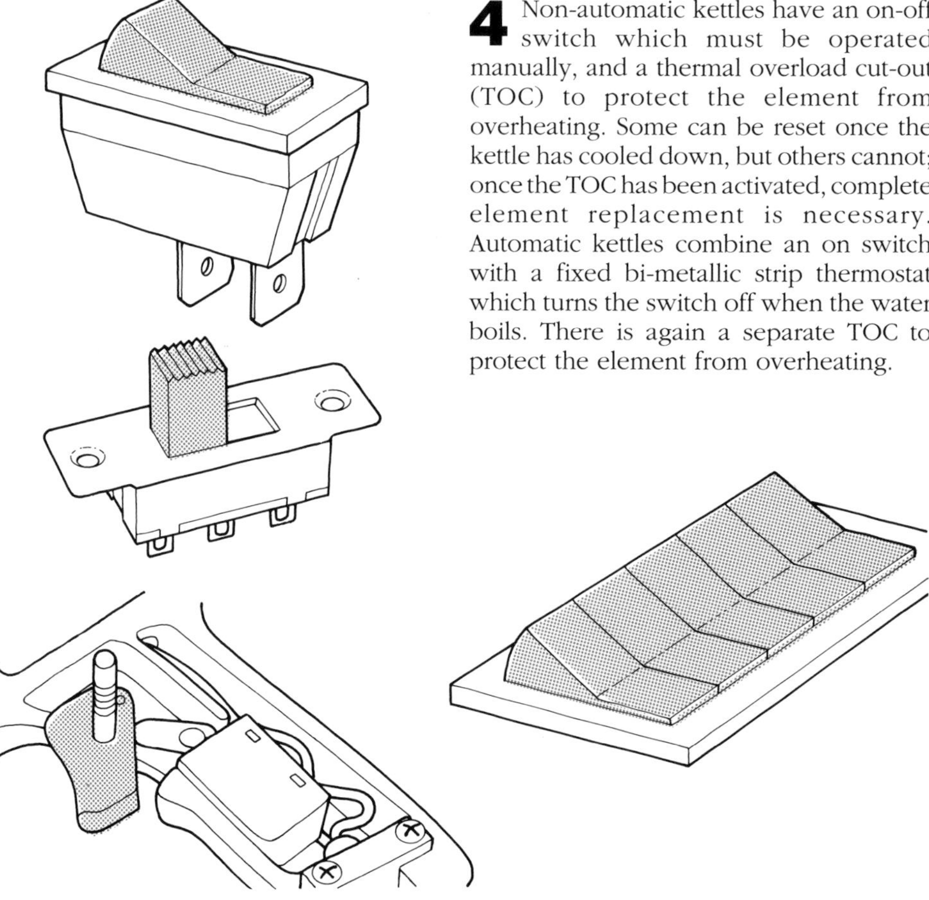

VARIABLE-SPEED SWITCHES

Some appliances, mainly d-i-y and garden power tools, have variable speed control. This is usually provided by means of an electronic speed control unit which interrupts the power supply to the motor at regular intervals. Increasing the pulsing rate increases the motor speed and vice versa. If the control unit fails, it must be completely replaced unless the fault is found to lie in the electrical connections to it.

TIMERS

Timers are used on appliances such as dishwashers and washing machines to control the sequence of different operations the appliance performs – opening and closing inlet valves, switching pumps on and off and so on. Within the timer there are either a series of *cams* on a central barrel (an edge-cam timer) or an etched disc (a face-cam timer) which is rotated by the cam advance motor. Edge-cam timers, the commonest type, are larger and deeper than face-cam timers. Next to the timer is the timing motor, which times all the functions of the machine. These motors are generally very reliable, but faults can develop with the timer unit. If they do, a complete replacement unit must be fitted.

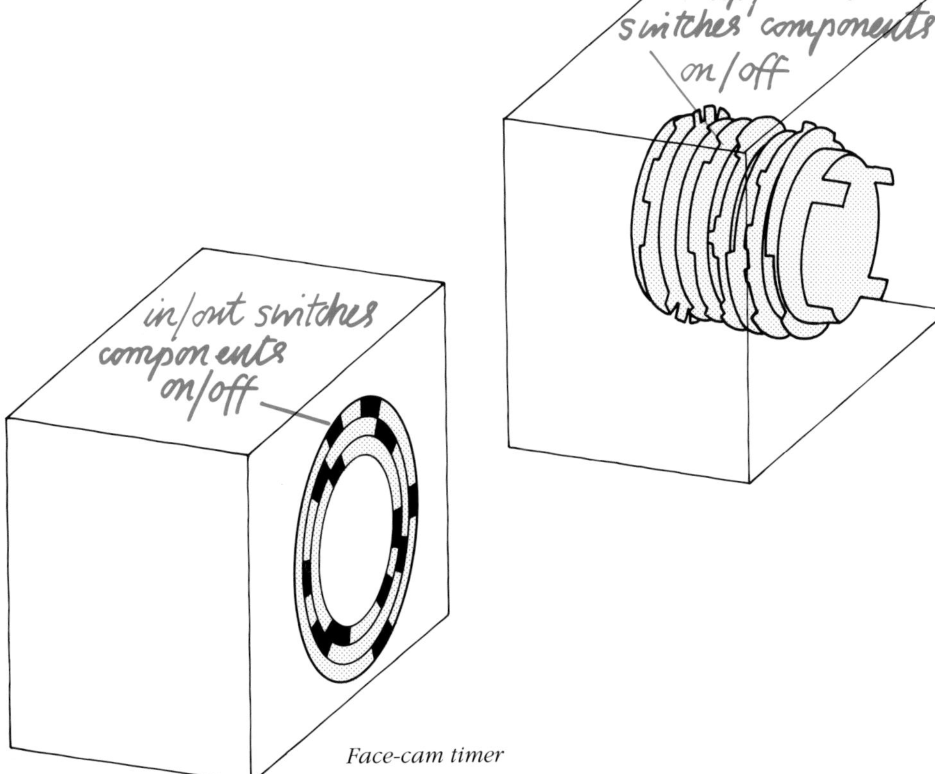

Edge-cam timer

Face-cam timer

FIXING YOUR

COFFEE MAKER

Coffee makers boil water from a reservoir and trickle it through a filter containing ground coffee into a jug on a heated plate

FAULTFINDER

This is a simple type of appliance based around a heating element, but complicated by the presence of water and easily clogged up by scale

THINGS YOU NEED

- **Tools for gaining access and for fitting parts**
- **Continuity tester**
- **Replacement parts as necessary**
- **Descaling liquid**

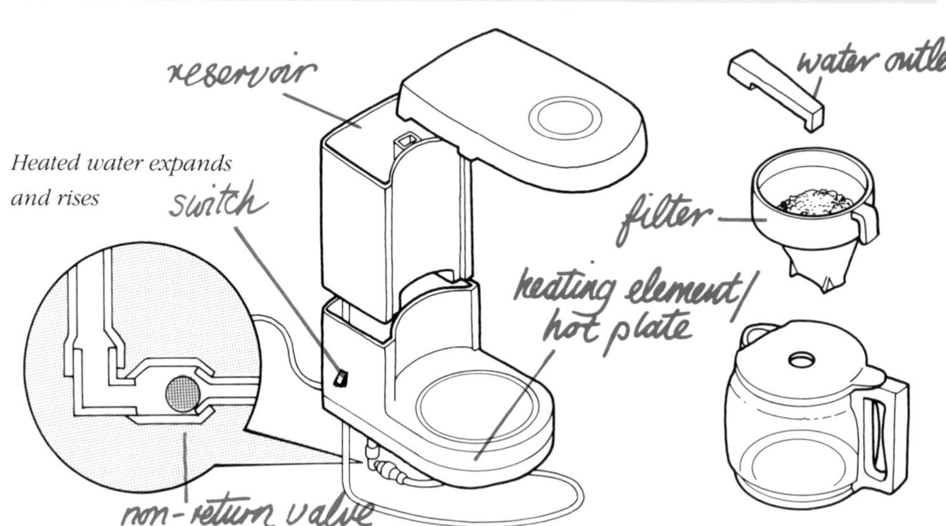

NO POWER	
Likely cause	*What to do*
Plug or flex fault	Rewire or replace as necessary
Internal wiring fault	Test for continuity, remake connections
On-off switch faulty	Replace
LIGHT ON BUT NO HEATING	
Likely cause	*What to do*
Internal wiring fault	Test for continuity, remake connections
Element failed	Replace
Thermostat faulty	Replace
Thermal overload cut-out (TOC) tripped or faulty	Test for continuity, reset or replace as necessary
HEATING BUT NO WATER TRANSFER	
Likely cause	*What to do*
No water in reservoir (will cause TOC to trip)	Fill reservoir
Scale build-up	Descale appliance
Non-return valve faulty	Replace
LIGHT OFF BUT APPLIANCE WORKING	
Likely cause	*What to do*
Internal wiring fault	Test for continuity, remake connections
Neon lamp failed	Replace lamp (sometimes part of on-off switch assembly)
LEAKS	
Likely cause	*What to do*
Jug not underneath filter outlet	Position jug correctly
Faulty seals between components	Replace seals if possible, take machine to service engineer otherwise
Cracked reservoir or jug	Replace if possible

FIXING YOUR

COOKER

Modern electric cookers and separate ovens and hobs often bristle with technology, but only microwave ovens are truly complex

FAULTFINDER – OVENS

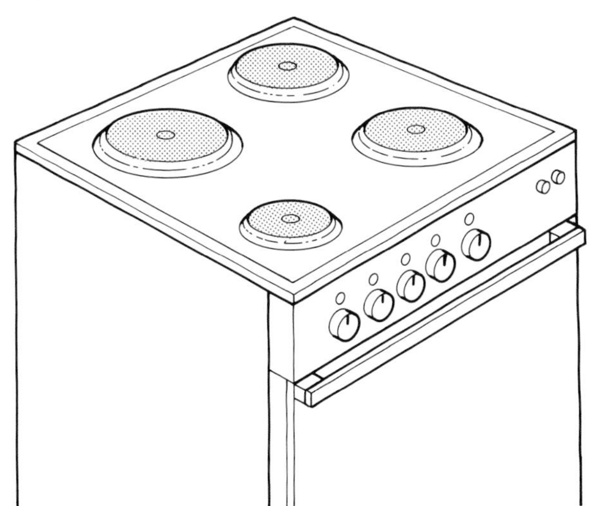

The basic components of conventional cookers – heating elements, temperature regulators and thermostats – have changed little from earlier models

THINGS YOU NEED

- **Tools for gaining access and for fitting parts**
- **Continuity tester**
- **Electrical screwdriver**
- **Replacement parts as necessary**

NO HEAT

Likely cause	*What to do*
Circuit fuse blown/Miniature circuit breaker (MCB) tripped	Trace cause (see pages 10-11), then replace fuse/reset MCB
Circuit wiring discontinuity	Check wiring to cooker switch and cooker, remake connections or replace cable as necessary
Total element failure	Replace
Thermostat failure	Test thermostat operation, replace if necessary

SLOW OR UNEVEN HEATING

Likely cause	*What to do*
Single element failure	Test for continuity, replace if necessary
Faulty thermostat	Test thermostat operation, replace if necessary
For fan-assisted ovens:	
Air intake blocked	Clear air intakes
Fan running slow	Check for debris on fan, clean off; replace fan motor if necessary
Fan not running	Check for continuity, replace motor if necessary

OVERHEATING

Likely cause	*What to do*
Thermostat failure	Replace

HEAT ESCAPING

Likely cause	*What to do*
Failed door seal	Replace seal and clips

FAILED OVEN LIGHT

Likely cause	*What to do*
Wear and tear	Fit replacement lamp, either from rear of cooker or after unscrewing cover inside oven
Damage to lamp cover	Replace

SEE PAGES 24-51 for how to carry out REPAIRS AND TESTS

FAULTFINDER – HOBS AND GRILLS

THINGS YOU NEED

- **Tools for gaining access and for fitting parts**
- **Continuity tester**
- **Electrical screwdriver**
- **Replacement parts as necessary**

NO HEAT	
Likely cause	*What to do*
Faulty wiring or connection to element	Check continuity and connections, repair as necessary
Element failure	Replace
Regulator failure	Replace
FAILED CONTROL PANEL LIGHT	
Likely cause	*What to do*
Wear and tear	Gain access to light and replace
Failed starter (fluorescent tube)	Replace starter

REPLACING AN ELEMENT

1 It is a relatively simple job to replace a hob element, although it is vital that an exact replacement is fitted with the same wattage, size and configuration as the original. Before starting work, turn off the cooker or hob at its isolating switch and remove the circuit fuse (or switch off the MCB) on the cooker circuit.

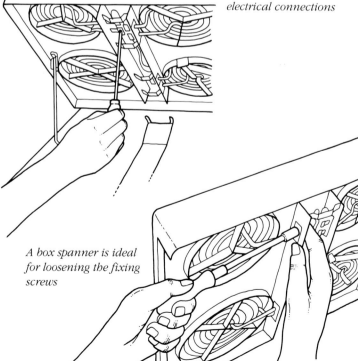

Unscrew or pull off electrical connections

A box spanner is ideal for loosening the fixing screws

2 Except with lift-up or swivel-type elements, it is generally necessary to raise the hinged top plate of the cooker to gain access to the element terminals. Some elements have push-fit electrical connections, others screw-on ones; remove these carefully. The element itself usually has threaded ends which are secured by fixing nuts. Release the old element and fit the replacement, making sure it is securely fixed. Then reattach the electrical connections, checking that the cables are routed correctly and are not trapped or in contact with hot surfaces. Replace the top plate if necessary and restore the power.

3 Replacing oven elements can be more difficult, depending on how easy it is to remove the necessary panels to gain access to them. Isolate the cooker or oven from the mains first. Then remove panels to expose the element and disconnect its electrical connections so you can test it for continuity. When you locate the failed element, release its fixing nuts. Ease the old element out and reverse the sequence of operations to fit the new one. Restore the power.

ALWAYS unplug an appliance before starting any work on it

TESTING AN OVEN THERMOSTAT

1 Turn the temperature control up from the off position to a low heat setting. Leave the oven to heat up for about ten minutes; the pilot light by the control knob should go out, indicating that the oven has reached the required temperature and the thermostat has cut out.

2 Open the oven door to allow some heat to escape. This should cause the pilot light to come on again, indicating that the thermostat has switched the element back on.

3 Turn the temperature control right down and check that the pilot light goes out. If it does not and the oven stays hot, the thermostat is not cutting out properly and needs replacing. Leave this job to a service engineer.

REPLACING A HOB REGULATOR

1 If a hob regulator needs replacing, it is essential to buy a new one that matches the old regulator's specification precisely. Isolate the hob completely from the mains before starting work on it.

2 Gain access to the regulator by removing the push-on control knobs from their spindles and unscrewing the cover plate behind them. Note the position of each knob relative to its spindle before removing it.

3 Make detailed notes and sketches of all the wiring connections before undoing any of them. Label individual cores if necessary to aid identification. Then disconnect them, unscrew the regulator mounting plate and remove the regulator by undoing its fixing screws or nuts.

4 Fit the new regulator to its mounting plate and remake the wiring connections. Secure the mounting plate and check that all the wiring is returned to its original position. Refit the cover plate, checking that any seals fit correctly, and replace the control knobs. Restore the power.

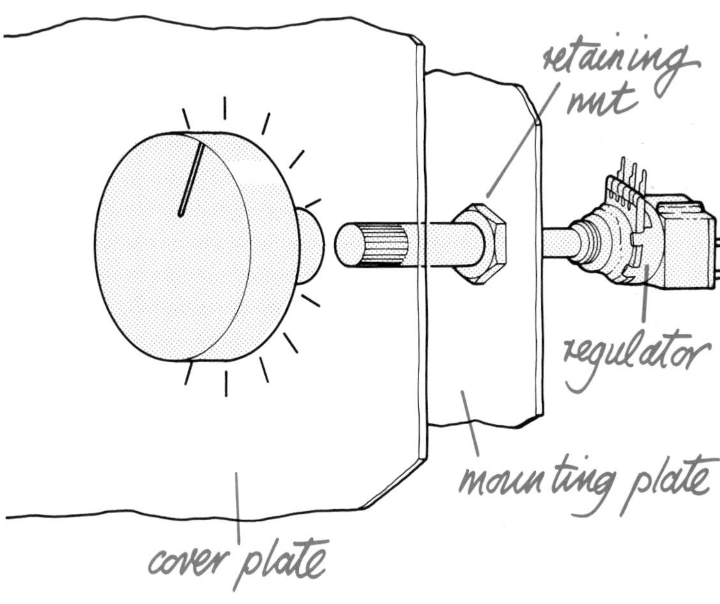

SEE PAGES 24-51 for how to carry out REPAIRS AND TESTS

FAULTFINDER – MICROWAVE OVENS

Microwave ovens are generally very reliable and are not suitable for d-i-y repair work. The advice given here deals with only the simplest operating faults

THINGS YOU NEED

- **Instruction leaflet**
- **Microwave-safe cookware**
- **Kitchen scales**
- **Cleaning materials**

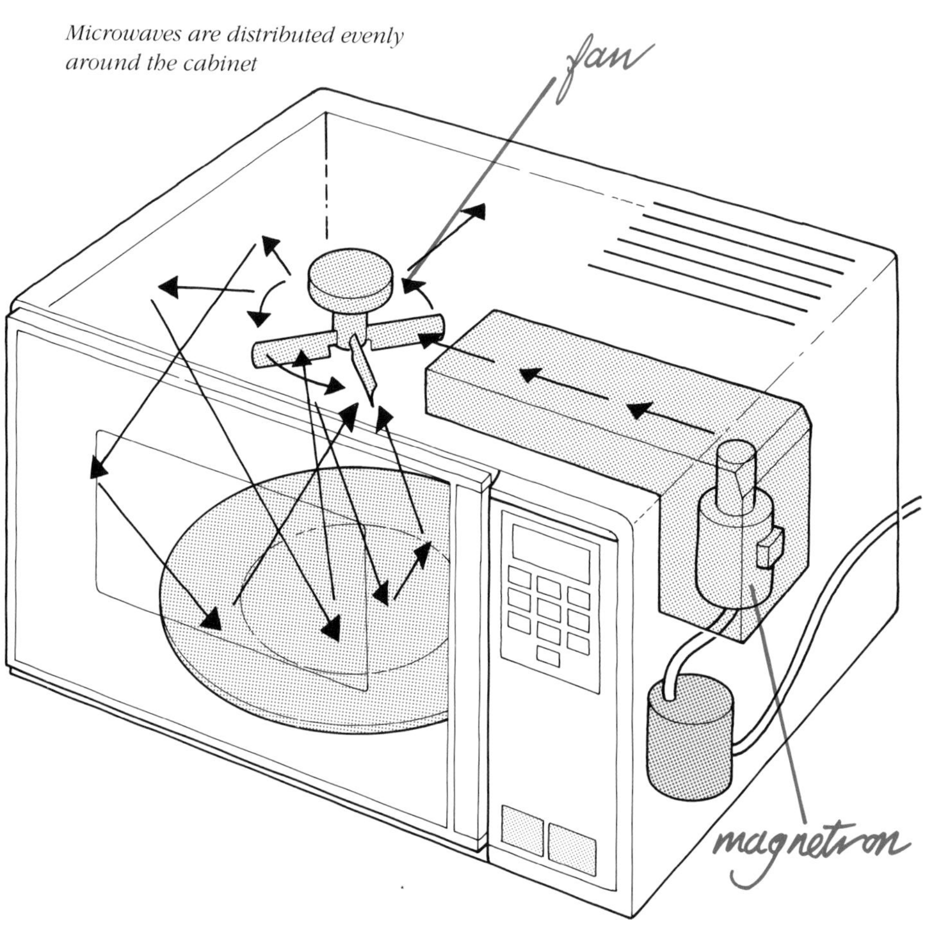

Microwaves are distributed evenly around the cabinet

CLEANING

Clean the oven compartment and the inner face of the door regularly with a damp cloth, using a little detergent to remove grease spots if necessary. Do not use abrasive cleaners. Mop up spillages as soon as they occur. Wipe the exterior of the oven and touch control panels with a barely damp cloth; do not use aerosol cleaners.

ALWAYS REASSEMBLE AN APPLIANCE BEFORE PLUGGING IT IN TO TEST YOUR REPAIR

ALWAYS unplug an appliance before starting any work on it

NO POWER	
Likely cause	*What to do*
Plug or flex fault	Rewire or replace as necessary
Door improperly latched	Open door and close again
Recent power failure, cancelling electronic display	Reset clock
Faulty timer or on-off switch on manual models	Call service engineer
Condensation in touch control pad	Move oven away from source of steam such as open saucepans, retest later to see if fault has cleared. Call service engineer if fault persists

ARCING, SPARKING OR BURNING	
Likely cause	*What to do*
Use of metallic containers	Use microwave-safe cookware only, avoid crockery with metallic glazes
Use of metallic ties, skewers, etc.	Do not use
Excessive use of cooking foil	Use for shielding only as recommended in microwave cooking instructions
Build-up of food particles in oven	Clean oven interior regularly

FOOD UNDERCOOKED	
Likely cause	*What to do*
Wrong cooking time selected	Check food weight and alter cooking time as appropriate
Wrong power setting selected	Alter power setting
Fault on magnetron	Call service engineer

FOOD OVERCOOKED	
Likely cause	*What to do*
Wrong cooking time selected	Check food weight and alter cooking time as appropriate
Wrong power setting selected	Alter power setting
Air vents blocked/obstructed	Keep all vents clear of blockages or obstructions, and ensure that there is enough clearance around oven (especially built-in types)

STEAM COMING FROM REAR VENT OR AROUND DOOR	
Likely cause	*What to do*
Steam from cooking vented with air cooling magnetron	Nothing
Door is not airtight (normal)	Nothing

FOOD CATCHES FIRE	
Likely cause	*What to do*
Overheating	Switch off or unplug oven, keep door closed until food cools

SEE PAGES 24-51 for how to carry out REPAIRS AND TESTS

FIXING YOUR

DISHWASHER

Dishwashers are great labour-savers and are also more efficient and hygienic than traditional hand washing

FAULTFINDER

Due to the presence of water and the wide variety of functions they perform, dishwashers break down more frequently than almost any other appliance

THINGS YOU NEED

- **Tools for gaining access and for fitting parts**
- **Continuity tester**
- **Replacement parts as necessary**
- **Spirit level**

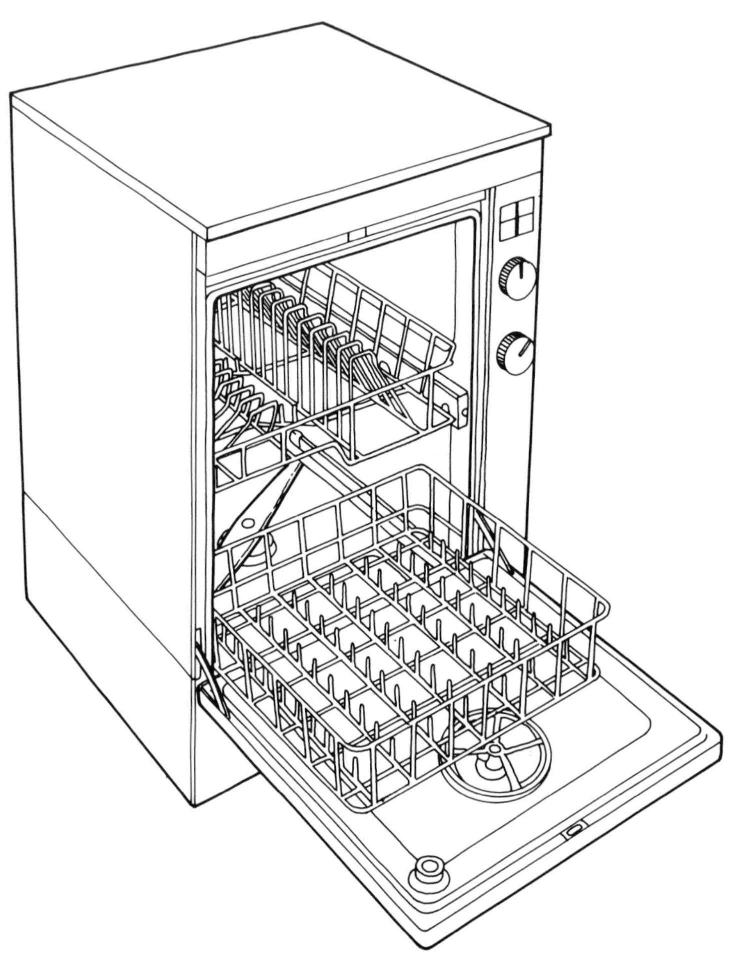

NO POWER	
Likely cause	*What to do*
Plug or flex fault	Rewire or replace as necessary
Water supply turned off	Restore water supply
Door not properly closed	Close door properly
Internal wiring fault	Test for continuity, remake connections
Door microswitch faulty	Replace
Timer faulty	Replace

NO FILLING ACTION	
Likely cause	*What to do*
Water supply turned off	Restore water supply
Filter before inlet valve blocked	Remove and clean filter
Inlet valve faulty	Replace
Timer faulty	Replace

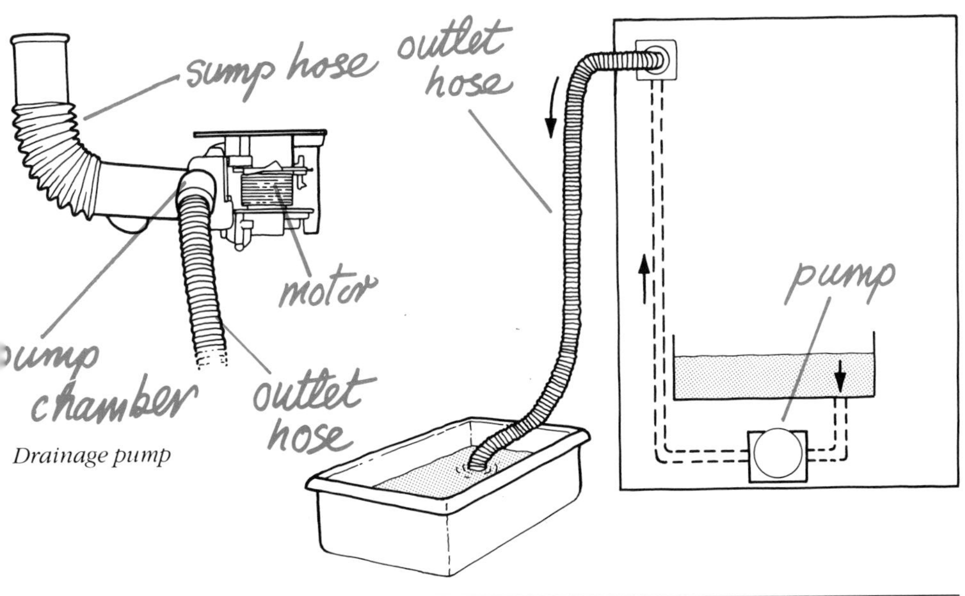

Drainage pump

NOTE: To empty a machine full of water, disconnect the outlet hose from its usual discharge point and place it in a bucket at floor level so the water is siphoned out. Raise the hose to stop the flow while you empty the bucket.

PROGRAMME INTERRUPTED	
Likely cause	*What to do*
Door opened during programme	Close door
Plug fuse blown due to wiring fault or low insulation	Test wiring for continuity, remake connections, check insulation with RCD
Internal wiring fault	Test for continuity, remake connections
Door microswitch faulty	Replace
Timer faulty	Replace
Heating element faulty	Replace
Overheat protector tripped	Trace and rectify cause of overheat, reset overheat protector

NOISY OPERATION	
Likely cause	*What to do*
Machine not standing level	Adjust feet and check for level
Incorrect loading of machine	Load machine as per instruction booklet
Spray arm fouling	Reposition offending object
Loose/worn spray arm mounts	Replace spray arms
Worn pump bearings	Replace pump

NO DISCHARGE ACTION	
Likely cause	*What to do*
Sump hose blocked	Remove hose and clear blockage
Outlet hose kinked/blocked	Unkink hose/remove blockage
Object in pump chamber	Remove object, check pump for damage, replace pump if necessary
Discharge pump faulty	Replace pump
Internal wiring fault	Test for continuity, remake connections
Timer faulty	Replace

SEE PAGES 24-51 for how to carry out REPAIRS AND TESTS

FAULTFINDER continued

THINGS YOU NEED

- **Tools for gaining access and for fitting parts**
- **Continuity tester**
- **Replacement parts as necessary**
- **Spirit level**

POOR WASHING ACTION

Likely cause	*What to do*
Incorrect wash cycle selected	Check instruction booklet for guidance
No detergent in dispenser	Fill detergent dispenser
Too little detergent	Check instruction booklet for correct quantities
Detergent dispenser faulty	Replace
No rinse aid in dispenser	Fill rinse aid dispenser
Rinse aid dispenser faulty	Replace
No salt in water softener	Fill salt compartment
Heavily soiled dishes not pre-rinsed	Rinse dishes in sink before loading or run rinse-and-hold cycle after loading
Overloading of machine	Check instruction booklet for guidance
Incorrect loading of machine	Check that items are properly loaded without any water traps
Filters full of food debris	Clean filters
Spray arms blocked/jammed/split	Remove blockages/replace spray arms
Unsuitable items washed	Check dishwasher suitability of all items washed
Thermostat faulty	Replace
Heating element faulty	Replace

POOR DRYING ACTION

Likely cause	*What to do*
Too little rinse aid dispensed	Adjust rinse aid dispenser
No rinse aid dispensed	Fill rinse aid dispenser, replace dispenser if faulty
Too much rinse aid dispensed	Adjust rinse aid dispenser
Door opened too soon	Allow load to stand at end of cycle
Thermostat faulty	Replace
Heating element faulty	Replace

MACHINE OVERFILLS

Likely cause	*What to do*
Water level pressure switch faulty	Replace
Inlet valve faulty	Replace
Timer faulty	Replace

MACHINE LEAKS

Likely cause	*What to do*
Machine not standing level	Adjust feet and check for level
Door seal misaligned/perished	Realign/replace
Air break unit (part of inlet system) blocked	Clean or replace
Pump seals faulty	Dismantle and clean pump, replace if badly worn
Sump/spray hoses loose or holed	Refit or replace hoses
Inlet/outlet hoses loose or holed	Refit or replace hoses
Thermostat seals faulty	Replace seals

MACHINE FLOODS	
Likely cause	*What to do*
Various faults	Isolate the appliance from the mains and turn off the water supply, then disconnect the outlet hose and lower it into a bucket to siphon off the water in the machine. Leave the door closed for up to half an hour if the machine is hot. Most machines have a flood protection device to switch off the machine if it overfills; this needs manual resetting.

HOW IT WORKS

- At the start of the programme, the machine fills to a pre-set level. The water level pressure switch sends a signal to the timer to stop the filling action and move on to the next step in the programme. The water is heated and softened by the built-in water softener.
- The wash pump then pumps the water at high pressure to the two spray arms to rinse the contents. The water runs down to the base of the cabinet, into the sump and then back to the pump again in a closed cycle. At a pre-set temperature or time the detergent container opens automatically and the actual washing cycle begins.
- When it is complete the dirty water is pumped out of the machine via a cleanable filter in the sump, and fresh water is taken in for the rinse cycles - one cold, the other hot with a metered measure of rinse aid added to help drying off. Finally the machine empties and the heat of the contents completes the drying process.
- The door latch features a microswitch which stops the machine working if the door is not properly closed. The machine will not work at all if the microswitch is faulty.

FIXING YOUR

ELECTRIC FIRE

Electric fires and radiant heaters are best suited to warming small rooms or for supplementing background heating

FAULTFINDER

In some heaters the element is exposed, in others it is enclosed in a tube, making the heater safer and suitable for use in a bathroom; always make sure you fit the right type of replacement element

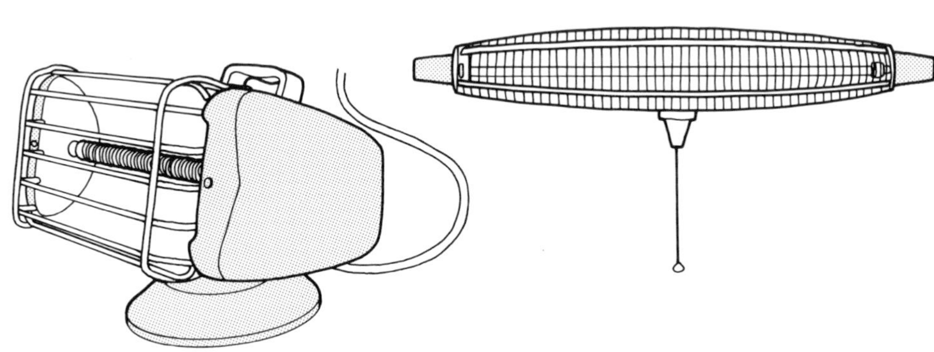

THINGS YOU NEED

- **Tools for dismantling and reassembly**
- **Continuity tester**
- **Replacement parts as necessary**

NO HEAT	
Likely cause	*What to do*
Plug or flex fault	Rewire or replace as necessary
Internal wiring fault	Check continuity, remake connections
Element failed	Replace
Main on-off switch failed	Replace
Broken pull cord (wall heaters)	Replace
NO FLAME EFFECT	
Likely cause	*What to do*
Failed lamp	Replace
Internal wiring fault	Check continuity, remake connections
Jammed reflector rotor	Reposition rotor

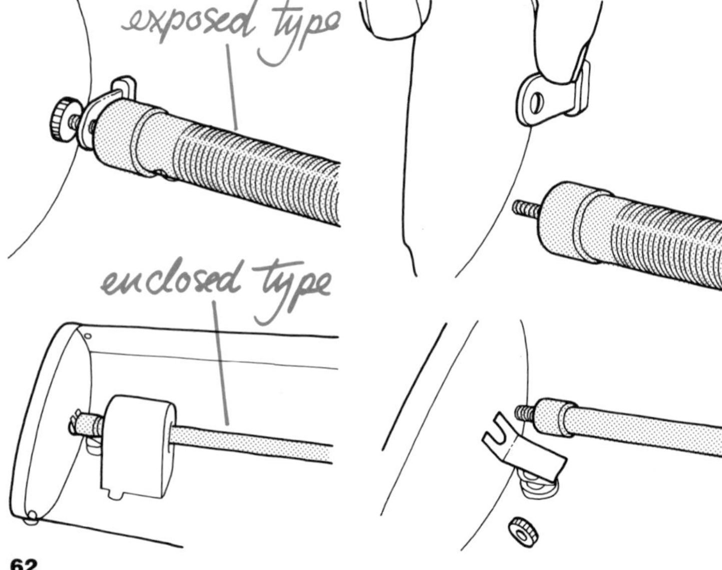

REPLACING AN ELEMENT

1 Unplug the fire, and examine the outer casing to locate screws holding the grille or casing in place. Remove them in a logical sequence, labelling each one for later replacement in the right place, to gain access to the element mountings.

2 Release the old element by undoing the securing nuts or releasing the spring clips as appropriate. Take it with you when shopping for a replacement to ensure that you buy an exact match of the right type and size, with the correct wattage and contact type. Reverse the dismantling sequence to fit the new element, replace the grille and test the fire.

EXTRACTOR FAN

Extractor fans and cooker hoods are invaluable for clearing the air in steamy or smelly rooms

FAULTFINDER

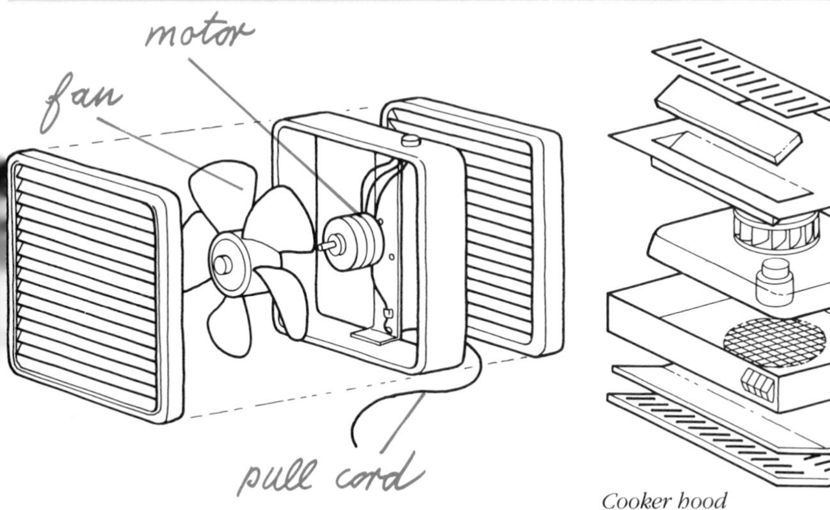

Cooker hood

Cooker hoods are extractor fans designed specifically for use above a hob or free-standing cooker, and work in exactly the same way

THINGS YOU NEED

- Screwdrivers
- Continuity tester
- Replacement parts as necessary
- Light oil

SEE PAGES 24-51 for how to carry out REPAIRS AND TESTS

NO POWER

Likely cause	*What to do*
Fuse failure	Check fuse in plug or fused connection unit (FCU), fit replacement fuse
Faulty flex connections	Check flex connections at plug, FCU and fan terminal block; remake as necessary
Failed switch	Test for continuity, replace if necessary
Broken pull cord	Replace
Burnt-out motor	Replace

NOISY OPERATION

Likely cause	*What to do*
Grease build-up on fan blades	Clean fan blades
Blocked filter	Clean or replace
Wear on fan or motor bearings	Lubricate bearings with light oil

DISMANTLING

1 Disconnect the fan from the mains supply. Then release the front grille so you can gain access to the screws securing the motor and fan assembly to the inner clamp plate. Undo them and lift the assembly out.

2 Undo the screw securing the fan blade to the motor shaft, and lift the blade off. You can now clean all the components; wash the grilles and fan blade in soapy water and clean the motor with a dry brush.

REPLACING A PULL CORD

1 Disconnect the mains supply and remove the front grille so you can gain access to the screws securing the switch unit. Undo them and lift off the unit.

2 Release the switch selector from the metal contacts securing it, and feed the new cord in through the guide in the fan body and round the pulley in the switch selector. Knot it through the hole in the fan body, reassemble the selector and switch unit, and test the switching operation. Restore the power.

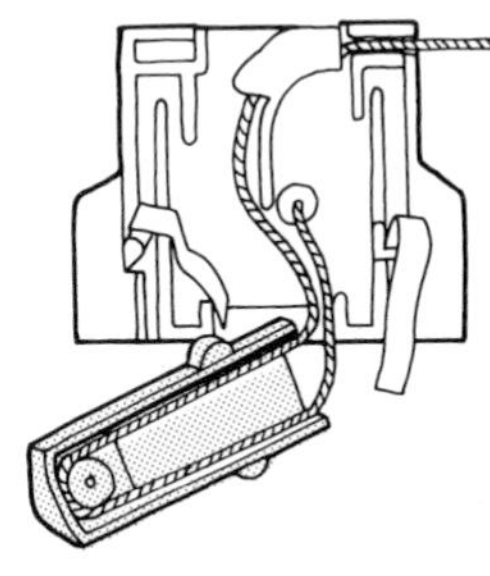

FIXING YOUR

FAN HEATER

Fan heaters are the most efficient form of electric room heater, combining a high heat output with rapid air circulation

Fan heaters usually have a shaded-pole induction motor and variable heat output

THINGS YOU NEED

- **Screwdrivers**
- **Continuity tester**
- **Replacement parts as necessary**

NO POWER	
Likely cause	*What to do*
Plug or flex fault	Rewire or replace as necessary
Internal wiring fault	Check continuity, remake connections
Thermal overload cut-out (TOC) tripped	Reset
TOC failed	Replace
Main on-off switch failed	Replace
NO HEAT	
Likely cause	*What to do*
Internal wiring fault	Check continuity, remake connections
TOC tripped	Check motor for free running, reset TOC
TOC failed	Replace
Heat selector switch failed	Replace
Heating element failed	Replace
NO MOTOR ACTION	
Likely cause	*What to do*
Fan or motor jammed	Check that moving parts rotate freely, reposition deformed fan blades; check that motor mountings are secure; clean and lubricate bearings if necessary
Motor failed	Check continuity of motor windings, replace if necessary

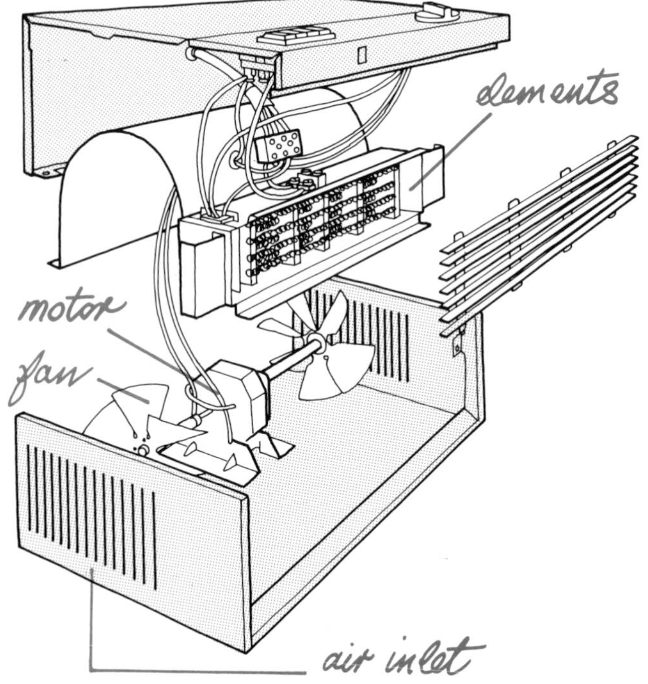

DISMANTLING

1 Unplug the heater, and examine the outer casing to locate screws holding the grille or casing in place. Remove them in a logical sequence, labelling each one for later replacement in the right place.

2 Clean all components and connections, then test for continuity and remake connections or replace failed parts as necessary. Reassemble and test.

ALWAYS REASSEMBLE AN APPLIANCE BEFORE PLUGGING IT IN TO TEST YOUR REPAIR

FIXING YOUR

FOOD MIXER

Food mixers are excellent labour-savers; the various models function in roughly the same way

FAULTFINDER

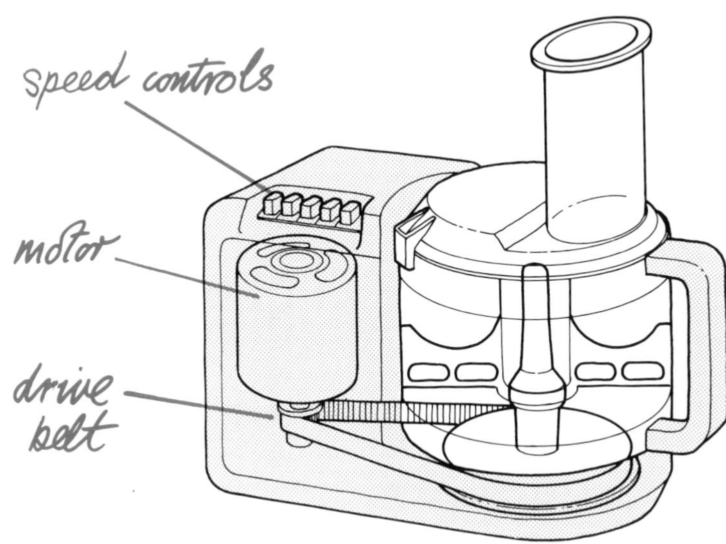

NO POWER	
Likely cause	*What to do*
Plug or flex fault	Rewire or replace as necessary
Internal wiring fault	Test for continuity, remake connections
Speed selector switch broken	Replace
Speed control module failed	Replace
Motor failed	Replace field coil or armature
FAULTY SPEED CONTROL	
Likely cause	*What to do*
Loose connection on selector switch	Test for continuity, remake connection
Speed control module faulty	Replace
UNEVEN RUNNING	
Likely cause	*What to do*
Debris inside casing	Open casing and clean
Worn motor brushes	Replace brushes
Overheated commutator	Clean commutator
Damaged gear train	Replace

THINGS YOU NEED

- **Tools for gaining access and for fitting parts**
- **Continuity tester**
- **Electrical screwdriver**
- **Replacement parts as necessary**
- **Light oil**
- **Grease**

DISMANTLING

1 Unplug the mixer from the mains and examine the casing to determine which screws to remove for access to the interior. Remove and label them, and lift off the outer casing.

2 Locate potential faults in the internal wiring or individual components using your continuity tester and remake faulty connections or replace failed components as necessary. Replace motor brushes if they are worn to less than about 6mm (¼ in) in length or are showing signs of sticking.

3 Clean out the interior and lubricate motor bearings with light oil and the gear train with a little grease. Reassemble.

SEE PAGES 24-51 for how to carry out REPAIRS AND TESTS

FIXING YOUR

FRIDGE & FREEZER

Fridges and freezers are generally reliable appliances, but can suffer from a range of faults

FAULTFINDER

The operating mechanism of fridges and freezers is unique to this type of appliance

THINGS YOU NEED

- **Tools for gaining access and for fitting parts**
- **Continuity tester**
- **Replacement parts as necessary**
- **Thermometer for checking temperatures**

ALWAYS REASSEMBLE AN APPLIANCE BEFORE PLUGGING IT IN TO TEST YOUR REPAIR

NO COMPRESSOR ACTION	
Likely cause	*What to do*
Plug or flex fault	Rewire or replace as necessary
Thermostat faulty	Check thermostat operation, replace if necessary
Starting relay faulty	Replace
Internal wiring fault	Test for continuity, remake connections
Motor/compressor seized up	Call service engineer
Thermal overload cut-out (TOC) faulty	Replace
Inadequate ventilation causing overheating of motor/compressor and tripping of TOC	Improve ventilation to appliance
Very low room temperature	Nothing

TOC TRIPS WHEN MOTOR STARTS	
Likely cause	*What to do*
Thermostat faulty	Replace
Starting relay or TOC faulty	Replace
Compressor faulty	Call service engineer
Overloaded cabinet	Reduce volume of stored food

CONTINUOUS OPERATION BUT NO COOLING EFFECT	
Likely cause	*What to do*
Loss of refrigerant	Call service engineer
Compressor faulty	Call service engineer
Pipework matrix damaged	Call service engineer

CONTINUOUS OPERATION WITH PARTIAL COOLING	
Likely cause	*What to do*
Very high room temperature	Reduce room temperature
Open door or faulty door seal	Close door/replace door seal
Overloaded cabinet	Reduce volume of stored food
Internal light remaining on	Check microswitch, replace if necessary

CABINET TEMPERATURE TOO HIGH	
Likely cause	*What to do*
Wrong thermostat setting	Alter setting
Icing on evaporator unit	Check/replace thermostat

SEE PAGES 24-51 for how to carry out REPAIRS AND TESTS

FAULTFINDER continued

THINGS YOU NEED

- **Tools for gaining access and for fitting parts**
- **Continuity tester**
- **Replacement parts as necessary**
- **Thermometer for checking temperatures**

CABINET TEMPERATURE TOO LOW

Likely cause	*What to do*
Wrong thermostat setting	Alter setting
Thermostat faulty	Replace
Thermostat capillary tube displaced	Reposition tube correctly
Thermostat capillary tube broken	Replace thermostat
Defrost heater faulty	Check/replace thermostat
Freezer fast-freeze switch left on	Reset switch
Faulty fast-freeze switch	Replace
Faulty solenoid valve on fridge/freezers with shared compressor	Replace solenoid switch
Very low room temperature	Nothing – fridge can only cool, not maintain a temperature independent of the room outside

NOISY OPERATION

Likely cause	*What to do*
Appliance touching surroundings	Move appliance to stand freely
Appliance not standing squarely	Adjust appliance feet
Loose shelving/contents	Adjust shelving/contents positions
Loose compressor mountings	Tighten mountings
Refrigerant pipework touching	Adjust pipework positions
Starting relay faulty	Replace

WATER IN CABINET

Likely cause	*What to do*
Drain tube blocked on auto-defrost fridges	Clear tube

HOW IT WORKS

Fridges and freezers circulate a refrigerant around a sealed cooling system. The motor/compressor unit draws in the refrigerant gas, compresses it and forces it into the condenser tubes, where the gas cools and liquefies at a temperature well below the freezing point of water. As it enters the evaporator inside the cabinet the liquid expands back into a gas, drawing heat out of the evaporator plate and the air in contact with it and so cooling the cabinet. Finally the gas is returned round the system to the compressor for the cycle to begin again.

SEE PAGES 24-51 for how to carry out REPAIRS AND TESTS

REPLACING A THERMOSTAT

1 Obtain a replacement thermostat to match the appliance make and model number. Then isolate the appliance from the mains, and examine it to determine the position of the thermostat and its capillary tube.

2 Gain access to the old thermostat control by prising off the selector knob, and removing the internal lamp cover and lamp if necessary. Undo the thermostat fixing screws and ease off the thermostat cover.

3 Make a note of the wiring positions before disconnecting anything. Then undo the connections and lift out the old thermostat. Follow the path of the capillary tube within the appliance and ease it out, noting the positions of any fixing clips. Reverse the dismantling sequence to fit the replacement thermostat unit and capillary tube.

REPLACING A DOOR SEAL

Split or faulty door seals allow warm moist air to enter the appliance, causing excessive icing and unnecessary overrunning of the compressor, which makes the appliance very expensive to operate.

1 Examine the existing seals to find out how they are fitted to the door edge, then obtain a matching set of replacement seals. Some fridges have door seals permanently bonded to the door, so you have to order a whole new door from the manufacturer – expensive.

2 Remove the old seals and fit the replacements, making sure that they are properly bedded in their channels and that they are compressed evenly against the door frame when the door is closed.

CLEARING A DRAIN TUBE

On fridges with an auto-defrost function, ice on the evaporator unit is periodically melted by the defrost heater, under the control of the thermostat. The melt water runs off the evaporator into a catchment channel along the back of the fridge, and is drained by a plastic tube that runs down the back of the appliance to a tray on top of the motor/compressor unit, where it evaporates.

1 The tube can become blocked by particles washed off the evaporator unit, or by mould growth, causing the melt water to accumulate in the bottom of the fridge.

2 Clear the tube using a length of flexible wire. Crimp one end of the wire round a small piece of folded cloth, feed the other end into the drain tube and use it as a pull-through to draw the cloth pad along the tube and clear the blockage.

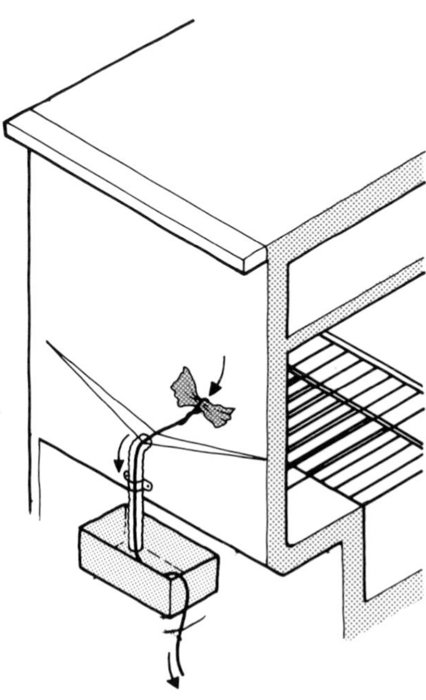

FIXING YOUR

HAIR DRIER

All hair driers work on the same principle, of driving a fan which blows air over a heated element

FAULTFINDER

The drier may have a simple on-off switch or a switch bank. The element is protected from overheating by a thermal overload cut-out

THINGS YOU NEED

- **Screwdriver or other tools for dismantling appliance**
- **Continuity tester**
- **Electrical screwdriver**
- **Replacement parts as necessary**
- **Light machine oil**

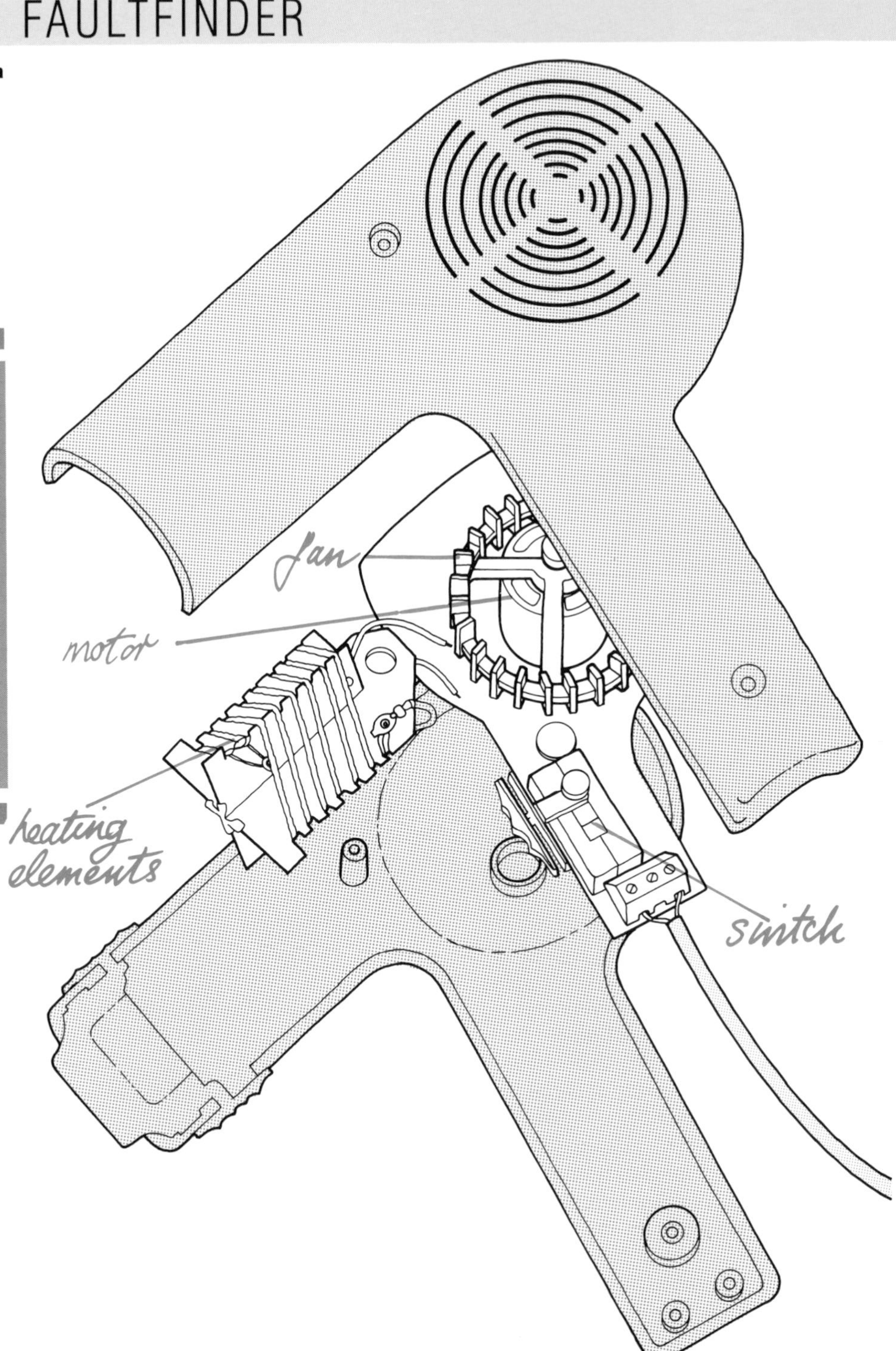

NO POWER

Likely cause	*What to do*
Plug or flex fault	Rewire or replace as necessary
Internal wiring fault	Test for continuity, remake connections
On-off switch faulty	Replace
Thermal overload cut-out (TOC) faulty	Replace

NO HEAT

Likely cause	*What to do*
Internal wiring fault	Test for continuity, remake connections
Heat selector switch faulty	Replace
TOC tripped	Clear air inlets of fluff/hair to allow unimpeded air flow over element
TOC faulty	Replace
Heater element faulty	Replace

HEAT BUT NO AIR FLOW

Likely cause	*What to do*
Internal wiring fault	Test for continuity, remake connections
Motor shaft jammed	Clear fluff/hair from motor shaft, lubricate bearings lightly
Motor burnt out	Replace
Bridge rectifier faulty (models with DC motors only)	Replace
Speed selector switch faulty	Replace

REDUCED FAN SPEED

Likely cause	*What to do*
Motor/fan shaft partly jammed	Clear fluff/hair from shaft
Motor brushes worn (models with brush motors only)	Replace
Motor/fan bearings worn	Lubricate lightly, replace bearings if available, replace motor otherwise

DISMANTLING

1 Hair driers are particularly prone to flex damage, especially where the flex enters the plug and the appliance casing. The casing itself is also easily damaged if the drier is dropped or knocked. You can temporarily repair casing cracks as soon as they occur with PVC insulating tape, but the casing must be completely replaced at the earliest possible opportunity.

2 Isolate the appliance from the mains, then inspect the casing to locate the positions of the fixing screws. Some models feature tamper-proof screws, so you may have to improvise a tool in order to undo them.

3 Unscrew the fixing screws, labelling them for later replacement in their correct positions. Open the casing and slide out the element, motor and fan unit so you can test each component and all the internal wiring for continuity. Remake faulty connections and fit replacement parts as required before reassembling and testing the appliance.

SEE PAGES 24-51 for how to carry out REPAIRS AND TESTS

FIXING YOUR

IMMERSION HEATER

Immersion heaters are fitted into most hot water cylinders, either as the sole source of water heating or as a back-up

FAULTFINDER

Immersion heaters have their own electrical circuit run from the fuse box or consumer unit. They are often run via a time switch

THINGS YOU NEED

- **Continuity tester**
- **Electrical screwdriver**
- **Replacement thermostat**
- **Replacement heater**
- **Immersion heater spanner**
- **PTFE tape or plumber's putty**
- **Small adjustable spanner**
- **Length of garden hose**

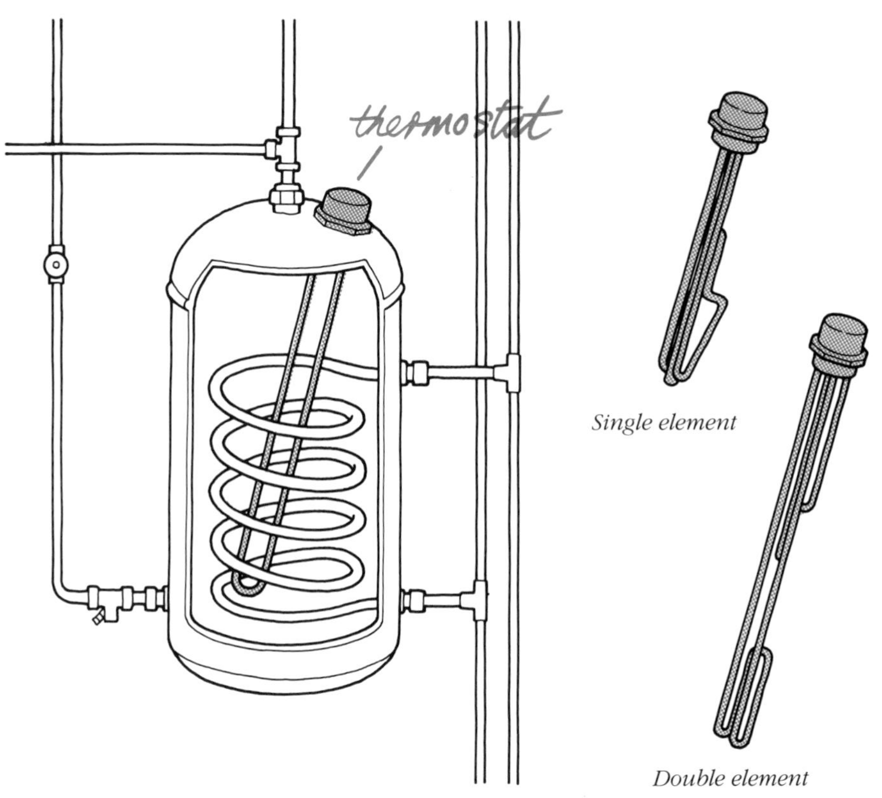

Single element

Double element

NO HEAT	
Likely cause	*What to do*
Circuit fuse blown/MCB tripped	See pages 10-13
Wiring fault at switch or heater	Check connections, remake as necessary
Flex damaged	Test for continuity, replace if necessary
Thermostat faulty	Replace
Element failed	Replace entire heater

WATER NOT HOT ENOUGH	
Likely cause	*What to do*
Thermostat set too low	Reset
Intermittent wiring fault	Check wiring, remake connections
Insufficient heating time	Alter timer settings
Thermostat faulty	Replace
No insulation on cylinder	Fit cylinder jacket

WATER TOO HOT	
Likely cause	*What to do*
Thermostat set too high	Reset
Thermostat faulty	Replace

SEE PAGES 24-51 for how to carry out REPAIRS AND TESTS

FIXING YOUR IMMERSION HEATER

HOW IT WORKS

Immersion heaters fit into a large round boss in either the top or the side of the hot water cylinder. Vertical types may have a single or a double element; the latter has a short element intended for heating small quantities of water for washing, and a long element which heats the whole cylinder, for filling a bath, say. This type is controlled by a two-gang change-over switch, often marked 'sink' and 'bath'. Horizontal types are fitted near the base of the cylinder; if the equivalent of a dual-element vertical heater is required, a second element is fitted near the top of the cylinder. Most immersion heater elements are copper-sheathed, but special alloy-sheathed heaters are used for longer life in areas where the water is hard. Each heater is controlled by a variable thermostat, which can be altered with a screwdriver.

Set a single-element thermostat or the upper element of a two-element system to 60°C (140°F), and the lower element of a two-element system to 75°C (167°F). In soft water areas, you can increase these settings by 5°C (9°F) without reducing the life of the element unduly.

The heater is supplied with power via its own circuit. This is run from the fuse box or consumer unit to a 20-amp double-pole isolating switch near the hot cylinder. Heat-resistant 1.5mm^2 three-core butyl rubber-sheathed flex links the switch to the heater terminals. If the heater is controlled by a timer, this is wired in between the switch and the heater. If two elements are fitted, a special two-gang change-over switch takes the place of the one-gang isolating switch, and two separate flexes run from it to the two heater terminals.

REPLACING A THERMOSTAT

To replace the heater thermostat, simply turn off the heater switch and disconnect the circuit at the fuse box or consumer unit, unscrew the thermostat cover and disconnect the flex cores from the terminals. Release the screw holding the thermostat to the heater boss and slide it out. Reverse the sequence to fit the replacement.

REPLACING AN ENTIRE HEATER

1 Turn off the heater switch and disconnect the circuit at the fuse box or consumer unit. Turn off the cold feed to the hot cylinder, and open a hot tap to drain the vent pipe. Then attach your hose to the cylinder draincock, and take the other end to the bath or to an outside gully. Open the draincock with a spanner and drain off enough water to lower the level in the cylinder below that of the boss. Then close it and remove the hose.

2 Unscrew and remove the thermostat cover from the old heater and disconnect the flex cores.

3 Unscrew the old heater with the special heater spanner and lift it out. Then fit the large sealing washer over the heater flange, and wind PTFE tape (or smear a little plumber's putty) on to the threads. Insert the new heater into its boss, carefully threading it down inside the heating coil in the cylinder. Tighten it down with the special spanner.

4 Reconnect the flex to the new thermostat and set it to the correct operating temperature. Restore the water supply to the cold feed pipe and close the hot tap once any air in the pipe has been cleared. Restore the electricity supply.

FIXING YOUR

IRON

As well as a heating element pressed against the soleplate, modern irons have a variety of steam and spray functions

FAULTFINDER

Correct thermostatic control and overheat protection are vital for safety and to avoid damaging clothes. Other functions simply improve performance

THINGS YOU NEED

- **Tools for gaining access and fitting parts**
- **Continuity tester**
- **Replacement parts as necessary**
- **Descaling liquid**

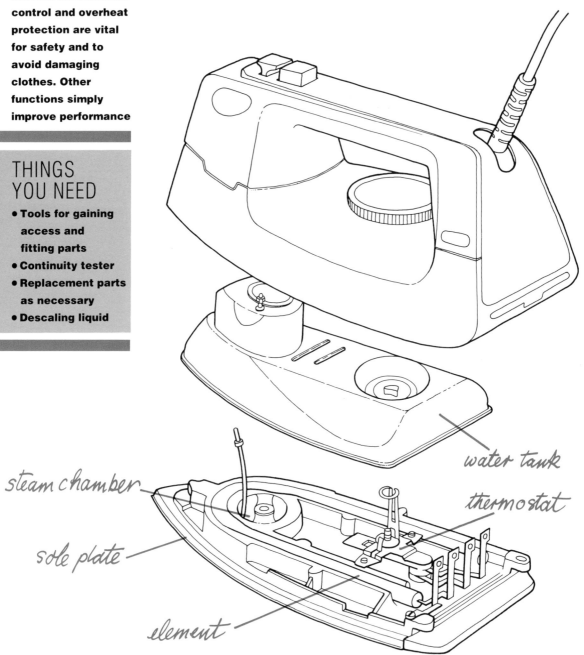

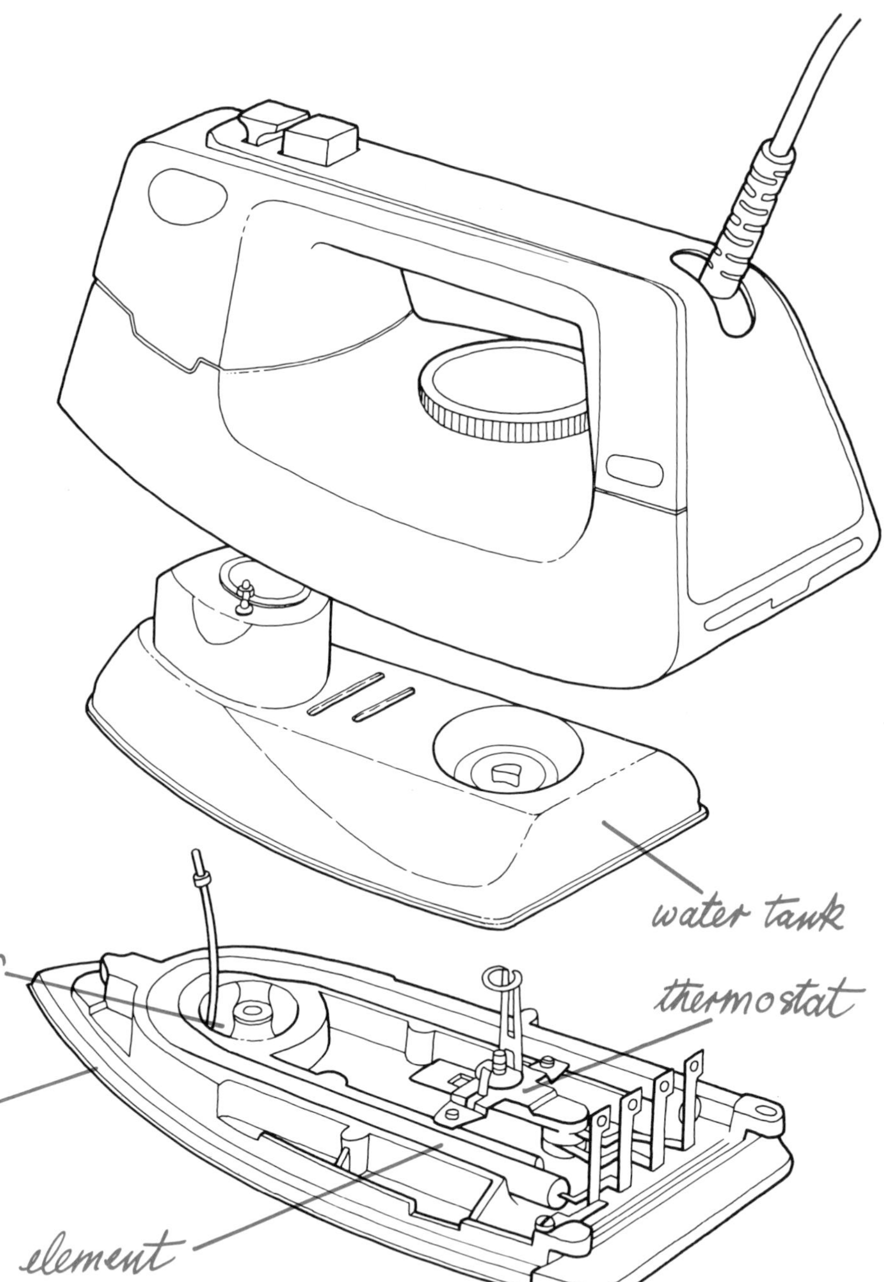

ALWAYS unplug an appliance before starting any work on it

NO POWER	
Likely cause	*What to do*
Plug or flex fault	Rewire or replace as necessary
Internal wiring fault	Test for continuity, remake connections
Thermostat faulty	Replace
Thermal overload cut-out faulty	Replace
Element faulty	Replace element/soleplate
OVERHEATING	
Likely cause	*What to do*
Thermostat faulty	Replace
Selector knob broken and rotating on thermostat shaft	Replace knob
NO STEAM	
Likely cause	*What to do*
Water tank empty	Refill tank
Incorrect selector knob setting	Select steam setting
Vents blocked by scale	Descale iron
Water control valve faulty	Replace
NO SPRAY	
Likely cause	*What to do*
Water tank empty	Refill tank
Spray nozzle blocked	Remove for cleaning

DISMANTLING

1 Isolate the appliance from the mains. Then examine it to locate the positions of the fixing screws that secure the cover plate over the flex terminal block and the filling nozzle assembly at the front of the iron (this may simply be clipped into place). Remove these to reveal the screws holding the iron body to the soleplate. Remove any push-fit control knobs at this stage after noting their setting positions.

2 Undo the main fixing screws so you can pivot the iron body back and reveal the soleplate, the water control valve, the thermostat and the thermal overload cut-out. Check all the wiring connections and the components, remaking loose connections and replacing faulty components.

DESCALING AN IRON

Most steam irons can be descaled in this way. Check with the manufacturer's instructions to make sure.

1 Buy a proprietary iron descaling liquid, and dilute it as recommended in the instructions. Pour the liquid into the tank through the filler nozzle.

2 Set the iron to steam and let it heat up fully. Then unplug it and stand it face down in the sink, resting on two slim wooden battens (pencils are ideal) to allow the descaling liquid to drain gradually through the steam outlet holes in the soleplate. After about half an hour, empty out any remaining descaling liquid from the tank, and fill and rinse it with clean water before using it again.

SEE PAGES 24-51 for how to carry out REPAIRS AND TESTS

FIXING YOUR

KETTLE

Modern kettles feature automatic switches, self-resetting overload devices and high-speed elements

FAULTFINDER

A kettle that is well looked after should keep on working for years. It will need regular descaling in hard water areas

THINGS YOU NEED

- **Tools for gaining access and for fitting parts**
- **Continuity tester**
- **Replacement parts as necessary**
- **Descaling liquid**

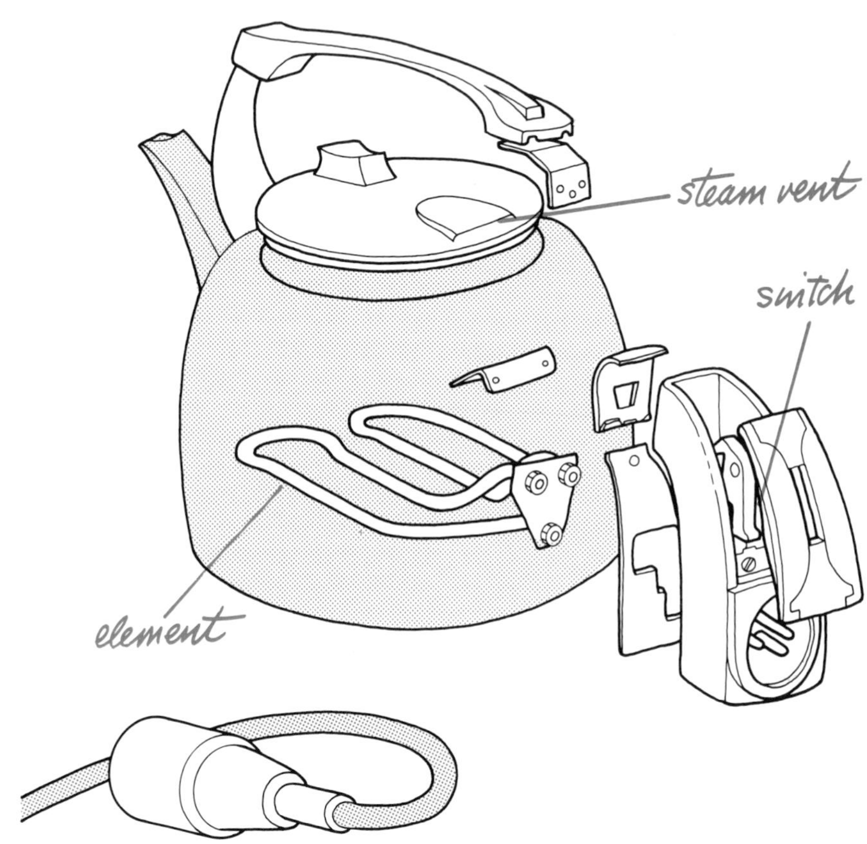

NO POWER	
Likely cause	*What to do*
Plug or fuse fault	Rewire or replace as necessary
Flex or connector damage	Replace lead
Loose connection of lead to kettle	Check fit of connector, examine pins for signs of overheating, replace lead
Thermal overload cut-out tripped	Reset if possible, replace if necessary
Contacts in switch faulty	Test for continuity, replace if necessary
Element failed	Test for continuity, replace if necessary and check plug fuse (probably blown)

NO AUTOMATIC SWITCH-OFF	
Likely cause	*What to do*
Lid incorrectly fitted	Refit lid correctly so steam can reach and operate bi-metallic strip
Steam tube blocked or filled with water	Empty kettle and invert to drain tube; descale tube
Bi-metallic strip corroded	Replace strip or entire switch
Switch actuating rod stuck	Clean out grease/dirt or replace switch

SEE PAGES 24-51 for how to carry out REPAIRS AND TESTS

ALWAYS unplug an appliance before starting any work on it

NO AUTOMATIC RESETTING AFTER BOILING	
Likely cause	*What to do*
Bi-metallic strip still hot	Allow strip to cool down
Bi-metallic strip needs adjusting	Turn adjustment screw fractionally
PREMATURE SWITCH-OFF	
Likely cause	*What to do*
Overheating within scaled-up element tripping switch off	Descale element regularly
Switch faulty	Replace switch
Bi-metallic strip overadjusted	Readjust fractionally
Leak into kettle switch area, blowing plug fuse or tripping RCD	Check for leaks (see below), replace switch if short-circuited
LEAKS	
Likely cause	*What to do*
Kettle overfilled	Fill only to 'max' level inside kettle
Kettle overboiling	Check time taken to switch off after boiling, adjust bi-metallic strip
Element fixings loose	Tighten fixings and observe
Split or perished washers	Replace
Joint between element and fixing plate failed	Replace element

REPLACING AN AUTOMATIC KETTLE ELEMENT

1 Obtain a replacement element to match the make and model number of the kettle. This will generally come complete with a set of replacement gaskets, washers and nuts.

2 Unplug the lead from the kettle. Examine the kettle to assess the likely order of dismantling the switch assembly and/or handle. Label screws as you remove them, so you can replace them correctly during reassembly. On some models, the switch earth pin has to be removed using a special hollow driver (included in the element kit).

3 With all the fixings removed, ease the switch away from the kettle body, taking care not to damage the gasket. Set it aside.

4 Undo the nuts holding the element to the kettle body with a spanner, remove the nuts and washers and lift the element out of the kettle. Discard the old internal gaskets, and clean the inner and outer surfaces of the kettle round the element hole to ensure good earth contacts (metal-bodied kettles only) and a leak-free fitting.

5 Fit new internal gaskets, then position the new element carefully, add new external washers and tighten the securing nuts. Offer the switch assembly up into position complete with its gasket, and reassemble.

6 Check for earth continuity between a metal kettle body and the socket earth pin. Then fill the kettle and leave it to stand for five minutes as a check for leaks. Finally, boil the kettle to check that it is boiling and switching off correctly.

HOW IT WORKS

Most automatic kettles rely on a bi-metallic strip to switch off the power when the water has boiled. As the water comes to the boil steam is channelled over the strip, which bends as it heats up and trips the switch off.

LIGHTS

Lights and lamps, whether table, desk or standard, have little to go wrong with them

FAULTFINDER

Flex damage is the most common problem, but switches and lampholders may also need replacing occasionally

NO LIGHT/INTERMITTENT OPERATION

Likely cause	*What to do*
Bulb failure	Replace bulb
Plug or flex fault	Rewire or replace as necessary
Poor bulb contact	Clean contacts, replace bulb if necessary
Loose connection in lampholder or switch	Inspect, remake if necessary
Switch faulty	Clean switch contacts, replace switch if necessary

THINGS YOU NEED

- **Replacement flex**
- **Stanley knife or side cutters**
- **Wire strippers**
- **Electrical screwdriver**
- **Replacement in-line switch**
- **Replacement lampholder**
- **Replacement switched lampholder**
- **Socket or open spanners**
- **Wire wool**

REPLACING THE FLEX AND LAMPHOLDER

Replacing the flex on many table, desk and standard lamps is no different in principle from working on any other appliance (see pages 38-9). However, the design of the lamp body may make it difficult to gain access to the flex terminals or to feed in the new flex. Some careful examination of the way the lamp was assembled is generally needed before work can begin.

Lampholders in many table and standard lamps are screwed on to a threaded insert, and it is a simple matter to unscrew and replace the lampholder. On some desk lamps, the lampholder is mounted on a metal bracket inside the fixed shade, and can be released only if you can gain access to the fixing nuts with a socket or open spanner.

1 Once access has been gained to the lampholder terminals, the screws can be undone to allow the flex to be disconnected. If the flex path is hidden within the body of the lamp, attach a length of string to the end of the flex, then pull out the old flex and draw the string through. You can then use the string to draw the new flex into place. Always use the correct type of flex – two-core for non-metallic lamps, three-core for lamps with a brass lampholder or other metal parts.

2 When rewiring the latter, take the earth core to the special earth terminal on the lampholder, and check for earthing continuity between the lamp body and the earth terminal.

FIXING YOUR SHAVER

Electric shavers have rotary or foil cutters and are available in battery- or mains-operated versions

FAULTFINDER

NO POWER	
Likely cause	*What to do*
Plug or flex fault	Rewire or replace as necessary
Voltage setting incorrect	Reset voltage selector
Shaver adaptor/socket fuse blown	Replace fuse (1-amp)
Batteries flat	Recharge/replace
Internal wiring fault	Test for continuity, remake connections
Motor brushes sticking/worn	Clean/replace
Stator coils faulty (foil types)	Test continuity, replace motor
Cutter jammed (foil types)	Clean or replace foil and cutter
SLOW/INTERMITTENT RUNNING	
Likely cause	*What to do*
Cutter/foil incorrectly fitted	Reposition correctly
Cutter/foil clogged or damaged	Clean and lubricate, replace if necessary
Batteries low	Recharge/replace
Motor brushes sticking/worn	Clean/replace
Yoke/spring faulty (foil types)	Replace yoke/spring
Flex damaged	Replace lead
Poor connection with mains lead	Check for wear, replace worn parts
Internal wiring fault	Test for continuity, remake connections
Poor battery contacts	Check/clean contacts
OVERHEATING	
Likely cause	*What to do*
Motor short circuit/overheating	Replace motor
Poor connection with mains lead	Check for wear, replace worn parts
Battery short circuit	Correct fault, replace batteries

A shaver should need little maintenance if used with care and cleaned regularly

THINGS YOU NEED

- **Tools for gaining access andfor fitting parts**
- **Continuity tester**
- **Replacement parts as necessary**
- **Light machine oil**

MAINTENANCE

Clean cutters after every use. Lubricate the end bearings of brush motors occasionally with light machine oil, and smear a little paraffin on cutters and foils for smooth running. The motor on foil types (a pair of stator coils driving an oscillating yoke rather than a rotating shaft) needs no lubrication.

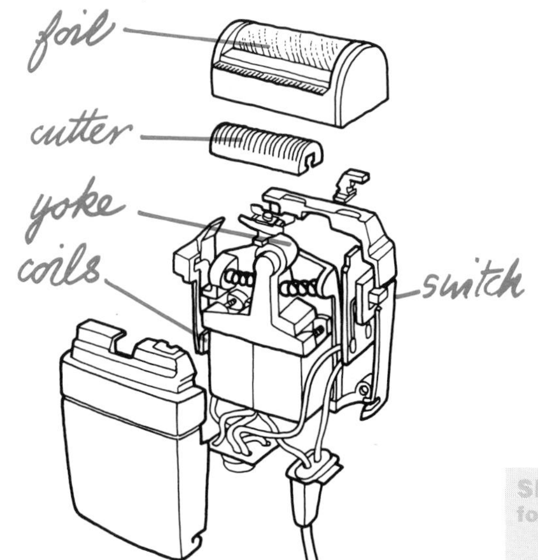

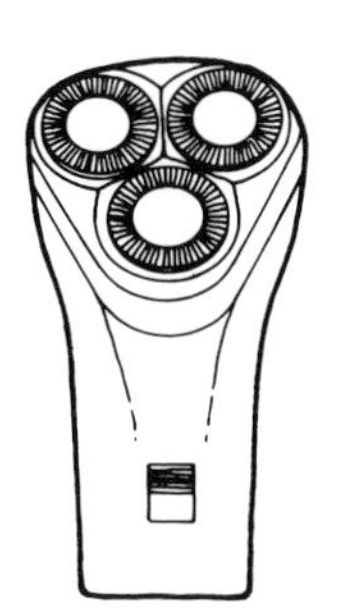

SEE PAGES 24-51 for how to carry out REPAIRS AND TESTS

FIXING YOUR

SPIN DRIER

Spin driers contain a perforated drum spun round by a motor to force out water from wet clothes

FAULTFINDER

A pump removes the water (on basic models the water simply collects in a basin at the bottom of the machine) and a brake stops the drum when the lid is opened

THINGS YOU NEED

- **Tools for gaining access and for fitting parts**
- **Continuity tester**
- **Replacement parts as necessary**

NO POWER	
Likely cause	*What to do*
Plug or flex fault	Rewire or replace as necessary
Internal wiring fault	Test for continuity, remake connections
Motor brushes sticking/worn	Clean/replace
Motor burnt out	Replace motor
Push-rod switch faulty	Replace switch
NOISY OPERATION/VIBRATION	
Likely cause	*What to do*
Clothes loaded unevenly	Reload drum correctly
Clothing between drum and jacket	Retrieve clothing
Brake binding	Adjust brake cable
NO DRUM ROTATION	
Likely cause	*What to do*
Drive belt slack/broken	Adjust/replace drive belt
Drum jammed	Retrieve clothing from between drum and jacket, check brake operation
NO BRAKING ACTION	
Likely cause	*What to do*
Brake cable slack/disconnected	Adjust/reconnect
Brake band worn	Replace
NO PUMP OPERATION	
Likely cause	*What to do*
Drive belt slack/broken	Adjust/replace
Pump blocked	Remove and clean
Hose kinked/blocked	Straighten/remove obstruction

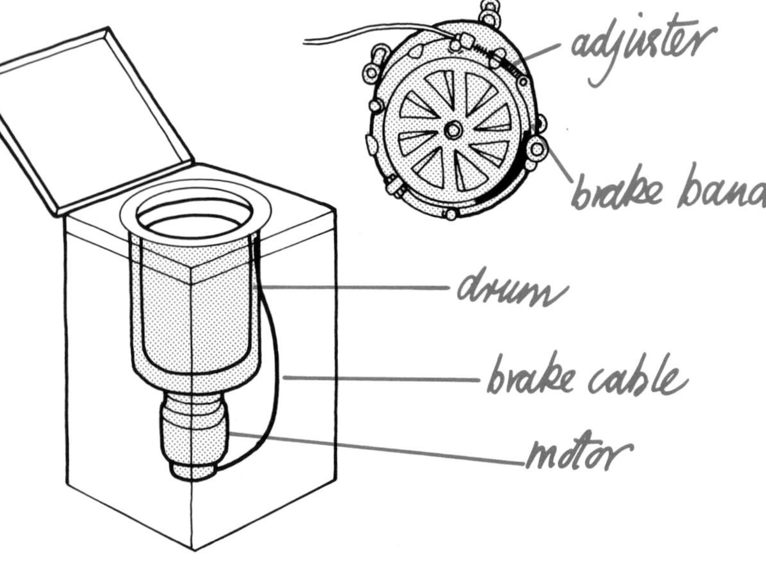

REPAIRING THE BRAKE

1 Isolate the appliance from the mains. Then depress the brake release button on top of the machine so you can release the end of the brake cable from its stop. Use a spanner to separate the adjuster nut from the button so you can free the cable nipple.

2 At the brake end of the cable, undo the locknut so you can screw the cable adjuster nut in fully and remove the cable from the brake arm. Reverse the sequence to fit the replacement cable.

3 To replace a worn brake band, disconnect the cable, unscrew the nuts and bolts securing the brake band round the base of the drum, remove the old band and replace.

FIXING YOUR

TOASTER

Toasters are essentially simple appliances which seem to suffer from more than their fair share of problems

FAULTFINDER

NO POWER	
Likely cause	*What to do*
Plug or flex fault	Rewire or replace as necessary
Internal wiring fault	Test for continuity, remake connections
Latch mechanism not engaging	Clean and check operation of mechanism
Latch switch faulty	Test for continuity, replace switch
Element failed (wired in series so others denied power too)	Test for continuity, replace element if available, otherwise fit new carriage with elements or replace toaster
TOAST BURNS ON ALL SETTINGS	
Likely cause	*What to do*
Latch mechanism sticking	Clean and check operation of mechanism
Trip thermostat faulty	Replace
Delatching coil faulty	Replace
Latch switch short-circuited in on position	Replace
Element which trips the thermostat failed	Replace if possible (see above)
TOAST UNDERDONE	
Likely cause	*What to do*
Trip thermostat faulty	Replace
Latch mechanism tripping early	Clean and check operation of mechanism, adjust if possible, replace otherwise
Design fault (trip thermostat cooling too slowly during repeat toasting)	Allow to cool between toasting, alter heat setting to compensate

The carriage mechanism and the elements can fail, or the toaster may simply perform below par

THINGS YOU NEED

- **Tools for gaining access**
- **Continuity tester**
- **Replacement parts as necessary**

LOOKING AFTER A TOASTER

1 Clean out toast crumbs regularly, either by inverting the toaster or by opening the crumb tray at the bottom if there is one. Use a small dry paintbrush to clean the toast carriage mechanism.

2 If toast jams in the mechanism, raise the carriage by hand. If the latch mechanism is engaged, unplug the toaster before freeing the jammed slice. Never poke metallic objects such as knives into the toast slot to free a blockage while the toaster is on; you may touch an element and receive a shock, and you may also damage the toaster.

3 Allow the toaster to cool down before putting it away. Do not coil the flex round the body of the toaster while it is still hot, since the sheathing will be damaged.

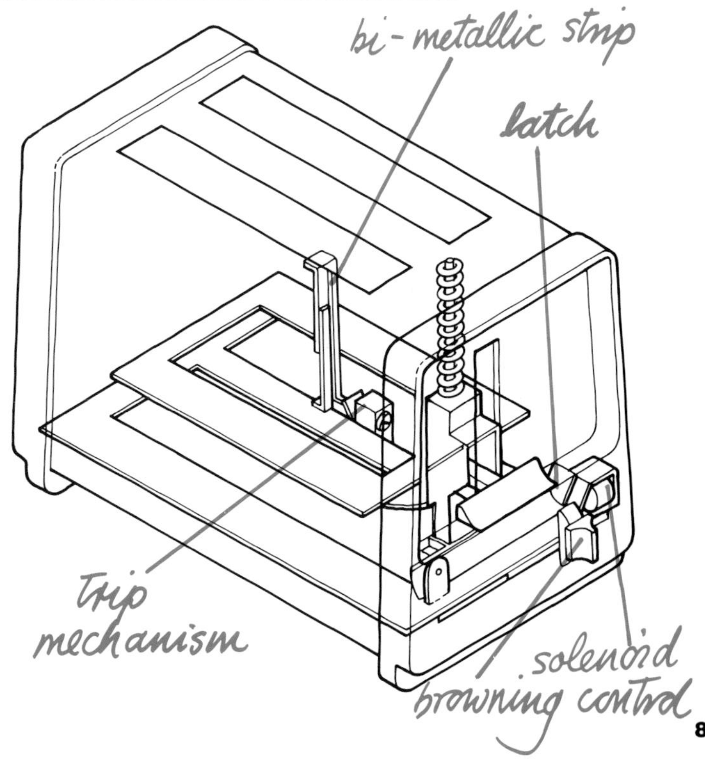

FIXING YOUR

TUMBLE DRIER

The horizontally mounted drum is rotated by an induction motor and warmed by heated air circulated by a fan

FAULTFINDER

The hot damp air may be removed by means of a vent to the outside or condensed within the machine

THINGS YOU NEED

- **Tools for gaining access and for fitting parts**
- **Continuity tester**
- **Replacement parts as necessary**

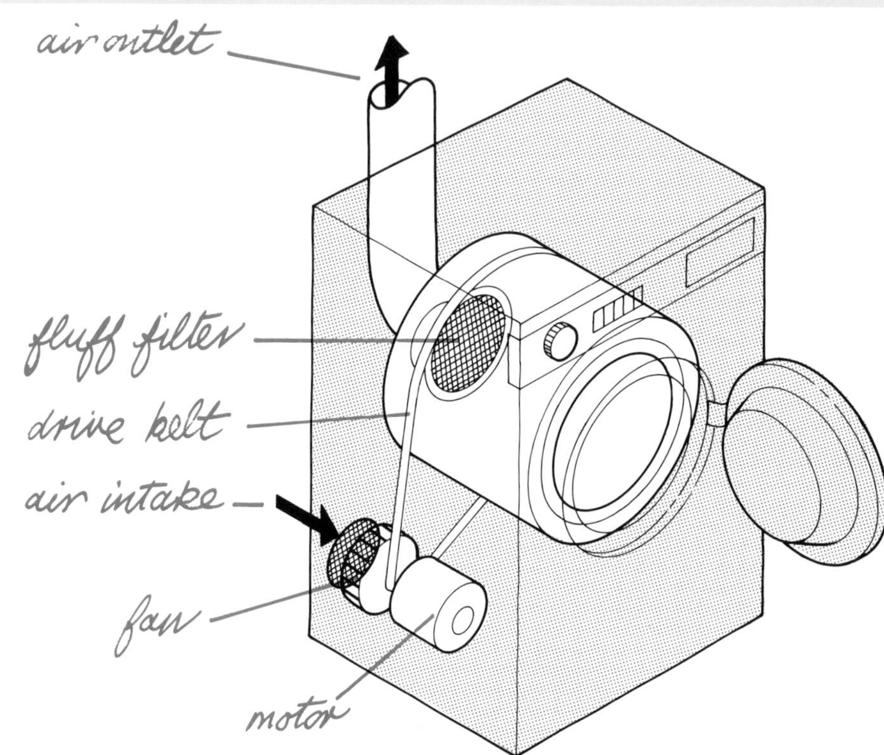

NO POWER	
Likely cause	*What to do*
Plug or flex fault	Replace or rewire as necessary
Internal wiring fault	Test for continuity, remake connections
Selector switch faulty	Replace
Door switch faulty	Check door closes properly, replace switch if necessary
Motor burnt out	Replace

INTERMITTENT OPERATION	
Likely cause	*What to do*
Plug or flex fault	Rewire or replace as necessary
Internal wiring fault	Test for continuity, remake connections
Door switch faulty	Check door closes properly, replace switch if necessary

NO HEAT	
Likely cause	*What to do*
Internal wiring fault	Test for continuity, remake connections
Heating element failed	Replace
Thermostat faulty	Replace
Thermal overload cut-out faulty	Replace
Heat selector switch faulty	Replace

ALWAYS unplug an appliance before starting any work on it

NO DRUM ROTATION	
Likely cause	*What to do*
Drive belt slack/broken	Replace
Motor burnt out	Replace
NOISY OPERATION	
Likely cause	*What to do*
Metallic objects in drum	Remove loose objects (dry clothes inside out to prevent zips and buttons from contacting drum)
Worn bearings	Replace bearings or call service engineer
EXCESSIVE CONDENSATION IN DRIER ROOM	
Likely cause	*What to do*
Warm moist air from drier being vented direct into the room	Install temporary or permanent ducting to take air to outside the house
SLOW DRYING	
Likely cause	*What to do*
Fluff filter clogged	Remove and clean (this should be done after each use)
Air intake or outlet vent blocked	Remove blockage
Machine overloaded or very wet load inserted	Load according to manufacturer's instructions
Insufficient fresh air supply	Open doors or windows in room, vent drier properly

FITTING DUCTING

When drying a full load of damp washing, an air-venting tumble drier will generate a great deal of warm moist air. If this is allowed to discharge direct into the room where the drier is situated, it will cause serious condensation on windows and other cold surfaces such as exterior walls and floors.

1 As a temporary cure for the problem, buy a length of 100mm diameter flexible plastic duct hose complete with an outlet connector of the correct size for your appliance. Plug in the connector and pass the other end of the hose out through a window, letting it discharge air well below window level. The hose can be removed when the drier is not in use. Make sure no other air outlets are left open.

2 For a permanent solution, cut a 100mm diameter hole in the house wall at a point as near to the machine as possible (ideally, behind it if it backs on to an outside wall). Plug the ducting hose connector into the rear air outlet, cut the hose down in length if necessary (leaving enough for the machine to be pulled out of its recess for servicing) and pass the cut end through the hole in the wall. If you have cavity walls, make sure that the hose reaches into the outer leaf of the wall, so moist air is not discharged into the cavity. Fit a louvred ventilator grille to the wall over the outlet hole and slide the appliance back into its recess.

CONDENSER DRIERS

These cool the damp air from the clothes so that it condenses to water and can be collected in a storage tray. They need no venting. The tray needs emptying periodically; a warning light on the drier indicates when this is necessary.

FIXING YOUR

VACUUM CLEANER

The vacuum cleaner has changed little since it was invented at the beginning of the century

FAULTFINDER

Recent models boast features that complicate the basic function

NO POWER	
Likely cause	*What to do*
Plug or flex fault	Rewire or replace as necessary
Internal wiring fault	Test for continuity, remake connections
On-off switch faulty	Replace
Motor brush sticking/worn	Clean/replace
Motor thermal overload cut-out (TOC) fault	Replace TOC
MOTOR SLUGGISH	
Likely cause	*What to do*
Motor brushes sticking/worn	Clean/replace motor brushes, check commutator for wear/damage
Commutator worn/damaged	Replace armature and motor brushes
Armature windings faulty	Replace armature or complete motor
Armature bearings worn	Replace armature bearings
Dirt/grease build-up on fan and within fan chamber	Remove fan, clean fan and chamber, check secondary filters
LITTLE OR NO SUCTION	
Likely cause	*What to do*
Internal blockage/full bag	Clear airways, empty/replace bag
Internal filters clogged	Clean/replace filters
Air leak via appliance casing/hose	Repair/replace damaged components

THINGS YOU NEED

- **Tools for gaining access and for fitting parts**
- **Continuity tester**
- **Replacement parts as necessary**
- **Dust bags**

SEE PAGES 24-51 for how to carry out REPAIRS AND TESTS

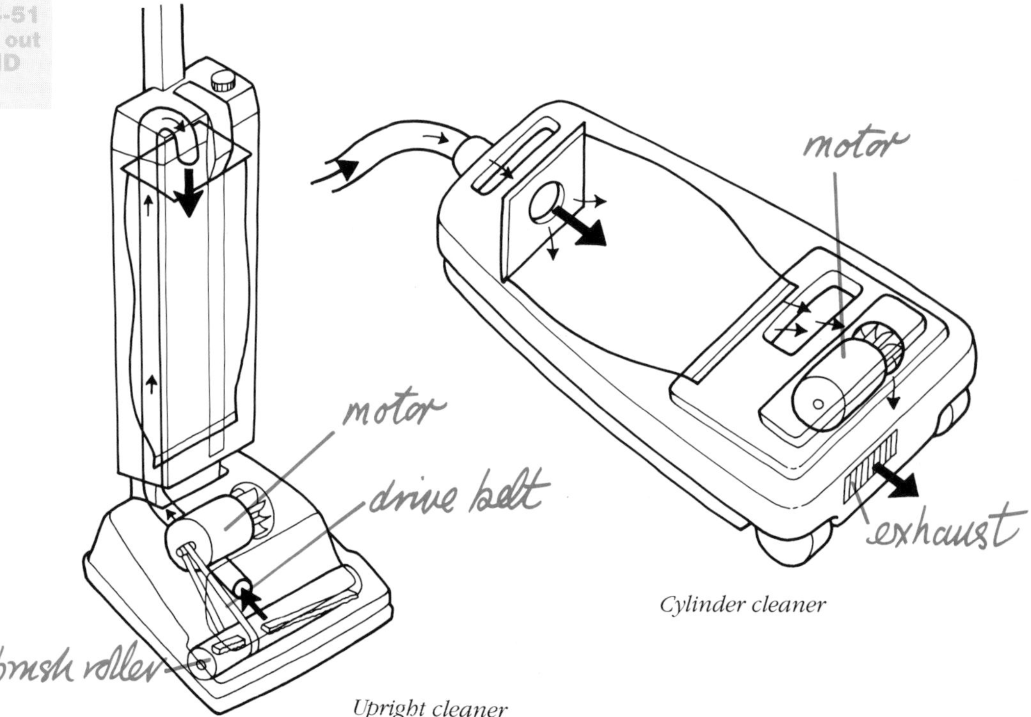

Cylinder cleaner

Upright cleaner

NO ROTATION OF BRUSH ROLL (UPRIGHTS)

Likely cause	*What to do*
Drive belt slipping/broken	Replace drive belt, check for free rotation of brush roll
Fibres/grit in end bearings	Remove if possible, lubricate bearings, replace bearings if necessary
Selector set for smooth flooring so disengaging brush roll	Set selector to 'carpet'

NOISY OPERATION

Likely cause	*What to do*
Dirt/grease build-up on fan and within fan chamber	Remove fan, clean fan and chamber, check secondary filters
Fan chipped/cracked	Replace fan, check motor bearings
Brush roll bearings worn	Replace
Brushes/beater bars loose on roll	Reposition/replace brushes/bars

DISMANTLING AN UPRIGHT VACUUM CLEANER

1 Isolate the appliance from the mains, then remove the cover plates (probably underneath the machine) and disengage the drive belt from the motor shaft. Use a screwdriver to prise out one end of the brush roll. Lift it out.

2 Undo the securing bolt holding the handle shaft to its support socket, and remove the handle. Unscrew and remove the pedal controlling the handle position. Then invert the machine again and undo the screws securing the handle socket to the appliance casing. Remove it.

3 Undo the screws securing the motor to the appliance chassis, disconnect the wiring to it and lift it out. Remove the fan from the motor shaft by holding the fan in one hand and turning the shaft clockwise (it has a left-hand thread).

4 To clean/service the motor, remove the casing screws, open the casing and clean all surfaces with a soft paintbrush. Check the brushes, commutator, armature and bearings, replacing parts as necessary before reassembling everything.

DISMANTLING A CYLINDER VACUUM CLEANER

1 Isolate the appliance from the mains, then examine the casing to locate hidden fixing screws, often found beneath the exhaust cover and filter. Remove them to allow the rear panel to be removed. Other fixings are often located underneath trim strips; undoing them allows other panels to be removed too.

2 Remove the cord rewind pedal and switch pedal; both are generally held in place by plastic retaining clips, and have springs underneath.

3 Remove further fixing screws round the cover of the main compartment to gain access to the motor and the cord rewind mechanism. You can now carry out continuity tests on all the electrical components.

HOW IT WORKS

The vacuum cleaner works by the simple principle of driving a fan with an electric motor to create a rapid air flow through the machine. This causes a vacuum at the suction end which draws in debris.

FIXING YOUR

WASHING MACHINE

The automatic washing machine is the most complex of all domestic appliances, and the one most likely to go wrong

FAULTFINDER

Washing machines combine motors, heaters, pumps, thermostats and a whole array of valves, switches and timing devices with plenty of water

THINGS YOU NEED

- **Tools for gaining access and for fitting parts**
- **Continuity tester**
- **Replacement parts as necessary**

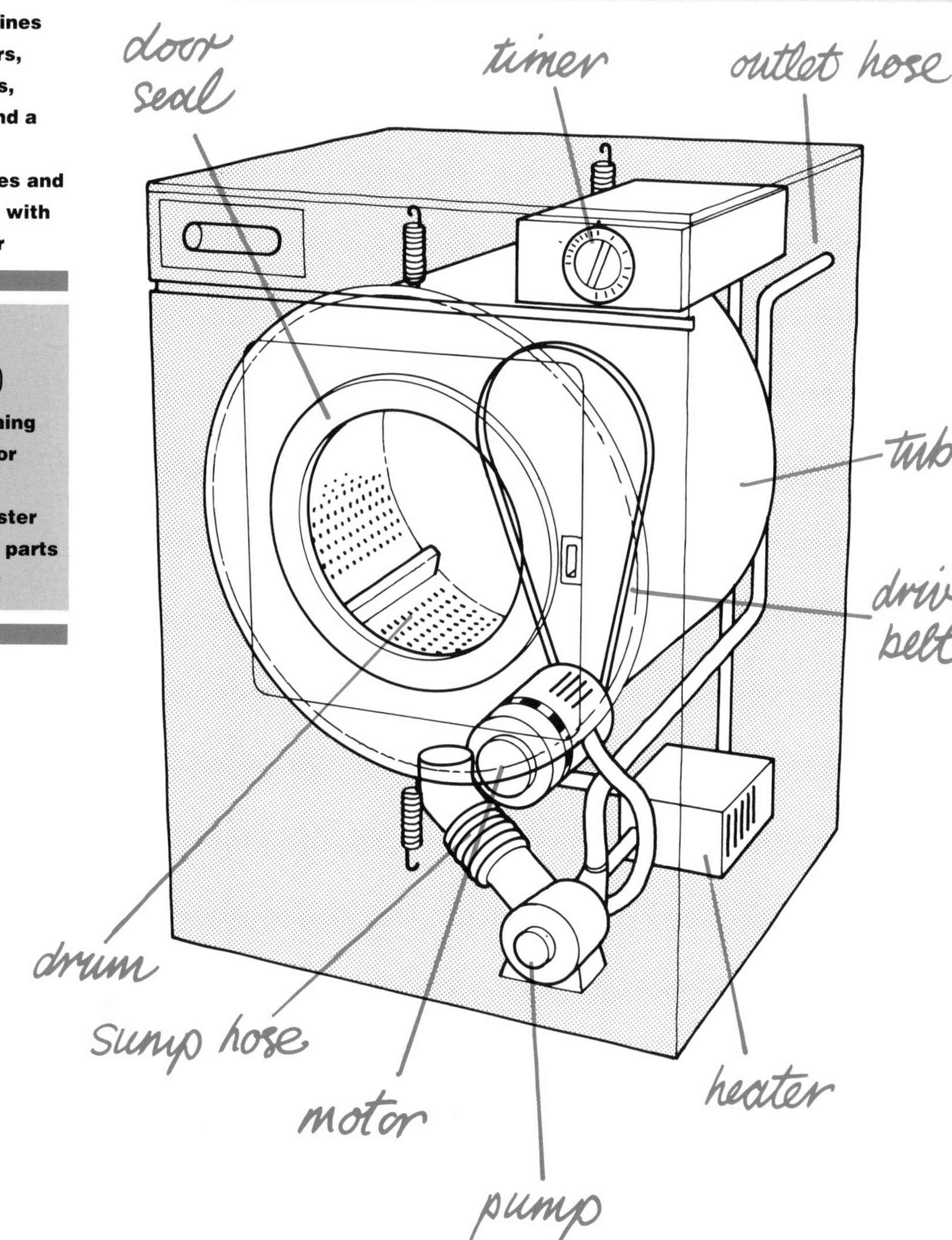

NO ACTION

Likely cause	*What to do*
Door not properly closed	Close door properly
Machine in rinse-hold mode	Reprogramme machine
Plug or flex fault	Rewire or replace as necessary
Water supply turned off	Restore water supply
Door interlock faulty	Replace door interlock
Internal wiring fault	Test for continuity, remake connections
Timer faulty	Replace

NO FILLING ACTION

Likely cause	*What to do*
Water supply turned off	Restore water supply
Filter before inlet valve blocked	Remove and clean filter
Inlet valve faulty	Replace
Timer faulty	Replace
Water level pressure switch faulty	Replace

MACHINE OVERFILLS

Likely cause	*What to do*
Siphonage through waste pipe causing continuous filling	Check instruction booklet and correct outlet hose arrangement
Water level pressure switch faulty	Replace
Inlet valve faulty	Replace
Timer faulty	Replace

POWDER NOT TAKEN

Likely cause	*What to do*
Low hot water supply pressure	Open supply stoptap, avoid using hot water elsewhere in the house during washing
Filter before inlet valve blocked	Remove and clean filter
Inlets to powder dispenser blocked with scale build-up	Remove dispenser and clean inlets
Outlet from powder dispenser blocked	Remove dispenser and clean chamber

ALWAYS REASSEMBLE AN APPLIANCE BEFORE PLUGGING IT IN TO TEST YOUR REPAIR

SEE PAGES 24-51 for how to carry out REPAIRS AND TESTS

FAULTFINDER continued

THINGS YOU NEED

- **Tools for gaining access and for fitting parts**
- **Continuity tester**
- **Replacement parts as necessary**

PROGRAMME INTERRUPTED

Likely cause	*What to do*
Siphonage through waste pipe causing continuous filling	Check instruction booklet and correct outlet hose arrangement
Plug fuse blown due to sudden wiring fault or low insulation	Test wiring for continuity, remake connections, check insulation with RCD
Thermostat faulty	Replace
Heating element faulty	Replace
Pump faulty	Replace
Inlet valve faulty	Replace
Timer faulty	Replace
Induction motor overheating, tripping thermal overload cut-out (TOC)	Trace and rectify cause of overheating, reset TOC
Motor faulty	Check capacitor on induction motors after shorting out the electric charge, replace if faulty; then check motor, replace motor/parts as necessary

NOISY OPERATION

Likely cause	*What to do*
Machine not standing level	Adjust feet and check for level
Machine vibrating against adjacent cabinets or appliances	Allow additional clearance if possible, otherwise place padding between units
Coins/metallic objects between inner and outer drums	Remove heater, lift out obstruction or manoeuvre into sump hose, disconnect hose and remove obstruction
Main drum bearing faulty (grating or rumbling noise)	Replace drum bearings
Motor bearing or pump bearing faulty (high-pitched noise)	Replace motor or pump
Drive belt poorly adjusted	Adjust drive belt tension
Suspension mounts worn/faulty (noise before/after spin action)	Renew suspension pads/springs/dampers as necessary

NO DISCHARGE ACTION

Likely cause	*What to do*
Sump hose/pump filter blocked	Remove hose and clear blockage
Outlet hose kinked/blocked	Unkink hose/remove blockage
Object in pump chamber	Remove object, check pump for damage, replace pump if necessary
Pump faulty	Replace
Internal wiring fault	Test for continuity, remake connections
Timer faulty	Replace

SEE PAGES 24-51 for how to carry out REPAIRS AND TESTS

NO DRUM ROTATION	
Likely cause	*What to do*
Drive belt slipping/broken	Check drive belt tension, replace if necessary
Motor overheating, tripping TOC (induction motors)	Trace and rectify cause of overheating, reset TOC
Motor faulty (brush types)	Check and replace motor/parts as necessary
Motor faulty (induction types)	Check capacitor after shorting out the electric charge, replace if faulty; then check motor, replace motor/parts as necessary
Motor speed control module faulty	Replace
Door interlock faulty	Replace
NO SPIN ACTION	
Likely cause	*What to do*
Door interlock faulty	Replace
Pump faulty, causing pressure switch to prevent spin action	Check/replace pump
Motor faulty	See above
Motor overheating, tripping TOC (induction motors)	Trace and rectify cause of overheating, reset TOC
Motor speed control module faulty	Replace
POOR WASHING ACTION	
Likely cause	*What to do*
Incorrect wash cycle selected	Check instruction booklet for guidance
No washing powder/liquid used	Fill dispenser
Insufficient powder/liquid used	Check instruction booklet for correct quantities, especially in hard water areas
Powder not taken into machine	See above
Overloading of machine	Check instruction booklet for guidance
Heavily-stained clothing not prewashed/treated	Check instruction booklet for guidance
Drive belt slipping	Check drive belt tension

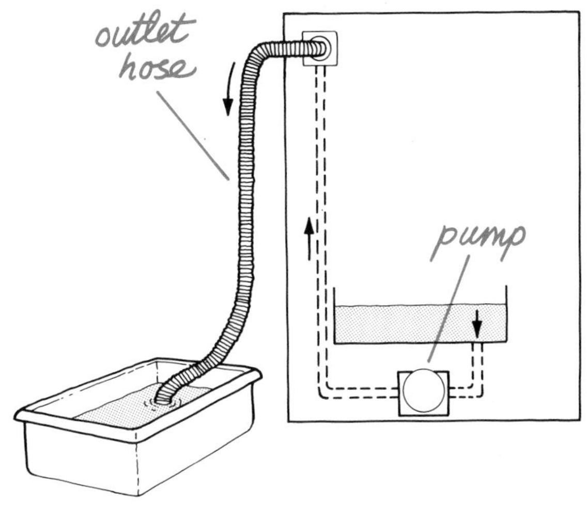

NOTE: To empty a machine full of water, disconnect the outlet hose from its usual discharge point and place it in a bucket at floor level so the water is siphoned out. Raise the hose to stop the flow while you empty the bucket.

FAULTFINDER continued

THINGS YOU NEED

- **Tools for gaining access and for fitting parts**
- **Continuity tester**
- **Replacement parts as necessary**

MACHINE LEAKS

Likely cause	*What to do*
Door seals misaligned/perished	Realign/replace door seals
Hose clips loose	Tighten hose clips
Dispenser hose perished	Replace
Sump hose perished	Replace
Outlet hose perished	Replace
Heater/thermostat seal faulty	Replace
Inlet hoses perished	Replace
Tub seals/grommets faulty	Replace

MACHINE FLOODS

Likely cause	*What to do*
Various faults	Isolate the appliance from the mains and turn off the water supply, then disconnect the outlet hose and lower it into a bucket to siphon off the water in the machine. Allow machine to cool, remove clothes, trace fault

HOW IT WORKS

- Washing machines agitate a perforated drum that contains the wash load inside a larger tub that holds the washing water. At the start of the cycle the inlet valves open and water flows in through the inlet hoses via the detergent dispenser. The water level pressure switch senses when it has reached a pre-set level and sends a signal to the timer to stop the filling action and move on to the next step in the programme. The water is then heated to the required temperature and the motor is engaged to turn the drum.
- At various points in the programme the timer activates the pump to empty the tub, opens the inlet valves to refill it (the last time via the conditioner dispenser) and signals the motor to perform the rinsing action and high-speed spins. Depending on the programme, the machine may pause full of water ('rinse-hold' or 'anti-creasing' mode) before the final spin dry – you have to press a button to instruct it to complete the cycle. A washer-drier includes a condenser tumble drier, which can be set to start automatically after the wash has finished.
- The door latch includes a switch, or interlock, which prevents you from opening the door for a minute or two. If it fails, the machine will not work at all. On most machines the switch also makes it impossible for you to open the door if the machine is full of water.
- The outlet hose has to be carefully positioned to prevent siphonage, a process which draws water out of the machine as it is trying to fill up. The outlet should be above the maximum level of the water within the drum and should have an air space between it and the drain tube. Instruction manuals give details.

FIXING YOUR

WASTE DISPOSAL UNIT

Waste disposers are motorised grinders which turn left over food and the like to a fine slurry which can be rinsed away

FAULTFINDER

NO POWER	
Likely cause	*What to do*
Plug or fuse fault	Rewire or replace as necessary
Internal wiring fault	Test for continuity, remake connections
Faulty on-off switch (if fitted)	Replace
Thermal overload cut-out (TOC) tripped	Reset
TOC faulty	Replace
NO GRINDING ACTION	
Likely cause	*What to do*
Grinding blades jammed	See below
Motor burnt out	Replace
INTERMITTENT ACTION	
Likely cause	*What to do*
Loose connection	Locate and remake connection
Broken flex core	Test flex for continuity, replace if necessary
Fault in speed controller	Replace
SLOW GRINDING AND BURNING SMELL	
Likely cause	*What to do*
Motor overheating through overwork	Check water is running through unit. Switch disposer off, allow to cool, check motor coils for continuity, replace coils/motor if damaged

Waste disposers are prone to jamming, especially if something like a teaspoon finds its way in, which can cause serious damage. The electrics must be well isolated from the water and waste compartment

THINGS YOU NEED

- **Tools for gaining access and for fitting parts**
- **Blade release tool**
- **Continuity tester**
- **Replacement parts as necessary**

FREEING JAMMED BLADES

1 If the disposer has a reversing function, try using this to free the obstruction. You may have to reset the thermal overload cut-out (TOC) first of all.

2 If the jam does not clear, isolate the disposer from the mains. Then try to remove the obstruction if possible, and use the special release tool supplied with the appliance to try to free the grinder blade. Some release tools fit over the hub of the grinder spindle; others are designed to engage on protruding fins on the blade. Insert the tool through the sink outlet and try to turn the blade both clockwise and anti-clockwise.

3 If the blade is still jammed, detach the motor unit from the top housing – some models have clip fixings for easy dismantling, others use bolts or wingnuts. Lift out the unit and remove the blockage from the grinder. Reassemble the unit, reset the TOC and test the disposer.

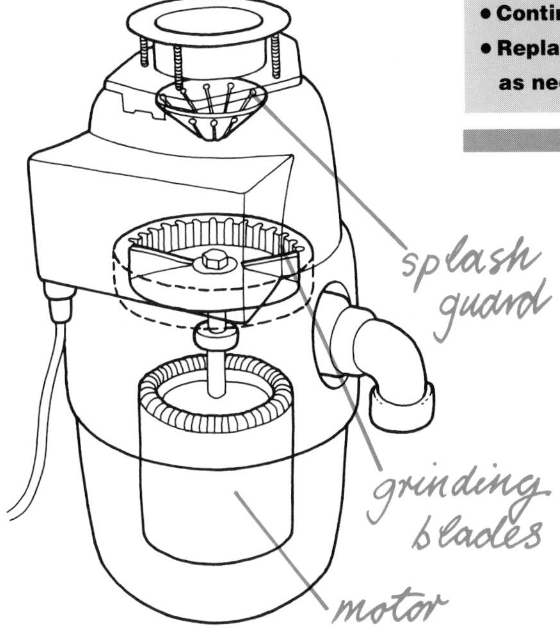

FIXING YOUR

WATER HEATER

Electric water heaters range from instantaneous units for a basin or shower to storage heaters for the kitchen sink

FAULTFINDER

It is unusual for a water heater to develop a fault. Limescale may be the culprit in hard-water areas

THINGS YOU NEED

- **Tools for gaining access and for fitting parts**
- **Continuity tester**
- **Replacement fuse (3kW types only)**
- **Replacement parts as necessary**

NO POWER	
Likely cause	*What to do*
Connection unit fuse/circuit fuse blown/ MCB tripped	Trace cause of fault, rectify and replace fuse/ reset MCB
Loose connection in switch/connection unit	Turn off at mains, remake connection
Flex damaged (3kW types only)	Switch off connection unit, replace flex
Internal wiring fault	Test for continuity, remake connections
NO HEAT	
Likely cause	*What to do*
Internal wiring fault	Test for continuity, remake connections
Thermostat faulty	Replace thermostat
Thermal overload cut-out (TOC) tripped	Reset
TOC faulty	Replace
Element failed	Replace
OVERHEATING	
Likely cause	*What to do*
Thermostat faulty	Replace
TOC faulty	Replace
REDUCED WATER FLOW	
Likely cause	*What to do*
Outlet tap not fully open	Open tap fully
Stoptap on supply pipe nearly closed	Open stoptap slightly
Internal scale build-up	Descale following manufacturer's instructions
Scale at outlet (e.g. shower head)	Descale following manufacturer's instructions

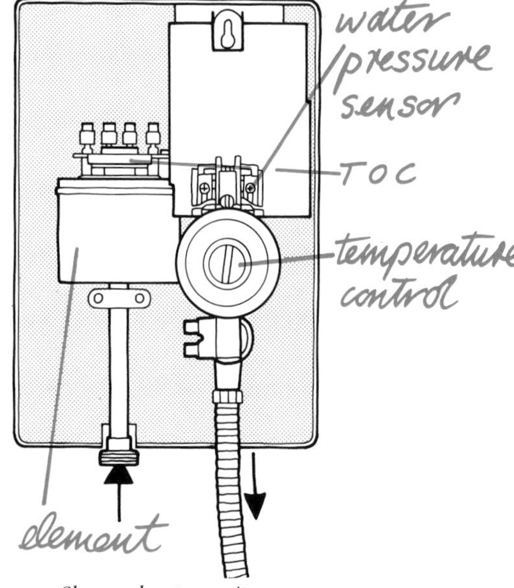

Shower heater unit

DISMANTLING

1 Isolate the heater from the electricity supply by switching off its double-pole switch or fused connection unit. Disconnect the circuit too.

2 Turn off the water supply to the heater at the stoptap on its supply pipe and open the outlet tap. Undo the casing screws and lift it off to gain access to the electrics. Test the continuity of all components and internal wiring connections from the main terminal block onwards.

3 Follow the manufacturer's instructions for descaling the unit if it appears to be furred up. You may have to disconnect the plumbing and electricity supplies first and remove the unit from its support brackets to enable you to introduce the descaling liquid.

ABOUT THE HOUSE

- FIXTURES AND FITTINGS
- PLUMBING
- WIRING
- CENTRAL HEATING
- SECURITY

FAILED

FIXINGS

Dozens of things around the house rely on sound fixings to keep them securely in place

LIGHT-DUTY FIXINGS

If fixings fail, repairing them can be more difficult than making them in the first place

THINGS YOU NEED

- **Assorted screwdrivers**
- **Replacement screws**
- **Woodworking adhesive**
- **Wood filler**
- **Dowels**
- **Plugging compound**
- **New fixing devices**
- **Power drill and bits**

1 If a screw has pulled out of wood – where it held a handle to a door, for example – it may have torn out some of the wood fibres too. Try packing out the hole with a match and driving the screw back into place. Alternatively (or additionally), dip the screw threads in woodworking adhesive before replacing the screw.

2 If this fails to hold, drill out the damaged hole and tap in a short length of wooden dowel of the same diameter as the drill bit. Smear some woodworking adhesive on the dowel first, and leave until the adhesive has hardened. Then drill a thin pilot hole and replace the screw.

3 In man-made boards, especially chipboard, screws pulling out can cause severe damage to the board. Repair it with wood filler, and try to remake the fixing elsewhere if possible. If it is not, glue in lengths of dowel or, where the fixing is into the board edge, drill a clearance hole and tap in a plastic wallplug. Make sure its wings are aligned to expand parallel with the surface of the board, not at right angles to it, and drive in the fixing screw.

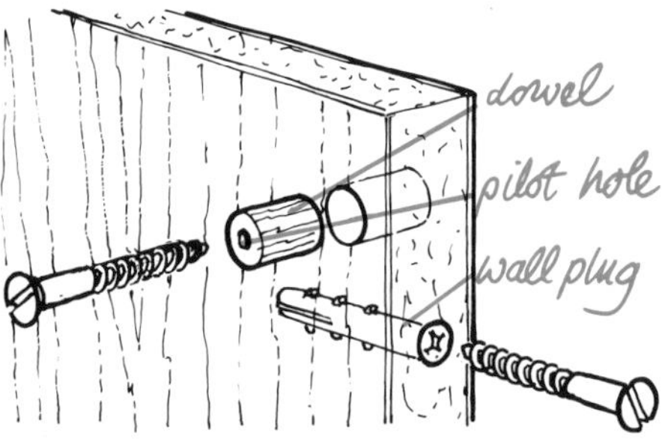

4 In masonry walls, the most frequently used light-duty fixing is the plastic wallplug. Drilling too large a hole, using too small a plug or fitting the wrong size of screw into it can all cause the fixing to fail. If it does, first try using a larger plug and a thicker screw in the original hole. If it still fails, pack the original hole with proprietary plugging compound. Then drill a new hole and remake the fixing or screw directly into the plugging compound – follow the instructions for the particular product.

CAVITY FIXINGS

1 In partition walls and ceilings clad with plasterboard, fixings are often made with cavity fixing devices of one type or another. These use various mechanical methods to help spread the load the fixing is carrying against the inner face of the plasterboard; some remain in place if the fixing screw is withdrawn, while others are lost in the cavity. In the former case, so long as the plasterboard is undamaged and the fixing screw is a tapered woodscrew rather than a straight bolt, try using a larger screw in the original fixing device. Otherwise use a new fixing device in the original hole.

2 If the fixing has pulled out and has also damaged the plasterboard, use a sharp Stanley knife to neaten the edges of the hole. Then prepare an offcut of plasterboard about twice as long as the hole, but narrow enough to be pushed through it. Drill a hole in it, feed a length of string through and tie a nail to one end. Pull the nail up against one face of the offcut, then butter some plaster on to the other face.

3 Slide the offcut into the hole, keeping hold of the string, and pull this to hold the offcut against the inner face of the plasterboard. When the plaster has hardened, cut off the string flush with the offcut and fill the recess with more plaster. Re-make the fixing once you have a smooth and fully hardened finish.

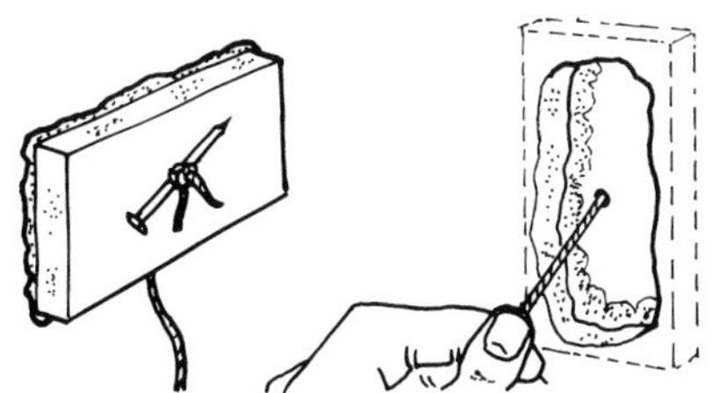

4 If there is a large hole in the plasterboard, cut out a strip between the two adjacent wall studs. Nail horizontal and vertical battens around the edges of the hole and nail a new patch of plasterboard to these. Fit a new cavity fixing.

THINGS YOU NEED

- **Offcuts of plasterboard**
- **Stanley knife**
- **Plaster**
- **Nails**
- **Hammer**
- **Timber**
- **String**

HEAVY-DUTY FIXINGS

1 Where a cavity fixing has failed, it may be preferable to provide timber support rather than to rely on another cavity device. In partition walls, cut back the plasterboard to the edges of the adjacent studs, nail a horizontal cross-piece into place between them. Screw the new fixing to the cross-piece if appearance doesn't matter; otherwise cover it with a plasterboard patch first.

2 In ceilings with access above (a loft, for example), drill down through the ceiling surface on both sides of the joist to indicate its position in the room below, and make the fixing into the centre of the joist. If no joists coincide with the required fixing position, fit a piece of board between the joists using battens at each side, and make the new fixing through the ceiling into the board.

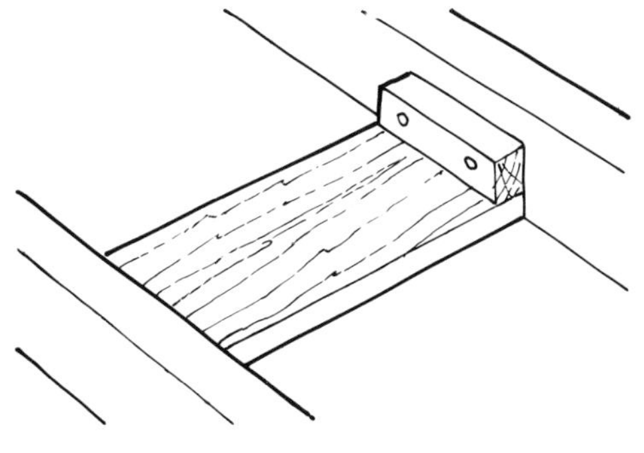

JAMMED FIXINGS

● If a fixing you need to undo will not budge, there are several methods you can use to remove it. If it is a screw with a slotted head, try inserting your screwdriver at a slight angle and then striking its handle with a hammer to turn the screw enough to free the threads. You can also use an impact screwdriver to do this if you have one. If this fails, try touching the screw head for several seconds with a hot soldering iron to expand the metal, then try to undo the screw.

● As a last resort, use a screw extractor. First drill a small-diameter hole down the length of the screw shank with a sharp twist drill bit. Insert the left-handed thread of the screw extractor anticlockwise into the hole and keep turning until the screw moves.

Heavy-duty fixings into partition walls and ceilings must be made either into the wall studs or ceiling joists, or into timber fixed between two studs or joists. You can buy an electronic detector (about £15).

THINGS YOU NEED

(See above)

FIXING YOUR

FLOORS AND STAIRS

Noisy floorboards and stairs are a nuisance; stairs that are damaged are a potential hazard

FLOORBOARDS

Most homes have some suspended timber floors consisting of boards of one type or another nailed to the supporting joists; the floorboards may creak, warp or shrink

THINGS YOU NEED

- **Claw hammer**
- **Nails**
- **Power drill and bits**
- **Screws**
- **Screwdriver**
- **Bolster chisel**

Slight squeaks may be due to floorboards rubbing against one another even though they are securely fixed. You may need only to work talcum powder into the gaps between boards to act as a lubricant.

1 The commonest problem with timber floors is that they develop annoying creaks as time goes by. Boards may creak because sections have been lifted for access to wiring or pipework below the floor, and have not been properly replaced. Locate the offending board and prise it up with a bolster chisel and claw hammer where it has been cut. Remove the old fixing nails, check that both its ends rest on a joist or on a batten – an extra block of wood nailed to the joist side – and secure the board back in place with screws rather than nails. Drill narrow pilot holes just shorter than the length of the screws and wider clearance holes the depth of the wider part of the screw (between the thread and the head). These holes let the screw go in smoothly without damaging the wood.

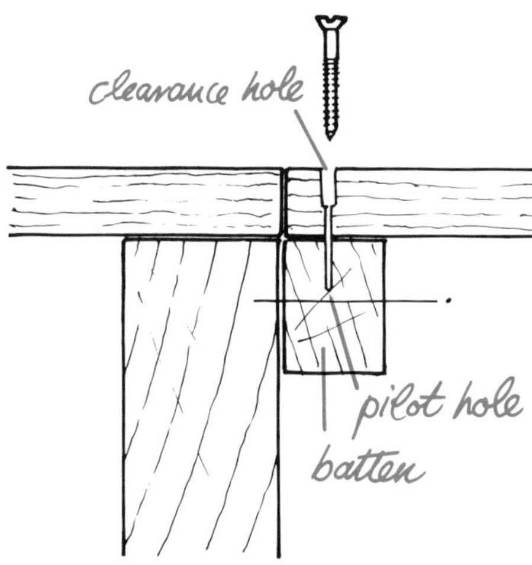

2 There are two common causes of undisturbed boards starting to creak. The first is warping; the timber used may twist along its length as temperature and humidity changes occur, and this can pull out the fixing nails, allowing the board to move against the joist below and rub against the nails or adjacent boards when it is trodden on. Cure the problem by screwing the board down tightly against the top of the joist. Drive the screws in beside the existing fixings.

3 The second cause of creaking is inadequate fixings; in this case the board is not secured to every joist it crosses, so can lift slightly and will creak against the joist when under load. This problem is very common with modern floors covered with chipboard rather than with solid timber floorboards. Cure it by nailing (or better, screwing) each affected board to every joist after making test drillings to identify the precise joist positions. Make sure you are not about to screw or nail through wiring or pipework. Secure chipboard panels every 300mm (12in) across the board as well as along the edges.

WARPED BOARDS

Warped board edges can show as ridges through carpets and thin floorcoverings such as sheet vinyl and cork. You can prevent this (and also conceal gaps between the boards) by putting down an overlay of hardboard or thin plywood before a new floorcovering is laid.

STAIRS

CREAKS

Staircases creak for the same reason that floorboards do: loose components rubbing against each other as the flight is used. In the case of stairs, the problem is usually caused by slight gaps opening up between the treads and risers through wear and tear, or because of slight settlement in the side walls supporting the staircase structure.

1 You may be able to alleviate the creaking by puffing talcum powder into the gaps, but it is better to attempt a more permanent cure.

2 First remove the stair carpet. Then insert an old chisel into the angles between the treads and risers to prise the two slightly apart, and squirt in some woodworking adhesive along the joint. Do this last thing at night, so the flight will not be used for several hours and the adhesive will have a chance to harden thoroughly. Then drill pilot and clearance holes at 150mm (6in) intervals down through the front edge of the affected treads into the top edges of the risers beneath, and screw the two securely together with countersunk screws.

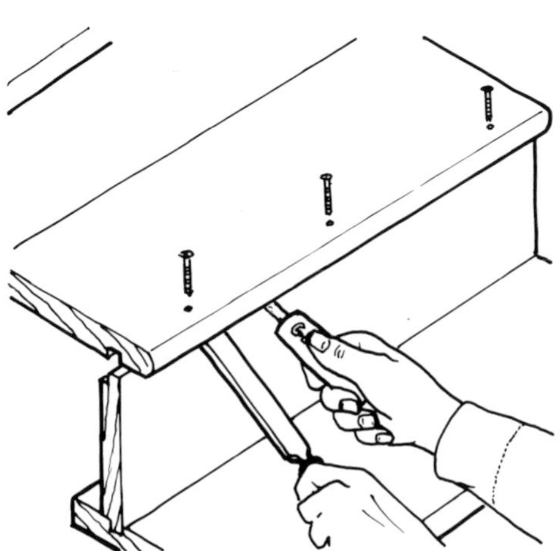

3 If you can gain access to the underside of the flight via an understairs cupboard, check that all the wedges securing the treads and risers are firmly in place in their slots in the staircase sides. Remove any loose ones you find, apply adhesive and tap them back into place with a mallet. Cut and fit new wedges if any are missing.

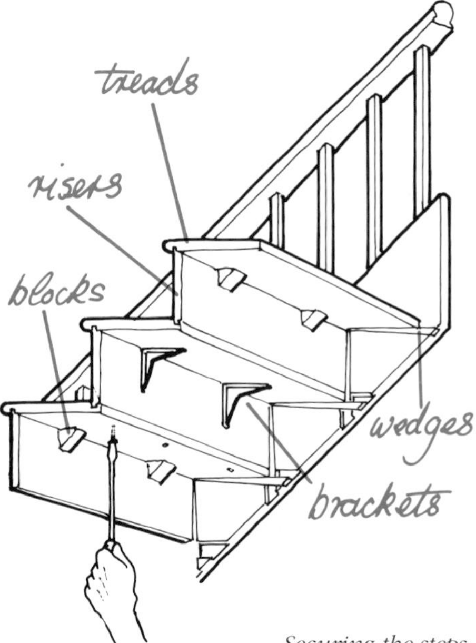

Securing the steps

4 Still working from below stairs, glue and screw triangular blocks of scrap wood into the internal angles between treads and risers or install L-shaped brackets. Drive screws up through the rear edges of the treads into the risers above.

Staircases are one of the most intricate parts of any house structure and can suffer from a variety of faults

THINGS YOU NEED

- **Talcum powder**
- **Power drill and bits**
- **Screws**
- **Screwdriver**
- **Woodworking adhesive**
- **Angle repair brackets**
- **Mallet**
- **Scrap wood blocks**
- **Power jigsaw**
- **Replacement nosing**
- **Hammer**
- **Nails**
- **G-cramps**
- **Tenon saw**
- **Handrail bolts**
- **Dowels**
- **Chisel**

THINGS YOU NEED

- **Talcum powder**
- **Power drill and bits**
- **Screws**
- **Screwdriver**
- **Woodworking adhesive**
- **Angle repair brackets**
- **Mallet**
- **Scrap wood blocks**
- **Power jigsaw**
- **Replacement nosing**
- **Hammer**
- **Nails**
- **G-cramps**
- **Tenon saw**
- **Handrail bolts**
- **Dowels**
- **Chisel**

TREADS

If the front edge of a tread – called the nosing – splits or breaks away, it needs repairing urgently since it could cause someone to trip and fall. Glue and screw split nosings back into place if possible; otherwise use a jigsaw to cut the damaged nosing away flush with the face of the riser beneath, shape a new nosing from softwood of the same thickness as the tread and glue and screw it in place.

BALUSTRADE

1 If any part of the stair balustrade becomes loose, attend to it immediately to avoid the risk of accidents. Secure the bottom ends of loose balusters into their recesses by running in some woodworking adhesive around them, by tapping in small glued wooden wedges alongside them, or by driving nails at an angle through the baluster into the surrounding wood. Use angled nails to secure the top ends of loose balusters to the underside of the handrail too. Repair loose joints between handrails and newel posts by attaching metal brackets.

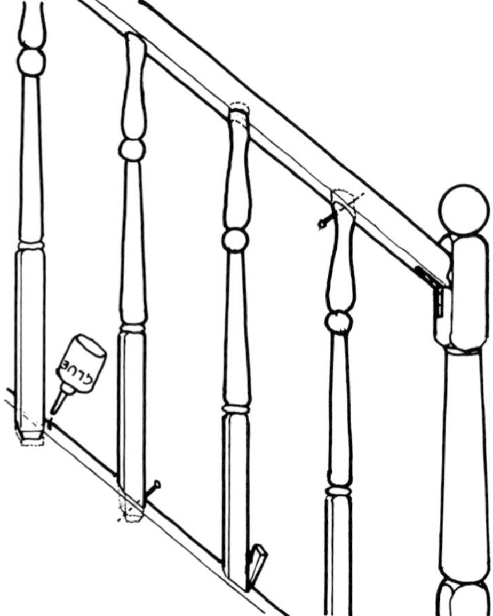

Securing the banisters

2 If balusters are cracked, squirt woodworking adhesive into the crack and hold the baluster together with a G-cramp until it has hardened. Badly damaged balusters should be replaced for the sake of safety. Hammer the baluster out at the top, striking it on the downstairs face.

3 Damaged handrails can be very dangerous. Repair minor cracks by gluing and nailing or screwing. For a more serious repair, splice in a new section. Cut out the damaged section and make a V-shaped cut in the exposed ends of the rail. Trim the new section of handrail to fit and glue it into place, clamping it firmly until the adhesive has hardened.

4 Alternatively, use dowels and handrail bolts. Make a straight cut in the handrail to remove the damaged section. Mark out the ends of the old and new section carefully, so they will align when you fit the bolts. Bore holes for the bolt and two dowels (these stop the handrail rotating) and chisel out recesses for the nuts. Apply woodworking adhesive to the dowels and the ends of the rails and tighten the nuts securely.

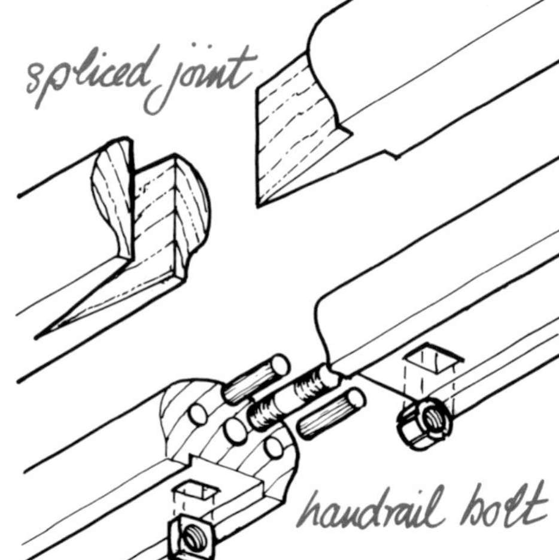

FIXING YOUR

DOORS AND WINDOWS

Wooden doors and casement windows cause problems when the wood changes shape. Sash windows need occasional maintenance

STICKING

1 If paint or varnish build-up is the likely culprit, cure it by stripping back to bare wood and then using a plane to remove a little wood so that there is a clearance of about 3mm ($^1/_8$ in) between door and frame. A Surform will remove the paint and do the planing job quickly but less smoothly. Paint or varnish the bare wood.

2 If the binding appears to be seasonal – worst in warm wet weather, non-existent in dry weather – moisture is being absorbed by the wood and is causing it to expand. If the door is properly decorated, the likely source of entry is via the traditionally undecorated top and bottom edges, so the door will tend to bind near the corners. Take the door off its hinges during a dry period when it's not binding and paint or varnish both surfaces before rehanging it.

3 If the hinge screws are loose, the door will hang away from the hinge side of the frame and will bind on the handle side. Either fit longer screws or drill out the existing screw holes, plug them with lengths of dowel covered with woodworking adhesive and drill fresh pilot and clearance holes for the screws.

Squaring up sagging corner joints with wedges and dowel

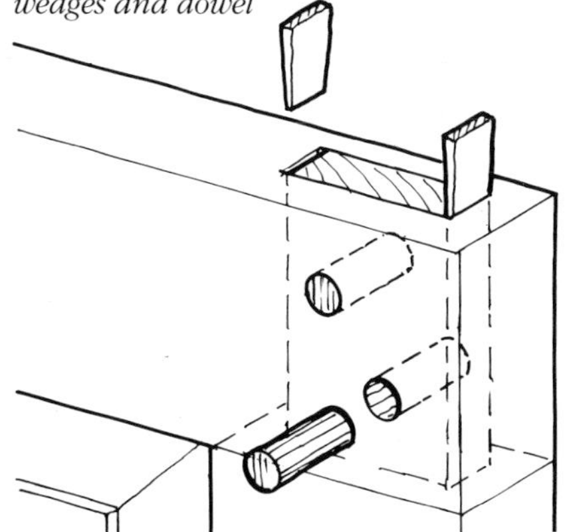

4 The corner joints on traditional framed-and-panelled doors may become loose with age and wear, allowing the door to sag so it catches the frame or floor. If the problem is minor, place sandpaper on the floor and run the door over it a few times. Otherwise, remove the door, laying it flat so its corners can be squared up, and drive slim glued wedges into all the tenon joints alongside the mortises. Next, drill two holes through the face of the door into each mortise and drive in lengths of glued dowel to lock the joint in place.

5 Cure a loose door frame by inserting timber packing between it and the masonry to hold it square, then drill holes through the frame and on into the masonry so you can insert long frame plugs. Push them in until the neck of the plug is flush with the frame, then hammer or drive in the screw contained within the plug to secure the frame to the wall.

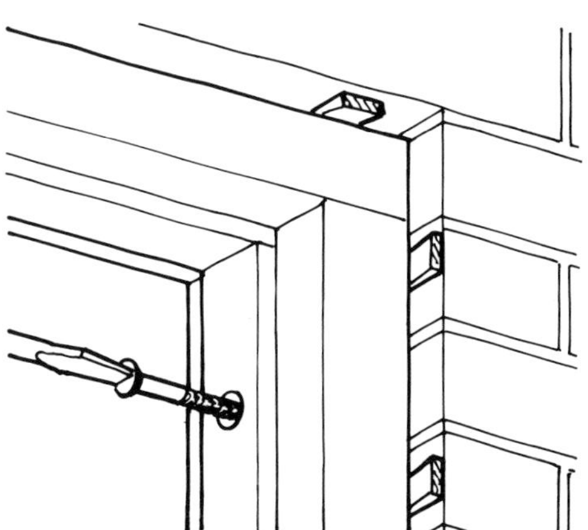

Curing a loose door frame

The commonest faults with doors are binding against the frame caused by a build-up of paint, expansion of the wood, problems with the hinges, sagging joints or loose parts in the frame

THINGS YOU NEED

- Abrasive paper
- Plane or Surform
- Paint or varnish
- Screwdriver
- Dowels
- Woodworking adhesive
- Timber wedges
- Power drill and bits
- Screws
- Frame fixings

NOT CLOSING

A door which won't close fully is not only annoying – it lets in draughts and cannot be sealed against a fire

THINGS YOU NEED

- **Screws**
- **Screwdriver**
- **Packing material**
- **Hinge**
- **G-cramps**
- **Timber boards and blocks**

1 If the hinge side of a door comes into contact with the door frame before the door is fully closed it's said to be hinge-bound. Hinge screws with heads that do not fit properly into the countersinks in the hinges or screws that are not driven in squarely may be the source of the trouble. Replace any over-large or misaligned screws.

2 It may be that the hinge is recessed too far into the frame rather than that any part of it is protruding. Remove recessed hinges and pack out the spaces behind them with sandpaper, card or hardboard – whatever gives the required thickness. The hinge should sit flush with the frame.

3 A warped door will not close if one corner – usually the top corner on the handle side – meets the frame before the rest of the door makes contact. Use G-cramps and timber boards to force the door back into shape. Gradually tighten the cramps over a couple of days until the door straightens. This method is not suitable for glazed doors. If the warp is on the hinge side, adding an extra hinge may cure the problem.

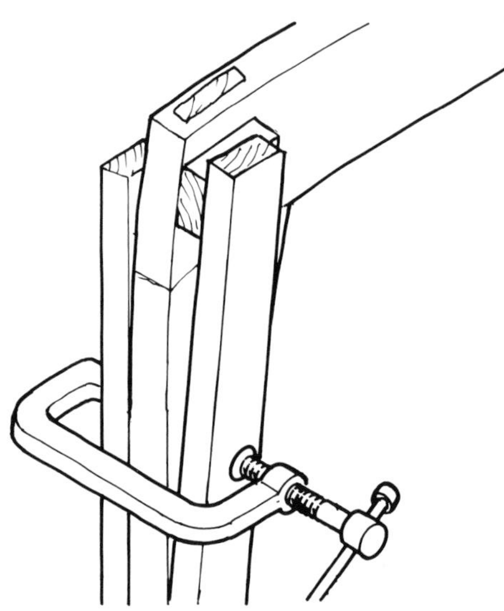

SASH CORDS

The most common major fault to affect sliding sash windows is a broken sash cord. Repairing them means taking the window apart, so replace all four cords even if only one breaks

1 To remove the sashes and gain access to the concealed weight compartments at each side of the frame, start by carefully prising away the vertical staff beads on the inside of the frame using a broad chisel. Label them and set them aside for re-use.

2 Lift the inner (bottom) sash on to the sill inside, support it with your body and cut through the unbroken cord against the edge of the sash. Hold the cord with your free hand and let it up gently to lower its weight to the bottom of the weight compartment. Set the sash aside.

3 To free the outer (top) sash, lever out the two parting beads that separate the sashes, lift out the sash as before and cut the unbroken cord(s). Save the beads.

4 Lever out the pocket covers to gain access to the weight compartments. The cover may be sealed up with paint (cut it with a sharp knife), or secured with a small screw. Then lift out each weight and its tail of cord, and label each one; they may be of different weights to balance the individual sashes.

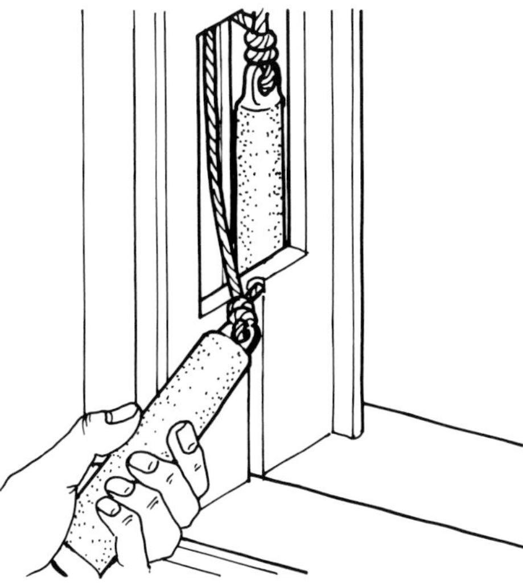

5 Mark the position of the cord end on the edge of each sash, then remove the cut pieces of cord from each weight and sash in turn, and make a note of the total length of each cord. Repair any loose joints, and take this opportunity to paint the normally inaccessible edges of the sashes and the sides of the frames. Oil the pulleys to make sure they run freely.

6 Cut the four new cords to the necessary lengths to match those they are replacing, adding about 100mm (4in) to allow for knots. Tie a weight small enough to pass over the pulley to the end of a piece of string and attach the new cord to the end of this; put a knot in the end of the cord to prevent it being pulled right through. Push the weighted end of the string over the pulley and retrieve it through the pocket. Draw the cord into position and tie it securely to its weight, then replace the weight in the pocket. Do this for all four cords and weights, and check that each pair of weights is separated by its parting slip – a thin strip of wood designed to stop the weights from banging together. Replace the pocket covers.

7 Hold up the outer sash first, and attach the cords to its sides with one nail to begin with, aligning the end of the cord with the mark you made earlier. Check that the sash will slide all the way up and down, and adjust the position of the cords slightly if necessary. Then drive two more fixing nails into the cord on each side.

8 Replace the parting beads, and repeat step 7 to fit the inner sash. Replace the staff beads all round, fill around the nail heads and repaint the beads to match the rest of the new paintwork.

THINGS YOU NEED

- **Old chisel**
- **Pliers**
- **Sharp Stanley knife**
- **Decorating tools and materials**
- **String and small weight**
- **Replacement sash cord**
- **Tacks or clout nails**
- **Hammer**
- **Tape measure**

Opening casement windows have similar problems to doors (page 99); broken windows are dealt with on page 22.

FIXING YOUR

FURNITURE

Furniture in the home has to endure a lot of wear and tear. Problem areas are joints, hinges and drawers

JOINTS

Joints, particularly in wooden chairs, work loose with time due to everyday use and to the wood drying out

THINGS YOU NEED

- **Mallet**
- **Abrasive paper and sanding block**
- **Chisel**
- **Woodworking adhesive**
- **Adhesive tape**
- **Sash or tourniquet cramps**
- **Wood for reinforcing blocks**
- **Power drill and bits**
- **Pencil and thin scrap of wood**
- **Tenon saw**
- **Dowels**
- **Screwdriver**
- **Screws**

1 If a framed piece of furniture such as a chair has joints that have worked loose, start by prising the joints apart. Use a mallet if necessary to separate different parts of the frame. Label the ends of each component so you can reassemble parts that look alike in their correct places.

2 Clean off the remains of the old adhesive with abrasive paper or a chisel. If tenons or rail ends have split, prise the cracks open, squirt in adhesive and use tape or a small cramp to hold the split closed while the adhesive sets hard.

3 Apply adhesive to tenons and rail ends, and reassemble the joints one by one. Wipe away excess adhesive before it has a chance to set. With the reassembly complete, use sash cramps or improvised tourniquet cramps to hold all the joints tight until the adhesive has set. Use scrap timber to prevent the cramps from bruising the wood, and make sure you do not overtighten the cramps and pull the frames out of square.

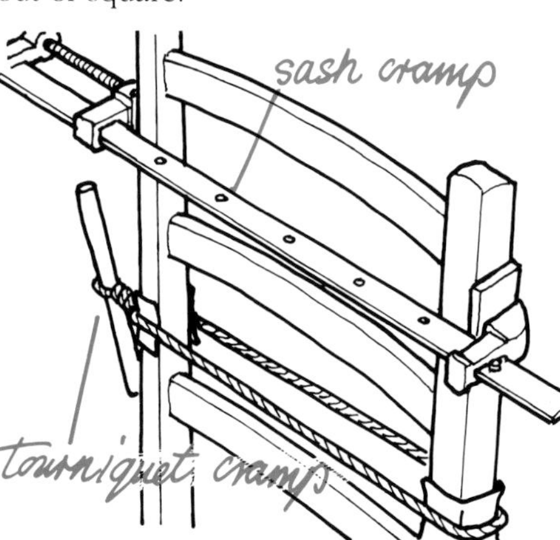

4 Reinforce mortise-and-tenon joints with countersunk or counterbored screws, or with glued dowels, driven into holes drilled through the joint. Fill counterbored holes with dowel plugs, stained or painted to match the surrounding woodwork.

5 Reinforce weak corner joints on chairs by shaping triangular corner blocks to fit in the angles beneath the chair seat. Glue and screw them into place.

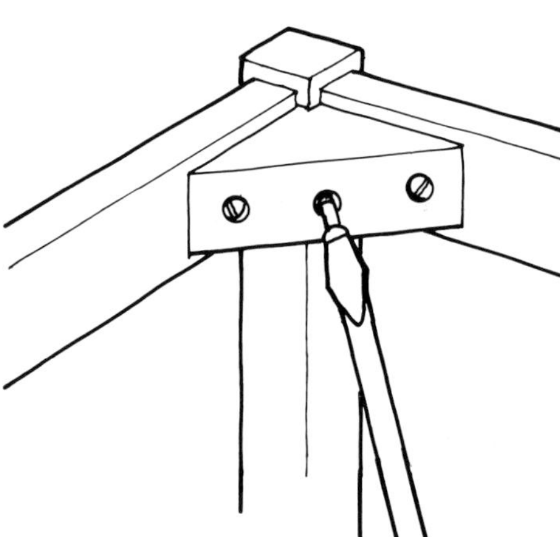

6 Where the fixing is into the edge of a veneered or plastic-faced chipboard panel such as in a kitchen unit, use a plastic wallplug with two expanding wings to make a secure fixing. Drill out the damaged screw hole and insert the plug so its wings will expand parallel to the board edge as the fixing screw is driven into it (see also page 94).

OTHER PROBLEMS

WOBBLY FURNITURE

To level uneven legs on wooden chairs, stools and small tables, stand the piece on a flat surface and insert card packing beneath the short leg until the piece is standing square and level. Then use a pencil and a scrap of wood about 3mm (1/8in) thicker than the packing to scribe a cutting line round each leg. Saw off the end of each leg at the scribed line, and sand the ends smooth.

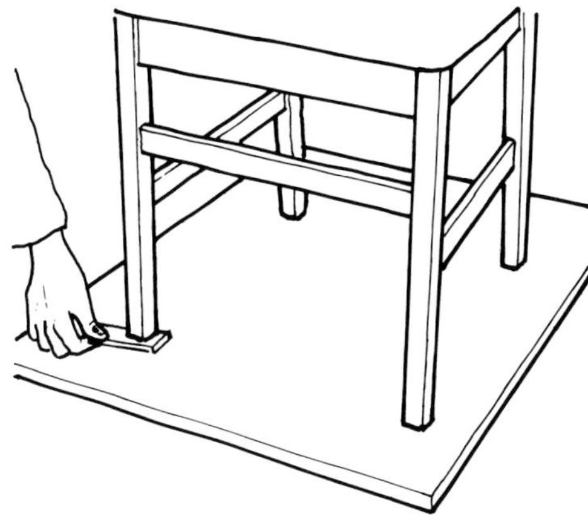

HINGES

Damage to hinge fixings on cupboard doors is caused either by the door being forced back too far when open, or by downward pressure on the top edge of the door. The result in both cases is either damage to the hinge itself or a tearing-out of the fixing screws, sometimes both. You may be able to re-secure the hinge by using larger screws, packing the screw hole with a match or applying woodworking adhesive to the screw thread before re-inserting it. Remove the screws, and buy a matching replacement hinge if necessary. Then drill out damaged screw holes and glue in lengths of dowel. When the adhesive has set, drill new pilot and clearance holes and replace the hinge screws.

STICKING DRAWERS

1 Drawers may not run freely because their corner joints are loose, or because frequent use has worn down the drawer bottoms where they slide on their runners. First try rubbing candle wax on the drawer and runners to lubricate the movement and prevent further wear.

2 If that is inadequate, repair loose joints by knocking them apart and re-gluing them, using a tourniquet cramp to hold the joints closed and the drawer square. Repair worn runners by gluing fresh strips of wood to the bottom edges of the drawer sides, and then planing them down until the drawer is a perfect fit and slides in and out smoothly.

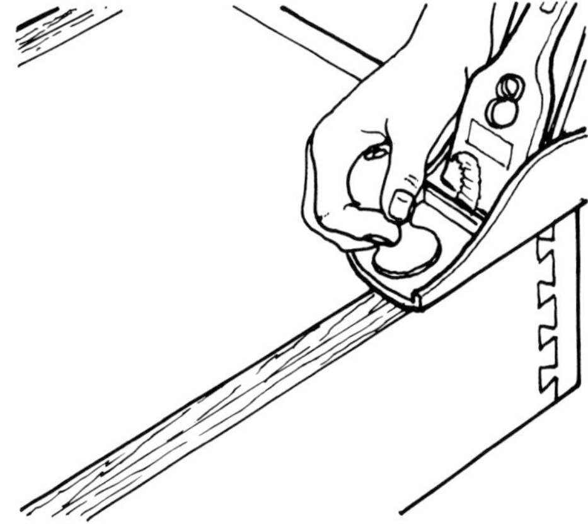

It's worth fixing minor problems as constant use will quickly make a more extensive repair necessary

THINGS YOU NEED

- **Candle**
- **Thin strips of wood**
- **Tenon saw**
- **Woodworking adhesive**
- **Mallet**
- **Plane**
- **Tourniquet cramp**
- **Power drill and bits**
- **Hinges**
- **Screws**
- **Screwdriver**
- **Dowels**
- **Wallplugs**

FIXING YOUR

PLUMBING

Irritating niggles and even some major problems can be sorted out without calling in a plumber

DRIPPING TAP

A tap that drips probably needs a new washer. If water leaks out of the top when the tap is on, the packing isn't properly adjusted

THINGS YOU NEED

- **Screwdriver**
- **Two adjustable spanners**
- **Replacement washer**
- **Replacement gland**

Old-style conventional taps usually have a capstan-style handle and a chrome 'easy-clean' cover concealing the tap mechanism (called the headgear); newer taps have shrouded heads. Supataps work differently.

CONVENTIONAL TAPS

1 Turn off the water supply to the tap (see page 14). With old taps, start by trying to unscrew the easy-clean cover with a spanner after wrapping it in cloth to protect the chrome plating. If it will not budge, try pouring some boiling water over it first.

2 Raise the cover so you can tighten the spanner on to the hexagonal part of the headgear and unscrew it. Use the second spanner to hold the tap spout and prevent the tap body from rotating as you do this. If the cover will not rise far enough, loosen the grub screw holding the tap handle to the spindle and remove the handle. Lift out the headgear.

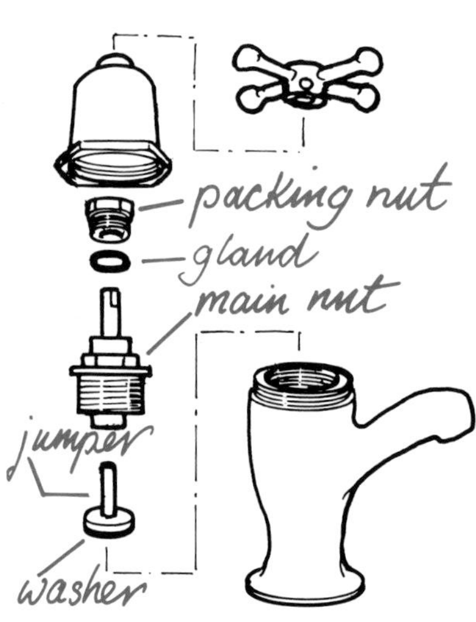

3 Pull out the jumper on which the washer is mounted, and remove the old washer (it may be held in place by a nut). Fit a new washer and reassemble.

4 With modern taps, prise off the hot/cold indicator disc on top of the handle and undo the retaining screw beneath it so you can pull the handle off. Then unscrew the headgear and replace the washer.

5 If the problem is that the tap leaks when it is on, adjust the packing. You don't need to shut off the water supply to do this. Remove the handle and easy-clean cover or the shroud and tighten the packing nut slightly. If that fails, remove the nut and replace the gland underneath – a rubber O-ring or wool coated in grease.

SUPATAPS

1 With Supataps you do not need to turn off the water supply. Turn the tap on and loosen the nut above the tap handle; keep on turning the handle to unscrew it from the tap body. The flow will increase initially, but as you remove the handle a valve inside the tap will stop the flow.

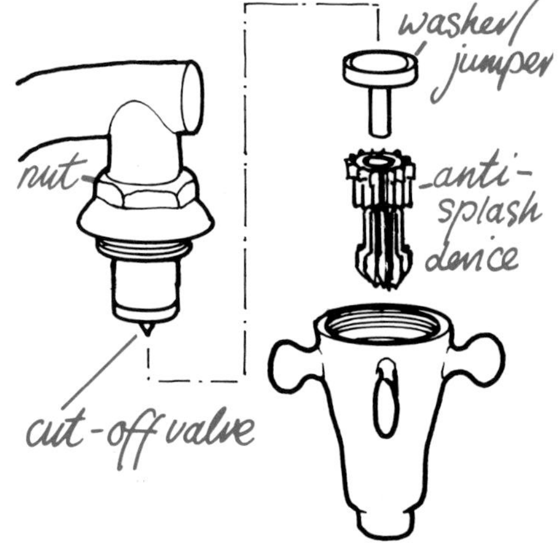

2 Knock the handle sharply against a hard surface to shake out the anti-splash device, and prise the jumper/washer unit out of it with a screwdriver. Fit a replacement, then reassemble the tap and tighten the top nut.

OVERFLOWS

1 Check what type of ballvalve is fitted to the overflowing tank/cistern. In the vast majority of homes it will be a brass Portsmouth-pattern valve with a piston. Modern installations may be fitted with an equilibrium or diaphragm type, the latter often made of plastic. Then turn off the water supply to the tank (see page 14). If the fault is in a WC cistern with no gatevalve on its supply pipe, cut off the supply to the cold water storage tank, drain it by opening the bathroom cold taps and then flush the toilet.

2 With a Portsmouth valve, remove the float arm by using pliers to pull out the split pin securing the arm to the valve body. Then apply penetrating oil to the screw cap on the end of the valve, and unscrew it. Use a spanner if necessary.

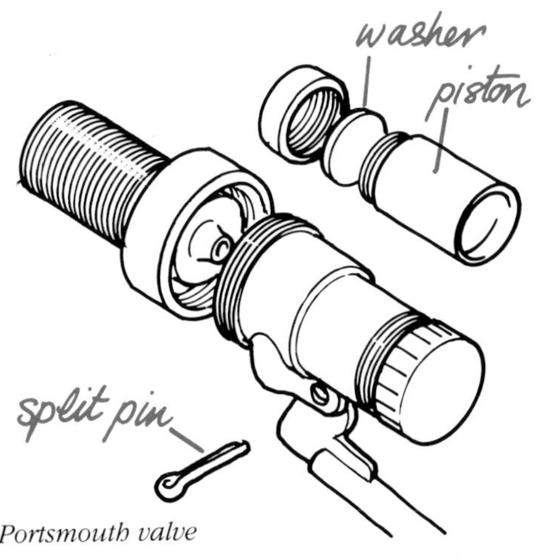

Portsmouth valve

3 Push the screwdriver blade into the slot in the underside of the valve body and lever out the piston. One-piece pistons have a slot in the side into which the washer slides; poke the old washer out and fit a new one. Two-piece pistons have the washer retained by a screw-on end cap; grip this with pliers and use a screwdriver in the piston slot to rotate the piston and so unscrew the cap. Push the old washer out of the cap and fit a new one. Reassemble the valve and restore the water supply.

4 Check that the tank/cistern fills to the correct level – just below the warning pipe. Bend the float arm up or down as necessary to raise or lower the water level. Lastly, unscrew the float from the float arm so you can check whether it contains water. If it does, tie a plastic bag round it as a temporary measure, and buy a replacement float.

5 With diaphragm valves, simply unscrew the retaining nut, remove the end cap and plunger and prise out the worn diaphragm with a small screwdriver. Note which way it was fitted and insert the new one the same way round, then reassemble the valve. Adjust the water level if necessary by using the small screw on the valve body.

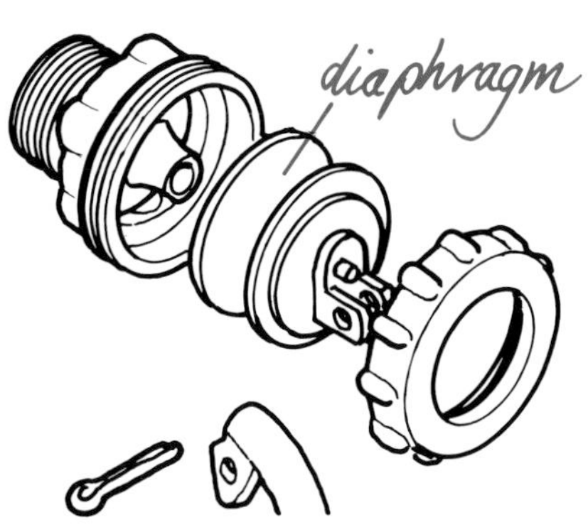

Diaphragm valve

Water storage tanks and cisterns are always fitted with a warning pipe to drain off the overflow if the automatic ballvalve fails to shut off the water supply. Drips from this pipe are often caused by a worn ballvalve washer

THINGS YOU NEED

- **Pliers**
- **Penetrating oil**
- **Adjustable spanner**
- **Screwdriver**
- **Replacement washer/diaphragm**

AIRLOCKS

Airlocks, caused by air becoming trapped in pipework, can stop the flow of water completely. They most commonly affect hot taps, but sometimes occur in radiators and heating pipework too

THINGS YOU NEED

- **Length of garden hose**
- **Jubilee clips/hose connectors**
- **Screwdriver**
- **Air release valve**
- **Hacksaw**
- **Adjustable spanners**

1 To cure an airlocked tap, connect one end of a length of garden hose securely to the spout with a hose connector and take the other end to the kitchen cold tap, which receives water at mains pressure rather than from the tank in the loft. Open the affected tap first, then the kitchen tap, so the mains-pressure water drives the airlock out of the pipework. The hose connector on the kitchen tap should incorporate a double-check valve to guard against any risk of back-siphonage.

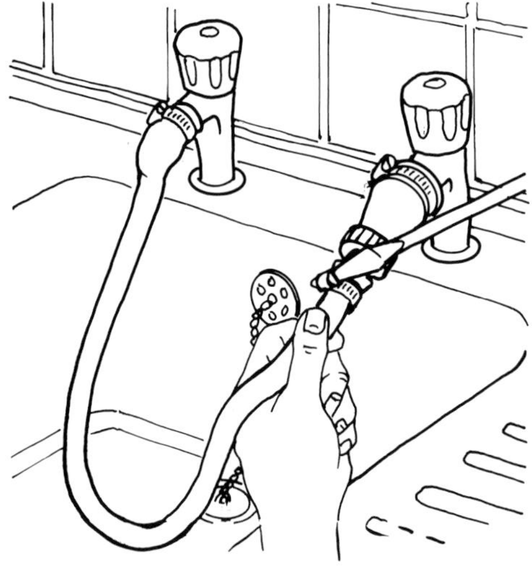

2 If the affected tap is a Supatap, unscrew and remove the nozzle (see page 104) and fit the hose directly to the tap outlet.

3 If the affected tap is a kitchen mixer tap, remove the swivel spout and hold a cloth firmly over the spout hole. Turn on the hot tap, then the cold one. Turn both off once the airlock is cleared, then remove the cloth and replace the spout.

4 If the problem recurs it may be that air is collecting at a high point in the pipework. Fit an automatic air release valve at the high point. Drain the pipe (see page 14), then cut out a piece of pipe and connect in the air release valve.

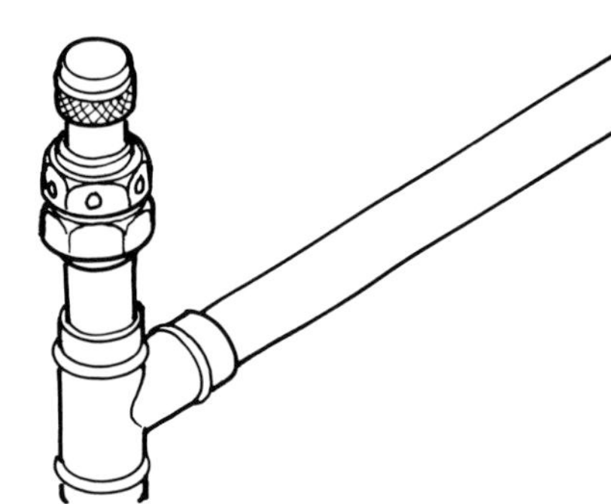

NOISY PIPES

Hot water pipes expand as they heat up and contract when they cool, causing irritating ticking noises. Other sources of noise include central heating pumps and faulty ballvalves

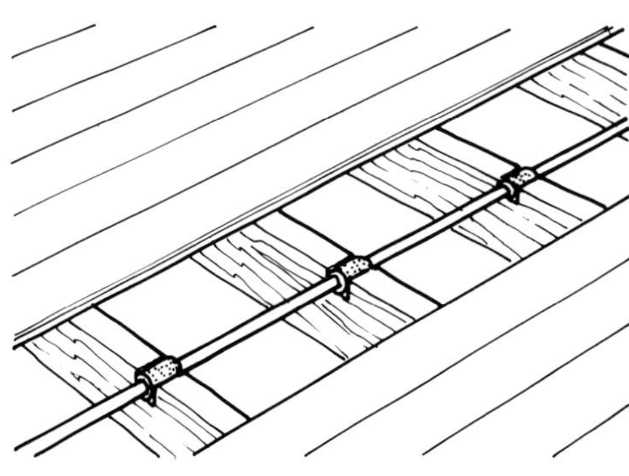

1 Lift floorboards to gain access to pipe runs causing expansion and contraction noises, and pack pipe insulation or glassfibre insulation pads round all points where the pipe passes through joists or walls. Add padding round the pipe where it is held in pipe clips, and remove any clips close to right-angled joints to allow the pipe to expand freely on either side. Add clips to support horizontal pipes at 1m (3ft) intervals for 15mm diameter pipe or 1.8m (6ft) for 22mm pipe.

2 If you suffer from water hammer – loud banging noises when a mains-pressure tap is turned off or when a ballvalve shuts – try closing the main stoptap slightly. Check the condition of tap and ballvalve washers and replace them if necessary. If an old ballvalve seems to be the cause of the problem, replace it with an equilibrium or diaphragm type.

3 A humming noise in the heating pipework may be caused by undersized piping being used or by the pump being run at too high a speed. The former is a design fault; reducing the pump speed slightly may cure the latter.

4 Banging noises coming from the boiler are often caused by a build-up of scale within the system. This can often be cured by draining the system down and treating it with a descaling solution before washing it through and refilling it with fresh water containing a corrosion inhibitor – see page 118.

THINGS YOU NEED

- **Pipe clips**
- **Power drill and bits**
- **Screws and wallplugs**
- **Pipe insulation**

JAMMED STOPTAPS

1 If the stoptap on the rising main has jammed in the open position, first try trickling a little penetrating oil down the spindle. Then use an adjustable spanner to apply more leverage to the tap handle, but do not overdo it: you may shear it off completely. If this fails, try heating the tap body with a blowtorch or hot air gun to see whether the expansion and contraction will free the jammed mechanism. Remember to let the tap body cool down before trying to operate the handle.

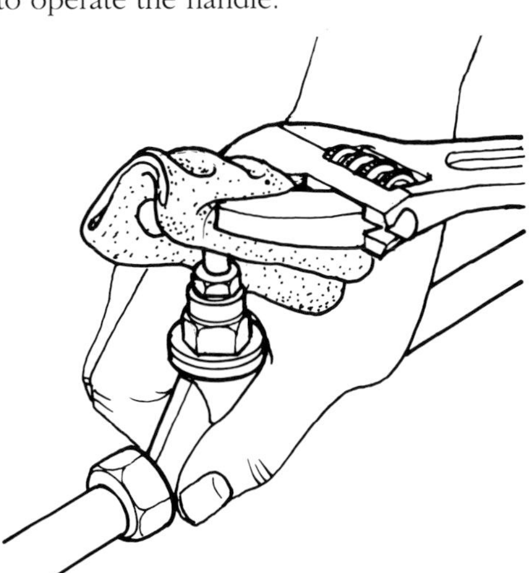

2 If all else fails, you will have to turn off the water supply company stopcock outside. You can buy special long-handled keys to operate this; but it's easy to improvise one. For stoptaps with bar handles, use a length of wood with a V-shaped notch cut in the end to turn the handle. For square-headed types use a length of copper or steel pipe with the end slightly flattened so it will fit over the tap head.

3 If you need to replace your stoptap, cut off the mains supply at the water supply company stopcock. Fit a length of hose to the draincock on the rising main just above the stoptap, take the other end outside and open the draincock to empty the rising main. Then remove the old stoptap and fit a replacement.

4 If a gatevalve on a low-pressure supply pipe jams, first try similar methods to those for freeing stoptaps. If they fail, operate the main stoptap or tie up the ballvalve float arm to stop the cistern refilling, then drain the pipe that the gatevalve controls by opening the bathroom taps. Finally remove and replace the gatevalve.

Most plumbing maintenance and repair jobs require you to be able to shut off the water flow and drain down the pipework

THINGS YOU NEED

- **Penetrating oil**
- **Adjustable spanners**
- **Blowtorch or hot air gun**
- **Outside stopcock key**
- **Garden hose**
- **Replacement stoptap**
- **Replacement gatevalve**

WC FLUSH PROBLEMS

The flushing mechanism fitted to WC cisterns usually gives years of trouble-free operation, but three problems can occur which cause inadequate flushing or no flush at all

THINGS YOU NEED

- **Adjustable spanners**
- **Screwdriver**
- **Replacement linkage**
- **Replacement diaphragm**

1 The WC's flushing action is caused by the water in the cistern being siphoned out when the handle is operated. A lever attached to the handle inside the cistern is connected by means of a wire linkage to the piston that works the siphon. If the WC will not flush, lift off its lid and check whether the linkage has become disconnected or has broken. Retrieve the linkage from the bottom of the cistern, or buy a replacement if it's broken, and fit it to reconnect the lever connector rod to the top of the piston.

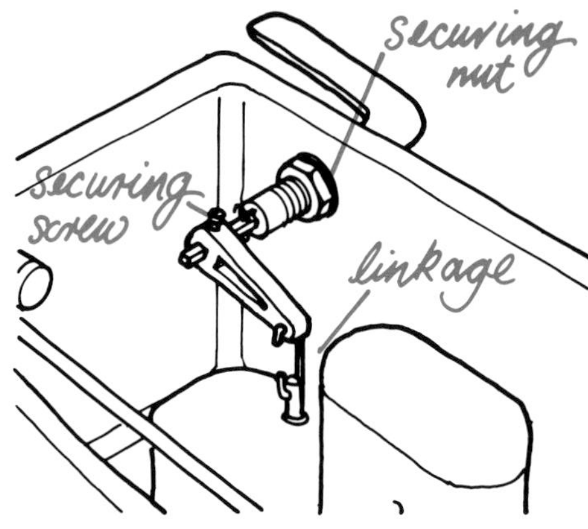

2 If the handle feels loose but still operates the flush mechanism, tighten the nut securing the handle to the cistern and also the screw securing the lever connector rod to the handle stem.

3 Inconsistent flushing may be caused by having too low a level of water in the cistern, or by a defective diaphragm inside the siphon assembly. If the water level does not reach the 'full' mark on the inside of the cistern, bend the arm of a metal ballvalve up slightly to admit a greater depth of water. With plastic ballvalves, turn the adjuster screw on the valve body to raise or lower the level of the float arm. Check that the cistern now fills to the correct level and test the flush mechanism. If the ballvalve appears to jam in use or the cistern overflow pipe drips constantly, remove and dismantle the valve (see page 105) so you can clean and lubricate it.

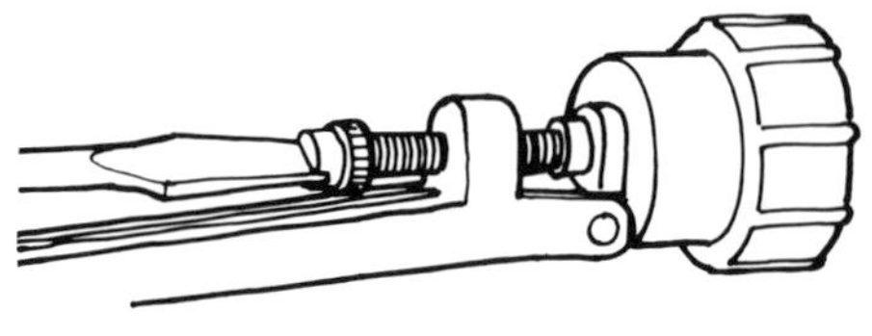

Adjusting the float arm height

4 If it still doesn't work properly, replace the diaphragm. First stop the cistern from refilling by operating the service valve on its supply pipe if one is fitted, or otherwise by tying the ballvalve arm up to a piece of wood spanning the top of the cistern. Then flush the cistern to empty it of most of the water, and mop out the rest with a sponge.

5 With an ordinary cistern, release the flush pipe by unscrewing the nut beneath the cistern. Move the pipe to one side and unscrew the backnut holding the siphon mechanism to the bottom of the cistern. With a close-coupled cistern, disconnect the supply and overflow pipes and undo the screws securing the cistern to the wall so you can lift it off the back of the pan to release the siphon. Disconnect the linkage between the siphon piston and the flush lever, and lift out the siphon.

6 Remove the plunger and spindle from the base of the siphon so you can examine the diaphragm that pushes the water up and over the siphon when the flush handle is operated. If it is split or badly worn, replace it with a matching one (or use it as a pattern to cut down a larger size). A rubber washer usually secures the diaphragm against the perforated plunger plate. Reassemble the siphon, replace it in the cistern, fit the backnut and reconnect the flush pipe or refit the cistern to the pan as appropriate. Replace the flush lever linkage, free the ballvalve so the cistern will refill, and test the flush mechanism. If it still does not flush properly, it is generally best to fit a whole new siphon unit.

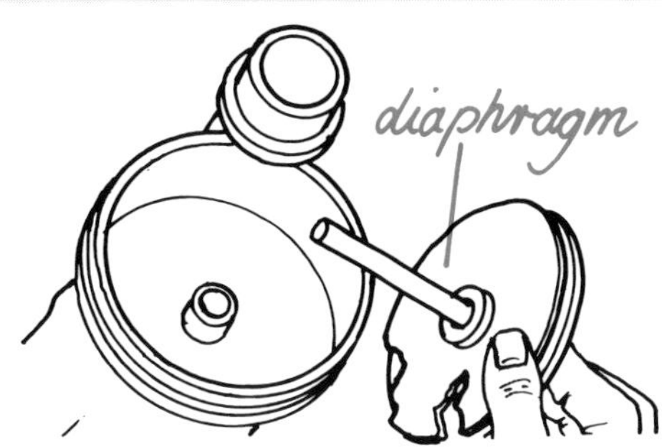

BLOCKED WASTE PIPES

1 To clear a blocked waste pipe in the bathroom or kitchen, try using a sink plunger first. Run a little water into the sink if none is there already. Block the overflow with a damp cloth, place the cup of the plunger over the open plug hole and pump it up and down vigorously.

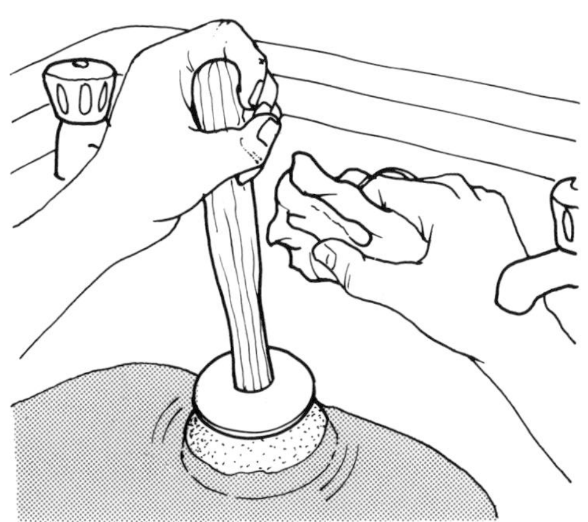

2 If this fails, you can try using a chemical drain cleaner. However, they have limited effectiveness against fat-based blockages, especially when the appliance is already full of water, and their major drawback is that if they do not work you are left with an appliance full of an unpleasant caustic chemical. Step 3 may be safer.

3 Gain access to the trap beneath the appliance (which can be tricky beneath baths and shower trays). Put the plug in, place a bowl or bucket below the trap and unscrew it so you can lift it out and clean it. Use an uncoiled wire coat-hanger or a plumber's snake to clear any blockage in the waste pipe itself. Then replace the trap and remove the plug. Flush the pipework through with hot water and washing soda to clean it out thoroughly.

4 If a WC is blocked or empties very slowly, remove any visible blockage from the trap if possible. Otherwise, the most effective way of clearing the blockage is to use a large WC plunger or to fit a rubber cleaning disc to a drain rod and use that as you would a plunger. If this fails, you could try using a plumber's snake.

5 Last of all, check whether the blockage is further down the drain run by lifting manhole covers outside. If the chamber nearest the house is empty, the blockage lies between it and the house. If it is full, check the other chambers down the run until you locate the site of the blockage. Hire a set of drain rods, screw them together, fit a plunger or scraper and feed them into the drain. Except at the first chamber, it is easier to push a blockage down the drain run from a full chamber to an empty one. When the blockage is cleared, flush the run through with plenty of water to remove silt and debris.

Blockages in waste pipes from baths, basins and sinks are usually caused by a build-up of soap scum, hair, fat and waste matter. WC soil pipes are often blocked by excess toilet paper, disposable nappies or even soft toys! **See also page 16**

THINGS YOU NEED

- **Sink plunger or force pump**
- **Chemical drain cleaner**
- **Coat-hanger**
- **Washing soda**
- **Plumber's snake (hired)**
- **Drain rods (hired)**

FAILED SEALANT

One potential source of dampness in the home is water penetrating the surfaces next to appliances such as baths, shower trays and sinks

THINGS YOU NEED

- **Sharp Stanley knife**
  or
- **Old screwdriver**
  or
- **Cold chisel and club hammer**
- **Self-adhesive sealing strip**
  or
- **Silicone sealant**
- **Mastic gun**
- **Screwdriver**

Leaks round bathroom appliances can cause serious damage to walls and floors, and to ceilings in rooms below the bathroom, while leaks round sinks can result in damage to the contents of the cupboard underneath and also swelling of chipboard worktops. The problem is compounded in bathrooms by the widespread use of plastic baths and shower trays which flex slightly in use, making it difficult to maintain a watertight seal between them and the bathroom walls.

1 In bathrooms, start by identifying the material used for the existing seal round the appliance. If it is flexible mastic or silicone sealant, use a sharp knife to cut it away. If it is a continuous plastic sealing strip, peel it off. If it is a hard-set filler such as tile adhesive, rake it out with an old screwdriver. If slim quadrant tiles have been used, chop these off carefully with a cold chisel and club hammer, taking care not to damage the adjacent surfaces.

2 Clean the edge of the appliance and any adjacent tiled or glazed surfaces thoroughly to remove soap, grease and any remaining traces of mastic, filler or adhesive. Then either reseal the gap with a self-adhesive sealing strip or pipe a bead of silicone sealant into it. Press sealing strips down firmly, and draw a moistened finger along the silicone bead to bond it well to the adjacent surfaces. Do not expect silicone to bridge gaps wider than about 6mm (¼ in).

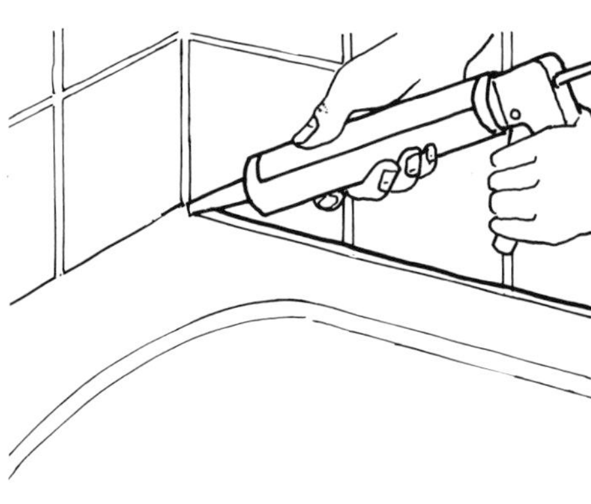

3 In kitchens (and where washbasins are set into vanity units), the seal should have been sandwiched against the edge of the cutout when the sink or basin was installed. If it was not, or if the seal appears to have failed, it may be possible to seal round the perimeter of the appliance with a bead of sealant. However, this rarely works with steel sinks because of the thinness of the material.

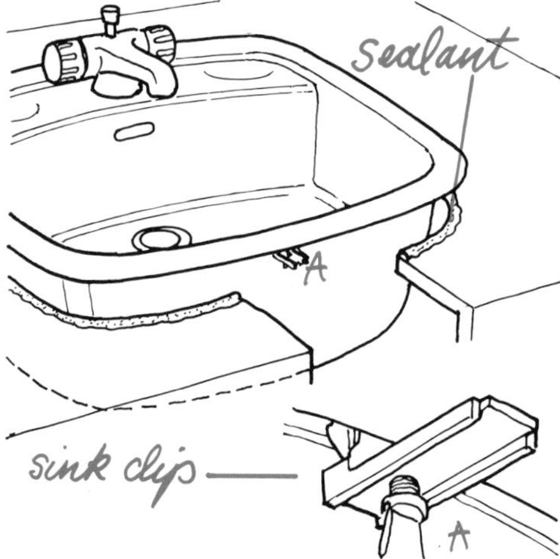

4 There is little alternative but to release the clips securing the sink to the worktop so it can be lifted out. There may be enough play in the pipework to allow you to do this without removing the fittings. Otherwise disconnect the trap from the waste outlet and undo the tap connectors after shutting off the water supply to the taps (see page 14). Run a generous bead of silicone sealant round the perimeter of the cut-out and bed the sink back into position. Wipe away any excess sealant that oozes out, then replace the clips and reconnect the trap and the supply pipework.

INSULATION

The Water Supply Bye-laws require new or replacement cold water storage cisterns to be fitted with a rigid and securely fixed cover which is light-tight and excludes insects, but is not airtight, and to be well insulated. Kits are now available from plumbing suppliers containing all the components needed for compliance with bye-law 30, including a cover, an insulating jacket, a screened breather valve, a sleeve for the vent pipe, and an overflow connector with insect screen and internal dip tube.

1 If you have an existing cistern that is uninsulated or poorly insulated, either buy a ready-made insulation jacket to match the shape and size of the cistern or wrap the cistern in loft insulation, tied on with string. Put a solid cover on top of the cistern and lay insulation over this too. Do not lay any insulation beneath the cistern, to allow a little warmth to reach it from the room below.

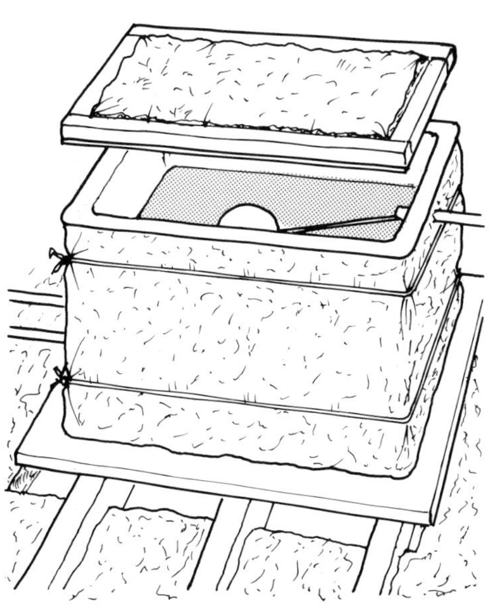

2 Fit a ready-made jacket to the feed-and-expansion tank too, or again cover it and wrap it in loft insulation material.

3 Insulate all pipework within the loft using pre-formed lengths of pipe insulation. Tape joints between lengths with PVC insulating tape, and either make cuts in the insulation at elbows and tees, or insulate joints with pipe wrap taped into position. Don't forget to insulate vent pipes as well.

4 Fit a ready-made insulating jacket to your hot cylinder, even if it already has pre-formed foam insulation on it. Make sure it does not cover the top of the immersion heater or cylinder thermostat, if either is fitted to the cylinder.

5 If access to the rest of the plumbing and heating pipework is possible (during redecoration, for example, when individual rooms are stripped and floorboards can be lifted), fit pipe insulation to all pipes carrying hot water, and also to any cold pipes run next to outside walls or under suspended ground floors. Pay particular attention to the rising main, which in winter is carrying water already close to freezing point.

6 Make sure pipework to outside taps is protected with waterproof insulation. One solution is to box in the pipework and then to fill the box with glass fibre insulation or expanding aerosol filler foam. In very cold weather, turn off the indoor stoptap controlling the pipe run to the tap, and leave the outside tap open.

Insulation is a vital component of your plumbing and heating systems, both for preventing freeze-ups in winter and for reducing heat loss from hot pipes and cylinders

THINGS YOU NEED

- **Bye-law 30 kit *or***
- **Insulation jacket for cold water tank**
- **Insulation jacket for feed-and-expansion tank**
- **Insulation jacket for hot cylinder**
- **Pre-formed pipe insulation**
- **Glass fibre pipe wrap**
- **PVC tape (such as electrical insulating tape)**
- **String**
- **Scissors**

FIXING YOUR

WIRING

Keep your electricity supply safe, functional and up to date. Always observe proper safety precautions

NEW LIGHTS

Many homes have just traditional pendant ceiling lights. If you want to fit a different sort of light fitting in place of one, you will have to carry out some modifications to the existing wiring

THINGS YOU NEED

- **New light fitting**
- **Round conduit box and fittings**
- **Timber batten and scrap wood**
- **Strip connectors**
- **Red PVC insulating tape**
- **Earth sleeving**
- **Screwdrivers**
- **Padsaw**
- **Wood screws**
- **Cavity fixings**

1 When you choose your new lamp, check to see what provision is made for connecting it to the house wiring. Many have a short length of flex (or separate live, neutral and earth cores) already attached; others (particularly fluorescent types) may have a terminal block inside the fitting. Check too to see whether the fitting has a flat base or one with enough space for the electrical connections to be made within it. If it is flat, you will have to create an enclosed recess in the ceiling to contain the connections, using a component called a round conduit box.

2 When you are ready to install your new light, first turn the power off at the mains (see page 10) and check that the light you are replacing no longer works. Then unscrew the cover of the ceiling rose you are removing and disconnect the pendant flex from its terminals.

3 If there is more than one cable connected to the rose terminals, label all the flex cores with tape tags, or else make a sketch of the wiring arrangement, before you disconnect anything, so you can remember which core went where. Note in particular whether there is a black cable core connected to the same rose terminal as one of the pendant flex cores; this will run to the switch controlling the light. It may have a band of red PVC tape wrapped around it. Disconnect all the cable cores and unscrew the old ceiling rose.

4 If your new light fitting has a hollow base, you can often connect the cables within this, using small plastic strip connectors – go to step 7. Otherwise the next step is to recess a conduit box into the ceiling, and to do this you will need access to the space above the ceiling – either via the loft, or by lifting a floorboard in the room above.

5 Hold the conduit box against the ceiling and draw a line round it. Then use a padsaw to cut a hole in the ceiling. Push the conduit box into it so its lip is flush with the ceiling surface.

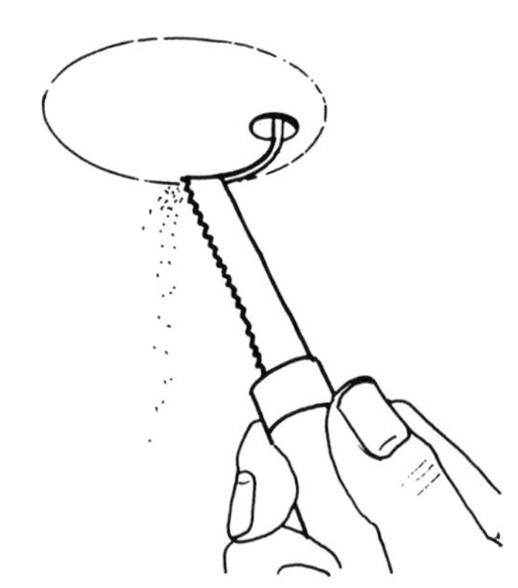

6 Cut a timber batten to fit between the ceiling joists flanking the hole, attach a wooden block to each end and screw through these into the sides of the joist so the batten just touches the top of the conduit box. Go back downstairs and screw the box to the batten.

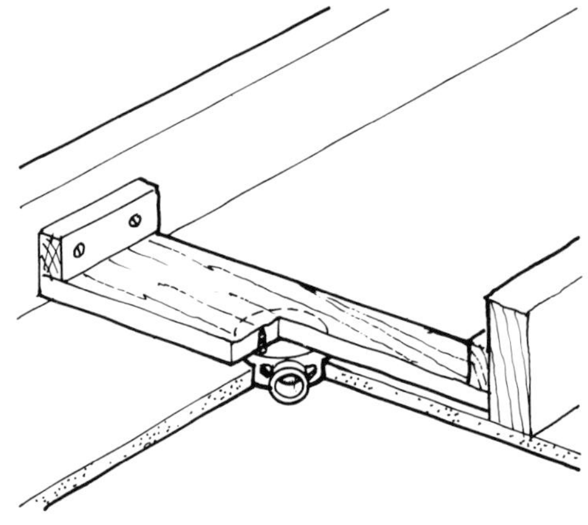

7 How you connect the new fitting to the circuit cables depends on how the old rose was wired up. If there was just one cable present and your new fitting has a terminal block, connect the cable cores directly to it – live (red) to the terminal marked L, neutral (black) to the one marked N and the earth to the one marked E.

8 If there was just one cable present and your new fitting has a flex tail, use three strip connectors to link the live (red) cable core to the brown flex core, the neutral (black) cable core to the blue flex core and the sleeved earth cable core to the green-and-yellow flex core.

9 If there was more than one cable present at the rose, one (which you labelled earlier) will be the switch cable and you will need four strip connectors to link the new fitting's flex to the circuit cables. Stick a band of red PVC tape to the switch cable if it's not there already. Link the black core of the switch cable to the brown flex core, and link any other black cable cores to the blue flex core. Connect all the earth cores together in the third strip connector and all the live (red) cable cores in the fourth. If any of the cable earth cores is bare, cover it with a short length of green-and-yellow PVC sleeving before connecting them up.

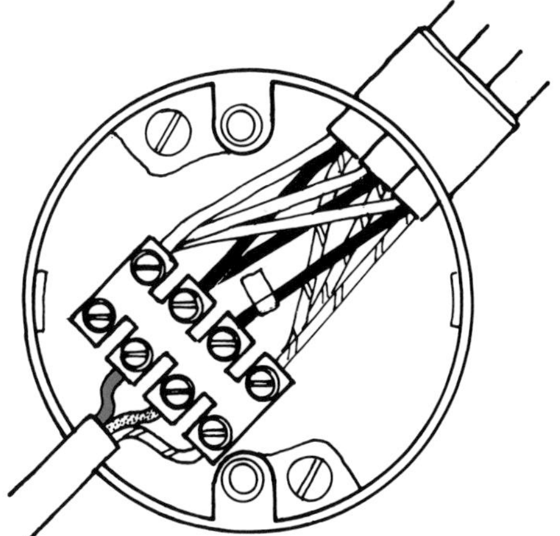

10 If you are using a conduit box, carefully push the strip connectors into the box and secure the new light fitting in position over it, either by screwing through the ceiling into the batten above or by using cavity fixing devices such as spring toggles. If the fitting has a hollow base, arrange the strip connectors within it and secure it to the ceiling. Some light fittings, such as spotlights, have small-diameter baseplates designed to be attached direct to the threaded lugs at each side of the conduit box, using small machine screws.

REPLACING ACCESSORIES

Wiring accessories – socket outlets and light switches especially – may need replacing because they have been damaged accidentally, because their switches are sparking or because they look old-fashioned

THINGS YOU NEED

- **Replacement accessory**
- **Replacement surface mounting box**
- **Screwdrivers**
- **Stanley knife**
- **PVC insulating tape**

1 If a wiring accessory or a plug is cracked and there is a risk of someone touching live parts inside, make an emergency repair with PVC insulating tape. Aim to replace the damaged component as soon as is practicable (it is sensible to keep one or two spare plugs in the house).

2 To replace a damaged accessory, first turn off the power to the circuit concerned (see page 10). Then undo the screws securing the faceplate to its mounting box, and pull the plate away from the box gently. Loosen the screws securing the cable cores to their terminals and pull them out. Throw the old faceplate away immediately, but keep the old fixing screws; the replacement accessory will come with metric-threaded machine screws which may not mesh with imperial-threaded lugs on an old mounting box.

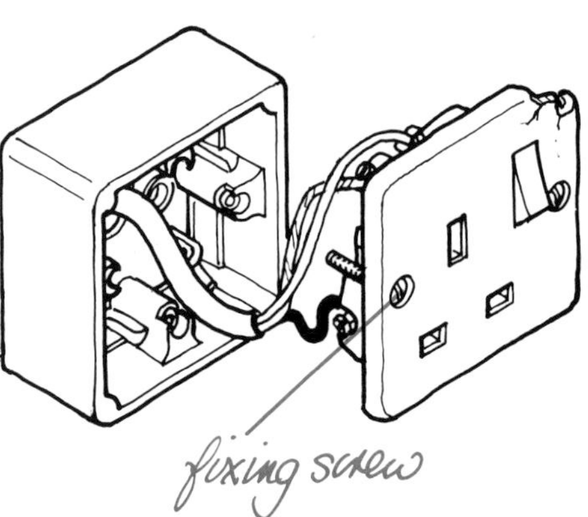

3 If the accessory is surface mounted and its plastic mounting box is also damaged, unscrew this from the wall after running a knife blade round it to cut through any paint or wallpaper sticking it to the wall. Fit a matching box after removing one of the knockouts – thin pieces of plastic in the back plate – to admit the cable(s).

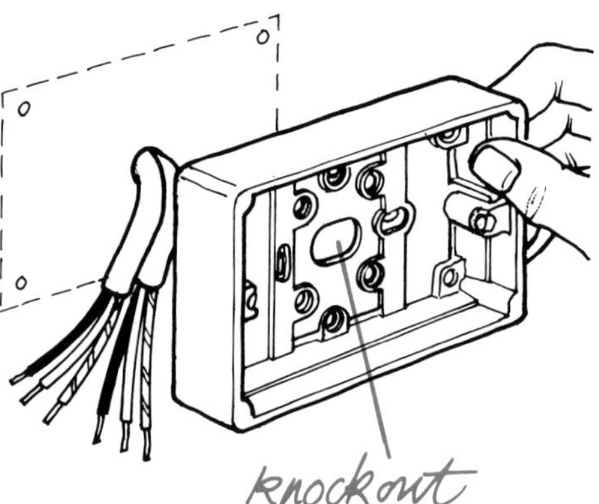

4 Reconnect the circuit cable cores to the terminals on the new faceplate. Fold the cable(s) neatly back into the mounting box and re-attach the faceplate (use new fixing screws if you replaced the mounting box).

5 If you need to open a ceiling rose so encrusted with paint that the cover will not unscrew, turn off the power and use a hammer (gently) to crack the edge of the cover so you can prise it off. Disconnect the flex and cable cores (see page 112), unscrew the rose baseplate, discard it and fit a replacement rose.

LIGHTING REPAIRS

FLEX

1 You may need to replace the flex of a pendant light because it is discoloured with age, because you want the fitting to hang lower (over a dining table, for example) or because it is worn and causes short circuits that blow the lighting-circuit fuse. Start by turning off the power at the mains (see page 10). Then unscrew the rose cover and disconnect the old flex. Lift down the lamp-holder and flex, unscrew the lamp-holder cover and disconnect the flex cores.

2 Cut a new length of flex and remove about 50mm (2in) of the sheath from one end. Strip the flex cores and connect them to the lamp-holder terminals. Loop the cores round their anchors and fit the lamp-holder cover.

3 Strip 100mm (4in) of sheath from the other end, prepare the cores and slip the flex through the rose cover. Connect the cores to the rose terminals, loop them over the flex anchors and replace the rose cover.

CORD-PULL

1 If the cord on a ceiling-mounted switch breaks below the two-part cord connector, unscrew this and fit a new length of cord.

2 If the break is between the connector and the switch, start by turning off the power at the mains (see page 10). Then unscrew the switch from its backing plate and disconnect the cable cores.

3 Undo the screws holding the terminal plate to the switch, holding it down with your other hand to stop the spring inside from 'exploding' the mechanism. Lift the plate slowly to expose the top of the cord anchor and pull the old cord out. Feed in a new length, knotting its top end securely, then replace the terminal plate. Fit the other end of the new cord to the upper part of the connector and reconnect the switch to its cable. Fix it back in place on the ceiling and attach the rest of the cord to the connector.

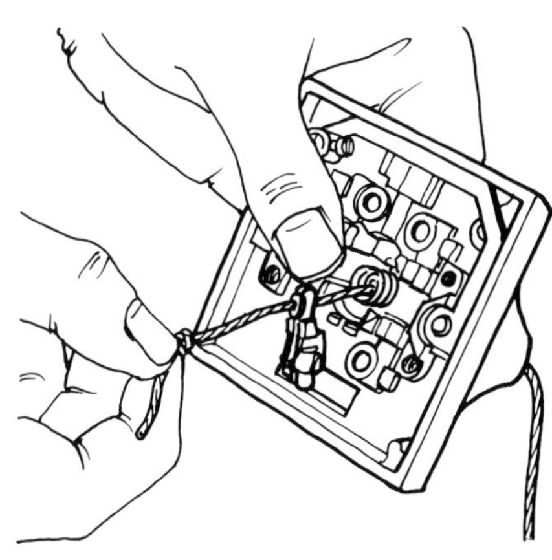

There are several other minor repairs to your wiring that you can carry out yourself when things go wrong, including replacing the flex on pendant lights, mending cord-pull switches and fixing faulty fluorescent lights

THINGS YOU NEED

- **Replacement two- or three-core flex to match existing type**
- **Screwdrivers**
- **Side cutters**
- **Stanley knife**
- **Wire strippers**
- **Replacement cord**
- **Replacement fluorescent tube**
- **Replacement starter**

FLUORESCENT LIGHTS
If a fluorescent tube fails to light or glows only dimly, replace the tube. If the tube makes repeated but unsuccessful attempts to start, or only the electrodes glow, try replacing the starter canister which plugs into the side of the fitting. If this does not work, replace the tube too.

FIXING YOUR

CENTRAL HEATING

Inefficient heating can make you uncomfortable and waste money. The cure is often very simple

COLD RADIATORS

All the radiators in a well-designed and balanced heating system should be at about the same temperature

THINGS YOU NEED

- **Air-vent key**
- **Pliers**
- **Spanners**
- **Length of garden hose**
- **Bucket**

1 If just one radiator is cold when the rest are hot, check whether the radiator valves are turned on and are working properly. Open the handwheel valve at one end of the radiator and remove the cover from the lockshield valve at the other end. Then turn it to full on with pliers or a small spanner, noting how many turns of the spindle this took so you can close it back to its original position later. If the radiator still won't heat up, no water is flowing through. One of the valves may have jammed shut and will need replacing – a job best left to a plumber.

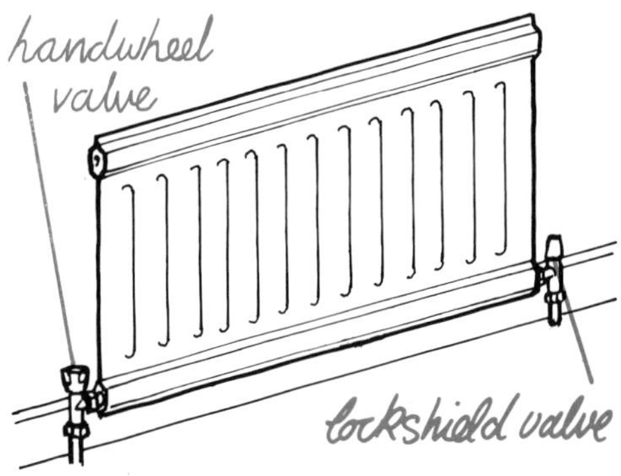

2 If the radiator is cold at the top but warm at the bottom, there may be a build-up of air or the gaseous by-products of corrosion in the system. Open the air vent at the top of the radiator with a vent key to see if air or gas is forced out as more

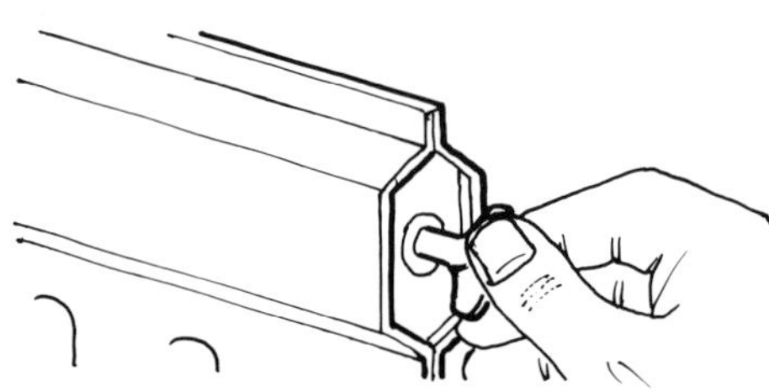

hot water flows into the radiator from the rest of the system. Close the vent as soon as water begins to splutter out, and check that the feed-and-expansion tank has water in it (it should be about one-third full when the system is running).

3 If the radiator is cold along the bottom but warm at the top, the cause could be a build-up of sludge (another by-product of corrosion in the system) which could eventually block the inlet or outlet valves. You may be able to get rid of this via a draincock, if one is fitted near the radiator, by connecting a length of garden hose to it and opening the plug with a small spanner. Run off some of the water and sludge into a bucket. Otherwise you will have to disconnect the radiator from its supply pipework, block its outlets with rag plugs and take it outside so you can flush it out with clean water.

4 If several upstairs radiators are cold, it is possible that the system is starved of water due to losses not being replaced via the feed-and-expansion tank. If it is empty, check the operation of the ballvalve and repair it if it is jammed shut (see page 105). Sludge in the pipework somewhere in the system could also be a cause; try increasing the pump speed for a short while to try to shift the blockage, or drain down and refill the entire system.

5 If all the radiators are cold, the likeliest cause is a jammed or failed pump, or a faulty motorised valve (if one is fitted) which is diverting water from the heating system. You may be able to free a jammed pump yourself (see right) or to fit a replacement pump or valve; otherwise call in a plumber for help.

6 If both radiators and hot cylinder are cold, the fault probably lies with the boiler or the system programmer. Check that the boiler is alight and that the programmer has a power supply. If both appear to be working properly, call in an expert to find the fault.

BOILER AND PUMP

1 With gas boilers, a common fault is the operation of the pilot light. This should burn continuously and light the main burners when the programmer switches their gas supply on. If it goes out, a heat-sensor prevents the main gas supply from coming on. You should be able to see the pilot light through an inspection window or by removing a front cover plate. If it is out, the jet may be blocked and will need cleaning and adjusting. Follow the boiler instructions for relighting it (most boilers now have piezo-electric push-button ignition devices); if this does not work but you can light the pilot light with a match, the ignition device is faulty.

2 If the temperature of the system seems too high or too low, the boiler thermostat may be faulty. If altering its setting produces no change in temperature, it will need replacing.

3 If the system is on but your radiators are cold, the fault may be a jammed pump. This can occur if the system has not run for a while (during hot weather, for example), or if sludge in the system blocks the pump impeller. On many pumps there is a slot on the end of the impeller shaft, usually visible on the outside of the pump casing, which you can turn with a screwdriver to attempt to free the impeller.

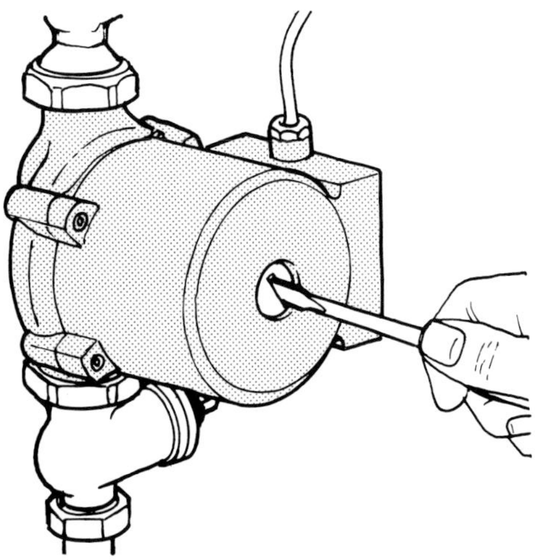

4 If this does not free the impeller, you will have to remove the pump for cleaning. It should be fitted with an isolating valve on the pipework at each side; turn these to the off position, disconnect the pump's power supply and undo the coupling nuts so you can remove the pump. Take it to the sink and run clean water through it while trying to turn the impeller with a screwdriver. When it rotates freely, replace the pump, open the isolating valves and bleed air from the pump chamber by opening the bleed screw on top of the casing. Then reconnect the power supply. Fit a replacement pump if it still fails to run.

You can often cure pump problems yourself, or else diagnose the fault and advise the service engineer to bring the right parts

THINGS YOU NEED

- **Screwdriver**
- **Spanners**

If your boiler stops working, first check that it has a power supply. This is provided by a fused connection unit, usually located near the boiler or programmer. Switch the power off, release the fuse holder and pull it out. Fit a new fuse, replace the holder and switch the power back on.

CORROSION AND SCALE

The biggest enemies of central heating systems are internal corrosion, which causes blockages and leaks, and a build-up of scale in the boiler and the system pipework, resulting in noise and inefficiency

THINGS YOU NEED

- **Chemical descaling liquid**
- **Chemical corrosion proofer**
- **Length of garden hose**
- **Draincock key or small spanner**
- **Radiator key**

1 If your system does not contain a corrosion proofer, corrosion will take place because of reactions between the different metals (copper pipe and steel radiators) used in the system. The result is a gradual eating away of the steel to form iron oxide – a thick black sludge which collects in radiators and can block pumps. Pin-hole leaks may develop, usually along the seams of radiators. Corrosion can be prevented by the addition of a special chemical to the water in the system. It pays to descale the system first of all using a chemical descaler, but if your system is more than about ten years old, you should get professional advice about which type of chemical to use. Otherwise you risk causing leaks as the scale is dissolved.

2 To introduce the descaler to the system, first shut off the water supply to the feed-and-expansion tank or tie up the ball valve to a batten across the tank. Attach a length of garden hose to the lowest draincock on the system, lead it to an outdoor gully, open the valve and run off a couple of buckets of water.

3 Close the draincock, then add the descaling liquid to the feed-and-expansion tank, following the maker's instructions, and turn the heating on to circulate the chemical round the system.

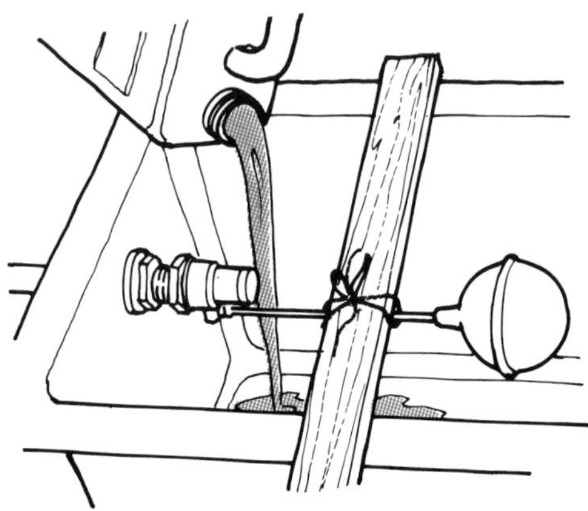

4 After the recommended time, switch off the heating and open the draincock to drain the system. As it empties, go round and open the radiator air vents, first upstairs and then downstairs.

5 When the system is empty, close the draincock, restore the water supply to the feed-and-expansion tank and refill the system, closing radiator air vents as each radiator fills. Switch the system on to pump the water round, then switch off again and drain it down for a second time.

6 Finally, refill the system and add the corrosion proofer at the feed-and-expansion tank. Make sure you use the right type; there are different chemicals for iron or steel boilers, for copper tubular types, and also for systems with aluminium rather than steel radiators. To avoid the risk of airlocks, you can refill the system from the bottom by connecting the hose from the draincock to a mains-pressure tap and closing radiator air vents as radiators fill up. Make sure you use a special hose connector containing a double-check valve to prevent the risk of back-siphonage occurring should the mains pressure drop while you are refilling the system.

GETTING RID OF

CONDENSATION

Condensation is the scourge of modern living, causing problems with interior damp and mould in the home

CHANGE YOUR HABITS

Every family produces a considerable quantity of water vapour through activities such as washing, cooking, bathing, even breathing. If the air in a room is fully laden with water vapour, the resulting condensation may be so heavy that it will actually run down surfaces and form puddles – on window sills, for example. And if it happens every day, air-borne mould spores will settle on these damp surfaces and begin to multiply, causing tell-tale black or brown stains on windows and walls.

1 Keep the doors of steamy rooms such as kitchens and bathrooms closed while cooking, washing or drying clothes, so moisture cannot easily reach other parts of the house. Open the window (and close the room door behind you) afterwards to let the warm moist air escape to the outside.

2 Sleep with bedroom windows or doors open slightly for extra ventilation. Each sleeper gives off half a pint of water during the night, and this will form condensation on windows and other cold surfaces unless it can escape.

3 Do not block up airbricks and ventilators – they are vital for air circulation, and help to get rid of moist air.

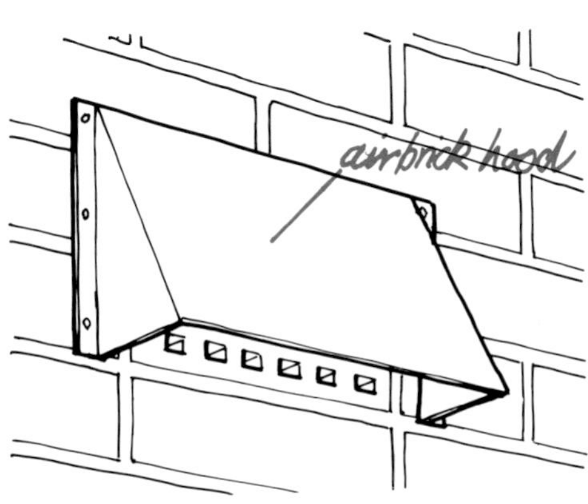

If airbricks cause draughts, fit hoods over them. Airbricks are especially important in rooms containing fuel-burning appliances; without adequate ventilation they will burn inefficiently, and may produce noxious fumes.

4 Improve the heating. Higher air temperatures mean less water vapour deposited as condensation (but also higher heating bills). As a compromise, go for continuous low-level background heating, even in unused rooms, rather than the traditional morning and evening burst. This keeps the whole house structure warm all the time, and so lessens the risk of condensation.

5 Wipe moisture up regularly from condensation blackspots such as window sills, tiled walls and shower cubicles (leave the cubicle door open to encourage air circulation). To discourage mould growth in these areas, wash them down regularly with a proprietary fungicide or dilute household bleach.

6 Avoid using paraffin heaters at all costs – each pint of paraffin burnt creates a pint of water vapour, which adds to the problem instead of curing it. If you have no central heating, electric convector heaters are the most efficient heating appliances to use.

Long-term condensation can affect the health of a house's occupants and in extreme cases can even damage its structure

THINGS YOU NEED

- **Better ventilation**
- **Better insulation**
- **Better heating**

Condensation occurs when air carrying water vapour comes into contact with a cold surface and is cooled down. Cold air cannot hold as much water vapour as warm air, and the result is that the excess moisture condenses into droplets and is deposited as liquid water on the cold surface.

NEW EQUIPMENT

In problem rooms like kitchens and bathrooms, you need controlled ventilation to get rid of the steam. Around the house, improving insulation will help

1 Install an extractor fan or ducted cooker hood (the recirculating type will remove smells but not water vapour) in the kitchen. You can fit a fan in the window, the wall or the ceiling, and it can be ducted to the outside air quite easily if your room has no suitable outside wall. The fan should be powerful enough to change the room's air at least ten times an hour.

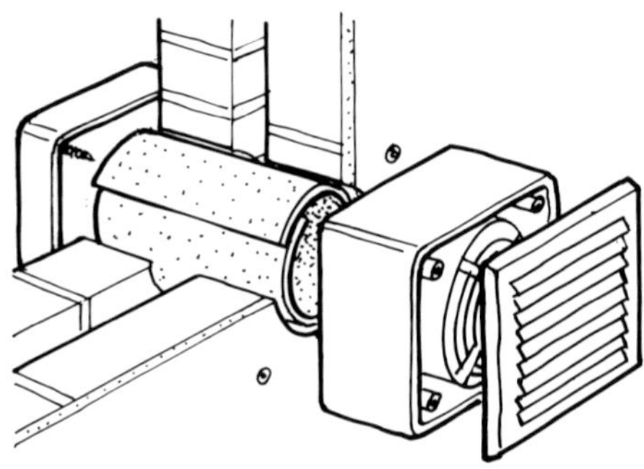

2 You can connect a fan to a device called a humidistat; this detects when the air humidity is rising, and turns the fan on automatically (and off again once the humidity has fallen).

3 In bathrooms, it may be more effective to link it to a time switch, so the fan will run for several minutes after the bathroom has been vacated.

4 Vent tumble driers to the outside, using flexible ducting. Drape it out of an open window or, better still, connect it permanently to a hole in the wall fitted with a grille to prevent rain penetration.

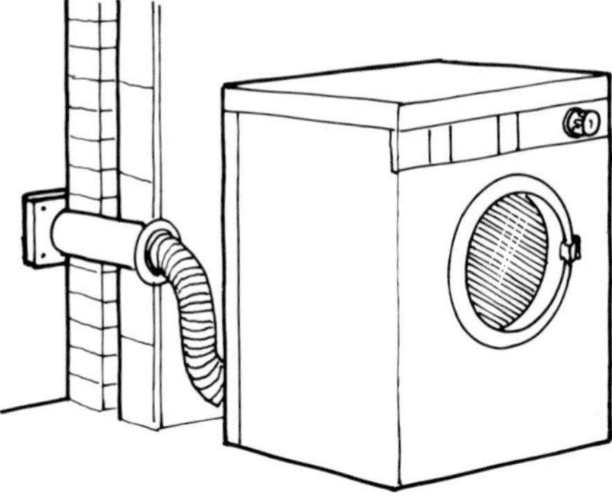

5 If you can keep cold surfaces warm, less condensation will form. Double glazing will help cut down condensation on problem windows. Sealed units are better than secondary glazing, since moist air cannot get between the panes, but even cheap disposable plastic film double glazing will bring some improvement.

6 On cold exterior walls, warm decorating materials like cork, blown vinyl wallcoverings and paper-backed fabrics will perform much better than paints and ceramic tiles. In serious cases, it may be worth having affected exterior walls dry-lined with insulating plasterboard, or even having cavity wall insulation installed. Both are comparatively expensive, but will pay for themselves quite quickly in terms of reduced heating bills as well as improving comfort levels inside the house.

7 Supply additional heating in problem rooms, using appliances such as electric convector heaters and oil-filled radiators that do not give off additional water vapour.

8 If all else fails and you still have a serious condensation problem, portable electric dehumidifiers may be the answer. They dry and warm the air, collecting the moisture in a reservoir which has to be emptied periodically, and can be moved from room to room as required. However, they have two drawbacks: they can be noisy – too obtrusive to run overnight in a bedroom, for example – and they are relatively expensive. But as a last resort, they often provide a permanent solution.

FITTING

HOME SECURITY

Security fittings are inexpensive and straightforward to fit; alarms offer additional protection and peace of mind

WINDOWS

1 Mortise rack bolts are set in a mortise in the opening casement or fanlight and are operated by a universal key which shoots a bolt into a recess in the window frame. Two-part window locks consist of two components which interlock when the window is closed. With some models, both parts are surface-mounted, while with others a bolt is shot into a hole in the window frame. Stay locks and bolts secure casement and fanlight stays in position, so they cannot be lifted if the window is broken. Lockable cockspurs replace the existing cockspur handle, and are locked with a key.

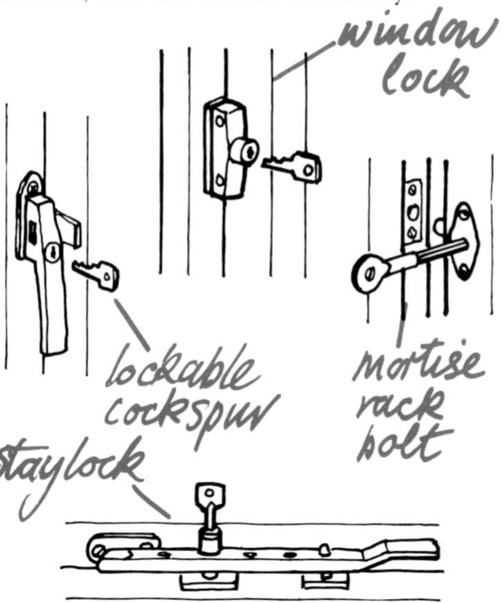

2 For metal windows, a range of slightly different types is available. Frame locks are secured to the leading edge of the window; when locked the protruding bolt overlaps the window frame and prevents the window from opening. Cockspur locks prevent the cockspur handle from being lifted, either by shooting a lockable bolt up underneath its fork or by locking the fork itself to the frame by means of a protruding bolt. Stay clamps fit over the metal casement stay and the fixed stay pin bracket, locking the two together.

3 For sash windows, there are three options. Sash locks are mounted on top of the meeting rails between the sashes; some shoot a bolt into the outer sash, while others have two parts which lock together. Dual screws consist of a threaded barrel which is fitted through the top rail of the inner sash, and into which a screwed bolt is driven to lock the two sashes together. Acorn stops are small studs screwed into the stiles (sides) of the upper sash to restrict the passage of the sashes past each other.

Fit locks to all opening windows. Choose from these varieties, depending on what type of windows you have

THINGS YOU NEED

- **Window locks**
- **Door locks**
- **Alarm system**
- **General tools**

DOORS

Good locks are the backbone of any home security system and will deter all but the most persistent housebreaker

1 Fit locks to all exit doors. Two types of lock are commonly used. The cylinder rim lock is surface-mounted on the inner face of the door, with the cylindrical lock body set in a hole drilled through the door stile. The keeper is usually surface-mounted on the door frame. The mortise lock is set in a deep mortise cut in the door edge, and is operated by a key inserted either from inside or outside the door. Here the keeper is recessed into the frame.

2 The most important security factor with any lock is its ability to be deadlocked. This means that the lock bolt cannot be pushed back once the door is locked and can only be freed with a key. Most mortise locks work like this; with rim locks the bolt may deadlock automatically when the door is shut, or may be deadlocked by an extra turn of the key. Some rim locks can be deadlocked from inside too. For maximum security, choose a lock that is certified as complying with British Standard BS3621.

3 For securing French doors which open outwards, a central mortise lock should be combined with lockable surface-mounted bolts screwed into place at the top and bottom of each door. The hinges are also at risk because their knuckles are on the outside, so it's also a good idea to fit hinge bolts. These are fixed steel pegs which are set into the closing edge of the door and fit into matching recesses in the door frame when the door is closed.

4 Most modern patio doors now incorporate key-operated locks which offer good security, but older types may rely solely on an internal catch. These should be fitted with a special patio door lock.

ALARM

When choosing an alarm system, consider the following points:

- The type of system you want (monitored alarms are best in secluded areas)
- The parts of the house needing protection
- The need for a panic button so you can set the alarm off from inside the house if you are in and detect intruders
- The siting of the control panel, and whether it will be operated by a key or a number code.

If you want to have the alarm professionally installed, check that the company is approved by one of the five alarm inspectorate institutions recognised by the police, and make sure the installer confirms that the system conforms to British Standard BS4737.

HI-TECH EQUIPMENT

- PORTABLES
- TV AND VIDEO
- HI-FI
- TELEPHONES
- COMPUTERS

WORKING WITH

ELECTRONICS

Circuitry has shrunk into microchips on a printed circuit board – you're unlikely to find the proverbial 'loose wire'

TECHNICAL TALK

Throughout this chapter we've tried to keep electronics jargon to a minimum, defining terms where necessary

Three terms crop up again and again:
Signal This is short-hand for the transmitted radio waves which are picked up by an aerial, or for the electric current passing in or between bits of equipment. Either way, the signal electronically represents the programme you watch or the music you listen to.
Level Short-hand for the strength of signal present at a particular point.
Frequency Any radio wave, sound wave or signal has a definable frequency specified in Hertz (Hz), kilohertz (kHz) or megahertz (MHz). So for example, Radio 4 is transmitted on a frequency of 198kHz in the long wave band. In the world of hi-fi, a loudspeaker with a good *frequency response* (specified in a range of Hz) will reproduce both low frequency (bass) and high frequency (treble) sounds accurately.

INITIAL ASSESSMENT

Run through this checklist to make sure there isn't a simple reason why a product appears not to be working

1 Check the plug fuse and make sure the socket works by trying another appliance in it. For battery-powered appliances, are batteries inserted and are they the right way round? Check that battery contacts are clean.

2 Check that all switches are on – for example, a computer may appear not to be working because the screen is not on.

3 Check connections between pieces of equipment and check selector switches – you may not be able to hear a cassette because the amplifier is switched to radio or because input and output leads have been confused.

IS IT WORTH REPAIRING?

With a cheap radio or cassette player that's out of guarantee, the answer is probably no if you can't fix it yourself by following the simple tips in this chapter. Even if a shop agrees to fix such a product, it's likely to cost as much or more than buying a new one. Frustrating though this is, bear in mind that fixing such products is a laborious and time consuming process, and the engineer's time has to be paid for by someone.

The same rule can unfortunately also apply to more expensive products: the laser in a CD player, for example, can be expensive to replace. If a product is only just out of guarantee, it would be worth asking the shop you bought it from if they would give you favourable exchange terms which would work out cheaper than a repair.

Miniaturised products such as mini-disc players, personal tape players, camcorders and micro-cassette dictaphones are often not worth repairing because they are difficult to fix and repairs are expensive.

SAFETY

- Switch off and pull out the mains plug when making or changing connections and especially if you have to remove any fixed cover.
- Don't let children push anything into openings in hi-tech equipment.
- Don't obstruct ventilation holes.
- Most important of all, don't tinker unless you know what you're doing. Simple checks can save you the cost and frustration of a service call, but the warning 'no user serviceable parts inside' means what it says.

ELECTRONICS REPAIR KIT

SOLDERING

Soldering is a useful skill to acquire even if you don't intend to do anything more than simple repairs to electronic equipment. Although most of the leads used to interconnect audio and video equipment can be bought ready-made, it's cheaper and sometimes more convenient to make your own or to repair faulty connections.

1 You need a lightweight soldering iron rated at no more than 18 watts, with a fine-pointed bit small enough to solder closely spaced connecting tags without melting the insulation on adjacent wires. You also need a roll of thin (22 gauge) solder.

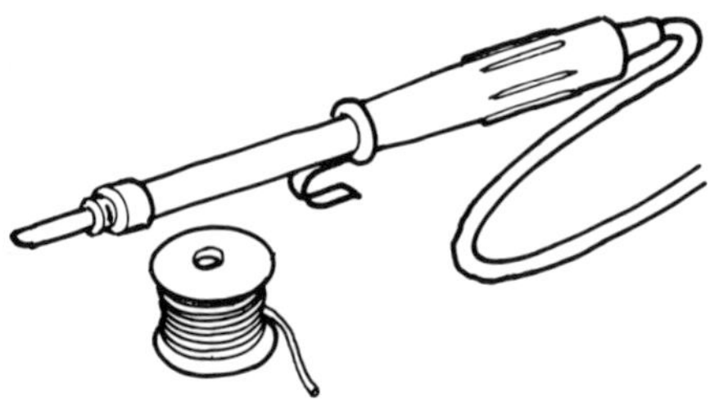

2 The key to successful soldering is to make sure the bare wire end and the metal tag you're soldering it to are both free of tarnish. This shouldn't be a problem with new plugs, but if the tag seems tarnished, clean it with a screwdriver blade or fine sandpaper until you see bright metal.

3 Strip the ends of the wire to the right length. Adjustable wire strippers are useful for removing first the outer plastic sheath (without damaging the woven wire screening which most audio and video leads have) and then the insulation on the inner conductors. Exactly how much insulation you need to remove for a particular plug needs to be determined by trial and error before you solder. Don't remove too much, or adjacent wires may touch when you put the cover back on the plug.

4 Pass the bare wire end through the tag, place the end of the solder on top, and apply the tip of the fully heated soldering iron just long enough for the solder to flow and wet both the tag and the joint.

5 Keep the joint still for a few seconds until the solder cools. The surface of the completed joint should be smooth and shiny.

6 Not all connectors use tags, which are rather outdated. There may be a pin, in which case you wrap the wire around the pin; with some very small connectors you may have no choice but to simply hold the wire against the terminal.

OTHER TOOLS

- A selection of small and medium-sized flat blade and cross point screwdrivers
- A selection of small and medium-sized Torx screwdrivers and a set of small Allen keys – see page 24
- A pair of wire insulation strippers adjustable for different diameters of wire
- A pair of miniature wire cutters and fine-nosed pliers. Cutters are better for cutting or trimming wires in confined spaces
- A small modeller's vice or 'third hand' clamp – extremely useful for holding work while soldering
- A multimeter or continuity tester – see pages 32-3
- Cleaning equipment: soft cloths, aerosol contact cleaner and special-purpose cleaning kits for products such as cassette machines.

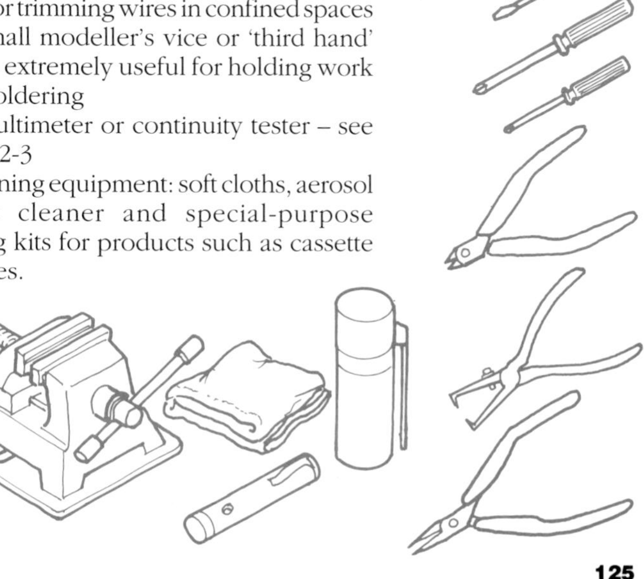

Tools can be bought from a d-i-y store or an electronics hobby store, which will also be able to supply many of the replacement parts you may need. The tools used for electronics repairs may already be in your tool kit for other electrical work, but you often need smaller versions for working in confined areas and with small and delicate components

FIXING YOUR

PORTABLES

A cheap product like a personal stereo can cost more to repair than to replace, but you may be able to get it going yourself

TUNING

FM can give better sound than MW even on a small portable, and stereo too, but many people find it difficult to get good reception on FM

1 The telescopic rod aerial needs to be extended for FM. Most have a joint at the base so that when fully extended the rod can be pointed in any direction. (The rod isn't needed for medium and long wave reception, but is needed if the radio has short wave.)

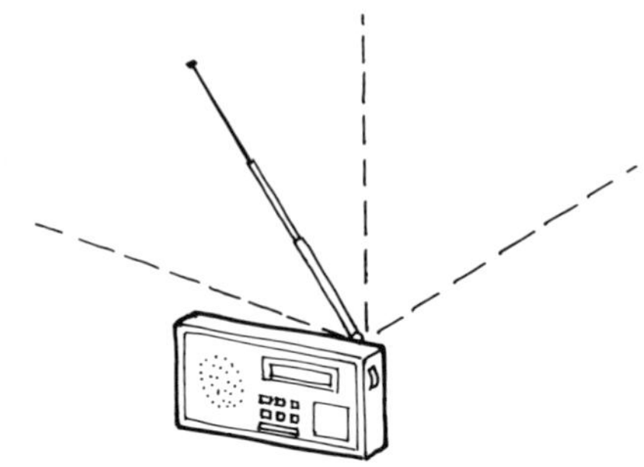

The listings in national newspapers specify a range of frequencies for national stations. To find out exactly which frequency is right for your area you will need to check a local publication.

2 Many modern radios have digital tuning: they can select a frequency (say, 91.3MHz) exactly and if you want, store it on a preset button for future selection, rather like on a TV. You can also scan along a waveband automatically, stopping at each station and storing it if you wish. Digital tuning is easier once set up than using the knob or thumbwheel found on older or cheaper sets, but you still need to make sure that you tune to the correct transmitter on FM: in many areas a BBC programme may be heard at several different frequencies and you need to ensure that you have selected the strongest signal.

3 On a set with rotary tuning, tune approximately to the correct frequency on the scale, then rock the tuning knob to and fro for the least distortion and background hiss, at the same time trying the effect of adjusting the aerial.

4 Angle the aerial in different directions for minimum background hiss and minimum distortion of your chosen station. FM reception unfortunately varies a lot from place to place: you can find for example that your set will work perfectly while you're holding it in mid-air but less well when you put it down on a worktop or shelf. It's worth experimenting.

5 Background hiss is more of a problem when receiving in stereo. In some cases you'll have to switch the set to mono to get acceptable results – it's worth checking when you buy a portable stereo that it has a mono switch for this purpose.

6 Interference can be caused by electronic equipment such as computers or CD players – try moving the radio away from these if they cannot be turned off.

HEADPHONES

Headphones are the first thing to check if the batteries are OK but you're getting no sound, sound in only one ear, intermittent sound or crackles

1 First, try to check the player with another pair of phones. Any type with the standard 3.5mm stereo jack plug should suit. If the fault is cured, go to step 3.

2 If there's no difference, another common problem is a faulty connection in the player's headphone socket caused by frequent insertion and removal of the plug. Unfortunately, replacing the socket or resoldering the connection to it (which sometimes fractures) is not an easy job unless you're used to such work. A squirt of contact cleaner aerosol can sometimes help if the problem is dirt rather than a broken connection. Treating the plug and socket gently from new can prevent the problem in the first place.

3 If the phones or their lead or plug are faulty, check whether the broken connection is at the plug end or near the earpieces by carefully putting pressure on each part while listening to some music.

4 If the moulded-on plug is faulty this can be cut off and a new plug fitted.

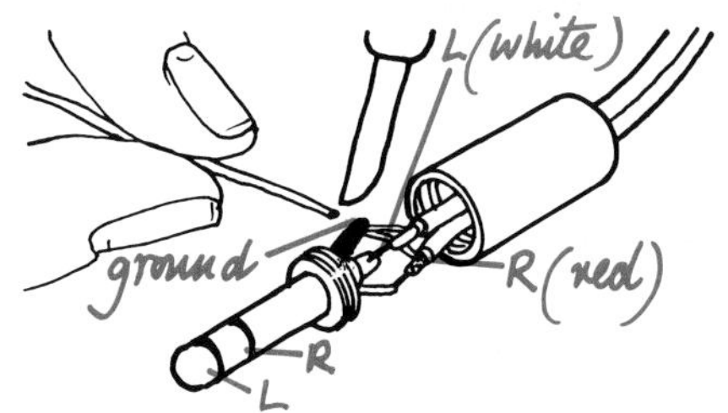

Note carefully how the solder tags in the new plug are connected to its tip, ring and sleeve. If there's a fault at the earpiece end it may be more difficult to repair.

5 Even if the phones cannot be repaired, it's much cheaper to buy new ones rather than buy a complete new player.

If the foam pads on your headphones are tatty you can buy new ones (in various sizes to suit) from audio and electronics shops. These just slip over the earpieces.

THINGS YOU NEED

- **Aerosol contact cleaner**
- **Soldering iron and solder**
- **Wire strippers**
- **3.5mm stereo jack plug**

OTHER PROBLEMS

● The telescopic rod aerials of portable radios sometimes snap off if mishandled. Replacements are available from dealers specialising in electronic components. Dismantle the cabinet, unsolder the connecting tag, remove the screw collar retaining the base of the aerial and fit the new one in a similar way. Don't attempt this on a set under guarantee or if you're not confident of being able to reassemble the set, as this is often the most difficult part of the job.

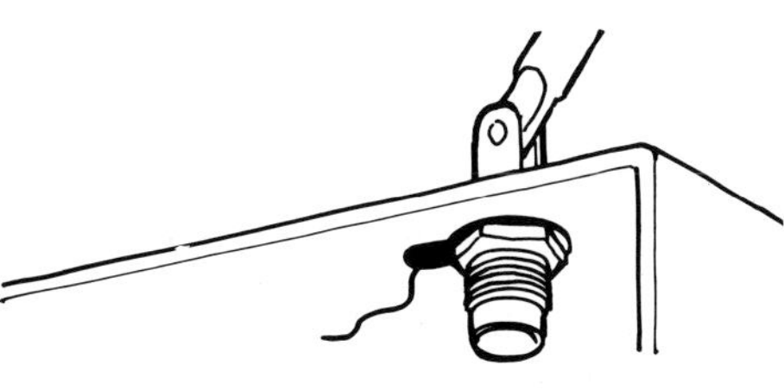

● A build-up of dirt or tape oxide particles on the tape head and moving parts of a personal stereo or cassette recorder can cause muffled sound, slow running or jamming. See Head cleaning, page 143.

● Faulty battery connections are another common problem causing total failure or crackling – see Faulty connections, page 129.

● Inserting the mains connector on a mains/battery portable generally operates an internal switch to disconnect the batteries during mains use. You need to remove this connector from the set (not just switch off at the mains wall socket) for the set to work off batteries. The internal switch is an occasional cause of intermittent operation but is difficult to repair. The detachable mains lead itself may be the culprit and new ones (complete with moulded-on plug) are available cheaply.

● Volume controls which crackle when adjusted are a common problem, especially on older equipment. If the body of the control is readily accessible on opening the set it is worth spraying it with aerosol contact cleaner, trying to aim the spray so that it penetrates the inside of the control.

THINGS YOU NEED

- **Screwdrivers**
- **Soldering iron and solder**
- **Replacement parts as in text**

USING

BATTERIES

Knowing your way round the different types and sizes will help you get top performance and save you money

TYPES

Batteries divide firstly into disposables you use once and throw away, and rechargeables that can be used many times. A single 1.5 volt battery is sometimes called a cell

DISPOSABLES

These come in different chemical formulations. It's not always clear from the names like 'long-life' or 'high power' which one you're getting.

Zinc chloride are suitable for low to medium current applications such as remote control handsets, clocks, calculators, torches and portable radios.

Alkalines are more expensive but have up to three times the capacity. They're best for products with high current demands especially if they're in use for extended periods. Examples are shavers, large radio-cassettes, personal stereos, motorised toys, video games and flashguns. They're also good if you want to rely on something to work properly after a long period of non-use: a smoke alarm or an emergency torch you keep in the car.

Lithium Cameras, watches and social alarm devices may use a special lithium type which is expensive but has a very long life. These are available from photo shops.

RECHARGEABLES

Rechargeable nickel-cadmium cells are, like alkalines, good for high-current extended use. You have to buy a charger unit and the cells themselves cost more than disposables but you'll save money in the long run. But rechargeables don't hold their charge well for long periods, so don't put them in products that aren't in frequent use. They may give a shorter life between charges than a disposable would with some products – a personal CD player, for example.

There's some evidence that it's better to let a set of cells run down and then recharge them fully rather than topping them up.

Nickel metal hydride rechargeable batteries are similar to nickel-cadmium cells but have twice the lifetime between charges and are more expensive.

SIZES

Some manufacturers use their own numbering system, but you should find the codes shown in the picture below on the pack somewhere. An 'L' added to the number means the battery is alkaline.

GETTING THE BEST RESULTS

- Be careful to insert batteries the right way round: wrong insertion will cause faulty operation and the batteries may overheat.
- Don't mix different types of cells in the same product, or mix new and partly used cells.
- Check 'use by' dates when buying.
- Don't try to recharge any type of disposable battery (with the exception of 'rechargeable alkalines', which work with a special charger) – there's a danger of explosion.
- When buying rechargeable batteries, always check the claimed capacity (in mAh) written on the battery or packaging. The greater this is, the longer the battery will run for between charges.
- Cells that are too run down to work, say, a personal stereo may still give months of use in a low-current product like a clock.
- Run the product off the mains wherever you have the option – this works out far cheaper.
- Don't leave cells in products for long periods – they may leak and corrode.

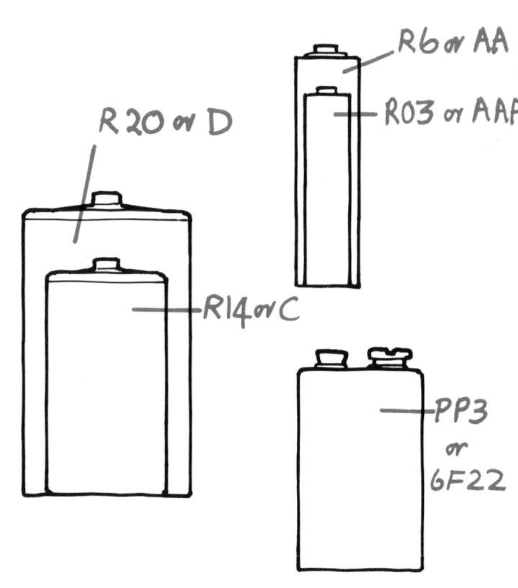

WATCH BATTERY

OTHER DISPOSABLES

Sometimes a camera's exposure meter may be operated by a button cell of the type also used in hearing aids. Take the old cell along when buying a new one to make sure you get the right type, but don't accidentally mix them up.

Quartz watches and credit card calculators usually use very small button cells, either the mercury oxide, silver oxide or lithium type. These should not be recharged.

Many watches show that the battery is nearing the end of its life by advancing the second hand every two seconds instead of every one. If you buy the battery from a jeweller they may add their normal fitting charge; try an electronics store instead.

1 Whether the watch back is easily removable depends on the type: some can be removed with a fine watchmaker's screwdriver. On others, very fine-nosed pliers can be used to grip recesses in the watch back and unscrew it.

2 Take care that the sealing ring which makes the watch water-resistant is replaced and correctly seated.

This can cost you several pounds in a jewellers, but in many cases it's possible to do this yourself

THINGS YOU NEED

- **Watchmaker's screwdrivers or fine-nosed pliers**
- **Replacement battery**

FAULTY CONNECTIONS

1 If batteries have been allowed to corrode in the set, the spring contacts in the battery compartment may be rusted. These can usually be restored with fine sandpaper provided you can get at them (not always easy).

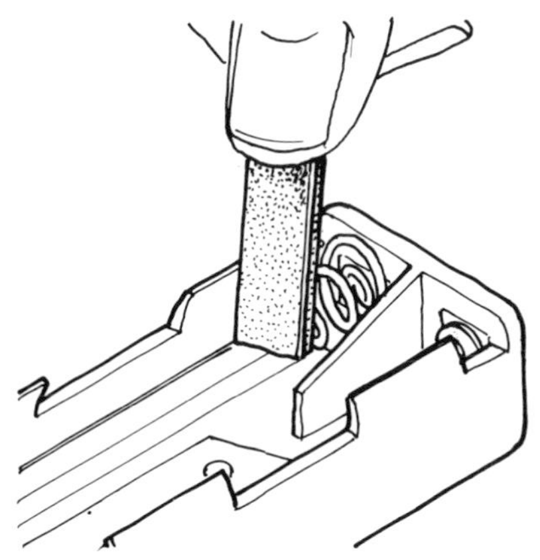

2 On sets with press-stud battery connectors it's quite common for the wire to break away from the stud. This can fairly easily be resoldered, and new press studs are available from component shops if necessary. There are two different sizes of stud, small for 6F22 (PP3) type batteries, and large for the PP9 type which is less commonly found in modern equipment. Make very sure that you get the positive (+) and negative (-) polarities correct.

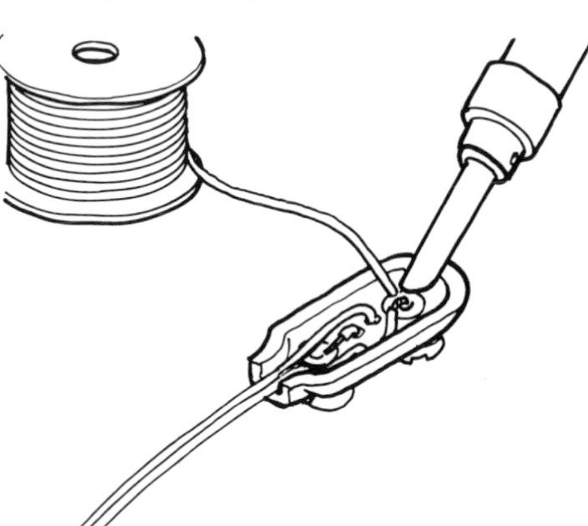

A common problem causing crackling or total failure is a faulty contact on battery connections

THINGS YOU NEED

- **Fine abrasive paper**
- **Screwdriver**
- **New battery connectors if necessary**
- **Soldering iron and solder**

TV AND VIDEO

Getting a new TV going used to be easy enough – plug in the aerial and switch on. It's not quite so simple these days

TRANSMITTERS

Understanding the way pictures are transmitted and received is the first step to getting a good picture

The UK is covered by about 50 main transmitters and a large number of less powerful *relays* which receive signals from the nearest main transmitter and re-broadcast them locally in areas where reception from the main transmitter would otherwise be poor.

A particular transmitter will transmit all five programmes: BBC1, BBC2, your local ITV region, Channel 4 and Channel 5. (In some areas, you may be able to receive signals from two or even three transmitters which would give you a choice of several ITV or other regional programmes, but you'll get the best reception from the transmitter whose service area you're in.)

CHANNELS

While the frequency of a radio transmitter is given directly as a number in kHz or MHz, the frequencies used by a television transmitter to carry picture and sound are usually quoted as a 'channel number' between 21 and 68. For example, the main transmitter for the West Midlands at Sutton Coldfield transmits on the following channel numbers:

BBC1	46
BBC2	40
ITV	43
Channel 4	50
Channel 5	37

Other transmitters use different channels. A local dealer should know the correct channels for your locality and there may be a list with the instructions for a new TV. Otherwise, the broadcasting companies themselves will be able to help you tune in to the right transmitter.

The use of the word 'channel' to mean two quite different things – the frequency a TV or VCR is tuned to or the name of a particular service (like Channel 4) – can be very confusing. We shall come back to this in the sections on setting up your TV and VCR.

AERIALS

Depending on where you live, you need an aerial designed for a particular group of channels:

A	21-34
B	39-53
C/D	48-68
E	39-68

Alternatively, you can use a wideband (W) aerial covering all channels 21-68 (but see below). So for Sutton Coldfield, you need a B or W group aerial. But there are over 30 relay transmitters in the same region and you may need a different aerial to receive from one of these.

The type of aerial you need also depends on how good a signal can be received in your locality. If you live within a reasonable distance of a transmitter, a simple and inexpensive aerial should be adequate.

AERIAL PROBLEMS

1 If your aerial was put up years ago it may be directed at the main transmitter rather than a newer and more local relay transmitter. It's likely that receiving from the relay will give a better picture, but this will in many cases mean buying a new aerial rather than simply adjusting the old one.

2 It's even been known for all the aerials in a street to be pointing in the wrong direction because each installer aligned the aerial with the one next door! This isn't the right way to do it: a professional installer should use a signal strength meter to ensure correct alignment. The waves which carry the signal are transmitted either horizontally or vertically, which requires corresponding orientation of the aerial elements.

3 If you buy a new set and the picture is disappointing, the aerial could be to blame for some of the faults you put up with on your old set. Aerials don't last forever: rain can corrode the connections or seep into the connecting cable; storms can twist the aerial or damage its mounting so it faces in the wrong direction. Try your set in a neighbour's house if you suspect aerial problems.

4 If you're on the fringe of a transmitter's service area, the signal may be relatively weak. Weak signals cause a grainy picture. A bank of trees or a hill between you and the transmitter may also weaken the signal. Most difficult of all, a tall building a mile or two away may reflect the signal so that your aerial receives it twice, causing ghosting. If you've got a Teletext set, a good signal is particularly important or the Teletext signal may be corrupted, causing 'nonsense' text.

5 In such cases a more complex, directional aerial will be needed to make the most of the signal picked up from one direction and strongly reject other signals. Such aerials have more metal elements and are more expensive.

6 If you go for a wideband aerial – for example to receive signals for more than one ITV region – it will need to be larger to give the same signal level as a single-group aerial.

DIGITAL TERRESTRIAL TV

The new digital terrestrial services offer you the usual five broadcasters plus many more. You can receive these by plugging a 'digital terrestrial receiver' into your existing TV – ideally, the programmes should be receivable using your existing TV aerial. In practice you may have to realign your aerial from a relay to a main transmitter or even upgrade it to a wideband aerial.

SATELLITE DISH AERIALS

You must pay a subscription to receive most satellite stations, which offer a wide choice of films, sport and special interests. Satellite systems can be installed with the aid of a helper. The receiver simply plugs into the back of your TV; aligning the dish to the satellite may take a whole day if you are inexperienced. You will need heavy-duty masonry drills, tools and mounting brackets (for wall mounting), a compass and elevation meter to align the dish, special coaxial cable to connect the dish to the receiver and an assistant to check the picture on screen. A good satellite dealer should be able to provide satellite location angles for your area and possibly a dish alignment meter. The new satellite transmissions are all digital, so go for a digital, rather than analogue, receiver and dish.

INSTALLATION

Installation isn't particularly difficult for a handy person with the right equipment, but working on a roof represents a considerable risk for the inexperienced. Your TV retailer will probably put you in touch with an aerial contractor, or they can be found in *Yellow Pages*. Because most people have their aerial installed by contractors, aerials (except set-top and caravan types) aren't readily available over the counter in electrical stores. But kits are available from d-i-y centres, including aerial, mast, and fixing brackets for mounting to wall or loft joists, or lashing the aerial to a chimney.

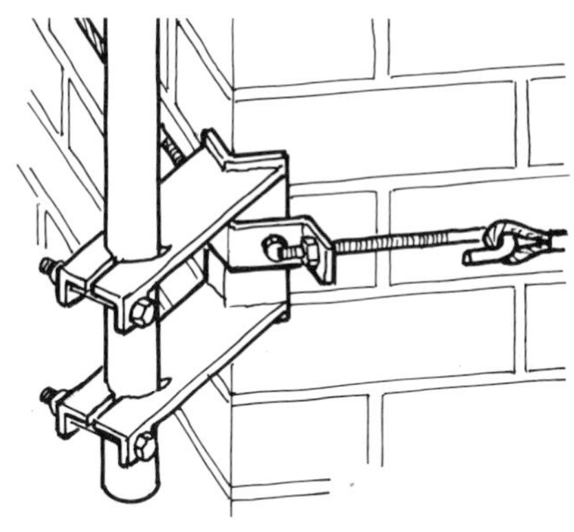

Chimney mounting kit

Do not attempt to put up a satellite dish on the roof or wall of a house unless you are experienced at doing light building work. It is possible to install a dish at ground level if you have a clear view in a southerly direction.

CONNECTORS

You can buy ready-made leads, or make them yourself if you can solder

THINGS YOU NEED

- **Appropriate plugs**
- **Screened cable**
- **Soldering iron and solder**
- **Wire strippers**

1 For all aerial connections low-loss coaxial aerial cable should be used. The coaxial plugs can be fitted without soldering, though it's preferable to solder the centre connection.

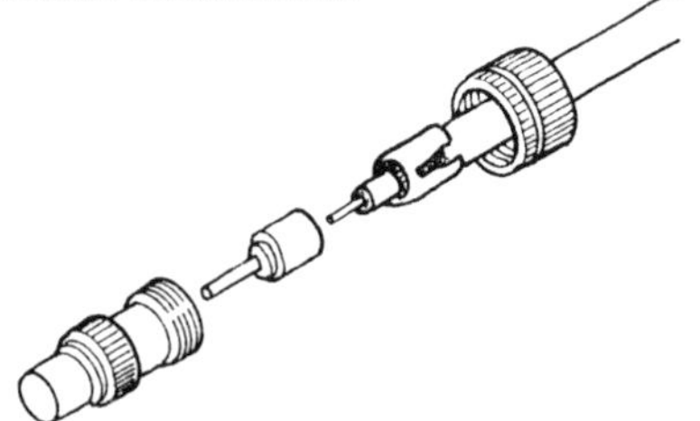

2 Any video or audio connection should be made with screened cable – this has a wire mesh round the inner conductors to screen them from interference and different numbers of cores depending on the job in hand. (Aerial cable is thicker and not suitable for other connecting purposes.)

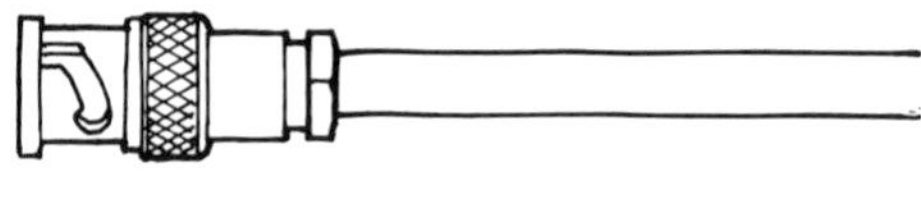

BNC plug, used mainly for older VCR connections; hard to solder – better to solder phono plugs and use BNC adaptor

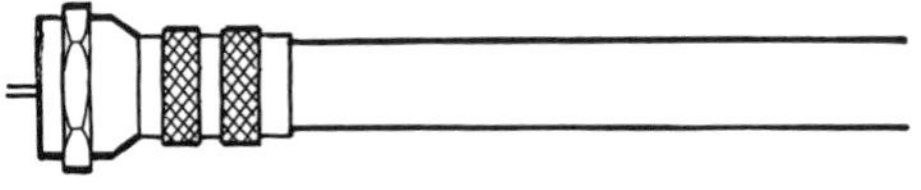

F-connector, used for satellite aerials and radio – comes in crimp-on or screw-on (better for d-i-y) types

Phono plug, used for audio (left = white, right = red) and video (yellow) connections

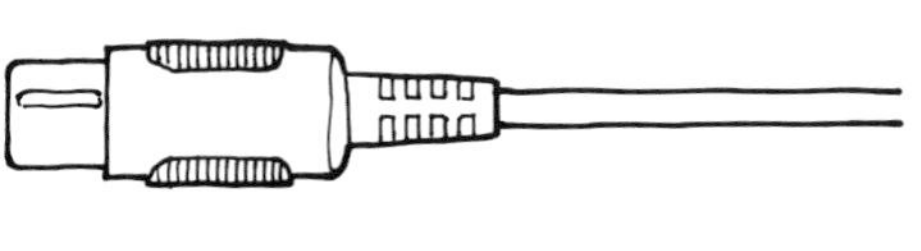

5-pin DIN, used for older audio – combines record and playback connections in one plug

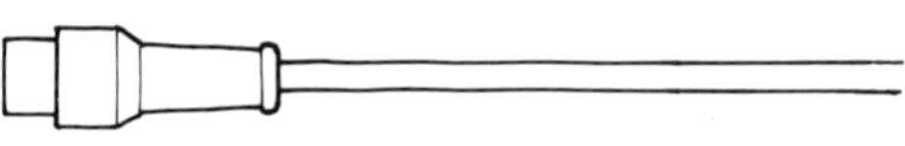

Y/C connector or S-connector – a four-pin plug used to connect Hi-band (S-VHS and Hi-8) VCRs to TVs

SCART CONNECTORS

1 Any new TV or VCR will have at least one SCART connection, sometimes called a Peritel or Euro connector. Broadly, SCART gives better picture and sound quality than the traditional aerial connection (including stereo sound).

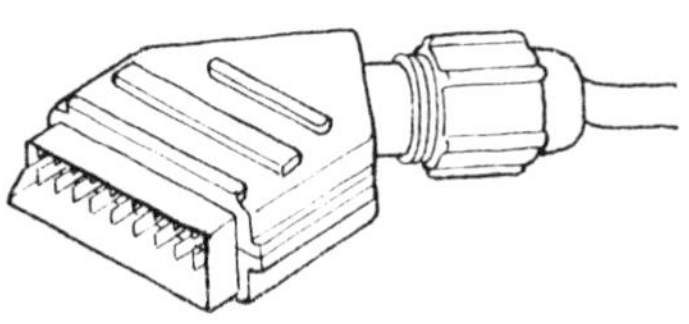

2 A standardised numbering system allocates individual pins in all SCART sockets to specific functions. Not all SCART leads or sockets make use of all 21 pins. In a SCART-to-SCART lead the audio and video outputs from one plug will cross over to the audio and video inputs of the other plug.

Scart pin connections

Ground (shield)	21		
Video out	19	20	Video or Luminance 'Y' in
Video ground	17	18	Ground
Red or Chrominance 'C' in	15	16	Video/RGB switching
Red ground	13	14	Ground
Green in	11	12	Data
Green ground	9	10	Data
Blue in	7	8	AV and widescreen switch
Blue ground	5	6	Audio in (left)
Audio out (left)	3	4	Audio ground
Audio out (right)	1	2	Audio in (right)

3 SCART extension leads are wired without any crossed-over connections, so that signals don't cross back over. The R, G and B (red, green and blue) connections are used instead of the traditional video connection in appliances where superior quality is possible, for example Digital Video Discs and digital TV. Some TVs allow their SCART connections to be used for Hi-band VCRs instead of the S-connector: in this case the *Video input* and *R input* pins are reassigned for the purpose. You can buy ready-made S-to-SCART leads.

MAKING CONNECTIONS

BASIC CONNECTIONS

1 The aerial lead plugs into the coaxial socket at the rear of the TV or VCR (usually marked *antenna in* or *UHF in* or *RF in*); the lead supplied with the VCR goes from the socket marked *UHF out* or *RF out* to the aerial socket on the TV. This 'loop-through' system can be used to connect several pieces of equipment in a chain. For best results from a VCR, and to ensure stereo sound playback from a NICAM VCR, a SCART lead should be used to connect TV and VCR. The simplest SCART connection carries two signals from the VCR to the TV – composite video plus audio (sound). This is often called AV (audio-video) connection, and is usually done by means of a SCART connector. Some older sets use BNC and phono plugs and sockets. The advantage of SCART is that there is only one lead, and interconnection is standardised and simple. Also, SCART allows for message signals so that the TV is automatically set to show the signal from the VCR when you play a tape.

Note: some SCART sockets are configured for input or output only, while others will perform both functions. Look closely at the socket labelling when deciding which SCART socket to use. Always refer to the instructions, TV and VCR, and check before you buy that the sets are compatible.

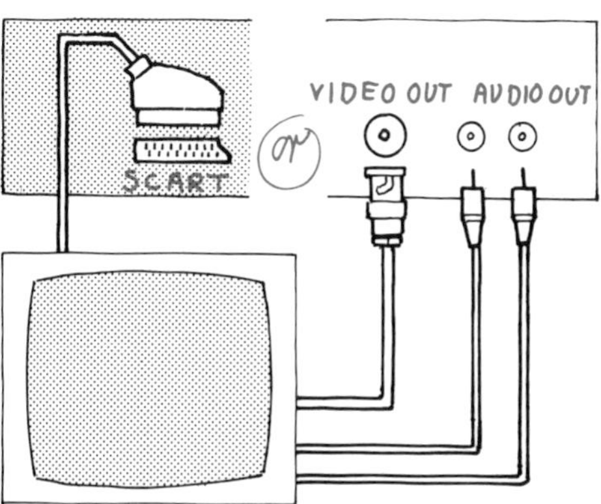

2 If you want to work more than one TV (or VCR) from the same aerial, this can be done using a special splitter or distribution box in a suitable place or places. Because you don't get something for nothing, the signal strength is reduced by splitting it between several sets, and many distribution boxes include an amplifier to boost the signal back to a strong enough level.

CONNECTING A VCR TO TWO TVs

The normal requirement here is to allow a video to be watched in different rooms – say the living room and a bedroom. You can use either an aerial switch or a splitter box so that a video game can be plugged in without removing the aerial, for example.

TV has become complicated because it's now part of a home entertainment network comprising video, satellite, stereo sound, computers, games and more. Connecting them all together successfully is half the battle

There is always a slight loss of quality when copying (or *dubbing*) a video on to another tape; results are best if the original is as good as possible. You can buy a video enhancer which goes between the two VCRs and may help to improve the quality of the copy. This also applies when editing camcorder recordings by copying from the camcorder to a VCR.

MAKING CONNECTIONS

It's clear that there are not only many different possible connector types but many different possible requirements – the diagrams on this page show some of the most likely ones, but others can be done on similar principles

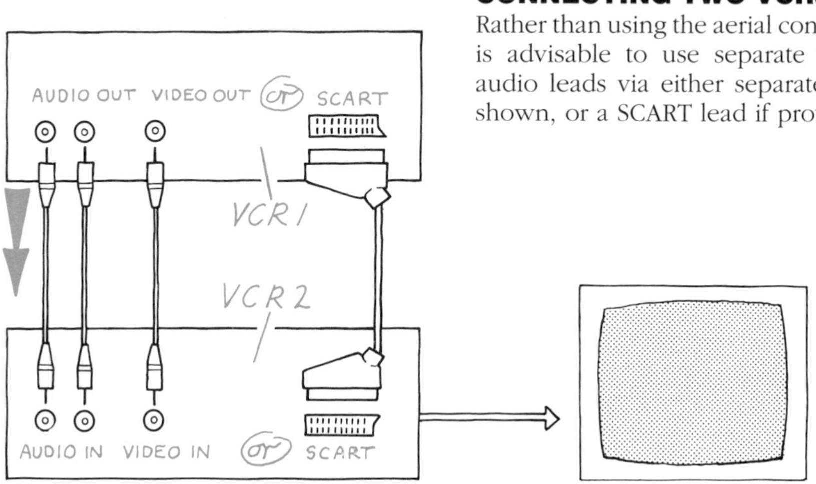

CONNECTING TWO VCRs

Rather than using the aerial connections, it is advisable to use separate video and audio leads via either separate plugs, as shown, or a SCART lead if provided.

Camcorders use phono connectors instead of SCART connectors for audio and video; Hi-band camcorders also have an S-connector. For convenient connection of camcorder to TV or VCR (for copying/ editing) many TVs and VCRs have phono and 'S' inputs on the front panel. If using the connectors you must manually select the appropriate input on the TV or VCR (usually designated AV or Aux) because unlike the SCART socket this is not done automatically.

COMPLEX CONNECTIONS

In all these cases you'll need to refer to instructions supplied with the VCR and TV to see exactly how these connections are made.

1 If you have an S-VHS VCR, a Hi-band camcorder, a Digital Video Disc player or a digital TV receiver, then keeping the Y and C signals (see right) separate can improve video picture quality. The Y/C connection can in some cases be made using the SCART system, though it will usually be necessary to switch to the Y/C mode on both the VCR and the TV. Unfortunately, because the SCART system was developed before the Y/C mode of operation was envisaged, some TVs may not allow this method of connection directly, but see step 3.

2 Alternatively, an S-connector (see page 132) can be used to carry the Y/C signals. Because the S-connector doesn't carry the audio you'll have to make a separate audio link using phono leads.

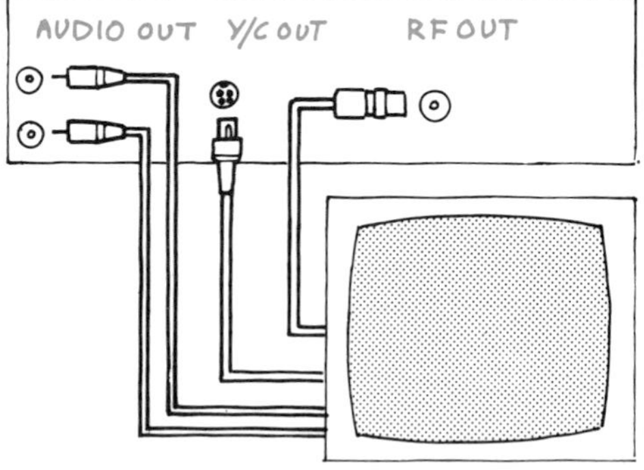

3 For older TVs without an S-connector or a Y/C-equipped SCART connector, but which do have SCART, the Y/C output from an S-VHS VCR can be connected to the TV using a separate RGB converter, available from the makers of the VCR. This converts the Y/C signal from the VCR's SCART to an RGB signal sent to the TV's SCART (see right). Make sure you use a lead equipped for RGB connections.

4 If you're using AV or Y/C SCART connections, you still need to make the conventional aerial connection so that the TV can receive TV broadcasts direct.

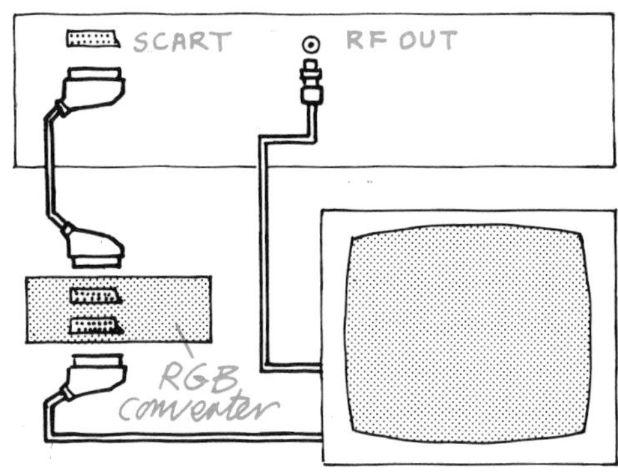

Using an RGB convertor to convert the Y/C signal

If you do a lot of home video experimenting it would be worth investing in a universal video connection kit which contains adaptors and leads to cover most possibilities.

SIGNALS

There are three sorts of signal (other than the aerial one) which may be used to carry the colour picture between the VCR and the TV.

- Composite video - this is a mix of the luminance signal (essentially the detail making up a black-and-white picture) and the chrominance signal (the additional colour information).

- Y/C signal - this is the luminance (Y) and chrominance (C) signals kept separate as they pass between VCR and TV. This may result in a better picture, especially from high-band VCRs (Super VHS and Hi-8) and prevent some kinds of picture interference caused by combining the chrominance and luminance signals.

- RGB (for red/green/blue) signal - normally the separate primary colours which make up a colour picture - are encoded into one chrominance (C) signal at the transmitter and only decoded inside the TV before being fed to the picture tube (if you look closely at the TV screen you can see that the colour picture is made up of minute red, green and blue segments). The RGB signals are sometimes fed separately, for example from a computer to a colour monitor, because this gives the best possible fine colour distinction and detail.

HI-FI CONNECTIONS

The NICAM sound quality from many broadcasts is of a high standard, and may not be optimally reproduced by your TV loudspeaker. If you want to play the stereo sound from a NICAM stereo VCR through your hi-fi system, the audio output sockets on your VCR allow this independently of the SCART system. A NICAM stereo TV may well have audio outputs for the same purpose. A hi-fi stereo VCR will also have audio input sockets; this lets you use the recorder as a sound-only cassette deck for recording from your stereo system.

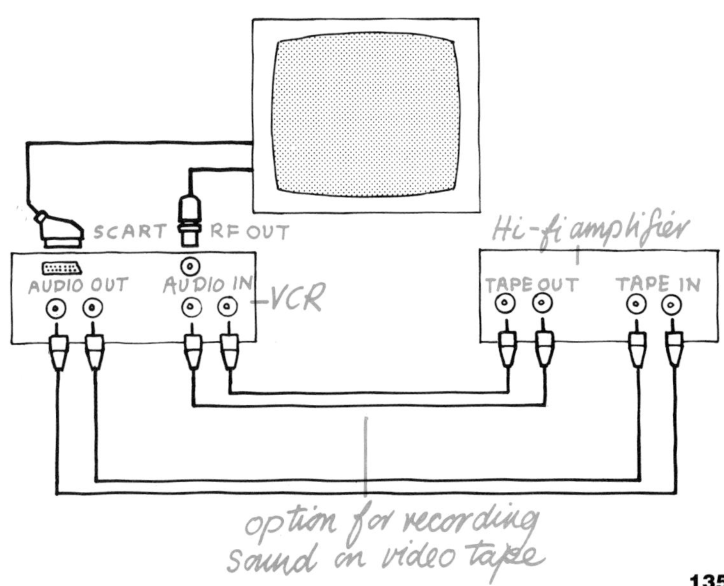

TUNING A TV

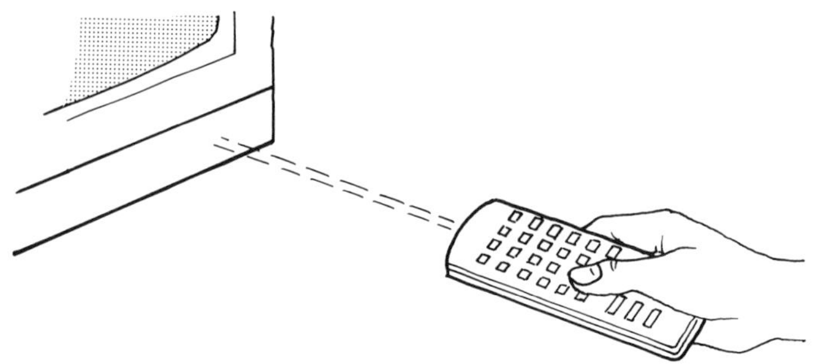

Most modern TVs and VCRs have fully automated tuning systems. Older TVs have a simpler electronic scan-and-store system requiring some input on your part. Very old TVs, particularly portables, will be totally manual with small tuning knobs or thumbwheels on the set for each 'preset' position

1 On a modern TV or VCR with fully automated tuning, the first time you switch it on it scans the UHF TV frequencies, picks up the strongest stations, identifies them using Teletext information and puts them in correct order (e.g. BBC1 on preset 1, etc.). Should you move to a new reception area, you can do this manually.

2 The scan-and-store tuning system starts at the lowest UHF channel number (21) and increases one number at a time until it finds a channel with a strong signal – likely to be from your local transmitter. It may then store this automatically in a selector position and continue scanning, or require you to 'skip' the signal (if it's not one you want) or 'store' it if you do.

3 Any station can be stored on any selector position, but most people find it convenient and logical to have their stations allocated to selectors as follows:

1	BBC1
2	BBC2
3	ITV
4	Channel 4
5	Channel 5

However, a scan-and-store system will usually line up the stations in order of increasing channel number, which isn't often the same. You can put this right, though: choose a selector position, cancel the channel number stored in it, and then enter the required channel number calculator-style using the remote control buttons, followed by 'store'.

4 You should end up with clear picture and sound on each selector position (usually five, though in some areas you may be able to receive alternative regional transmissions, so that more than five selector positions on the TV will be occupied).

5 Once you've got a basically satisfactory picture, you may need to adjust contrast, brightness and colour controls for the best results. Do this on a studio programme as some films or outside broadcasts make it less easy to judge the picture.

6 Most modern sets have +/- buttons on the remote control for increasing or decreasing picture and volume settings. Older sets may have conventional knobs on the set. With +/- controls there's usually a 'normal' button which returns the controls to typical settings which you can specify. In many cases you will need to make only small adjustments.

7 If contrast and brightness are way out of adjustment, start by turning the colour right down so you get a black and white picture. Contrast and brightness adjustments are inter-related: aim for a contrast setting which is high enough for black elements in the picture not to turn grey, then adjust brightness to suit. Finally advance the colour to a natural setting: skin tones or grass are a good guide here.

8 Very old TVs had extra adjustments – sometimes on the rear of the set – which occasionally needed attention if the picture broke up into lines or rolled vertically. Few modern TVs have these adjustments accessible to the user.

POOR RECEPTION

1 On an older set, you may need to fine-tune the stations after scanning and before storing, or the TV may have selected a non-local transmission. Check for better reception on other transmitter channels.

2 If picture quality is poor on all or most channels, aerial problems are likely. You can check this out by trying another TV if one is available.

If your TV picture is replaced by a bright vertical or horizontal line, switch off the set and arrange for a service call

TUNING A VCR

1 In the basic way of connecting the VCR to the TV using the UHF aerial cable, the TV sees the VCR's output as an additional 'station', and the first step is to set up a spare channel selector on the TV to take the VCR's output. VCRs have a switch at the rear to produce a special test pattern (usually a vertical black and white bar accompanied by a steady audio tone). The selector on the TV allocated to the VCR (usually marked video or AV) is the one to use.

2 Tune the 'video' preset on the TV until the test pattern is clear and steady, then switch off the test pattern.

3 If you're using SCART you don't have to tune in the selector button on the TV to suit the VCR's output. The TV is automatically switched to video when playback is selected on the VCR. If you use the SCART connection you still need the aerial connection between the VCR and the TV for the TV to receive TV broadcasts.

4 Next tune the VCR to receive each of the available channels. The procedure is similar to tuning a TV (see left). Most modern VCRs use a fully automatic tuning system. If your VCR has Video Plus programming, stations should be allocated to the presets in correct order, otherwise Video Plus will record the wrong channel.

5 With the TV switched to video, select each of presets 1, 2, 3, 4 and 5 in turn on the VCR; you should get clear picture and sound on each. (In some areas you may be able to receive alternative regional transmissions, which means that more than five VCR presets will be used.)

If the remote control operation is erratic, check the batteries and ensure that the handset has not been dropped or had liquid spilled on it. If you need a replacement, your retailer should be able to supply a pre-programmed universal remote control (which should work with all models).

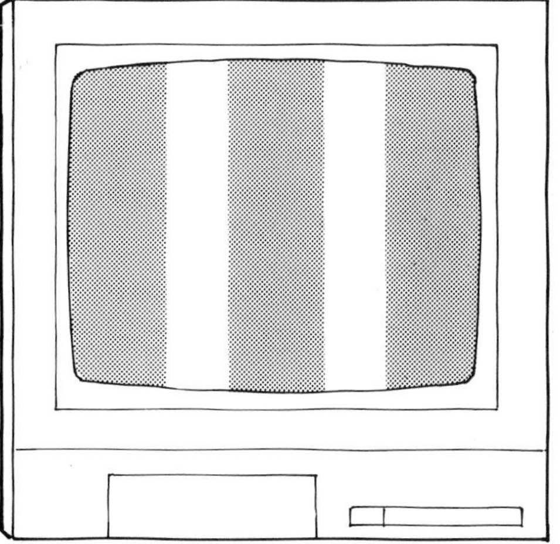

THE MILLENNIUM BUG

Some VCRs may not cope with the year 2000 date change or the ensuing leap year. These checks will highlight any problems with your VCR.

1 Set the date to 31-12-99. Set the time to 23:58. Return to normal mode (so the clock starts to run).

2 Record what happens when the time passes midnight (what day/date does it show? Note: 1 January 2000 is a Saturday).

3 Next set the date to 28-02-00 and proceed as above. Note: 29 February 2000 is a Tuesday.

4 If your VCR does not recognise the leap year, reset it to the year 1972 (a leap year when the days of the week fell on the same dates as they will in 2000). This should let you make timed recordings with your VCR.

VCR PROBLEMS

Work through this checklist to identify the fault in the TV or VCR that's causing trouble

POOR TV PICTURE

1 If reception is poor via the VCR's tuner (TV set to VCR output, VCR not playing a tape), but OK when you select a station on the TV, you may need to fine-tune some or all of the VCR presets. You may have a VCR preset tuned to a transmitter which is not your local one – try to find a better picture on another channel number. Alternatively, the TV may not be properly tuned in to the VCR.

2 If you're not using SCART, the UHF output of the VCR (that feeds the TV) may be suffering interference from other broadcasts. Most VCRs have the UHF output at around channel 37; unfortunately, in many parts of the country this channel has been allocated to Channel 5 broadcasts. If you get wavy patterns on the screen when receiving the VCR output but not other stations, or you are getting interference on Channel 5, try adjusting the output frequency of the VCR slightly. There is usually a small hole at the back which allows adjustment with a fine screwdriver blade. Adjust this output so it uses a channel well away from the five main broadcast channels and retune your TV to the corresponding channel. Modern VCRs do not have this screw adjustment; instead the required output channel is selected during installation (see page 136). See the instruction manual for directions.

NO PICTURE

Your VCR obviously has to be left on all the time to keep the timer going and record programmes while you're out. When it's switched to standby (or timer record) your TV still receives an aerial signal so it can work normally, but you won't get picture or sound on the TV's video setting. And if you unplug or switch off your VCR altogether for any reason, you won't be able to get a TV picture at all unless you reconnect the aerial lead directly to the TV. Some TVs show a blank screen instead of interference if they are not tuned in to a strong signal; this can also happen if the aerial is not plugged in.

POOR PICTURE ON PLAYBACK

1 This may be related to a particular tape – perhaps one you've hired from a video shop. Play another tape known to be good – if this OK, the problem is clear. For tapes not recorded on your own VCR you may need to adjust the tracking control for best results – see the instruction manual. On the latest VCRs tracking adjustment is automatic, so you shouldn't experience this problem.

2 If other tapes are similarly poor on playback, check TV reception via the VCR (TV set to VCR output, VCR not playing a tape). If picture is poor, check TV tuning.

3 If TV picture via the VCR is OK but playback is poor, a possible cause is contamination of the video heads. A typical symptom of dirty heads is the picture breaking up or white flecks in the picture, though this can also be caused by faulty or poor-quality video tapes. You're more likely to suffer from dirty heads if you rent a lot of videos. Unlike audio cassette heads, these are deep inside the machine and you shouldn't attempt to clean them directly yourself. Video cleaning cassettes are available; they may help if the problem is slight but if the heads are seriously contaminated you will need a professional service.

4 Dirty heads will probably affect any new recordings you make as well as playback. You could try comparing a new and an older (known to be good) recording by playing them on someone else's VCR.

5 If new recordings are poor but playback of older and hired ones is OK, check the VCR's tuning.

6 If both TV and VCR recordings deteriorate at the same time, but old tapes and hired ones are OK, you've probably got an aerial problem.

SATELLITE RECEIVERS

All major UK satellite broadcasts, including the BSkyB channels, are carried by the Astra satellites. One group carries analogue TV channels and can be picked up with one dish; a newer, differently positioned group carries digital satellite broadcasts and requires a fixed dish pointing in another direction. More complex systems used by enthusiasts to receive other satellites have a larger dish which scans the sky using a *positioner* connected to the receiver indoors.

1 It's quite possible to link satellite receiver, VCR and TV in a chain or *loop-through* arrangement. The satellite receiver output is seen as an extra channel which can be tuned in to both TV and VCR and then recorded and/or viewed direct using the UHF connectors.

2 As shown, SCART connectors give a better picture and stereo sound. For products with just one SCART socket, you will need a two-way SCART adaptor or switch. The diagram below shows how to connect things up so that the TV can show video or satellite and the VCR can record from satellite. In modern satellite receivers this arrangement is inbuilt and two or more SCART sockets are supplied, making connection much simpler (see right).

For equipment with two SCART sockets the adaptor will not be needed

3 There may also be alternative sound-only services on a particular satellite channel, obtainable by retuning the sound frequency. The satellite receiver presets are usually pre-programmed for Astra – for other services or satellites you will have to tune in and store frequency, polarisation and sound channel. Digital satellite receivers don't need tuning in. TV and radio channels are selected using the broadcaster's electronic on-screen programme guide (EPG).

SATELLITE PROBLEMS

If 'sparklies' – white or black streaks or spots sometimes caused by heavy rain or snow – occur check the receiver channel tuning. If this does not work the installer should check the dish alignment. Channels lower in power than others may show sparklies owing to the strain on the receiver; the only solution may be a larger dish. On digital satellite receivers, picture break-up into square blocks, jerkiness or freezing could indicate a problem with the alignment of the dish or its connecting cable.

New interference problems with your VCR may be the result of it sharing an output channel with the satellite receiver. Adjust the VCR output tuning electronic (see page 137), then retune the TV's video preset to match

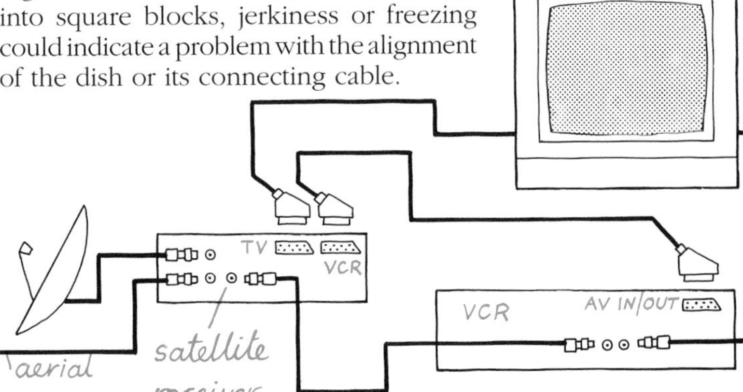

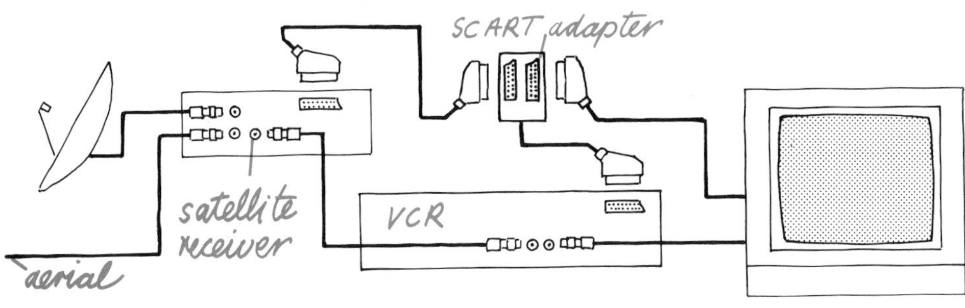

SORTING OUT

HI-FI EQUIPMENT

Buying a hi-fi system is only half the battle – it has to be well set up to give the best results

SETTING UP

If you buy a package, setting it up should present few problems; separate components are more complicated to connect together but usually offer better-quality sound

Many specialist hi-fi separates manufacturers now design the components in their range to match visually, so it is possible to effectively buy a package from them. However, if you want a system that uses remote control choose one that operates all these components from a single remote.

1 Some systems are made all in one piece (even if they're designed to look like 'separates' from the front) and need only the speakers and the mains supply connected.

2 Some package systems are made up of separate items which need connecting together in the same way as components purchased individually. Phono plugs are usually used to carry the audio signals between each of the sources (record deck, cassette deck, radio tuner, CD player) and the amplifier. There may also be other interconnections on some makes of system which allow 'intelligent' switching – for example, the amplifier would automatically switch to radio if you pressed one of the station selector presets on the radio tuner – or which carry power from one unit to the other.

3 The 'phono' input is for the record player and isn't suitable for use with other source equipment because it's designed to accept the low-level signal from the record player's magnetic cartridge. You would hear bad distortion if you connected a CD player to it, for example.

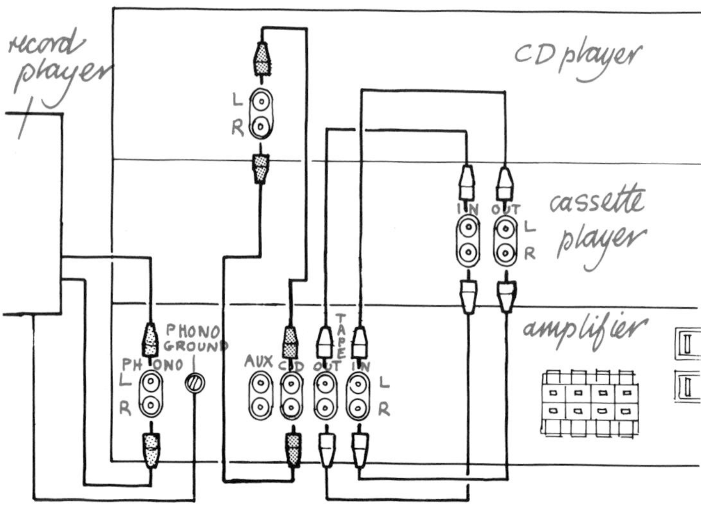

4 In some cases packages may need more than one mains lead and plug; on the better designed systems only one is needed and power is distributed internally or by means of rear connections. If you have a system that needs several mains connections it would be worth buying a compact mains adaptor with four or six outlets taking special small plugs.

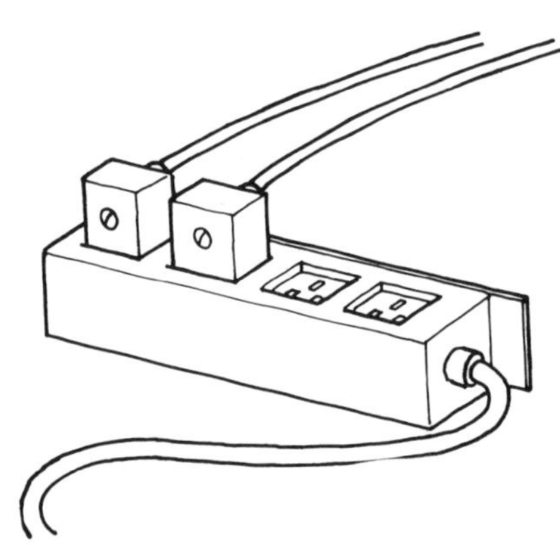

5 You usually need to remove transit screws or internal packaging material from record and CD players before you use them. Keep these carefully and put them back if you have to transport your system.

6 If you're using a record deck make sure that the system (or at least the deck) has a firm support, or you may experience problems with groove jumping. This can be a problem with CD players to some extent, too.

RADIO TUNER

1 Most systems come with a simple T-shaped wire aerial for FM radio. This may perform adequately where there's a strong signal from the transmitter; try pinning or taping it to the wall both horizontally and vertically to test for best results. But in many areas you'll need a better FM aerial to get good noise-free stereo reception. This may be fitted in the loft or preferably on the roof. In areas with very poor reception you may need a more complex aerial: consult an aerial specialist.

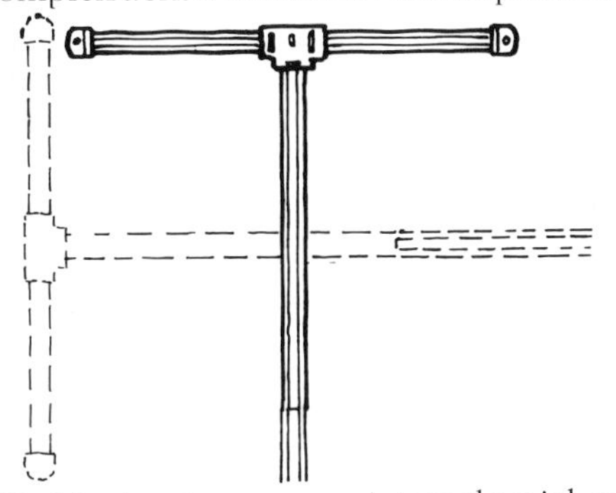

2 Most systems use an internal aerial, an external loop or a simple wire at the back of the set for AM. If a loop or a wire it's worth adjusting its position to get as good reception as possible, although AM transmissions always sound woolly compared to FM. There can also be a lot of interference, especially at night.

3 Most radio tuners nowadays have preset station selectors with a scan-and-store system like a TV (see page 136), but there will also be a means of searching for stations other than the preset ones. On some older designs, if you switch off the system at the mains for more than a day or two, you may find that the presets need to be reset. Some modern tuners have Radio Data System (RDS). This automatically displays the station name and other information in the digital display. Some models will automatically switch to BBC news or traffic announcements when they occur.

SPEAKERS

1 Position the speakers roughly as shown; generally it's best to place them symmetrically in the room about two to three metres apart, away from walls and corners and at about the height your ears will be when you're sitting to listen. Don't put them on the floor unless they are designed to do so – you can buy special floor stands if they're not going on shelves. Try experimenting: moving speakers into a corner or nearer a wall will tend to increase bass response; treble response and the overall acoustic of the room are affected by the amount of soft furnishings.

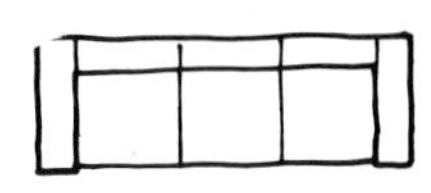

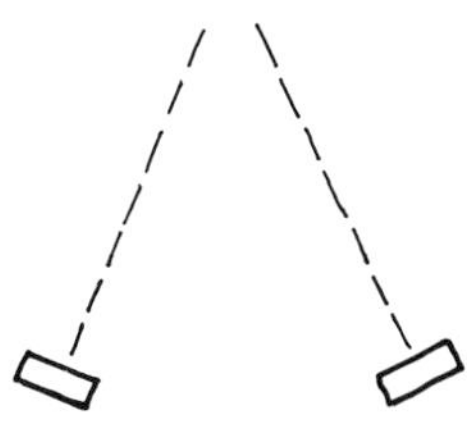

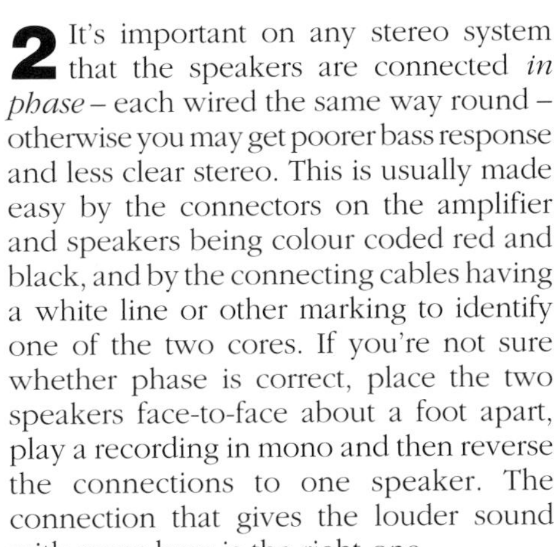

2 It's important on any stereo system that the speakers are connected *in phase* – each wired the same way round – otherwise you may get poorer bass response and less clear stereo. This is usually made easy by the connectors on the amplifier and speakers being colour coded red and black, and by the connecting cables having a white line or other marking to identify one of the two cores. If you're not sure whether phase is correct, place the two speakers face-to-face about a foot apart, play a recording in mono and then reverse the connections to one speaker. The connection that gives the louder sound with more bass is the right one.

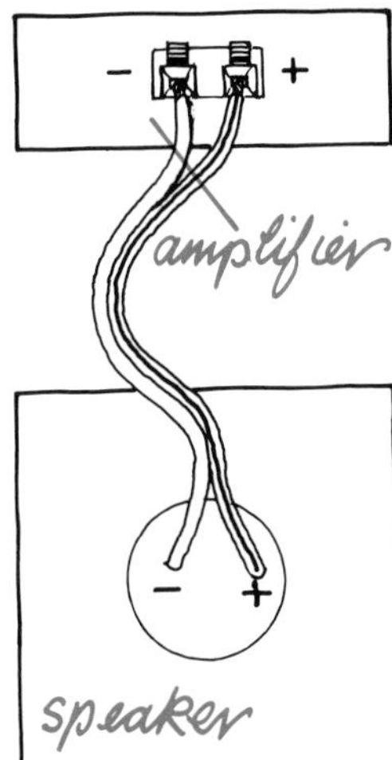

BUYING SEPARATES

If you're not fully confident, there's a lot to be said for buying from a hi-fi specialist who will advise you, let you listen before buying, and preferably set the system up in your home.

- **If you're buying a record deck as separate turntable, pick-up arm and cartridge, matching and installing them correctly is crucial.**
- **Matching amplifier power output in watts to the required power input of the loudspeakers is important. You don't need an exact match, but beware of having insufficient amplifier power. The power output per channel 'RMS' or 'EIAJ' is the one to look for in specifications.**
- **There are few problems matching CD players, tuners or cassette decks technically to the amplifier; go for a rough match on quality.**

HI-FI PROBLEMS

Sound quality may deteriorate over time – cleaning is often the answer. Poor sound from new calls for some adjustments

CD PLAYER

An ageing CD player's laser may lose power or its tracking may become misaligned, causing CDs to skip or click as if scratched. At first the problem may show on only a few discs – causing you to blame the discs. Unfortunately, replacing the laser can be expensive

1 On a portable player where the laser lens is accessible, finger marks or dust on the lens can prevent correct operation. Clean it carefully with a camera lens cleaning cloth.

2 If you get sticking or jumping or audible ticking behind the music on a particular CD only, the disc has probably been scratched or marked; if it's brand new and shows this problem it's probably a faulty pressing and the record shop should change it. If the problem shows up on several or most of your CDs, your player needs servicing.

3 Light marks on a CD can be removed with a disposable wipe or moistened soft cloth. Wipe the non-label side of the disc radially (from the centre outwards). If a disc has been scratched or scuffed badly it may be worth trying a CD repair kit that contains various grades of special micro-abrasive pads to repolish the surface.

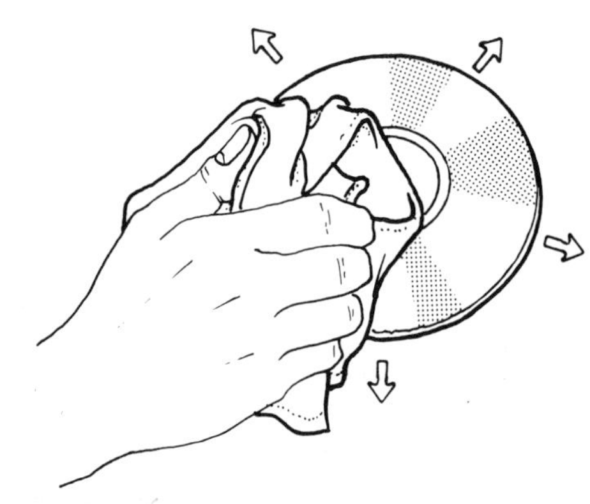

RADIO

1 Most reception problems can be solved by paying attention to the aerial (see pages 130-1). Check also that you're receiving national programmes from the right transmitter and not a weaker signal on a different frequency. Look in your local newspaper.

2 Clicks or more continuous interference can be a problem. A particular source can be interference from the CD player electronics – if possible, switch off the CD player when using the radio, or position it further from the tuner. Personal computers are also a common source of interference.

INTERFERENCE

1 It's quite a common problem to suffer loud clicks through the speakers, caused by things like fridges or the central heating switching on and off. Most of this interference is carried along the mains wiring of your house. It's best if possible to suppress the interference at source – plug-adaptor suppressors are available to plug the offending appliance in to. If the problem still isn't cured you may need to have suppressors fitted to the appliance.

2 Fitting a similar suppressor where your stereo plugs into the mains may help; so may keeping the mains lead(s) as separate as possible from the speaker and other interconnecting cables of the system.

3 Continuous buzzing or whining may be caused by tools like electric drills or kitchen appliances. However, it's less of a problem, as they are generally in use for only a short time.

CASSETTE PLAYER

HEAD CLEANING

1 The cheapest and most effective way to clean tape heads, pinch roller and capstan is to use cotton buds and isopropyl alcohol. You can either buy these together as a kit from hi-fi shops or use ordinary cotton buds sold by chemists and a small bottle of isopropyl alcohol (also available from most chemists). Don't use any other solvent, as this may damage the heads or plastic parts.

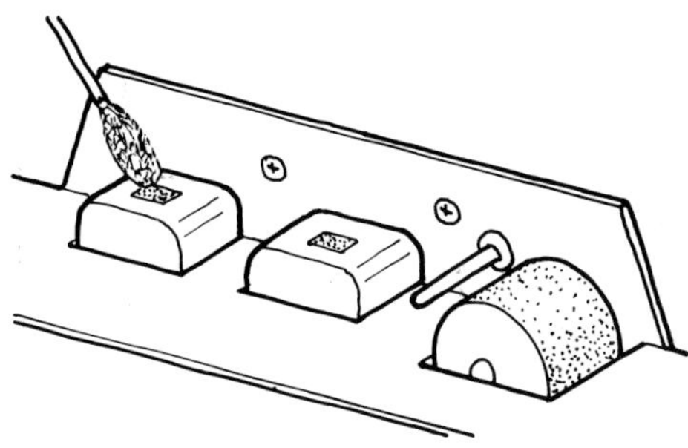

2 With some cassette players – especially the car type – the heads and drive mechanism are very difficult to reach without taking the unit to pieces. In these cases a mechanical cleaner is a better bet. You dampen the pads with a little fluid before playing the cassette. Other types of cassette-shaped cleaners use a fabric tape or slightly abrasive tape. On the whole these work less well.

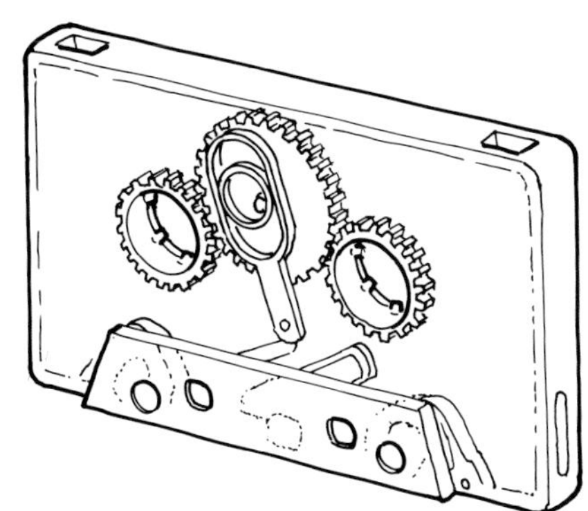

Mechanical head cleaner

RECORDING AND PLAYBACK

1 If your cassette deck has manual switching for different types of tape (ferric, chrome or metal) make sure you use the correct setting, especially when recording. If your deck doesn't have such switching, it either selects the correct tape setting automatically (check the instructions) or can record only on ferric tape (this is often the case with cheaper systems). Note however that any cassette player can play back commercial music cassettes recorded on chrome tape.

2 Ensure that the correct Dolby noise reduction is switched on if you're playing back a tape recorded using Dolby B or C.

3 *Bias* is an inaudible high frequency signal added to the music during recording. Different makes of tape may need slightly different amounts of bias to give optimum treble frequency response. If you want the best sound it's worth experimenting with different tapes. Alternatively, some hi-fi cassette decks have a variable bias control which you can adjust by trial and error until you get the best results with the tape you're using.

4 Too much level going on to the tape can cause distortion. Cheaper decks usually adjust the recording level automatically; hi-fi decks let you adjust the level manually and have recording level indicators. Keep the peak levels – those reached by the loudest passages of music – as high as possible without getting distortion. If levels are too low the recording will sound hissy when it's played back.

5 If your recording level is adjusted automatically and tapes sound hissy, try using chrome tape (assuming that your recorder will accept it) as hiss levels are usually inherently lower.

Regular cleaning of the tape heads and adjacent parts is essential for good-quality sound. This is always the first thing to try if you're getting woolly treble reproduction, speed variation or damaged tapes

THINGS YOU NEED

- **Cotton buds *or***
- **Mechanical head cleaner**
- **Cleaning fluid (isopropyl alcohol)**

If cleaning the tape path doesn't improve matters or you are experiencing jammed tapes, then the tape head or rubber guide roller is probably worn out or misaligned. These can be replaced if spare parts are available.

RECORD PLAYER

A turntable is easier to adjust and repair than complex electronic hi-fi components

THINGS YOU NEED

- **Small soft brush**
- **Cleaning fluid (isopropyl alcohol)**
- **Record cleaning products**
- **Small mirror**
- **Very small screwdriver**
- **Fine-nosed pliers**
- **Replacement parts as required**

1 If sound quality is poor from new, the alignment of the pick-up cartridge in the arm, or the downward tracking force on the stylus, may be at fault. Check that the stylus appears vertical viewed from the front (placing the stylus on a mirror helps with this). The tracking force (in grams) is recommended by the cartridge manufacturer; many record players have a calibrated dial for setting this.

2 Deterioration over a period may be due to stylus damage, wear or accumulated dust and dirt. The stylus can be cleaned with a small soft brush and proprietary cleaning fluid or isopropyl alcohol, wiping from the back to the front.

3 If your records are very dusty, use a low-priced combined velvet pad and brush. An antistatic spray will help to prevent static build-up which attracts dust.

CHANGING THE STYLUS

Make sure you get the correct type – the brand name and reference number are usually printed on the body of the cartridge. The brand name will not necessarily match that on the rest of the player. If it's an older type of stylus you may need to order it through a retailer. In some cases the stylus is push-fitted – note how the old one goes on before removing it. Sometimes a small screw has to be removed. A small mirror can help you see what you're doing.

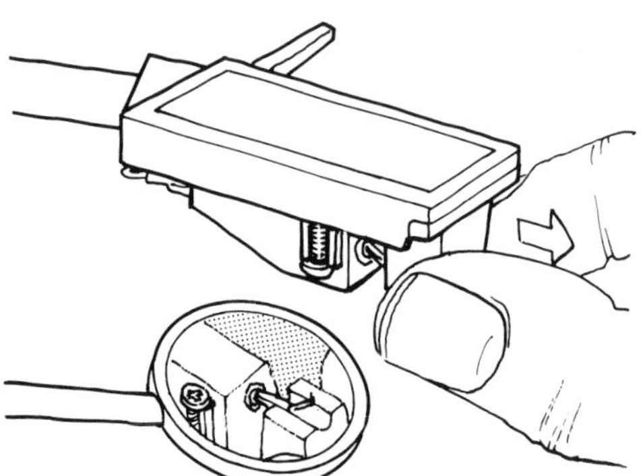

CARTRIDGE

1 Sometimes the fine wires connected to the rear of the pick-up cartridge come adrift or break off, causing hum or loss of sound on one channel. Check these – if push-on tags are loose, they can be tightened by pulling them off and squeezing them gently with fine pliers before replacing them.

2 If the cartridge is faulty you may get distorted sound or no sound on one or both channels; it's usually possible to buy a replacement cartridge from a hi-fi or components shop, but there are so many different shapes and sizes that you will probably need specific advice.

3 The wires connected to a cartridge usually have a standard colour code: red for the right signal, green for right 'earth', white for the left signal, blue for left 'earth'.

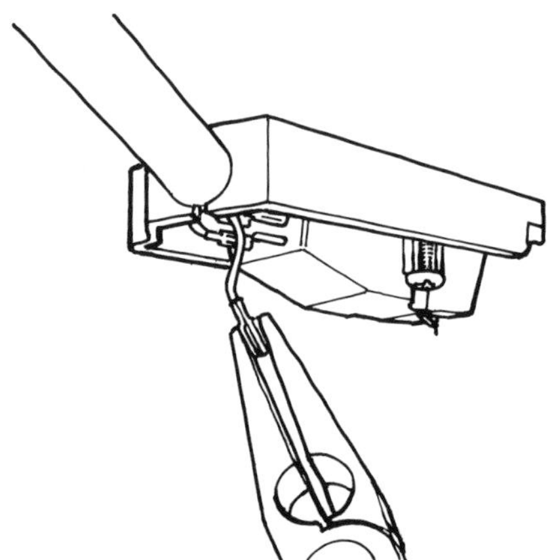

Improving the fit of push-on tags

OTHER HI-FI PROBLEMS

1 A continuous hum or buzz may be an internal fault but is more likely to be due to a faulty interconnecting lead. If the woven wire screening of an audio lead isn't correctly connected to a plug, hum may result. Check also that all plugs are pushed fully home in their sockets – but switch off first.

2 If hum occurs only when using the record player on a separates system, it is probably because the separate single earth wire is not connected to the terminal provided on the amplifier. Alternatively, the fragile wires connected to the cartridge at the end of the pick-up arm may have broken or fallen off. The push-on connecting tags can be resoldered if the wire connected to them has broken, but pull the tag off the cartridge first or the heat from the iron may damage the cartridge. Hum can also be caused on record and cassette players by the amplifier's power transformer – try spacing the units further apart.

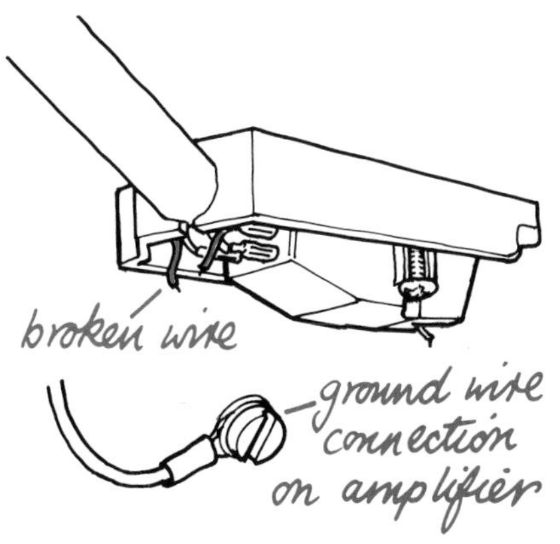

3 Complete failure calls for the usual checking processes that apply to any item – mains plug, fuse – but check all the connections too. It's not uncommon for problems in stereos to occur on one channel only. This makes it relatively easy to locate the fault by swapping over a set of connections left to right and right to left and seeing whether the fault moves to the other channel. For example, if the problem stays on the same side when you swap the speaker connections over, then one speaker is not working. If the record player is sending a signal on only one channel, it may be a connection problem or the cartridge may be faulty. Switch off before changing the connections – this is not just for safety reasons but to avoid damaging the equipment.

4 If one sound source shows a fault, try borrowing another unit to plug into its amplifier input to check the amplifier. You can try cassette decks and radio tuners in each other's inputs, but don't do this with record decks or CD players as the signal levels are different.

5 Some loudspeakers have fuses fitted which are supposed to blow if you play the system so loudly that the speakers might be damaged. Some amplifiers have fuses to protect them against similar overload or the loudspeaker wires being short-circuited accidentally. If a fuse blows, you'll get no sound on the channel affected – you can check this by the swap-over technique described above. After checking for obvious faults, replace the fuse with exactly the correct type as described in the instructions. For an amplifier fuse, do this once only; if it blows again immediately, get the amplifier serviced.

TELEPHONE

Advancing technology and the fact that equipment can be bought as well as rented has revolutionised the domestic phone

EXTENSION SOCKETS

Once you have a master socket, you can easily add an extension to another part of the house

THINGS YOU NEED

- **Extension kit or individual items:**
  adaptor
  telephone cable (special four-core type)
  fixing clips
  extension socket
- **Screwdriver**
- **IPC tool (see text)**

1 The easiest way to add a socket is to buy one of the kits available from telephone shops. These plug into the master socket and contain an adaptor so that the original socket facility is still available for use; a length of cable; clips to fix the cable to wall or skirting board; and the extension socket itself. If the cable in the kit isn't long enough for your purposes you can buy the individual items and as much cable as you require separately.

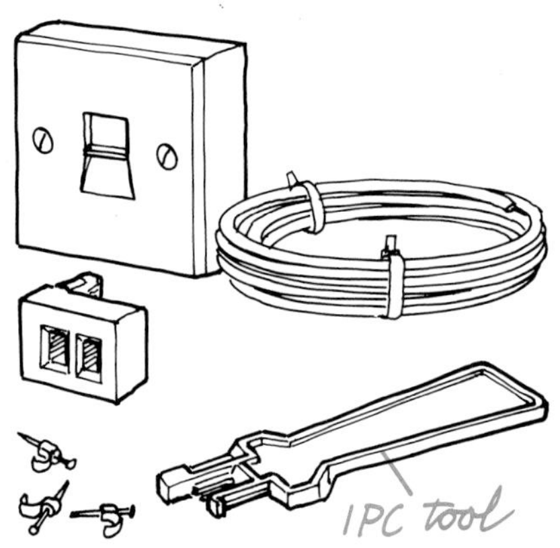

Telephone extension kit comprising adaptor, extension lead, telephone cable, fixing clips, extension socket (different from a master socket) and IPC tool

2 Telephone sockets and junction boxes have insulation piercing contacts (IPCs). As their name implies, they cut through the insulation on the slim cores in telephone cable and make electrical contact as the cores are pressed into the terminals with the IPC tool. The cores are colour-coded and are always connected to the terminals in the order shown; some cables contain six cores, others just four (omitting the two green-and-white cores 1 and 6 which are not used domestically).

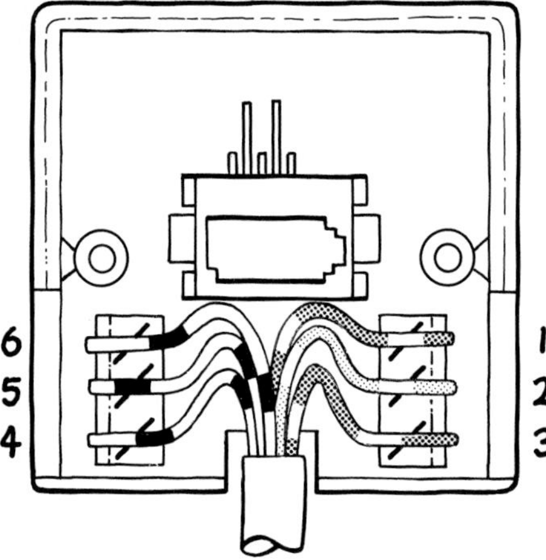

1 = green with white ring
2 = blue with white ring
3 = orange with white ring
4 = white with orange ring
5 = white with blue ring
6 = white with green ring

LEGAL REQUIREMENTS

You're allowed to wire in and use whatever telephone equipment you choose provided that:

1 Your telephone service provider has installed a master socket (where its phone line ends inside your premises) of the type shown.

2 The equipment carries the green circle symbol indicating that it has been approved by BABT. A small amount of telephone equipment and accessories can be sold legally but not used. These often carry a red 'prohibited' triangle. In theory, BT could detect that you were using prohibited equipment and take action against you.

3 If you are wiring up several extension sockets in series, connect the outgoing cable cores inside each socket on top of the incoming cable cores, following the same colour order. Do the same inside junction boxes too.

4 You can of course use a similar kit to run a further extension from the first one. However, although you can have as many sockets as you like, the number of phones in use at one time is limited. Any phone you buy has a REN number marked on it (usually 1 or 1.5). This indicates how much power it needs from the telephone line to make it ring. If the RENs of all the phones in the house add up to more than four, you're likely to find that some or all of the phones won't ring. If you need to increase your REN allocation above 4, you can buy a mains-powered REN extender box. Most cordless phones have a REN number that is much less than 1 (despite what they may claim). You can safely increase your number of phones by using these.

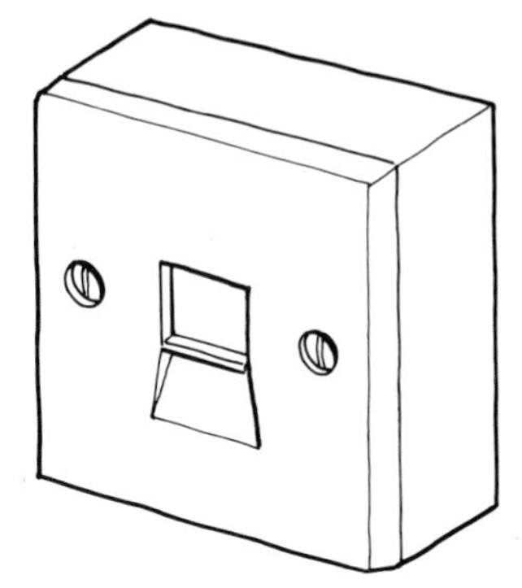

MASTER SOCKET
You have to pay for BT or another telephone company to fit this. If you've got an old-fashioned telephone you'll have to replace it with one with a plug to fit the socket. You can rent a phone from BT, but these days it's cheaper to buy one.

5 If you find that a particular length of cable isn't long enough for the extension you're planning, you can buy a special junction box. This can also be used if you want a T-junction in the extension wiring at some point.

6 As a simple alternative you can buy portable extension leads in various lengths for temporarily using the phone in different rooms.

OTHER EQUIPMENT

If you simply can't hear the phone all over the house, you can buy an extra ringer which will plug into any extension point. But in this case a cordless phone which will ring anywhere in the house or garden may be a better bet.

If young children are likely to unplug the phone without you realising, you can buy a locking plate which screws in place to prevent this. You can also get a plug-in device which can be used to prevent all outgoing calls except 999 calls, or only calls in certain categories (such as international calls or premium rate 0898, 0836 and 0860 calls). For a small rental fee BT can supply a 'call line identification' service. This is a small box which stores and displays the numbers of everyone who has recently dialled you, and will display the number of a caller when the phone is ringing. This is a useful deterrent against nuisance callers.

FEATURES

Modern telephones come equipped with a bewildering variety of features. Some of the most useful to look out for are single button memories for your regular numbers, a last number redial button, a display to show the number you have dialled and the length of the call time, and a loudspeaking 'hands free' option.

ANSWERING MACHINES

In most cases all you need is a mains supply socket close to the phone socket

THINGS YOU NEED

- **Dual socket adaptor**

If you don't have an answering machine, 'Call Minder' services can store your messages digitally at the exchange for a rental fee. These can record a caller's message while you are using the phone, but can't indicate whether calls are waiting and may be difficult to use with a fax machine.

1 In some cases the answering machine plugs into the BT socket and your phone plugs into a socket on the back of the answering machine. In other cases, a dual socket adaptor is used (this is usually supplied) so both items can be plugged into the wall socket.

2 Many answering machines automatically cut the outgoing message if you pick up an extension phone after the machine has answered. This may apply only if the phone is plugged into the machine itself.

3 As with any cassette equipment, cleaning the tape heads occasionally (see page 143) is a good idea. If the machine is heavily used you'll need to replace the tapes every so often as well. Older machines use standard audio cassettes. It is best to avoid C120 tapes when replacing these as they are fragile. More recent models use a single microcassette: replacements can be bought from phone or office equipment shops.

4 The latest answering machines do not use tape but store the messages digitally. They are more reliable and work much quicker than single tape machines so the caller is not kept waiting for the 'beep'. The disadvantage is that total message capacity is limited if you get a lot of calls.

FAX MACHINES

A fax lets you receive and send written information, drawings or photographs down a telephone line for the same cost as a phone call

1 Most low-priced models print on special heat-sensitive paper – make sure you get the right type for your machine. More expensive machines use plain paper, which does not deteriorate so quickly. You can copy documents using a fax machine, but the results are not as effective as those you achieve with a photocopier.

2 You probably have only one phone line at home: if you simply plug the fax machine into the master socket or an adaptor, you won't be able to use the fax and the phone at the same time. Heavy fax users should rent another line for the fax; charges depend on whether the extra line is for residential or business use.

3 Light users could get the sender to phone first. Fax machines can be set to manual answer – when the phone rings, you lift the handset and if you hear the fax tone, press a button on the fax machine to receive the fax.

4 Alternatively, you can buy a phone/fax switch which plugs into the BT socket: both your fax machine and phone (or answering machine) plug into the switch. Most modern fax machines have a fax switch built-in (some include a phone and answering machine as well). When another fax machine calls, the switch directs the call to your fax machine; if there's no fax signal the call is directed to your phone. But you still can't use both phone and fax at the same time. If you're buying a fax switch, try to get one which simulates the normal ringing tone when it answers, otherwise your callers, hearing the ringing tone stop, may hang up before you answer.

5 A fax machine has a REN number like a phone – if the RENs on all your phone equipment add up to more than four then not all the phones may ring.

6 If you use an answering machine together with a fax machine, the answering machine could answer first and try to record the fax. To solve this ensure that the answering machine is plugged into the socket in the fax machine and not connected via a dual socket adaptor, or buy a fax machine with an inbuilt answering machine.

THINGS YOU NEED

- **Phone/fax switch *or***
- **Second phone line**

To test your fax for year 2000 compliance, follow the instructions given for videos on page 137.

CORDLESS PHONES

1 You plug the main unit – the base station – into the phone socket and an adjacent mains socket. More recent cordless phones have standard batteries fitted to the base station so that it will still work during a power failure. But it's probably best to have an ordinary phone as a standby.

2 Older cordless phones were prone to interference from nearby radio stations, and it was common for neighbouring phones to interfere or conversations to be heard on portable radio. In 1998 two new frequency bands were allocated to improve performance. Eight VHF channels are allocated for analogue phones, which don't need the long wire aerials required by original versions. They can search for a 'free' channel and offer greater security. A new compact generation of digital cordless phones known as DECT have advanced features but cost more. The range of all cordless phones should cover all the rooms in a typical house and extend into the garden.

3 With most cordless phones you can press a button on the base station to page the person who has the handset with a bleep; in some cases the reverse as well. Some have a full intercom facility which allows conversation between the base station and the handset.

4 When the handset is away from the base station it uses its rechargeable battery for power. This is recharged when the handset is returned to the base. Talking uses the battery up quickest. Rechargeable batteries run down even if not used, so you should charge the handset every few days, or leave it on charge at night.

5 If you break off the aerial from your handset, replacements are available quite cheaply from component specialists. But don't try this unless you're confident that you can dismantle and reassemble the handset satisfactorily. More recent designs use short flexible aerials which don't break.

A cordless phone can save you from installing extensions all over the house, and can be used in the garden too

It's best to unplug a cordless phone from the telephone socket and the mains supply if there are thunderstorms about, as some cordless phones can be damaged by high voltage surges from lightning.

This section gives you some ideas on how to upgrade your PC

ADDING INTERNAL DEVICES

Whenever you are connecting anything new to your PC, make sure that it is switched off and unplugged from the mains. To gain access to the inside of your PC, simply unscrew and remove the outer casing. Most IBM-compatible PCs are constructed from standard components, making it possible to modify your system easily

All add-on devices come with the appropriate 'driver' software which has to be installed. If you're using Windows 95 or 98, many of these devices are 'plug and play' – meaning that the computer recognises them as a new device and prompts you for the installation. For the most popular devices Windows may even find the appropriate drives already installed in the driver library.

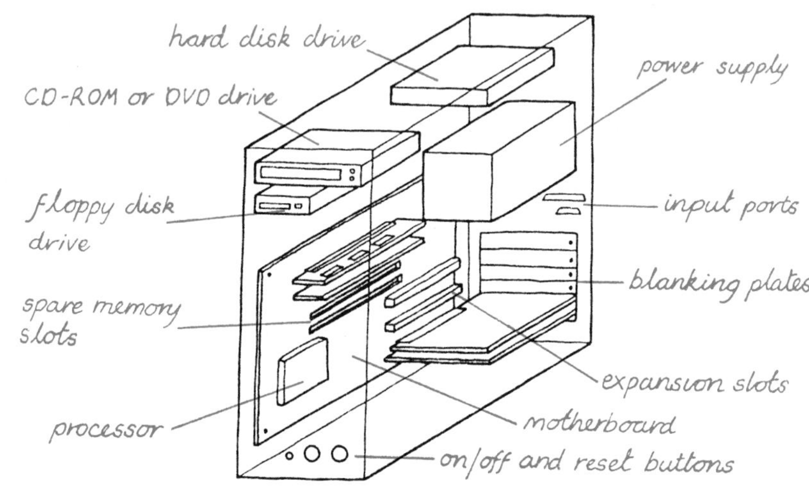

Inside a tower processor. You will find the same components inside differently shaped processor units

UPGRADING YOUR HARD DISK DRIVE

If you have installed a lot of programs you may be running out of hard disk space. The best solution is to add a second 'slave' hard drive (it's tricky to replace the main drive).You can buy these with several gigabytes (Gb) capacity, but if you are running early versions of Windows you may need a disk partitioning program to divide the disk into smaller sections.

1 Set a jumper (a small link) on the new drive to designate it as a slave. Inside the PC should be two spare connectors, a small plug to provide power to the drive and a wider multipin plug for the data. If there are no spare connectors, you can buy adaptor leads.

2 If your PC runs Windows 95 it should detect the new drive automatically. If not, you must access its BIOS (Basic Input Output System) – settings which appear on a series of screens when you turn on the PC – to get it to detect the new drive automatically.

ADDING MORE MEMORY

Increasing the amount of RAM (random access memory) is usually the most effective and cheapest way of increasing your PC's performance, particularly if you have upgraded Windows, run multiple or complex graphic applications or use the Internet.

1 The motherboard should have two spare slots alongside the existing memory. The new memory must match the existing memory – check the manual before buying. On older computers memory is usually installed in pairs, so to increase your PC from 16Mb to 32Mb you need two 8Mb cards.

2 Take care when plugging in the new memory. Most types require you to angle the card slightly when putting it in the slot, then to rock it upright until it clicks into place.

3 To confirm that it has worked, watch the memory check counter during the boot sequence when you turn on the PC.

ADDING EXPANSION CARDS

You can add internal cards into slots provided at the rear of the motherboard (there are two sorts of slot: the older, larger ISA type or the newer PCI type). Options include a TV/radio tuner, an internal modem, graphics upgrades such as a '3D' card for games, sound cards and many more specialist applications.

INSTALLING A CD-ROM OR DVD DRIVE

A wide selection of multimedia software is available on CD-ROM including games and encyclopaedias. You add a CD-ROM drive rather as you would a hard disk drive (see above), using the PC's spare internal power supply plug. The CD-ROM multiway data cable normally connects to the 'secondary' drive connector on your motherboard. You may need to run and install 'driver' software to get the system to recognise the drive – unless you're running Windows 95 and the CD-ROM is plug and play-compatible. Most new CD-ROM software requires a high-speed drive: aim for 4x speed minimum. The new generation of Digital Video Disk (DVD) drives also play standard CD-ROMs and are installed the same way.

This chapter is not intended to give detailed instructions. For these, consult your manuals or other information supplied. *The Which? Guide to Computers* explains how computers work in greater detail.

ADDING EXTERNAL DEVICES

ADDING A PRINTER

The best choice of printer for normal home use is a colour 'inkjet' printer; if you only expect to print out word-processed documents then a mono printer should suffice.

1 First, plug the printer into the parallel (LPTl) port at the rear of your PC.

2 Next, install the correct software driver. This will be supplied on a disk with the printer, or may be in the Windows 95 'install new hardware' driver library.

Many external devices such as printers and modems are available second-hand. This can be a good way to buy add-ons if you do not require complex or high-speed performance

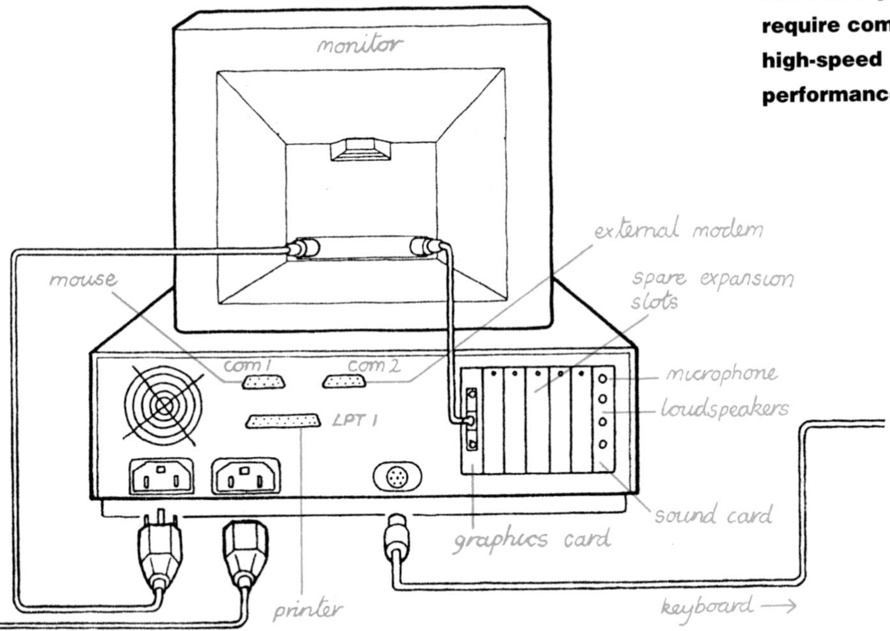

ADDING A MODEM

A modem lets you connect to the Internet, and send and receive electronic mail (email). External modems are usually the most versatile and convenient to use. V90 modems give the highest-speed Internet connection – pages appear more quickly so your phone bill will be lower. If you mainly want an Internet connection for email, you should be able to get by with a slower modem.

1 Plug the modem into the spare serial (COM) port at the rear of your computer (usually COM2 – your mouse uses COM1), then into your telephone socket and the mains adaptor. You must then install the driver software.

2 To get connected to the Internet and email you must subscribe to an Internet Service Provider, a large number of which operate in the UK. Suitable 'registration' software is readily available from such companies and is often given away with computer magazines. This software will install all the necessary applications.

CONNECTING A SCANNER

Scanners let you enter printed pictures or text pages into your computer for editing, incorporation into documents and printing. Most connect to the computer through the printer port: the printer then connects to the back of the scanner (faster 'SCSI' models may be supplied with a card that you install inside the PC). Once the scanner is connected you must install the software driver provided. Often, other useful software applications are supplied to help you edit photos or graphics: for example, 'optical character recognition' (OCR) converts scanned-in text so that it can be edited by a word processor.

OTHER ITEMS

- Zip and Jaz drives provide portable disk storage with capacities of 100Mb and 1Gb respectively – much larger than conventional floppy disks. They can be connected externally or internally.
- If you connect a digital camera to your computer you can download images.
- Joysticks provide better control with games and are usually connected through a sound card. Expensive versions provide some tactile feedback to the controls.
- You can connect a microphone to your sound card and digitally record voice commands, use speech recognition software or even talk to friends over the Internet.

THE MILLENNIUM BUG

Modern computers, including home computers, have a real-time clock inside which keeps track of the time and date. In a PC these clocks identify the year by the last two digits only so the computer identifies 1989 by the number 89. The problem occurs on the year 2000. Will your PC realise that it is the year 2000 or will it think it is 1900? If the latter it could get the days of the week mixed up. To further complicate things, some computers and software that correctly identify the year 2000 may then fail to realise that it is a leap year. If you are running any 'date sensitive' software programs - e.g. accounting software - the bug could cause you serious trouble.

- The more recent PCs running Windows 95 should be bug-free (but note that software is not guaranteed).
- Earlier computers which do not 'roll over' from 1999 to 2000 can be 'forced' into 2000 by entering the date manually in DOS. This need be done once only. A small number of PCs will not be correctable.
- Apple Mac computers should not have a problem because their operating system was designed to cope (though some software written for Macs may not be compliant).
- Although it may be possible for you to 'fix' your computer yourself, there may be side effects. For this reason it is best to use a purpose-designed Y2K software program to check your computer.
- The most versatile of these will interrogate the various clocks inside the computer, install a correction program if necessary and also check any software packages you have installed, reporting back on any problems.
- If a software package has a problem you can often obtain an upgrade via the Internet.

DIY AND GARDEN

TOOLS

- HAND TOOLS
- POWER TOOLS
- GARDEN TOOLS
- LAWNMOWERS

FIXING YOUR

HAND TOOLS

It doesn't take long to amass dozens of different hand tools. Many will last a lifetime with the minimum of care

CHISELS AND PLANES

Sharp-bladed tools such as wood chisels need regular maintenance to keep them in good working order

THINGS YOU NEED

- **Combination oilstone**
- **Light machine oil**
- **Honing guide**

  or
- **Bench grinder**

1 Chisels and most plane irons have two angled faces (bevels) at the cutting end. The steeper honed bevel forming the cutting edge is at about 30° to the blade, and the shallower ground bevel is at about 25° to it. To sharpen the cutting edge, the blade is held at 30° to the surface of an abrasive material – an oilstone or a grinding wheel. The ground bevel is gradually worn away by repeated sharpening, and a new ground bevel must eventually be formed.

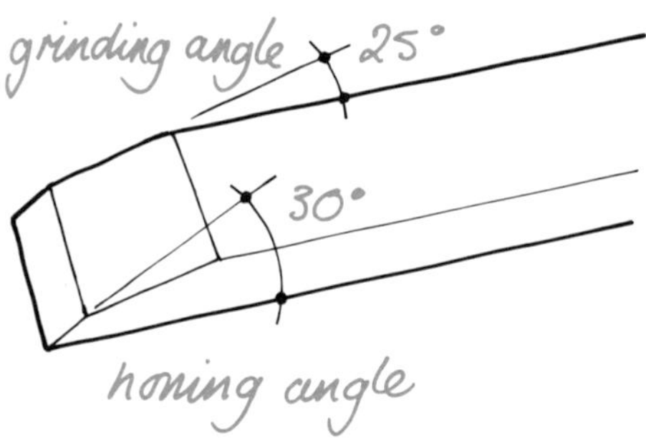

2 Put a little oil on the oilstone, and hold the blade or iron flat side down on the stone. Rub it up and down a few times to remove any high spots and to spread the oil evenly over the stone.

3 Clamp the blade or iron in a proprietary honing guide, which ensures that you sharpen the blade at the correct angle; it is difficult to maintain this otherwise. Rollers on the guide allow you to drive the blade backwards and forwards, producing a perfectly straight and square honed bevel.

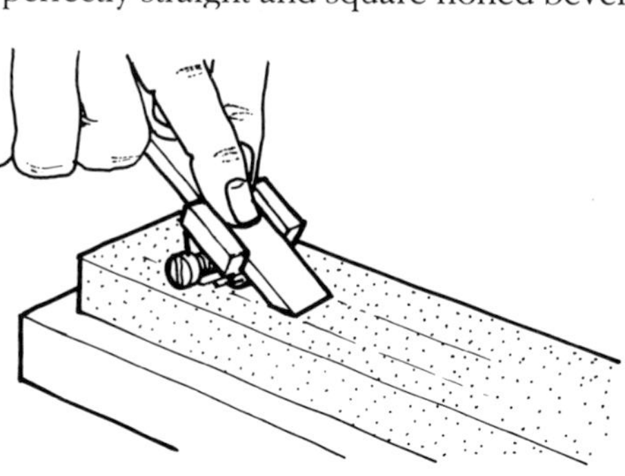

4 The honing process produces a thin burr of metal which curves over on to the flat back surface of the blade. When you can feel this with a finger, turn the tool over and rub its flat face lightly on the stone; this turns the burr over the other way. Continue honing lightly on both faces until it breaks away. The blade is now ready for use.

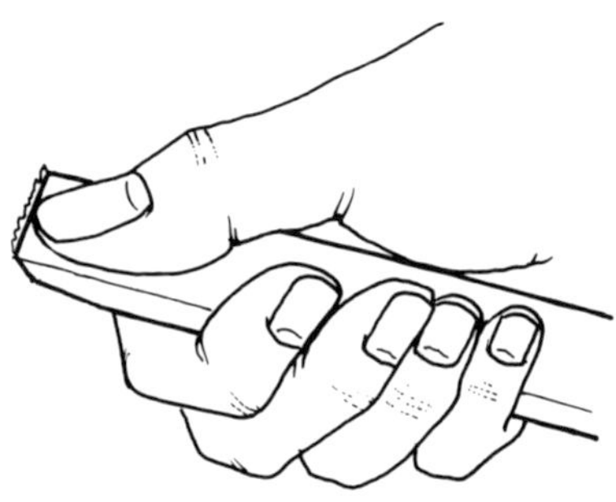

5 If you are using a bench grinder to sharpen chisels and plane irons, *always* wear safety goggles and use the machine's safety guard to prevent sparks from flying into your eyes. The wheel should revolve towards you (into the tool's edge), and you should hold the blade against the tool rest so you keep the honing angle correct. Press it lightly against the edge of the wheel (never the face), and remove it every few seconds so it can cool off. With plane irons, move the cutting edge from side to side against the wheel to sharpen it evenly.

OTHER TOOLS

● Most modern panel and tenon saws have hardened teeth which cannot be sharpened in the traditional way. Keep the blade clean and free of rust, and always fit the blade guard when the saw is being stored. Replace the saw when the teeth become blunt.

● You can sharpen twist drill bits with a proprietary powered drill sharpener. Simply switch the sharpener on and insert the drill, which will have its cutting tip automatically reground to the correct angle.

● Sharpen flat wood bits with a fine file or a slipstone. Clamp the bit in a vice, point upwards, and lightly abrade each side of both the spear point and the shoulders of the bit, keeping to the existing cutting bevels.

● If the tip of a straight-tip screwdriver wears to a slight curve or becomes chipped through unorthodox use, grind it back to a straight edge using a bench grinder. Take care not to overheat the blade or you may weaken it.

HAMMER HANDLE

1 Check that wooden handles on hammers are sound and secure. If not, buy a replacement handle. Clamp the hammer head in a vice, drill several holes in the top of the old handle and pull it out with pliers. If it won't budge, hammer the handle out using a punch.

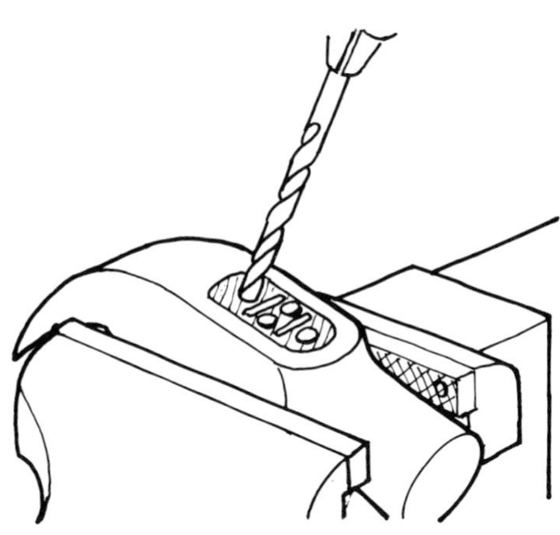

2 Cut two slots in the new hammer handle to take the wedges, then drive the head on. Saw off excess wood, and hammer in the two wedges to lock the head to the handle.

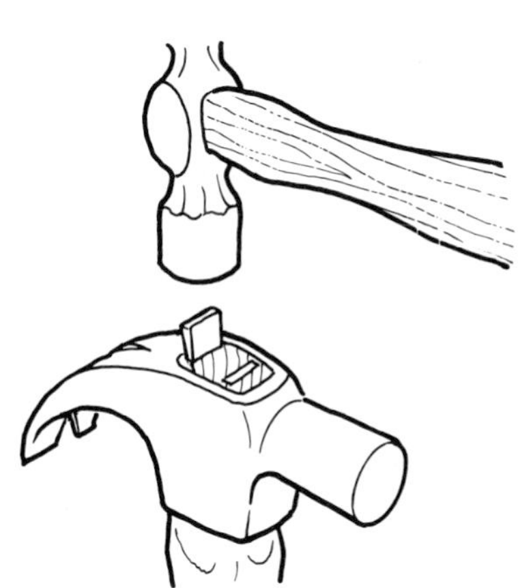

Drill bits need to be sharp to be effective; other tools can have their life prolonged by simple repairs

THINGS YOU NEED

- **Fine file or slipstone**
- **Drill sharpener**
- **Woodworker's vice**
- **Bench grinder**

For hammer:

- **New hammer handle**
- **Hammer wedges**
- **Power drill and bits**
- **Tenon saw**
- **Spare hammer**
- **Pliers or punch**

POWER TOOLS

Modern power tools are extremely durable and reliable if used properly and with care

COMMON FAULTS

The wear and tear of regular use can lead to faulty connections, but these are easy to track down. Worn brushes are another common and quickly cured problem

THINGS YOU NEED

- **Screwdrivers**
- **Hexagon (Allen) keys**
- **Continuity tester**
- **Replacement plug and flex**
- **Replacement carbon brushes**
- **Other parts as required**
- **Gearbox grease**

NOT WORKING/CUTTING OUT

1 Unplug the power tool from the mains and check that the flex is properly connected within the plug. Remake loose connections as necessary and ensure that the flex sheathing is secure in the cord grip. Test the fuse.

2 Open the tool casing to reveal the main terminal block, and check that the flex connections are sound and that the flex is securely held by its grommet. Remake loose connections as necessary.

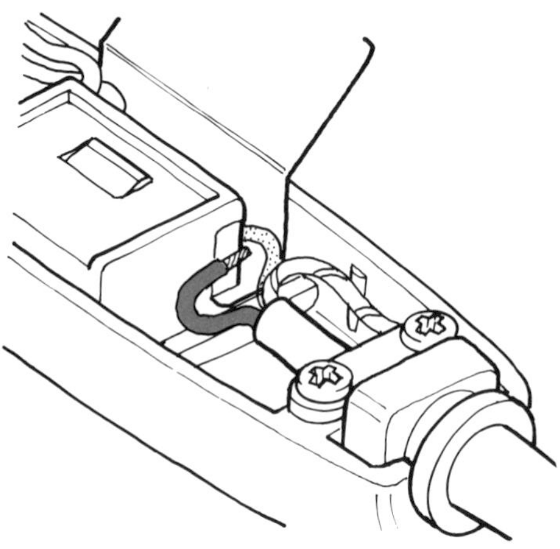

3 Check the condition of the flex. If it is visibly chafed, cut or burnt, replace it. If it appears intact, use a continuity tester (see page 32) to check the integrity of each flex core, again replacing the whole flex if one is broken.

4 Use your continuity tester to check the tool's switch, touching the probes to the switch terminals with the switch in the 'on' position. Replace the switch if it proves to be faulty.

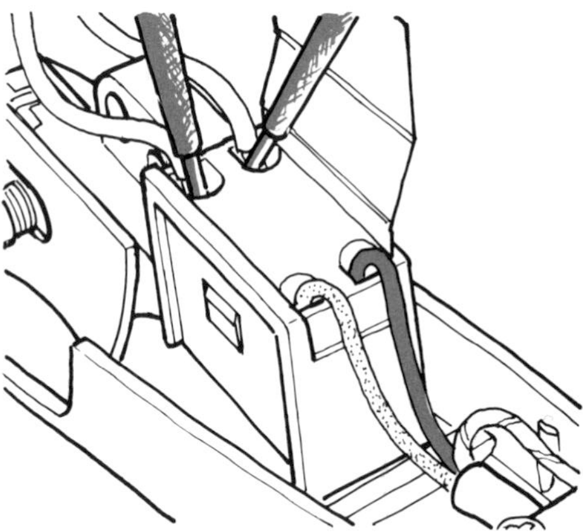

5 Check for continuity between the switch and the motor terminals, and remake loose connections or replace cores as required.

6 If all is well up to this point, the fault lies within the motor itself, or in an electronic speed control unit on variable-speed tools. If a thermal overload cut-out or overheat fail-safe device is fitted, check it for continuity and reset or replace it as required. Lastly, with cordless tools, check that batteries are recharging properly. See pages 42-5 for information on repairing motors, pages 48-9 for thermal cut-outs and pages 50-1 for switches and other controls. Alternatively, return the tool to the manufacturer's service agent for repair.

SLOW/NOISY MOTOR

1 Check for wear and free movement of carbon brushes. Replace brushes and springs if necessary and clean the brush slides with a cotton wool bud. Before reassembling the tool, clean the motor and the inside of the casing to remove dust, grease, wood shavings and the like. See pages 42-5 for more details.

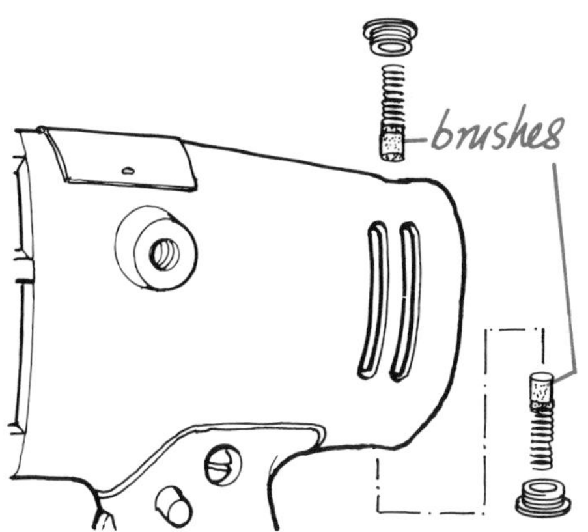

2 If the tool still doesn't work properly, other motor components may be at fault: either replace them or fit a new motor if individual parts are not available.

3 Inspect the gearbox for signs of wear or lack of lubrication. Lubricate and renew parts as appropriate.

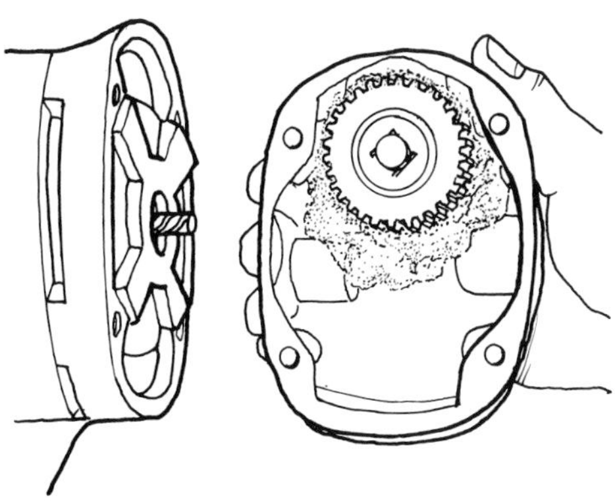

4 On cordless tools, check that batteries are recharging properly, and replace old battery packs if necessary.

OVERHEATING

1 Make sure that air vents are not obstructed; change the way you hold the tool or clean the blocked vents as appropriate.

2 Check whether the motor brushes are sparking excessively, and replace them as necessary. Lastly, check whether the commutator or armature has short-circuited as a result of overwork, and replace the component or the whole motor if they have.

FIXING YOUR

GARDEN TOOLS

As with d-i-y hand tools, many garden tools will give years of trouble-free service if they are well treated

HAND TOOLS

Wooden handles and cutting blades are the two components that may need occasional attention

THINGS YOU NEED

- **Replacement tool handle**
- **Hammer or mallet**
- **Power drill and bits**
- **Screwdriver**
- **Round-headed wood screws**
- **Chisel, plane or Surform**
- **Woodworking adhesive**
- **Fine file**

WOODEN HANDLES

The wooden handles on many garden tools are prone to two sorts of failure: splitting or breakage as a result of excessive leverage being applied, and pulling out of the tool head. Both are simple to put right.

1 If a handle breaks, remove any nails, screws or rivets holding the stump in the socket of the tool head, and pull the two apart. Drill the heads off rivets and rust-bound screws. If the stump remains stuck, try driving a long woodscrew into its end, secure the screw in a vice and use a hammer to knock off the tool head.

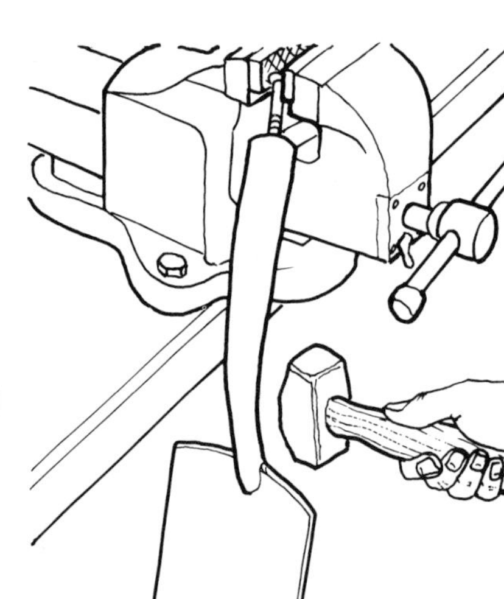

2 Buy a replacement handle, and cut it down to match the length of the original if necessary. Then use a chisel, block plane or Surform to taper the end of the new handle until it is a snug fit in the tool socket.

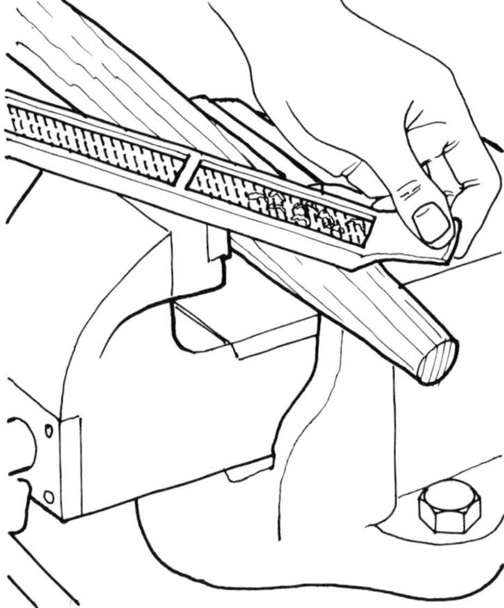

3 Stand the tool up and drive the handle securely home with a hammer or mallet, after checking that it is correctly aligned with the tool head. Then secure the head to the handle by driving a round-headed woodscrew through the hole in the socket.

4 If a handle simply pulls out of its socket, check whether the wood is split round the fixing. If it is, either repair the damage with woodworking adhesive or cut off the damaged end, taper the handle slightly and reattach it as in step 3.

BLADES

1 To keep garden shears in good condition and cutting well, clean and dry them after use and oil the pivot bolt regularly. Tighten it slightly if it appears loose; when properly adjusted, the blades should just open under their own weight. Treat secateurs similarly.

2 Check that the blade tips just cross each other when the shears are closed; if there is a slight gap, grip each blade in turn in a vice and file down the back stops behind the pivot point slightly.

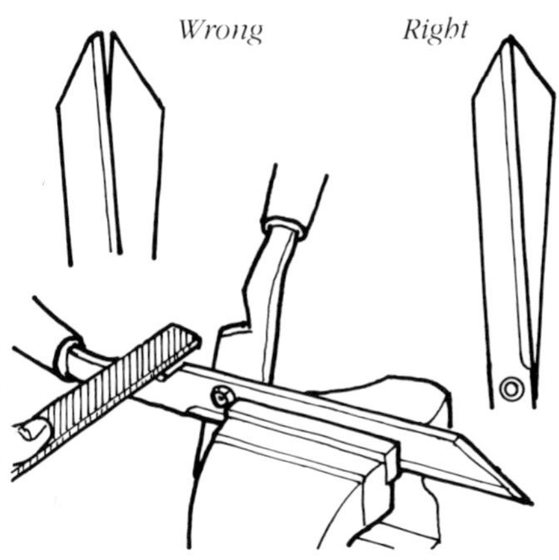

3 Sharpen shear blades with a fine-cut flat file. Grip each blade in turn in a vice and use the file at a shallow angle to the ground cutting bevel. If the blades are nicked or chipped, they will need the bevel regrinding – a job best left to a specialist tool repairer.

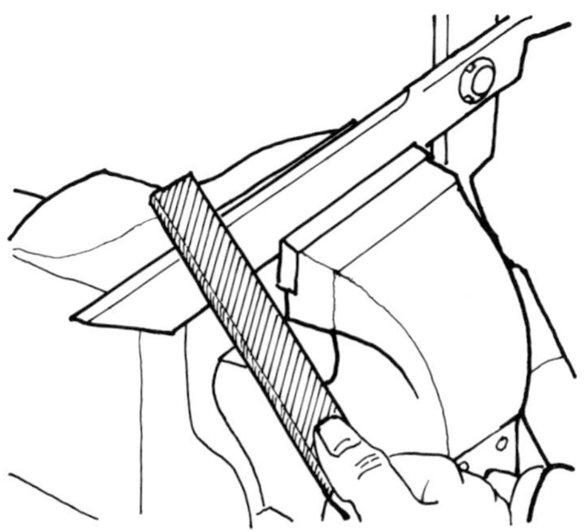

4 Use a file or a bench grinder to restore the cutting edge to tools such as spades and edge trimmers.

5 If the tines on a fork are bent as a result of excess leverage being applied to the handle, grip the crossbar securely in a vice between two scraps of wood. Then force the tine back into position by hand or with a heavy hammer.

TOOL CARE

The best way to ensure a long life for your garden hand tools is to clean and dry them thoroughly after use, and to store them somewhere dry to prevent rust forming on metal components and rot attacking wooden ones. Remove rust as soon as it begins to form using wire wool, and oil any moving parts regularly with light machine oil. Wipe down untreated wooden tool handles with linseed oil from time to time and coat metal surfaces with lubricating oil or a moisture-dispersing aerosol lubricant before putting them into winter storage.

POWER TOOLS

All garden power tools need occasional maintenance to keep them working well

THINGS YOU NEED

- **Strimmer spool and line**
- **Lubricating oil**
- **Screwdrivers**
- **Spanners**
- **Wire brush**
- **Fine file**
- **Replacement saw chain**

1 Look after any garden power tool as you would a d-i-y tool. Keep it clean, handle it with care so you do not crack casings, break handles or strain the flex, and store it in a dry place. Regularly check the condition of all flexes and extension cords; if the latter is on a drum, uncoil it fully before use to prevent the flex from overheating. Make sure that air vents are kept clear of grass cuttings or other debris so motors cannot overheat.

2 If the tool runs intermittently or not at all, overheats, or is sluggish or unduly noisy in use, follow the sequence of checks and maintenance outlined for d-i-y power tools on pages 156-7. Alternatively, return the tool to the manufacturer's service agent for repair.

SAFETY

Whatever type of power tool you are using, always make sure you use a residual current device (RCD) to provide protection against the risk of shock. This is especially vital with any bladed tools such as a hedgetrimmer, which can easily cut through its flex. You can use a plug-in RCD adaptor, or have a socket containing an RCD installed specifically for use with power tools. You need a high-sensitivity type RCD even if your house circuits are protected by a whole-house device.

When using a chainsaw, always wear a helmet with visor and integral ear protectors, safety gloves and stout boots with steel toecaps. Add special safety trousers made with chain-clogging material and protective gaiters if you do a lot of chainsaw work.

STRIMMERS

Strimmers use replaceable nylon line as the cutter, and you will from time to time have to fit a replacement spool of line. This may be mounted on the end of the motor shaft underneath the machine on basic strimmers, or on the handle on so-called command feed models. In either case it is a simple job to release the spool holder and fit the replacement spool. With shaft-mounted spools you may have to open the strimmer casing first, so you can hold the armature still while you unscrew the spool holder. Take this opportunity to clean out the motor casing, check the condition of the motor brushes and apply a little oil to any sleeve bearings.

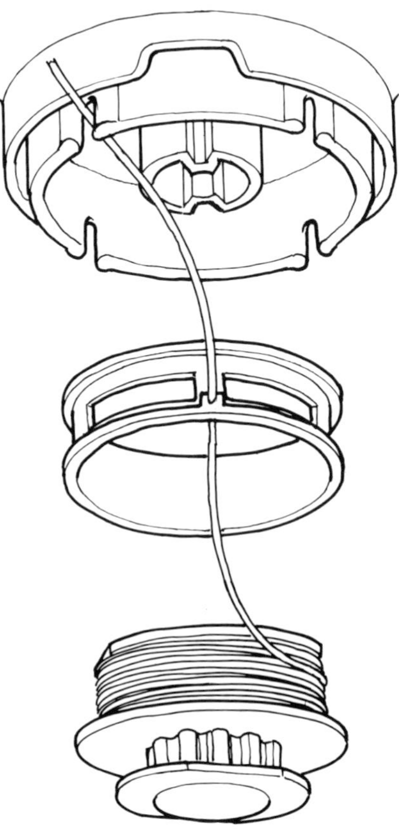

Spool fitting for a basic strimmer

HEDGETRIMMERS

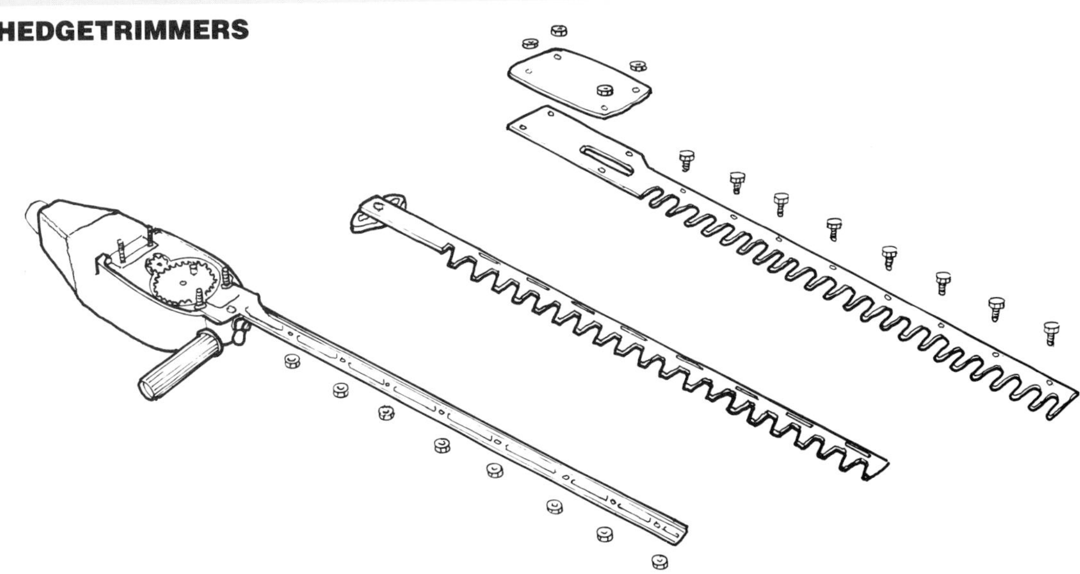

1 Hedgetrimmers need more regular maintenance than most other garden power tools. Wipe the blades clean with an oily rag after every use, and remove any dried-on clippings with a wire brush.

2 If the build-up becomes very heavy or the tool's cutting action becomes impaired, unplug and strip down the machine so you can clean and sharpen the blades individually. Open the casing or remove the cover plate to gain access to the blade mountings. Then undo the blade bolts and lift out the blades (some machines have one fixed and one moving blade, others two moving blades).

3 Clean them thoroughly, then mount them in a vice and use a fine file to sharpen the teeth, following the original sharpening angle as closely as possible. Reassemble the blades, close the casing or refit the cover plate, then line up the bolt holes and replace the blade bolts.

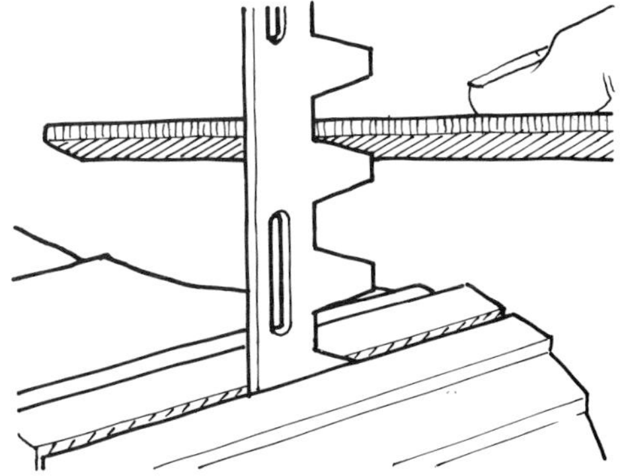

CHAINSAWS

Chainsaws need regular lubrication, and occasional adjustment and replacement of the saw chain. Follow the manufacturer's maintenance instructions carefully when carrying out any work on the tool.

FIXING YOUR

LAWNMOWER

A poorly maintained lawnmower can be a hazard: always make sure yours is safe and dress suitably when you use it

SAFETY AND MAINTENANCE

Regular servicing and maintenance make for better lawnmowing

THINGS YOU NEED

- **Scraper**
- **Lubricating oil**
- **Screwdrivers**
- **Spanners**
- **Replacement rotary blade**
- **Fine file**
- **Straight-edge and hammer**
- **Coarse grinding paste**

There are more different models of lawnmower than almost any other tool, d-i-y or garden, but all fall into two main types – cylinder or rotary – and are powered either by mains electricity or by petrol.

1 *Always* use a residual current device (RCD) with an electric mower (see Safety on page 160 for more details). *Always* wear closed shoes with stout toecaps when using any rotary mower.

2 Clean the blades and remove any grass cuttings that are blocking air vents or are trapped round bearings, drive chains and other rotating parts before putting the mower away after every use. Wipe the blades with an oily rag, and scrape off any compacted deposits of crushed grass and mud from the mower body. Unplug electric mowers from the mains and disconnect the spark plug of petrol-driven mowers before cleaning.

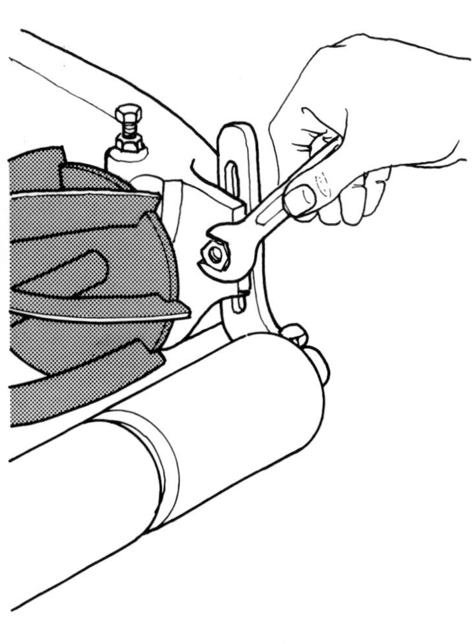

3 Before using your mower, check that all bolts or wingnuts holding the handle to the mower body are tight, and that adjustable wheels or rollers are set level to guarantee an even cut. Lightly oil the adjusting screws from time to time. Make sure that the bottom blade of cylinder mowers is correctly adjusted, and that the blade-retaining nut is secure on rotary motors. Check the flex and plug condition on electric mowers, and on petrol-driven models check the oil and fuel level and make sure the spark plug lead is connected. Lubricate as recommended by the mower manufacturer.

4 If an electric mower runs intermittently or not at all, or is sluggish or unduly noisy in use, follow the sequence of checks and maintenance outlined for d-i-y power tools on pages 156-7. Alternatively, take it to the manufacturer's service agent for servicing or repair.

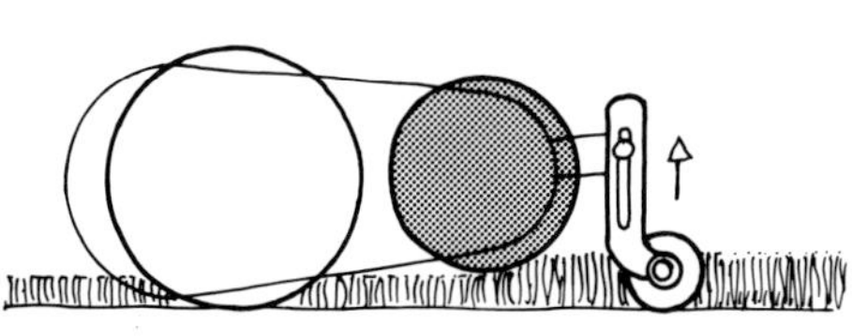

5 If an electric cylinder mower's motor runs normally but the blades do not rotate, suspect a broken drive belt. These are often made of plastic and can break if the cylinder is repeatedly jammed by long grass. Unscrew the casing over the drive wheels, remove the broken belt, fit a new one and replace the casing.

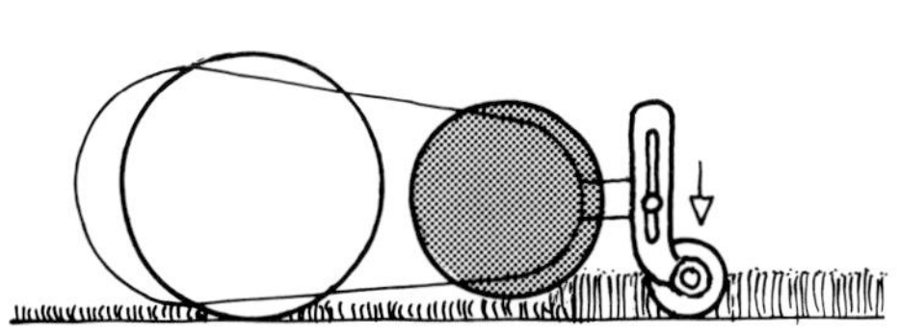

Adjusting the height of the cut of a cylinder mower by altering the roller position

6 Some electric mowers are fitted with a thermal overload cut-out to protect the motor from burning out if the blades are jammed. If yours has one and it trips, allow the machine to cool down and attempt to trace the cause of the problem before resetting the button.

7 Unless you are conversant with petrol engines, leave repairs to the manufacturer's service agent. Modern mower engines are extremely reliable, and if serviced every season should need no further maintenance.

BLADES

THINGS YOU NEED

- **Scraper**
- **Lubricating oil**
- **Screwdrivers**
- **Spanners**
- **Replacement rotary blade**
- **Fine file**
- **Straight-edge and hammer**
- **Coarse grinding paste**

1 Most rotary mowers have a bar blade, usually metal but occasionally plastic. To replace it, first unplug electric mowers and disconnect the spark plug on petrol-driven types. Then up-end the machine, hold one end of the blade to prevent it from rotating and undo the centre bolt with a spanner. Remove the bolt and any spacers after noting which way up the blade is fitted, clean the mounting and grease the bolt. Fit the new blade and the spacers and replace the bolt. Check that it is fully tightened.

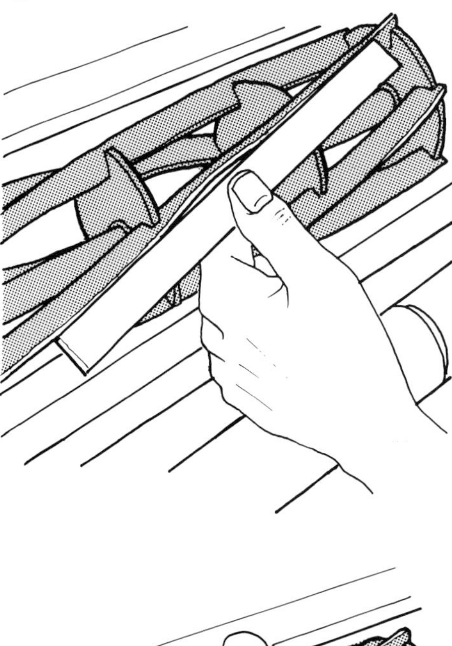

Straightening the blades on a cylinder mower

2 If the blades on a cylinder mower are deformed by hitting a stone, straighten the bent section with some gentle hammer blows. Use a straight-edge to check your progress. File down any nicks that cause the blades to catch once you have straightened them.

3 You can sharpen cylinder blades by grinding them against the bottom blade. Make sure the cylinder is free to rotate by disconnecting the drive belt/chain or removing a gear wheel, and use a brace, ratchet or box spanner on the cylinder gear locking nuts to turn it. Adjust the bottom blade until it just touches the cylinder, then smear some grinding paste on the cutting edge of each blade and rotate the cylinder backwards. Adjust the bottom blade periodically as the grinding continues, to keep it in contact with the cylinder. When each blade has a continuous ground line along its length, wipe off the remaining paste from both sets of blades.

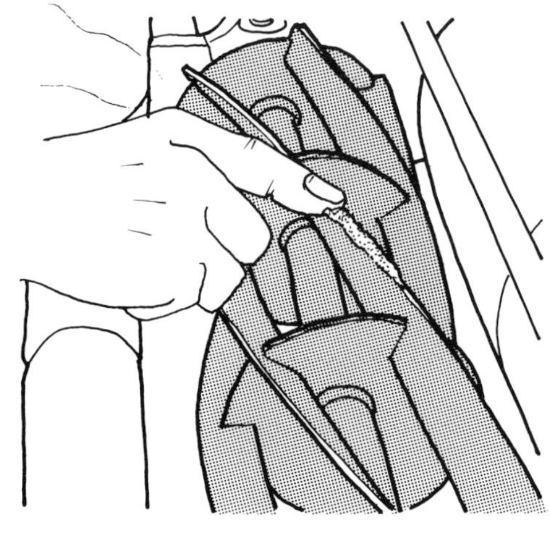

FIXING YOUR BICYCLE

- WHEELS AND TYRES
- BRAKES
- CHAIN AND GEARS
- RIDING POSITION

WHEELS AND TYRES

You don't need to be a master mechanic to look after your bike. Just a few tools can keep you pedalling in comfort and safety

PUNCTURES

If you get a flat tyre while you're out on your bike, don't try to ride home on it: it's not safe and you'll probably wreck the tyre and the wheel rim

THINGS YOU NEED

- **A spanner to fit the wheel nuts**
- **2 or 3 tyre levers**
- **Puncture repair kit: patches, rubber solution, scrap of sandpaper, wax crayon**
- **Talcum powder**

1 First, find where the air's getting out. As well as examining the inner tube, look for obvious external damage to the tyre, or something stuck in it, before you remove the tube. If you pump the tyre up, you may be able to find the leak by listening for escaping air. Dab spit or soapy water on the valve – if it bubbles, it's leaking and needs to be re-tightened or replaced.

2 Loosen the bolts or open the quick-release mechanism holding the wheel in the frame and take out the wheel. Let out any remaining air so that the tyre can be squeezed between the brake blocks. Some brakes have a release lever to make this easier. If it's the back wheel of a bike with derailleur gears, putting it into top gear (the smallest of the cogs) will make it easier to unravel the wheel from the chain.

3 Use the tyre levers to ease the edge of the tyre up and over the rim of the wheel. Take care not to pinch the inner tube. If you don't have any tyre levers, you can improvise with spoon handles. Work one side of the tyre off the rim all round, unscrew the valve retaining collar, push the valve through the hole in the rim and take out the inner tube.

4 If you still don't know where the puncture is, pump in a little air. You may be able to hear or feel the air from the puncture if you feed the tube past your ear. Alternatively, work the tube through a bowl of water: bubbles will mark the puncture. Mark it with the wax crayon and dry off the tube. Check the corresponding position on the tyre, using the valve hole as a point of reference, to make sure that the culprit isn't still stuck in the tyre.

5 Pick out a patch to fit. Use the sandpaper to clean up the area around the puncture and to provide a key for the adhesive. Spread an even coating of rubber solution around the hole, a little larger than the patch. When the rubber solution is dry, remove the backing from the patch and smooth it down, working from the centre outwards to make sure that no air gets trapped under it. Rub talcum powder over the entire inner tube so that no sticky patches remain. Alternatively, use self-adhesive patches.

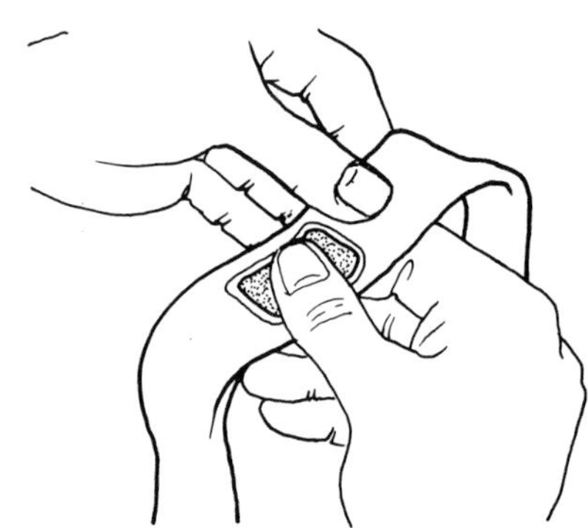

6 To replace the inner tube, first push the valve inside the tyre and out through the hole in the rim. Inflate the tube a little and work it back inside the tyre (don't twist it). Starting at the valve, ease the tyre back over the rim. You will need to push hard to get the last bit of the tyre back on – try soapy water if it's difficult. Take care not to pinch the inner tube against the wheel. Replace the valve retaining collar.

TYRE PRESSURES Keeping tyres inflated to the right pressure makes the bike go faster with less effort and makes the tyre last longer. The recommended pressure is printed on the side of the tyre. You can buy a pressure gauge from a bike shop.

7 Replace the wheel, squeezing the tyre to help it pass between the brake blocks. For back wheels, you must wrap the chain around the sprocket before slotting the axle into the forks. Centre the wheel between the forks, tighten the wheel nuts or quick-release and pump up the tyre.

8 Any quick-release mechanism should be correctly tensioned when replacing the wheel. Older bicycles may not have 'captive' cones; if in doubt, put the wheel in the same way it came out.

9 You may prefer not to repair punctures on the road. Carry a spare inner tube and repair the tube at your leisure. For emergency repairs to small punctures (e.g. those due to thorns) you can use aerosol sealant, but will have to repair the puncture or replace the tube later. A different type of inner tube sealant can be added to the tube in advance, ready to seal a small puncture when it occurs. Also, the inside of the tyre can be lined with a hard plastic strip to give added resistance to sharp objects. However, if you continuously get punctures check that the tyre is not over-inflated but within recommended limits, and investigate the condition of the tyre and inner tube.

RIMS AND SPOKES

The wheel rim is held in place by the spokes, which are pushed through holes in the hub and screwed into the rim. Turn the nipples at the rim with a spoke key to adjust the tension of the spokes. You should be able to set the brakes closer to the rim and to control braking more effectively once the wheels are true.

ADJUSTMENTS

1 Spin the wheel holding a pencil near the rim and observe how much the position of the rim alters in relation to the pencil. A 'true' rim will appear to be stationary. If the wobble exceeds half an inch (1.3cm), you may need a new wheel and will certainly need a bike shop to do the repair.

2 Deflate the tyre; remove it if it looks like a major job (see Punctures). Pluck the spokes: they should all make a similar pinging noise. Turn loose spokes anti-clockwise to even up the tension.

3 You must replace nipples which cannot be turned or which spin uselessly. If there are over four, contact the bike shop. To remove and replace them you must remove the tyre and the tape strip which protects the inner tube from the spokes.

4 Hold the pencil steady at the lip of the rim (where the rim stops and the tyre starts) and spin the wheel. Gradually move the pencil closer until it marks the high spots on the rim as the wheel spins. Tighten the spokes by the marks and loosen those opposite to make the wheel round. Work half to one turn at a time and keep re-checking the wheel.

A wheel that isn't straight is annoying and can be dangerous. Broken spokes must be replaced to keep the wheel in shape

THINGS YOU NEED

- **Pencil or chalk**
- **Spoke key**
- **New spokes and nipples as required**
- **File**
- **Tyre levers**

You may need:

- **Freewheel removing tool**
- **Wheel rim tape**

After repairs to the rim or spokes have been completed, it is best to apply new wheel rim tape before replacing tyre and inner tube as described in Punctures.

5 Spin the wheel with the pencil held at the side of the rim (where the brakes make contact) to mark side-to-side wobbles. Again working half to one turn at a time, but in groups of four to six adjacent spokes, tighten the spokes opposite each mark and loosen those beside it. Re-check until you reach a reasonable compromise.

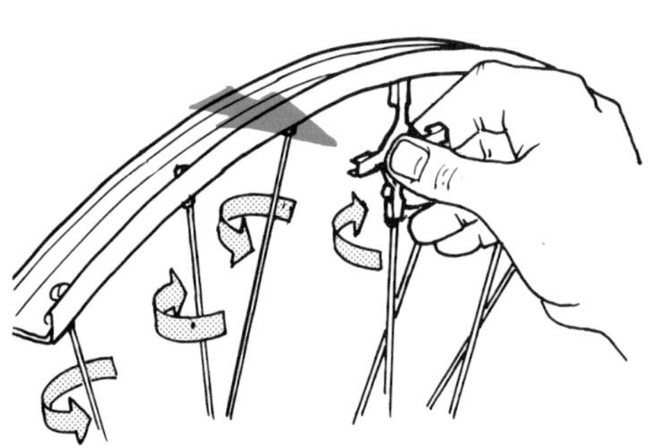

6 File down any heavily tightened spokes protruding on the inside of the rim that could puncture the inner tube.

BROKEN SPOKES

1 Remove the tyre, inner tube and protective rim tape. If the broken spoke is on the cog side of the rear wheel on a bike with derailleur gears, you will also have to remove the freewheel with a special tool in order to gain access to the spoke holes in the hub. The special tool can vary according to different makes of freewheel. Many bike shops will remove the freewheel for you.

2 Remove the broken spoke at both hub and rim end and take it to the bike shop for an exact replacement.

3 Push the new spoke through the hole in the hub so that the head is on the opposite side of the hub from the adjacent ones. On almost all bikes the spokes touch where they cross; weave the new spoke through the old ones copying the pattern used elsewhere on the wheel.

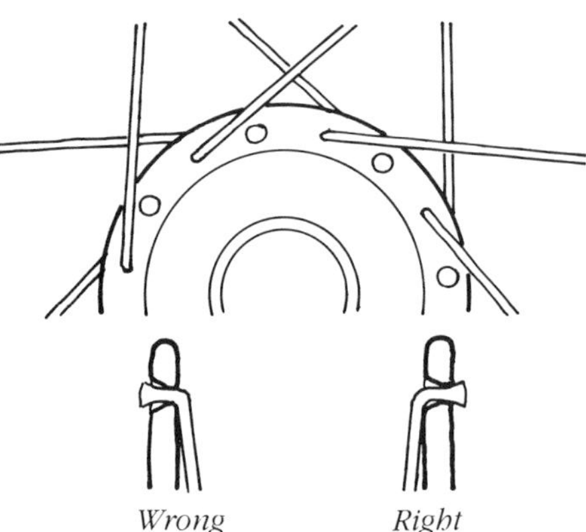

4 Join the spoke up with the nipple protruding through the rim and tighten it up until the tension matches the other spokes. Set the wheel true (see Adjustments) and file down the end of the spoke if it is protruding towards the inner tube.

DENTED RIMS

Small bulges in the rim can be repaired with a G-clamp. If the bulge is on both sides, gradually tighten the clamp against it to even out the rim. If the bulge is on one side only, spread the load on the undamaged side to avoid forcing it out of shape. A small block of wood will suffice.

WHEEL BEARINGS

Bicycle wheels spin on ball bearings which roll on outer cones incorporated in the wheel hub and inner cones on the axle. At least one of the inner cones will be adjustable.

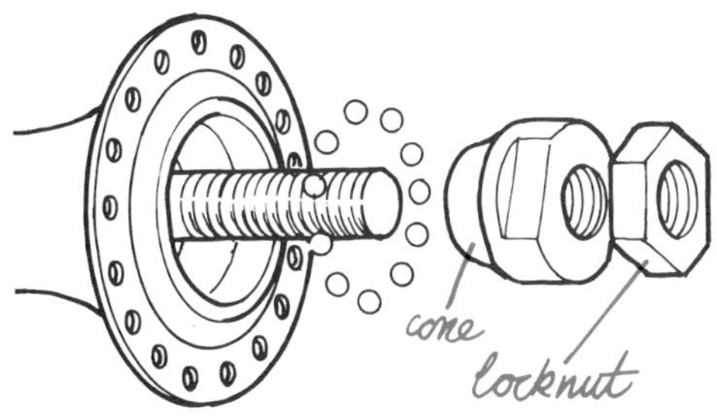

1 To check the wheel bearings, turn the bike upside down and stand it on the saddle and handlebars. Check the bearings by pushing sideways on the wheel rim: if there's any free play, the bearings at least need to be adjusted. The wheel should turn smoothly with very little noise or friction. If it's noisy, stiff or rough, the chances are that the bearings are worn and should be replaced.

2 To replace the bearings, first slacken the wheel nuts or open the quick-release mechanism and remove the wheel. You'll have to deflate the tyre or release the brake adjustment to allow it to pass between the brake blocks.

3 Remove the wheel nuts and slacken the cone locknuts. Unscrew one of the cones with care: the ball bearings are loose in the hub and will fall out once the cones have been removed. The cones have flat surfaces cut into them so that you can grip them with a thin spanner. Pop out the dust cap with a screwdriver, taking care not to scratch the bearings or the hub.

4 If you're putting in new ball bearings, replace the cones as well. Clean out old grease and dirt from the wheel hub, and use fresh grease both to hold the new balls in place during assembly and to lubricate them subsequently.

5 Replace the cones and locknuts, doing them up no more than finger-tight. Replace the wheel in the forks for the final adjustments.

6 To adjust the wheel bearings, rest the wheel in the forks but don't tighten the wheel nuts yet. Tighten the cones with your fingers until the wheel turns freely, but without any sideways free play. Tighten the locknuts against the cones, holding the cones in place with the thin spanner. Check the wheel, and if all is well tighten the wheel nuts and restore the brake adjustment or pump up the tyre. If not, the cones will have turned while you were tightening the locknuts: slacken them off and repeat step 6.

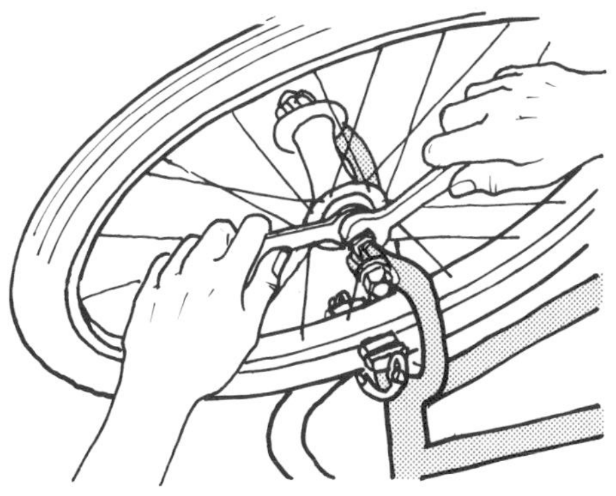

Worn or badly adjusted wheel bearings make it harder work to pedal your bike, but it's a relatively easy job to keep them smooth and friction-free. Badly adjusted bearings will wear out quickly

THINGS YOU NEED

- **A spanner to fit the wheel nuts**
- **A thin spanner to fit the cones and cone locknuts – purpose-made ones are available from bike shops**
- **Grease**

OTHER BEARINGS
Other bearings, in the pedal crank and the steering mechanism, usually work in the same way as wheel bearings, though some have ball races where the balls are held together in a cage. This makes them easier to handle.

FIXING YOUR BRAKES

Worn brake blocks and badly adjusted brakes are dangerous: not only is it difficult to stop the bike, but it's harder to control it while braking

BRAKE BLOCKS

Side-pull and centre-pull brakes operate from a single pivot in the centre of the forks; the cantilever brakes used on mountain bikes have a separate pivot for each brake block on either side of the forks

THINGS YOU NEED

- **Selection of spanners or hexagon keys**
- **Hammer**
- **Pliers**
- **'Third hand'**

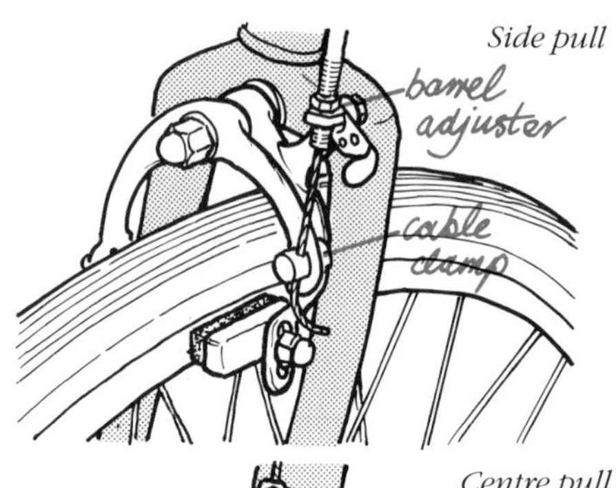

Side pull

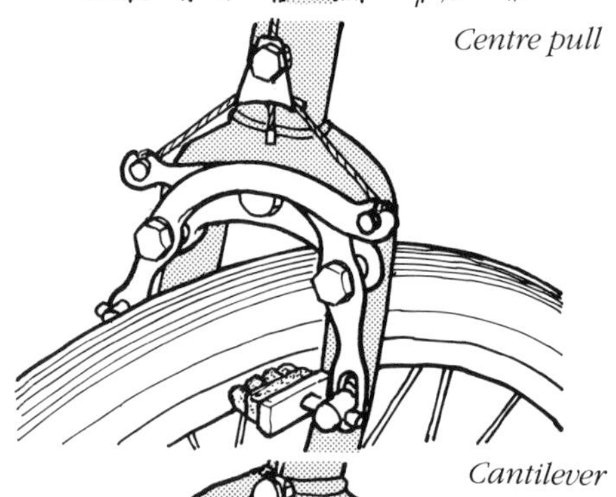
Centre pull

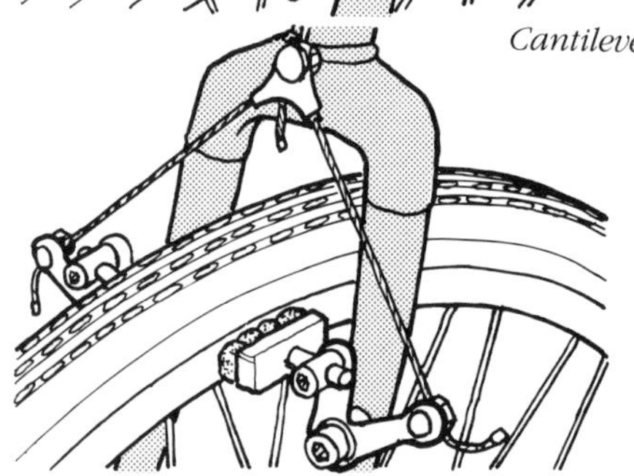
Cantilever

Your brakes can only be as good as the brake blocks themselves. When buying new ones, you need to know whether the wheel rims on your bike are steel or alloy, since these use different types of block. If you're in doubt, check with a magnet: it won't stick to alloy but will to steel. For side-pull and centre-pull brakes, you may be able to buy just the brake blocks themselves, and fit them to the original brake shoes. For cantilever brakes, the blocks are almost invariably moulded on to the shoes and you have to buy them as a unit.

SIDE-PULL AND CENTRE-PULL BRAKES

1 Release the clamping nut on the cable from the brake lever, so the brake blocks spring away from the wheel rim. Remove the brake shoes by undoing the domed nuts holding them to the brake arms.

2 Brake shoes that can be separated from the blocks are three-sided: the blocks fit in like a dovetail joint and can be pulled out of the fourth side (use a screwdriver or pliers). Fit the new blocks by hammering them gently into place.

3 Refit the shoes, making sure that the open side of the brake shoes faces rearwards, otherwise the blocks may pop out the first time you put on the brakes. Make sure that the blocks on each side are properly aligned with the rim of the wheel.

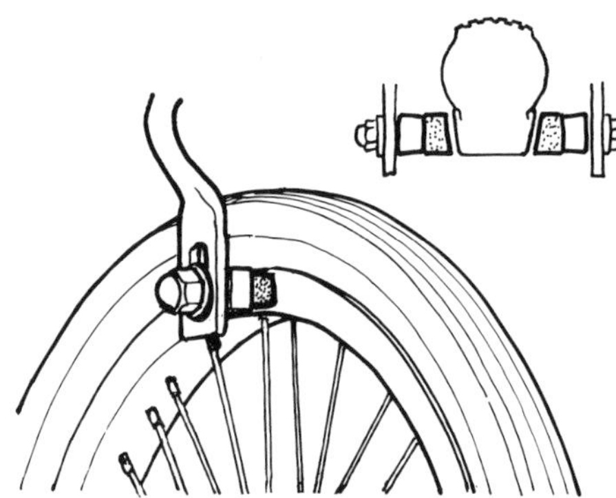

Where the brake design allows, set up the blocks very slightly 'toe-in' (when braking, the action of the wheel squares up the blocks). This can help to reduce squealing from resonating brake components – but not if they are poor-quality.

4 Adjust the brakes (see right).

CANTILEVER BRAKES

1 Squeeze the brake blocks together on to the wheel rim and remove the stirrup cable connecting the brakes on either side of the wheel.

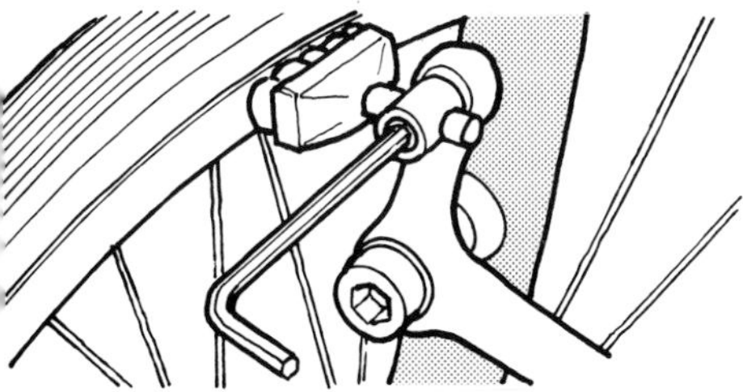

2 Using a hexagon key (left), slacken the socket-headed screws holding the studs on the back of each brake shoe, remove the old brake shoes and replace them with the new ones.

3 Replace the stirrup cable and adjust the socket-headed screws so that the brake blocks contact the wheel rim at the correct angle.

4 Adjust the brakes (see below).

HEXAGON KEYS
Many modern bikes, particularly more expensive models, have socket-headed screws in place of many nuts, such as those for adjusting the saddle. Hexagon (or Allen) keys are used – 4, 5 and 6mm are the most commonly required sizes.

ADJUSTMENTS

SIDE-PULL BRAKES

1 Screw in the barrel adjuster as far as it will go. Release the cable clamp.

2 Squeeze the brake blocks together on to the wheel, pull the cable through the clamp with pliers and re-tighten the cable clamp. A 'third hand' (available from bike shops) is a device which will hold the blocks against the rim, leaving you free to pull the cable through with one hand and tighten the clamp with the other.

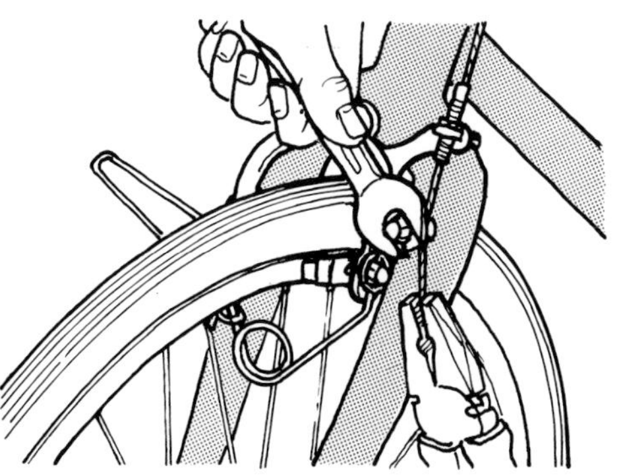

CENTRE-PULL AND CANTILEVER BRAKES

1 Screw in the barrel adjuster as far as it will go. Squeeze the brake blocks together on to the wheel and release the stirrup cable.

2 Release the cable clamp, adjust the length of the cable as required and re-tighten. Take care not to twist or kink the brake cable. Replace the stirrup cable.

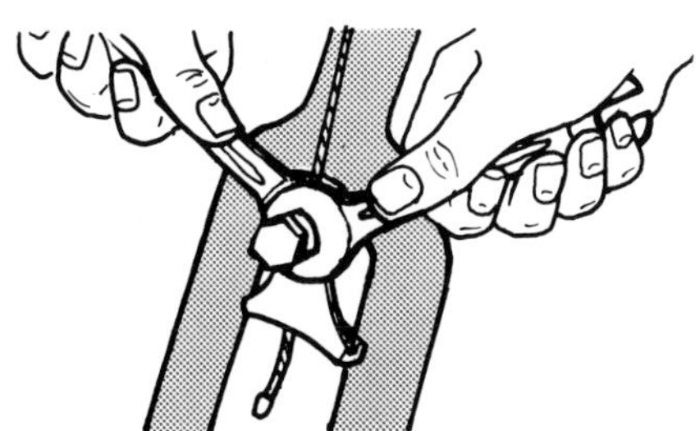

ALL BRAKES

3 Fine tune the brakes using the barrel adjusters to take up the last of the slack in the cable, leaving a gap of about 3mm ($^1/_8$ in) on each side. Straighten the wheel if it rubs at any point (see Rims and spokes on page 167).

Most bikes have two brake adjustment mechanisms. Larger adjustments are made by slackening the cable clamps, pulling the cable through and re-tightening. Fine tuning is achieved using barrel adjusters on either the brakes themselves or the brake levers

FIXING YOUR

CHAIN AND GEARS

Dirt, age and poor adjustment can all cause the chain to come off or problems with changing gear

Keep the chain and gears free of grime and lightly lubricated. Adjustments should keep you going; major problems usually mean some parts are due for replacement

THINGS YOU NEED

- **Adjustable spanner**
- **Selection of spanners and hexagon keys**
- **Cleaners and lubricants**
- **Screwdriver**
- **Pliers**

You may need:

- **Chain rivet removing tool**

WEAR AND TEAR

1 If you have trouble changing gear or the chain comes off, check first that the relevant parts – chain, gear changers, cogs – are clean and well lubricated. Excess grime can clog mechanisms or prevent the chain and cogs fitting together snugly; lack of lubrication can make joints cease up or prevent cables from moving smoothly.

2 If you hear a regular clunking noise or the chain comes off, check the cogs for bent, chipped or heavily worn teeth. Bent teeth can be straightened using an adjustable spanner, but chipped or worn ones mean the whole cog should be replaced – easy enough by the pedals (the front chainrings just bolt on), but less so at the back.

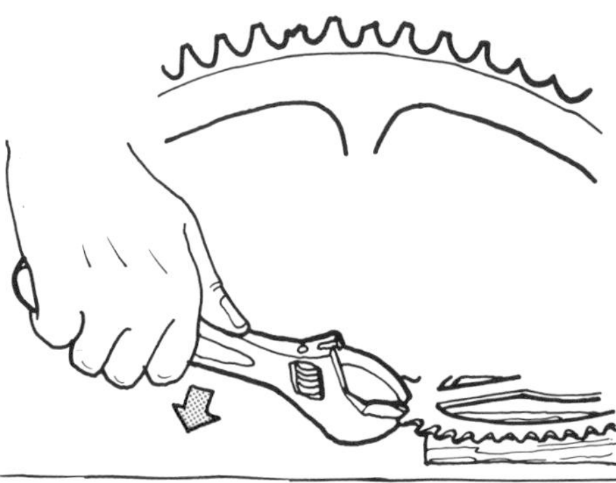

3 Check the chain for excessive wear: chains do need replacing every now and then. Try lifting the chain away from the teeth somewhere on the front chainring. If it clears the teeth it definitely needs replacing. On non-derailleur bikes you just pry off the master link with a screwdriver to remove the chain; on derailleur bikes you need to use a special tool to open one of the rivets.

ADJUSTMENT

On derailleur bikes the derailleurs can throw the chain off when you change gear or make it impossible to put it into the highest or lowest gears if they are poorly adjusted. Sturmey-Archer hub gears can fail to engage or slip out of gear for the same reason.

DERAILLEUR GEARS

1 If the gears are slipping or the changing action is stiff, the problem is with the shift lever. Tighten the tension screw – this has a wing or a coin slot to make it easy – so that the spring in the derailleur on the other end of the cable won't pull it out of position, but not so tight that the lever cannot be moved comfortably.

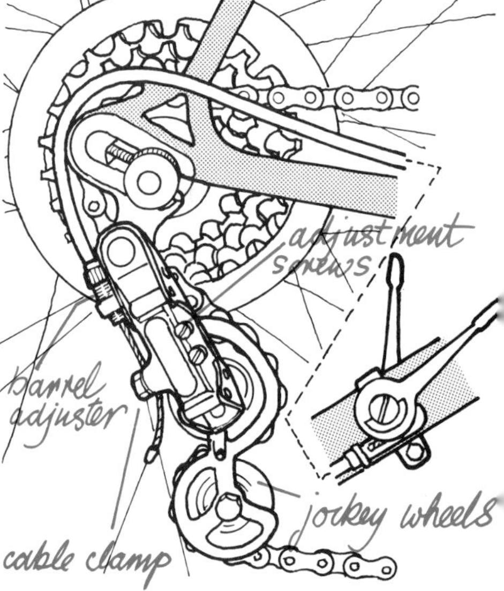

2 If you need to pull the shift lever all the way back to get the chain on to the largest cog at the front or back, or the chain won't even make it on to that cog, then the cable is slack. Try using the barrel adjuster on the derailleur if there is one. If that is insufficient, put the bike into top gear, with the lever pushed forward, loosen the cable grip and pull the slack through using pliers.

3 If you can't get the chain on to either the smallest or largest cog, but the cable tension seems to be OK, then the adjusting screws on the derailleur mechanism need seeing to. This is definitely the case if the chain goes into the wheel or off the end when you go for the low or high gears. Two tiny screws, often marked H and L for high and low, limit the range of movement of the derailleur. If they are not obvious, move the shift lever back and forth and watch for where the mechanism makes contact with them. Adjust the rear derailleur so that the small jockey wheels below the cogs are vertically in line with the inner and outer cogs at the limits of the travel.

4 If you have a front derailleur too, this needs to be set up so you can change cogs without throwing the chain off. Adjust it so that the chain will go into the highest gear on the largest cog and the lowest gear on the smallest cog without the chain rubbing against the front derailleur cage. You should now be able to get into all the gears without the chain rubbing, although it might be necessary to move the lever slightly to compensate for the extremes.

5 Greater problems with rubbing than that or a continuing tendency to throw the chain off may mean that the cage is not straight or is not correctly positioned vertically. Loosen the clamp that holds the mechanism to the bike and slide it into place – in line with the cogs and a quarter to half an inch above the teeth.

3-SPEED HUB GEARS

1 If the gears are not changing properly or the bike is drifting in and out of gear, try adjusting the cable. Put the bike in top gear, loosen the locknut on the barrel adjuster (near the hub) and tighten the cable until there is just a little slack. If the barrel adjuster won't tighten the cable enough, move the clip which holds the cable to the frame forward a little.

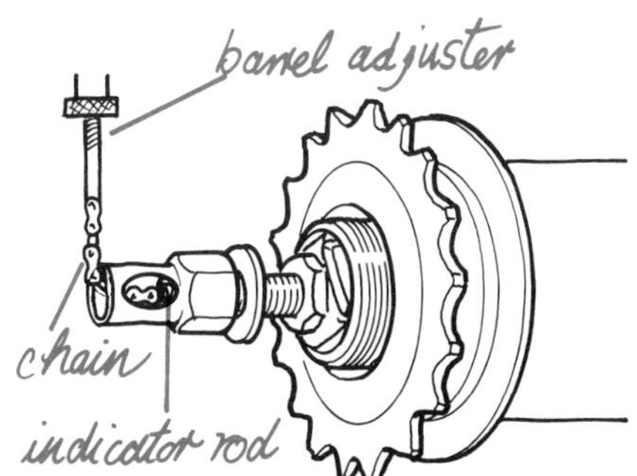

2 If the gears still don't work, look at the indicator rod where the cable goes into the hub. This should be exactly even with the end of the axle when you are in second gear. Use the barrel adjuster to line it up. If that doesn't do it, disconnect the barrel adjuster so you can turn the indicator rod by holding the connecting chain. It should be finger-tight. Reassemble, adjust the cable tension as before and try again.

3 The problem is elsewhere if the gears still won't work properly. Check that the cable is moving freely. Try putting penetrating oil into the hub to free parts which could be stuck.

MODERN 'INDEX' GEARS
These use special cables which are very resistant to stretching and rely on that fact to set up the gear change with click stops on the lever movement or with push-button mechanisms to get you up or down one gear. They need to be set up carefully – which the shop should do when you buy the bike – and should then need little or no adjustment.

A shift trigger or twist grip that is stiff or damaged is best replaced. Twist grips start to slip after a while and could well be the source of gear-changing problems.

SETTING YOUR

RIDING POSITION

Provided that your bike is the right size for you, you should be able to achieve a safe and comfortable riding position

SADDLE

Setting up the saddle and handlebars this way gives maximum efficiency. Take your bike on a good long ride to get used to the change and make sure it is comfortable

THINGS YOU NEED

- **Spanners or hexagon keys to fit the clamp below the saddle and the adjusting nut at the top of the handlebar stem**
- **Small block of wood**
- **Hammer**

1 Ideally you should feel a slight stretching behind your knee when you put your heel on the pedal at its lowest position. You should also be able comfortably to touch the ground with the toes of both feet.

2 To adjust the saddle height, slacken the clamp at the top of the seat tube. Pin the rear wheel between your knees and twist the saddle from side to side to raise or lower it. Re-tighten the clamp. The saddle tube may be marked to show the greatest height to which it should be adjusted. If not, don't raise the saddle so that less than one third of the tube is still inside the frame.

3 Some saddles can also be adjusted fore and aft. Undo the clamp underneath the saddle and adjust it so that the tip is about 5cm (2in) behind the centre of the bottom bracket. Stand the bike by a door frame or other vertical to check this. Your knee should be directly above the pedal when it's horizontal.

4 Set the angle of the saddle so the tip is level with the back. If this proves uncomfortable, lower the tip very slightly.

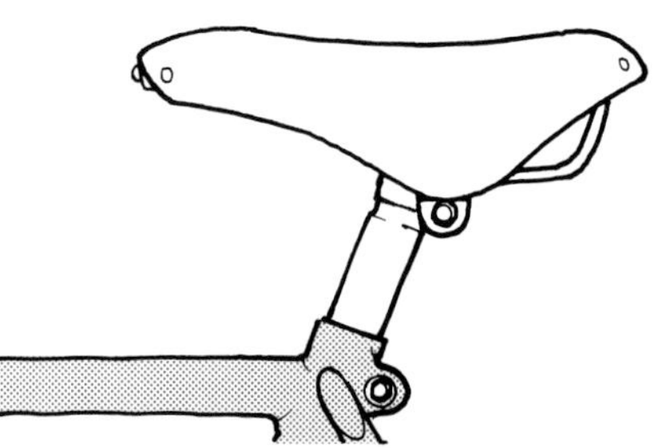

HANDLEBARS

1 The handlebars should be at the same height as the saddle. Slacken the adjusting nut at the top of the stem (a few turns only – don't undo it completely), protect the nut with a block of wood and tap it with a hammer to release the tapered clamp inside the stem, using penetrating oil if the stem is resistant. Set the handlebars at the saddle height and tighten the nut. You may have to readjust the front brake cable after changing the handlebar height.

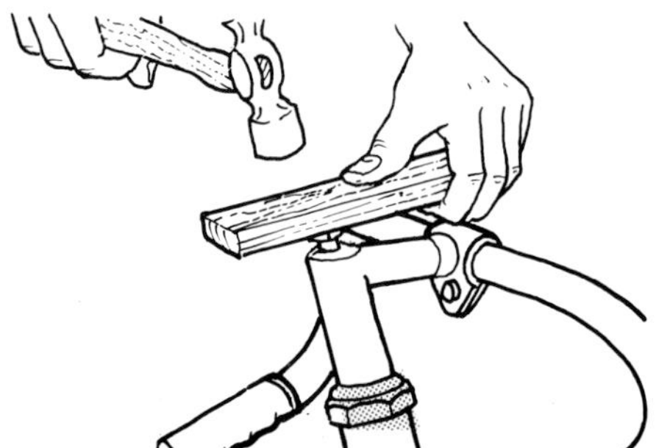

2 The distance from the tip of the saddle to the handlebars should correspond to the length of your forearm from the back of the elbow to the fingertips. If the distance is way too long or too short, you can buy handlebar stems of different sizes to compensate.

FIXING YOUR CAR

- MAINTENANCE
- SIMPLE REPAIRS
- RUST AND DENTS
- STARTING PROBLEMS

EVERYDAY

MAINTENANCE

Your car needs regular attention if you are going to avoid the risk of bigger bills later on

OIL

Routine maintenance tasks on virtually every car are simple and straightforward, and shouldn't take you more than fifteen minutes each week

THINGS YOU NEED

- **A lint-free rag**
- **Engine oil**

Oil is needed for many parts of your car, but the three major areas are the engine, gearbox and, in rear-wheel-drive cars, the back axle. While the oil level in the engine needs particular attention, that in the gearbox and axle rarely needs looking at outside a service interval. As doing these last two jobs is such a messy, awkward task without a full garage hoist, it is best left to the professionals.

1 To check the engine oil accurately you need to park the car on level ground. Open the bonnet, switch off the engine and do nothing for a couple of minutes to allow the oil to drain back to bottom of the engine.

2 Some cars, notably French models, have a gauge on the dashboard which gives a read-out of the oil level. Usually you have to let the car stand for a while with the engine off, then turn the ignition key just one notch so that the instruments light up, but don't start the engine. The gauge should give a clear indication if oil needs adding – though check the car handbook for full details of how to take an accurate reading.

3 On the majority of cars you will need to find the dipstick. This is usually a long steel rod with a hook or handle on the top, which pokes down into the sump. Finding it is usually straightforward, but if you have difficulty the car handbook will help. Be sure not to confuse it with the gear-box dipstick on automatic cars. Pull the dipstick up and out of the engine, catching any drops of oil with your rag. Wipe the dipstick clean.

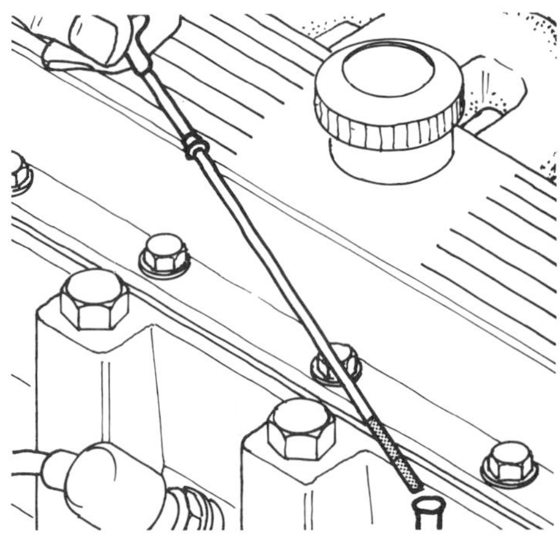

4 Look closely at the lower half of the dipstick. It will have two marks, the lower one the minimum oil level, the upper the maximum. Reinsert the dipstick into the engine as far as it will go, then remove it again. Holding it horizontally, note the oil level.

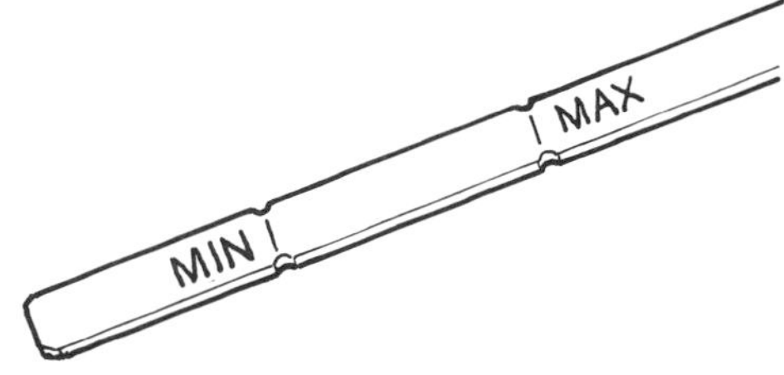

5 If the level is near the minimum mark, you should add some oil to the engine. Replace the dipstick. Remove the oil filler cap on the top of the engine (some unscrew, some just pull off). Pour in the oil. The engine will probably take about a litre of oil between the maximum and minimum marks on the stick, so add just half that before you take another reading on the dipstick (allow a couple of minutes for added oil to drain to the bottom of the engine).

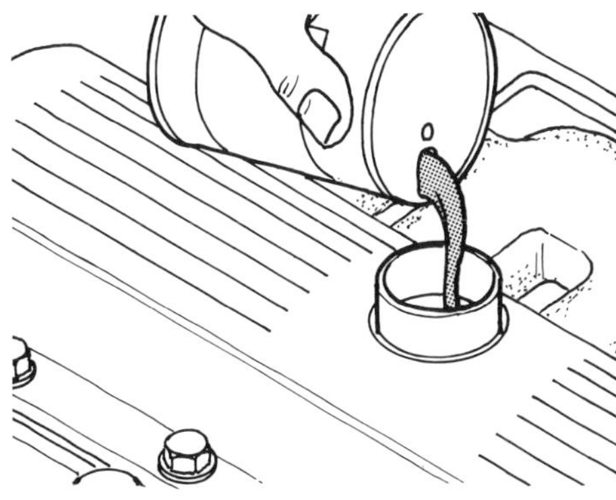

6 Do not fill past the maximum level on the dipstick – it's better to fall a little short if anything. Once the level is right, replace the oil filler cap and dipstick, and wipe clean any oil drops from the engine.

CHOOSING ENGINE OIL

Most car manufacturers recommend a range of brands of oil. But any proprietary multi-grade oil you buy from a filling station, garage or car accessory shop is likely to be satisfactory. Even own-brand oils will be OK, provided the grade and specification match the vehicle manufacturer's requirements for your engine. More expensive oils don't necessarily give better protection immediately, but they do work well for longer, so make sure you stick to the service requirements for changes if you pick a cheap one. Diesel and turbo-charged engines often need a special engine oil.

RADIATOR AND COOLING SYSTEM

All but a few cars use water to cool the engine and to provide warmth for heating the interior. The VW Beetle, VW vans, Citroen 2CV and Porsche 911 account for the majority of the exceptions – these engines are usually air cooled.

1 Before setting about checking the level in the cooling system, the car should have been parked on level ground and the engine allowed to cool down – i.e. left for at least 30 minutes.

2 Open the bonnet and find the coolant reservoir or expansion tank (a clear or semi-clear plastic container, connected to, but not necessarily right up against, the radiator). You should be able to see through this container and judge whether the coolant level is correct by the marks on the side of the container. It is not necessary to top up these systems frequently, but if the level is below the 'minimum' or 'cold' mark then coolant should be added (see overleaf).

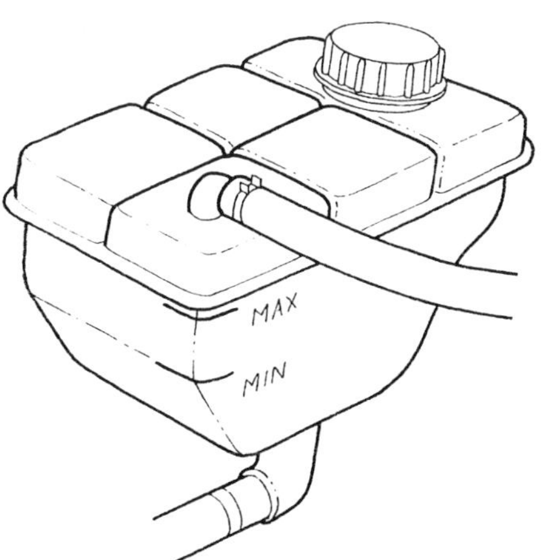

You need to keep an eye on the coolant level in the engine and check the power of the antifreeze before the cold season each year

THINGS YOU NEED

- **A rag**
- **Engine coolant**

Older vehicles may not have an expansion tank – the coolant level is checked by removing the cap normally found on top of the radiator. If the level is more than 20mm below the filler neck the level will need topping up.

THINGS YOU NEED

- A rag
- Engine coolant

3 Place a sizeable cloth over the top of the cap, and twist slowly. At this stage some steam or water may escape through the cap if you haven't allowed the engine to cool down enough. Stand clear and let things settle down. Then continue twisting until you can remove the cap completely.

4 Strictly speaking, you should top up the cooling system with a mixture of water and antifreeze or the special coolant recommended by some manufacturers. That way you know that in the winter the engine is still properly protected. However, it is acceptable to use plain tap water in emergencies, and then replace the coolant at a later date. Replace the cap when you have finished, making sure you have tightened it fully.

WASHER BOTTLE

A properly working windscreen washer system is a legal requirement. Special washer additives add to the cost but result in a cleaner screen and reduce the risk of freezing

THINGS YOU NEED

- Clean tap water
- Windscreen washer additive

1 Open the bonnet and locate the windscreen washer bottle. Usually this is a white translucent bottle through which you can judge the water level. Do not confuse this with the radiator expansion tank, which will have a hose connecting it to the radiator. The windscreen washer bottle will have small tubes running from it and may have wires running to it for the electric pump. On recent cars the bottle is often hidden, with only the cap and neck visible – look for the tubes and wires or a windscreen symbol on the cap.

2 Remove the top of the washer bottle. Add a dose of washer additive (the packaging will state how much) then top up the bottle with plain tap water. Replace the cap and close the bonnet.

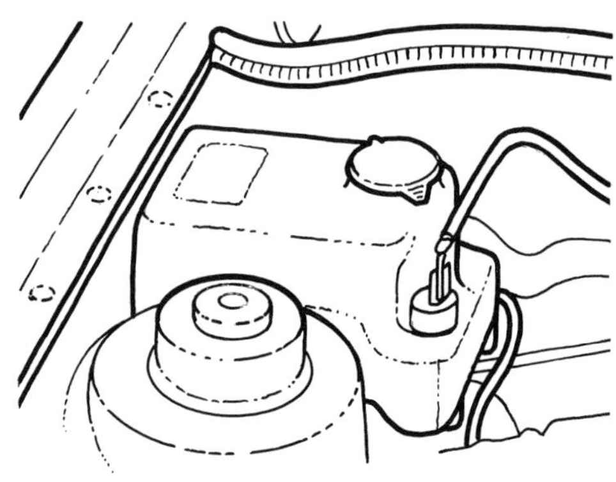

BRAKE AND CLUTCH FLUID

WARNING

Brake and clutch fluid is nasty stuff: not only will it harm your skin and eyes, but it will strip off paintwork in seconds. Take great care in handling it and as far as possible avoid any drips or splashes.

1 Brake fluid gradually absorbs water, which leads to ineffective brakes. That's why you need a complete change at regular intervals, and why you should avoid using fluid from a half empty can which has been standing around. Buy fluid in small quantities just for the job in hand.

2 Locate the master cylinder reservoirs for the brakes and clutch (not all cars have hydraulic clutches). The containers are usually clear or semi-clear with markings for minimum and maximum levels. If the level is low, it will require topping up.

3 Remove the top of the master cylinder reservoir. Wrap the top carefully in a rag and place in a convenient position within the engine compartment.

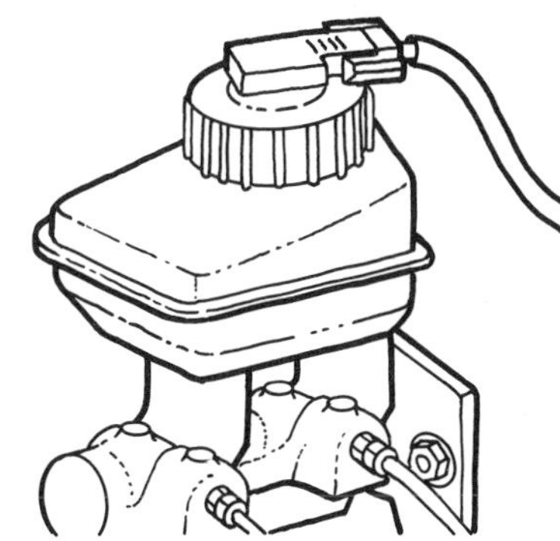

4 Using only fresh fluid, top up each reservoir to the 'full' mark; replace the caps and close the bonnet. Use brake and clutch fluid as specified by the vehicle manufacturer. If you need to add fluid regularly, consult a garage.

Fluid levels should be checked regularly to keep your brakes and clutch working efficiently. The entire brake fluid should be changed every two years – a job only for the experienced or a garage

THINGS YOU NEED

- **A lint-free rag**
- **Brake fluid (check the grade in your car handbook)**

POWER-ASSISTED STEERING FLUID

1 Locate the power-assisted steering fluid reservoir under the bonnet – usually a translucent or black plastic container.

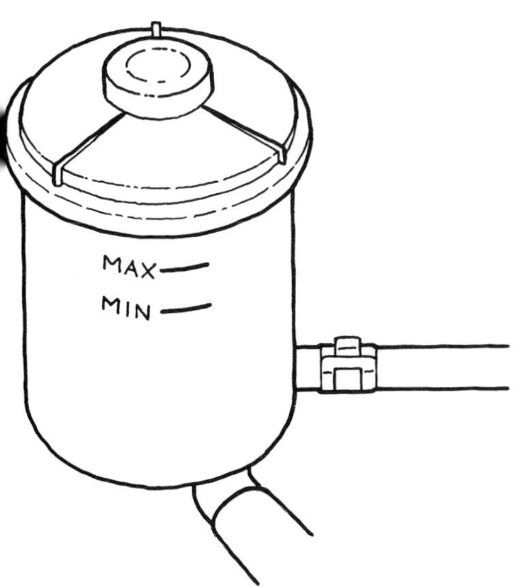

2 Check the level with the engine turned off, by viewing from the side if the container is translucent and marked with minimum and maximum levels, or by removing the cap. This may have a small dipstick or there may be level marks inside the container.

3 If the level is low, top it up with the fluid recommended by the vehicle manufacturer.

4 If the fluid level needs regular topping up, get a garage to investigate.

If your car has power-assisted steering (PAS), the fluid level should be checked regularly and replenished if necessary

THINGS YOU NEED

- **A lint-free rag**
- **PAS fluid (check the grade in your car handbook)**

AUTOMATIC GEARBOX FLUID

If your car has an automatic gearbox, the fluid level should be checked regularly. Driving with too much or too little fluid can damage the transmission

THINGS YOU NEED

- **A lint-free rag**
- **Automatic transmission fluid (check the grade in your handbook)**

Most automatic gearboxes have a dipstick for checking the fluid level. Some only require checking during routine services and the method for checking the fluid level varies between manufacturers, so it's best to check the vehicle handbook for the precise details. However, the following method can be used as a rule of thumb.

1 Check the fluid level when the engine and gearbox are warm – drive the vehicle about ten miles if the engine is cold. If the gearbox is hot, say after driving in city traffic in hot weather, allow it to cool a little before checking the level.

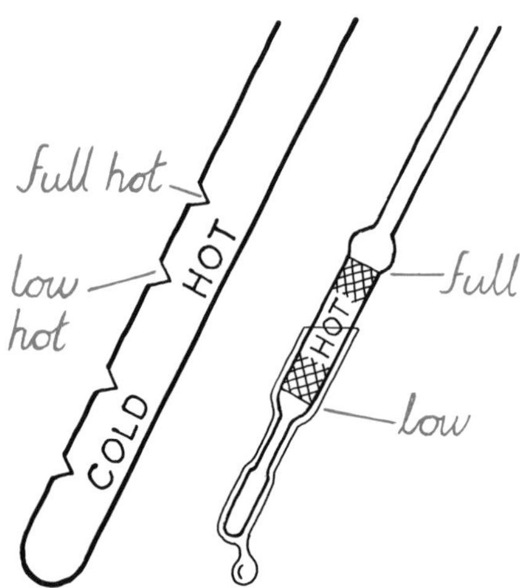

2 Park the vehicle on level ground with the drive selector in 'Park' or 'P', with the handbrake applied and the engine idling.

3 Locate the dipstick. Do not confuse this with the engine oil dipstick – if in doubt consult the car handbook. Remove the dipstick and wipe it clean, replace it in the tube and then withdraw it to check the level.

4 The dipstick may be marked with 'hot' and 'cold' levels. Check the level against the 'hot' markings for maximum and minimum levels – see illustration.

5 If the level is low, replenish it using fluid of a specification recommended by the vehicle manufacturer. If it is necessary to correct the level on a regular basis or if the level is too high, consult a garage.

LOOKING AFTER

TYRES

Modern tyres are tough, hard wearing and give very high levels of grip. But they need checking over periodically

CHECKING TYRES

1 Decide whether you want to check tyre pressure at home with your own gauge and pump, or to use one on a garage forecourt. Don't forget to check the spare wheel too.

2 Tyres should be checked cold, so if you do use a garage, make sure it's only a local one that's a short run away. Remove the dust cap over the tyre valve. Press the gauge on to the valve and compare the reading with the correct pressure given in your car handbook.

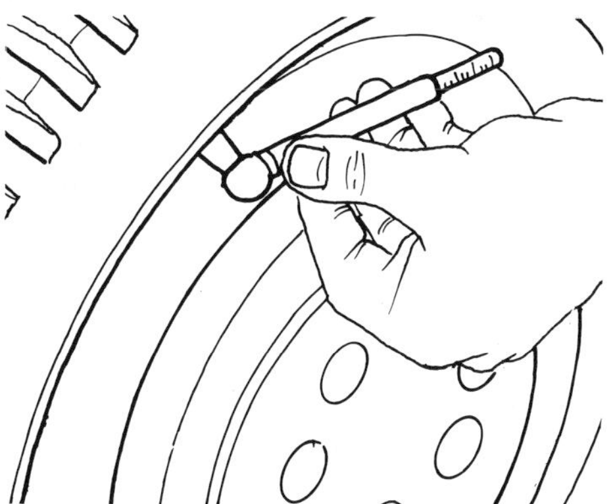

3 If the pressure is too low, inflate the tyre with your foot pump or the garage air line. If it is too high (and this isn't caused by the tyre being hot because it's been driven on for some time immediately prior to checking) let some air out by pressing down on the valve stem with a small screwdriver or the edge of the valve cap. Don't forget to replace the cap when you have finished.

4 You can check the life left in your tyres by measuring the tread depth. Push the core of the measuring tool into the tread of the tyre, remove it and take a reading. You should do this across several points over the width of the tyre as wear is not always even. The more tread a tyre has, the more grip you'll get in wet conditions, so just because a tyre has a tread depth above the legal limit, it doesn't mean it gives as good a performance as it would if it had a greater tread depth.

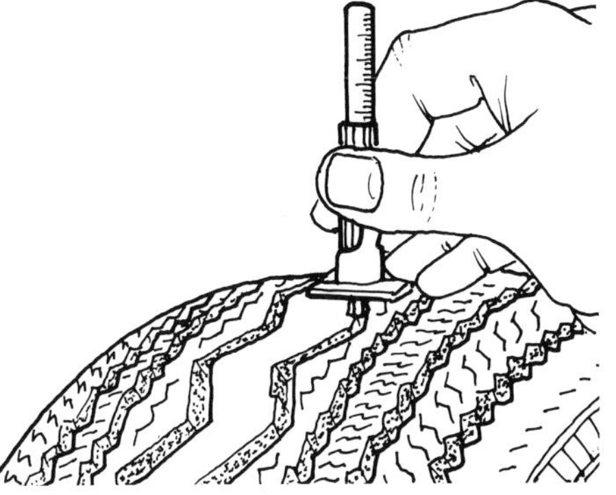

5 Look hard at the sides of the tyres for splits or bulges. If you do find any, or see any suspicious-looking projections from the tread of the tyre, change to the spare and get it checked out by an expert.

The major attention required by your tyres is routine checking of pressure. If the pressure falls, they may provide less grip, wear more quickly and, in extreme circumstances, 'blow out'

THINGS YOU NEED

- **Tyre pressure gauge**
- **Foot pump**
- **Tread depth gauge**
- **Small screwdriver**

CHANGING A WHEEL

Don't drive on a flat tyre – aside from being dangerous it will almost certainly mean your tyre will need replacing rather than merely repairing. Just get yourself to a safe spot and change the wheel

THINGS YOU NEED

- **Spare wheel**
- **Jack**
- **Wheel brace**

1 Choose a safe spot on firm ground as far away from passing traffic as possible – this is particularly important if your puncture is on the driver's side of the car. Pull the handbrake firmly on, switch on the hazard lights and keep an ear out for passing traffic.

2 Remove the spare wheel and jack. All cars have a jack and a brace for removing the wheel nuts or bolts tucked away somewhere. The usual place is in the boot (under the carpet or in a side pocket) or under the bonnet. Before using the jack, remove the wheel trim (they usually just pull off, or are levered off with the end of the wheel brace) and then loosen by half a turn each nut on the wheel you want to remove.

3 Check in your handbook for the correct place to locate the jack under the car and approved jacking procedure. In most cases the jack will be positioned along the side under the doors – you might find the correct position marked on the bodywork. Put the jack in place and raise the car until the wheel is clear of the ground.

4 Remove the wheel nuts or bolts completely, then lift off the punctured tyre and wheel. Put this to one side and put the spare into position. Some cars have protruding bolts on the hub over which you slip the wheel – pretty straightforward. Others have bolts which you screw in, so you have to make sure that the holes in the wheel for the bolts align with those underneath on the hub. Lightly tighten the nuts or bolts with the wheel brace.

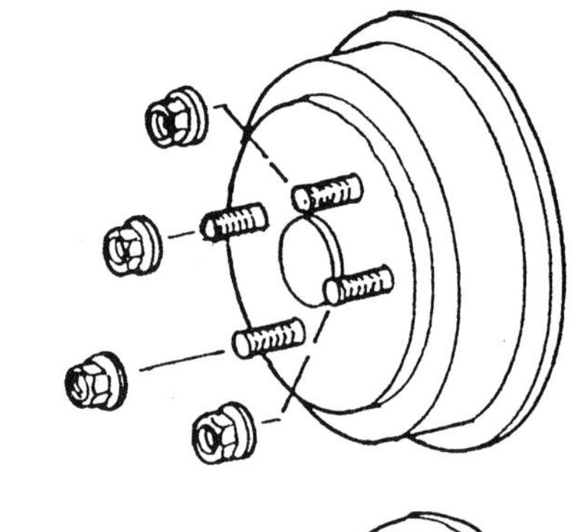

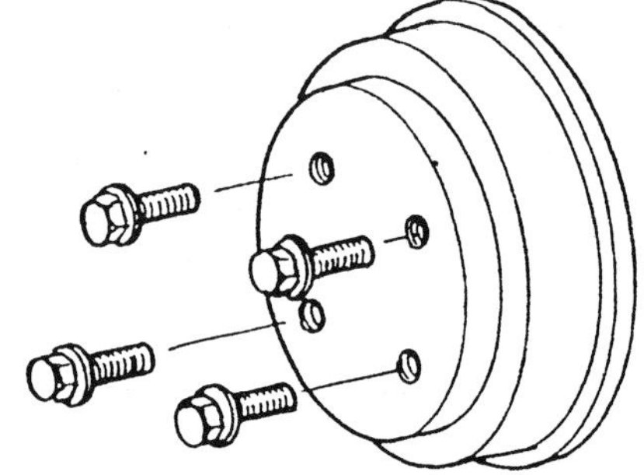

5 Now lower the jack to the ground and tighten the nuts/bolts firmly – putting a foot on the brace will help if you don't have sufficient weight behind you to tighten as much as you'd like.

6 Replace the wheel trim, and return the spare, jack and brace to their correct locations.

7 Make sure the punctured tyre is repaired or replaced ready for next time.

FIXING YOUR

WIPERS

There's no point putting up with ineffective wipers and washer jets: all the problems are quick, cheap and easy to put right

WIPER PROBLEMS

SMEARING

The root cause of smearing is invariably some form of deposit on the screen which the rubber blade cannot cope with. Polish or wax intended for the paintwork should never find its way on to the glass as it leaves a thin film which resists water. The other common problems are dead insects, bird droppings and deposits from certain types of trees.

1 With a little luck, a good additive in your washer bottle will clear these deposits away. But if that does not turn out to be the case, a proprietary glass cleaner will do the job, as will the special cleaners found in car accessory shops specifically aimed at dissolving dead flies.

2 A cheaper option is simply to wipe the windscreen with newspaper and methylated spirits.

STREAKING

Streaking of the windscreen, where the wiper appears to miss out a section in the middle of the glass, is usually due to the blade becoming jammed.

1 Pull the wiper arm away from the windscreen until it is locked in the upright position.

2 Next you need to check that the blade is perfectly clean (if not wipe gently along its length with a clean cloth) and undamaged, and that it is free to move within its mountings.

3 If it's jammed, try slightly bending open the tabs which hold the rubber blade onto the arm.

4 If this doesn't cure the problem you'll need a replacement blade.

The very edge of the wiper blade is a thin strip of rubber which squeezes the water off the screen. It usually works efficiently, but a few common problems occur

NEW BLADES

There are two main ways in which the wiper blade (the rubber bit and its metal carrier) can be attached to the metal wiper arm. In every case, replacement is simply a reversal of the removal procedure. Prices and quality of arms and blades vary, so shop around.

● The oldest design is where the blade can be pulled straight off the arm after a small clip in the connector is depressed to unlock it.

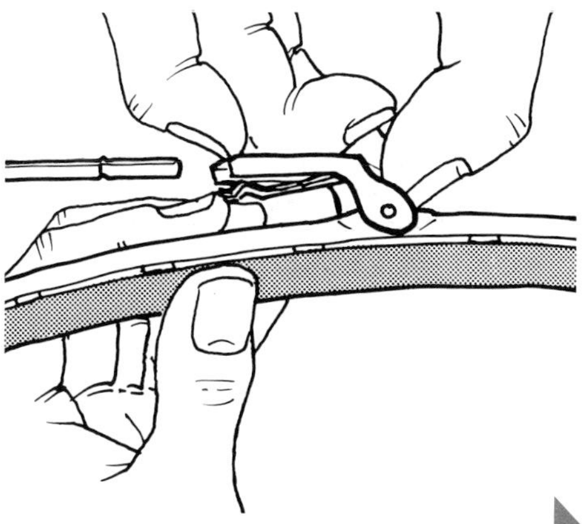

The rubber blade on a windscreen wiper won't last for ever – the atmosphere gradually makes it harder and more brittle; ice can cause splits and tears

THINGS YOU NEED

- **Screwdriver**
- **Replacement wiper blade**

● The second type has a large hook on the end of the wiper arm. Removing the blade is simply a matter of pulling the arm away from the screen as far as you can (it will usually lock into this position) and then twisting the wiper through 90° so that it can easily be uncoupled. There is a plastic insert holding the blade in place, which you'll need to unclip, perhaps with the aid of a small screwdriver, before the wiper blade will come free.

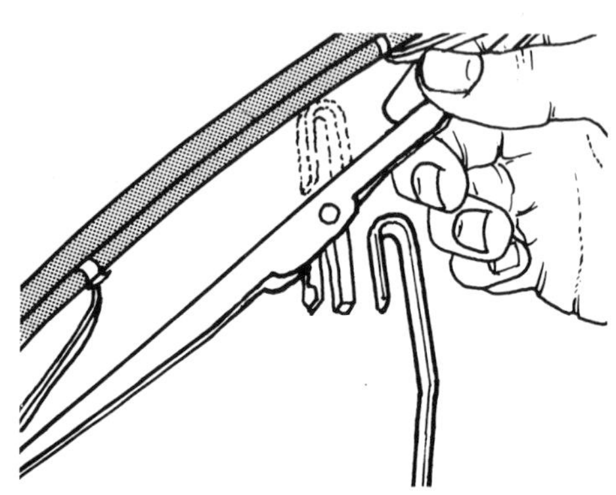

WASHERS

The usual problem with windscreen washers is that they are not pointing at the right part of the windscreen. Adjustment is very straightforward

THINGS YOU NEED

- **Needlework pin**

1 Make a mental note of where the water hits the screen at low and high speed. When you are driving faster the air flow over the car will tend to force the jet lower down the screen, so the final adjustment has to be something of a compromise.

2 Each outlet for the washer consists of a small, movable sphere with a tiny hole. Stick the pin in this hole and move it up, down or side-to-side until you think you have it right.

3 Remove the pin and try out the washer. Continue making fine adjustments until you have got it right.

4 You may find that you'll need a little further fine tuning after you have given the car a road trial.

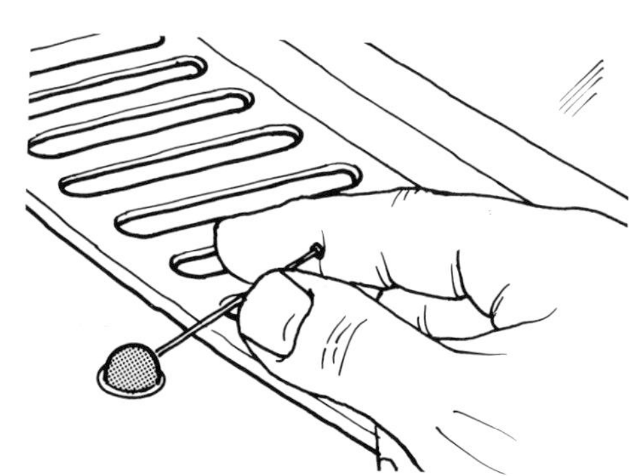

FIXING YOUR

ELECTRICS

Many of a car's functions – both essential and non-essential – are electrical, and they are usually very reliable

FUSES

1 The first trick is to find the fuse box, which tends to be hidden away. Your car handbook will tell you the location and the specification of all the fuses you need. The most common places to find the fuses are behind a panel beneath the steering wheel or on the lower part of the dashboard on the passenger side, inside the glove box – also perhaps behind a panel or at the very top – or under the bonnet. Turn off the ignition and switches before removing and replacing fuses.

2 You could find anything from just a couple of fuses on a car like an old Mini, up to something like 30 on a modern car. If you are lucky there will be a label on the lid of the fuse box to tell you which fuse covers which electrical function. Alternatively, this will certainly be noted in your car handbook. If you are stuck without any information, you can remove each fuse in turn and inspect it for failure. Car manufacturers often supply a fuse removal tool in the fuse box or its lid.

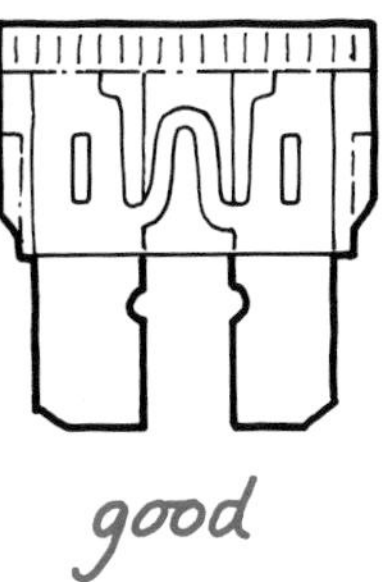

good

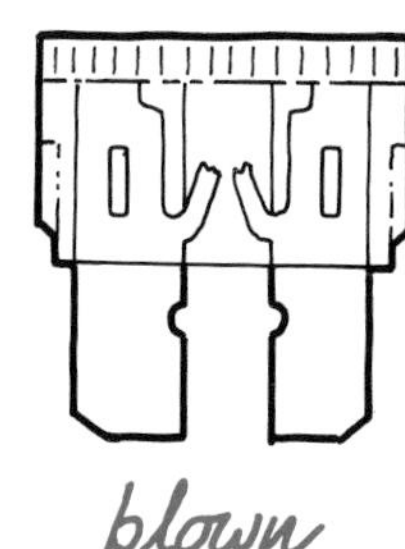

blown

3 Remove the suspect fuse and have a close look at it. From one end to the other runs a thin strip of metal. If this appears broken, it's certain that the fuse has blown. Check the rating for this fuse in the car handbook: if you are lucky there will be a chart on the lid of the fuse box giving the ratings, and the fuse box may even hold a spare. Get a replacement of the correct rating from your dealer or car accessory shop. (It's usually worth buying a spare at the same time, in case the problem reappears.) If the blown fuse was of a different rating to that noted in the handbook, that may be the reason for the failure in the first place. Never replace a fuse with one of a higher rating than recommended by the manufacturer.

4 Insert the new fuse and test out the function which previously hadn't worked. If the original problem was just caused by a faulty fuse, you should be back in business. If there's something more serious amiss, the fuse will blow again and you'll have to get the car checked over by a professional electrician.

If anything electrical in your car stops working, the first thing to check is the fuse

THINGS YOU NEED

- **Fuse removal tool**
- **Replacement fuse**

BULBS

It's a legal requirement that all of your car's lights work, even in daylight hours. So check regularly that all, including the brake lights, come on when they should

THINGS YOU NEED

- **Screwdriver**
- **Replacement bulb**

HEADLAMP BULBS

The majority of headlamps have a traditional type of bulb, the replacement of which is covered below.

1 Open the bonnet of the car and locate the back of the headlamp unit, which projects back towards the engine compartment. If it is covered with trim or has a protective cover, remove this.

2 The electrical wiring to the bulb will be plugged into the back – pull this free, holding the block, not the wires.

3 The bulb may now just pull out, or need to be twisted free or unclipped, or need a fixing ring unscrewed first to free it.

4 Take great care not to touch the bulb with your fingers – always use a holder or cloth. If you do accidentally touch it, wipe the bulb clean with methylated spirits.

5 Put the new bulb into position – it may have lugs around the edge that allow you to fit it in only one position. Replace the fixing ring if appropriate.

6 Reconnect the wiring, and replace the trim or protective covering.

SIDE, BRAKE AND INDICATOR LIGHTS

Bulb replacement usually involves accessing the rear of the light unit; for example, for a rear light it will be necessary to find the back of the light unit in the vehicle boot space.

1 Some trim or covering panels may need to be removed to gain access to the unit. Several bulbs may be contained in one complete unit (for say, brake, indicator and fog lights), which is usually held in place by plastic clips or locking tongues. Release of these clips should allow access to change the failed bulb.

2 Some light units require the lens to be removed before you can access the bulb. The lens will normally be clipped into position or you may have to remove fixing screws. When replacing the lens unit, take care not to over-tighten any screws as this may cause the plastic to break.

3 Reassembly is normally the reverse process.

AERIAL

PUSH-IN AERIAL

If you are not bothered about putting retractable aerials up and down, then you might find the simple push-in type of replacement attractive. All you need to do is remove as much as possible of the original broken aerial, but leaving the base in place on the bodywork. Then take the wedged end of the replacement, and push it down as far as possible into the socket. Of course you can't retract this type of aerial, and removal isn't really practicable. There's also a small chance that reception will be inferior too, but for the price – just a couple of pounds – you might feel the simplicity of the idea is worth the risk.

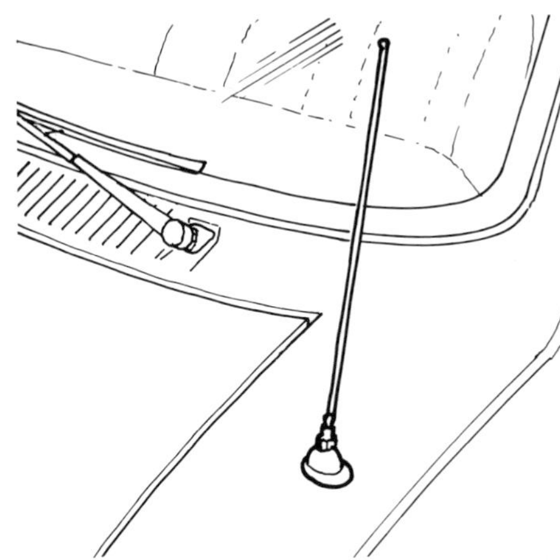

There's little to stop a car radio aerial lasting forever, except car washes, low trees and vandals. Replacements are cheap, though the job is a bit fiddly to do properly

THINGS YOU NEED

- **Push-in replacement aerial**

or

- **Retractable aerial**
- **Open-ended spanners**
- **Adjustable clamp wrench**
- **Aerosol can of dismantling oil**

ROOF AERIAL

Roof-mounted aerials are usually screwed on to a base-plate. This makes replacement a simple matter of unscrewing what's left of the old one, and screwing in the replacement. In this case it's advisable to get a replacement from the main dealer for your make of car as it will have been specially designed to give the best reception.

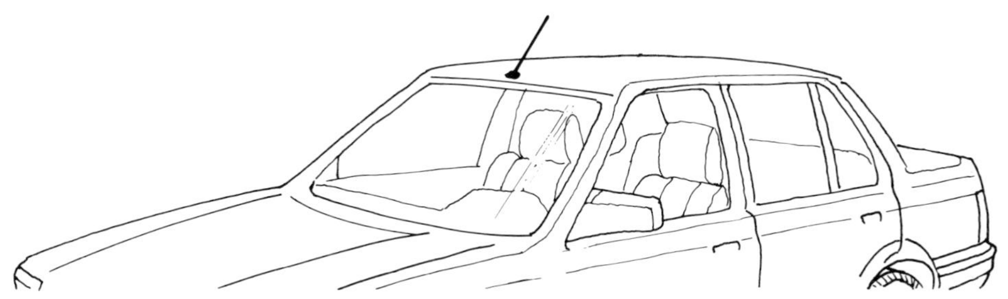

RETRACTABLE AERIAL

1 Replacing a manually retractable aerial is more involved (electric aerials are basically similar but with more wiring – they are not specifically covered here). You will need to gain access to the area beneath the aerial mounting point – probably underneath the front or rear wing. This area could need cleaning before you start. You may need to remove an inner wing cover to get at the mounting.

2 Spray dismantling oil on the nut retaining the aerial mounting under the wing. Leave the oil to penetrate then remove the nut with an open-ended spanner. You may need to grasp the top of the aerial mount with the adjustable clamp wrench to prevent it turning as you unscrew the nut – use a helper.

3 Remove the radio from its position on the dashboard of the car. Unplug the aerial from the back (the aerial cable is usually the thickest black one, the plug has a single pin in the centre).

4 Carefully feed the old cable from the radio back through to the aerial position, noting the route it takes so that you can insert the new cable in the same way. Remove the remains of the old aerial and cable.

5 Replacement is a reversal of the above procedure. With your new aerial you will almost certainly get detailed instructions about exactly where all the washers, grommets and nuts should be positioned – follow these to the letter.

CAR STEREO

Getting better sound from your car stereo isn't merely a matter of spending money on a more expensive system. It could well be that you'll get more from your existing stereo by making a few adjustments

THINGS YOU NEED

- **Screwdrivers**
- **Spanners**

IMPROVING RADIO RECEPTION

Crackly interference can be incredibly irritating. Usually it is confined to the radio rather than the cassette.

1 It is worth checking the radio aerial connections, including the aerial mounting and earth to the vehicle body. To ensure that the aerial earth has a good contact with the vehicle body, remove any rust or dirt that would prevent a good earth being made.

2 Next remove the radio unit and check that all connections to the rear of the unit are secure. Tighten any that are not.

3 If there is no improvement seek help from an auto electrician.

IMPROVING SOUND QUALITY

While expensive equipment will undoubtedly produce better quality sound than that fitted as standard to most car makes, there are ways to make improvements at little cost.

1 The main cause of indifferent sound quality is not the main stereo unit mounted in the dashboard but the speakers, particularly where these are not part of the original vehicle design. The first thing to do is to check the location of each speaker and reassess whether it might not be better repositioned.

2 The speaker should be mounted on a very rigid base. Look at each speaker location in turn. Those on the top of the dashboard are usually pretty firm and are anyway difficult to reposition. The same goes for speakers mounted in the front footwell, which are invariably screwed into a metal part of the body structure.

3 Common areas of weakness are speakers mounted in doors or on tilting rear parcel shelves. If you have a door-mounted speaker, remove the door panel to see how rigidly it is fastened. To do this you will have to unscrew the armrest, window winder, the cover over the speaker and possibly the cover over the door handle. Some of the screws retaining these parts will be hidden under covers which will need to be prised off. The door panel itself is held in place by screws and/or push-in clips. With clips you just have to prise up a corner and then ease the whole panel free – sometimes you have to be pretty forceful.

4 Inspect just how the speaker has been mounted. If it is screwed through to some metal part of the door structure, fine, leave well alone. If it is merely mounted on a floppy part of the door panel you'll be certain to improve the sound by mounting it somewhere more rigid. Look at the structure of the now exposed inner door skin – is there a place where the mounting screws for the speaker could be attached to metal? Any repositioning you do has to take into account the downward movement of the window as well as the fact that you'll leave an exposed hole where your speaker was (easy enough to cope with by fastening a dummy speaker cover in place). Alternatively, you might beef up the floppy door panel with a stiff piece of plywood with a central hole for the speaker.

5 At the back of the car about the worst place for the speakers is in fancy pods on a folding parcel shelf. Consider repositioning them in the rear pillars – if you pop off the lining to the sides of the back window, you could well find an obvious mounting point for a speaker designed in by the car manufacturer.

Whatever you do, never cut holes in structural parts of the car. Though it is acceptable to drill small holes to screw the speakers in place, large holes for the main body of the speaker could significantly weaken the structure of a car.

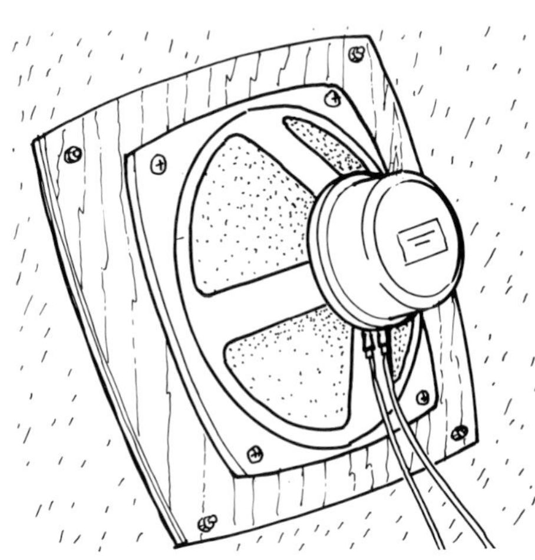

Mounting speakers on a stiff piece of plywood can improve sound quality

LOOKING AFTER

BODYWORK

Repairing minor knocks and scratches will maintain a car's appearance without costing much – and it will help keep rust at bay

RUST

Rust is usually what finally finishes off a car, so it pays to look out for the first signs and attack them as early as possible

THINGS YOU NEED

- **Sharp knife or screwdriver**
- **400-grade wet-and-dry abrasive paper**
- **Rust preventer**

1 Rust is often more widespread than it appears to be from the surface, and unless you neutralise it all you will find it continuing to spread under the paint. So with a sharp knife or small screwdriver, scrape away the paint around the area of the rust. You'll find that it will come away easily as the rust has loosened the paint's grip on the metal. Then with the wet-and-dry abrasive paper, used wet, rub down the area to remove the worst of the rust.

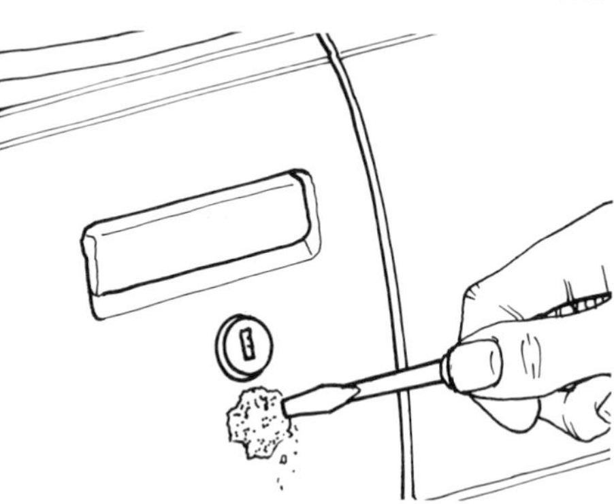

2 Allow the area to dry and then apply the rust-preventing treatment, following the manufacturer's instructions. Usually you paint this material on and leave it for a few minutes. It has the effect of changing the colour of any remaining rust and making it less liable to recur.

3 It may be tempting to use power tools to prepare the bodywork – grinders and rotary wire brushes are very good at removing all signs of rust. But they also cause damage to the sound metal beneath, which to the amateur means the next stage – preparation before painting – becomes a more difficult task.

TOUCHING UP PAINTWORK

Getting a 'new car' finish with home repairs is as good as impossible. But if you want to improve the appearance of your car because it has gone rusty or has had a slight scrape, d-i-y repairs are quick and very economical

1 After the rust has been dealt with there will almost certainly be a rather rough surface to the metal. Paint placed direct on to this will have no effect on the blemish, so it needs smoothing with cellulose stopper. This is a rapid-drying filler that is easy to sand smooth. Ensuring that the entire area is dry, apply the stopper to the affected area so that the finished level is a touch higher than the surrounding surface.

2 When the stopper is dry – after 20-30 minutes – smooth the surface with the abrasive paper until it is flush with surrounding paintwork. Using the paper wet helps to wash away the waste and gives a smoother finish.

3 Touch-up paint is supplied in small pots or tubes with a brush built into the lid. The popular colours are available at car accessory shops, but dealers will sell the lot, including the more unusual ones. Shake the container hard for at least a couple of minutes to ensure the paint is thoroughly mixed. Then withdraw the lid and brush, taking care to wipe the excess paint on the throat of the container as you do this. Starting with just a little paint at a time, brush over the damaged area and leave to dry. Don't go back and forth over the same area because it will roughen. If you don't get the coverage you need, wait 15 minutes or so and put on another coat.

4 If it is just a paint chip that needs covering up, and the damage hasn't reached the metal beneath, preparation can be confined to washing with clean water. After drying, put the tiniest blob of touch-up paint you can get away with into the chip, then work it carefully but quickly to the edges.

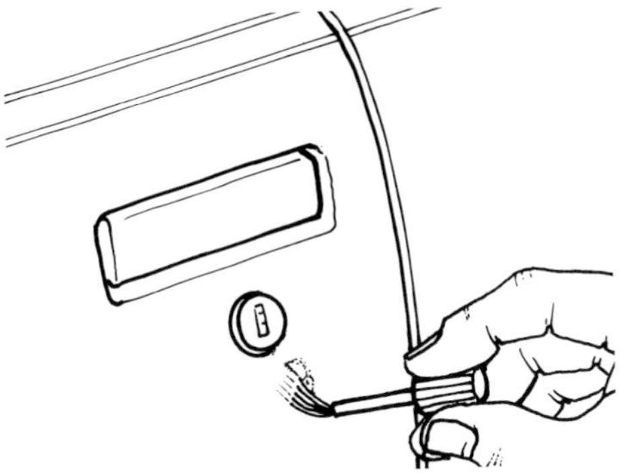

THINGS YOU NEED

- 400-grade wet-and-dry abrasive paper
- Cellulose stopper
- Touch-up paint
- Clean, lint-free cloth

SMALL DENTS

1 The dented area must be thoroughly cleaned and all the paint removed – see the section on removing rust. The paintwork surrounding the dent should be blended into the bare metal with the abrasive paper.

2 Measure out the two ingredients of the body filler – resin and hardener – according to the instructions and mix together. The amount of hardener you use will alter the time the paste takes to set; warm weather speeds up the hardening too.

3 Scoop the paste into the dent and smooth over with the plastic spatula supplied. With deep dents (more than 10mm; 3/8in) it will be easier to fill a shallow layer, allow it to dry, then finish off with a second layer. The paste should be built up higher than the surrounding bodywork.

4 As soon as the filler gets hard (perhaps 10-30 minutes) sand it into shape with the orbital sander, taking great care not to damage surrounding paintwork. Final finishing off should be done by hand with the wet and dry paper, used wet. Wash the repair down with clean water and allow to dry.

5 Protecting the undamaged areas with newspaper and masking tape, spray a coat of primer paint over the repair according to the instructions on the can and allow to dry. Any blemishes still remaining can be filled with cellulose stopper (see Touching up paintwork).

6 Once you are satisfied with the finish, apply the top coat of paint. It will never be possible to get a perfect finish with either an aerosol or brush application, but it will be possible to make a big improvement for little cost. The key is not to apply too much paint at once – you can always put another coat on once the first has dried.

THINGS YOU NEED

- Body filler paste
- Sharp knife or screwdriver
- Orbital sander
- 400-grade wet-and-dry abrasive paper
- Rust preventer
- Clean, lint-free cloth
- Primer and top-coat paint

PROBLEMS WITH

STARTING

Starting problems are the most common reason for a 'breakdown'. The cause can usually be narrowed down to one of four common faults

The checklist gives a logical order for tracking down the problem. Further on is more detail on how to deal with each fault

Vehicle immobilisation and security systems will prevent engines from starting unless they are deactivated. Check the vehicle or immobiliser handbook for instructions on correct use.

1 **When you turn the key in the ignition, does the engine turn more slowly than usual?**

YES

You've probably got a flat battery, or possibly a poor connection at the battery.

SOLUTIONS

- Check the battery connections
- Recharge the battery – takes several hours
- Use jump leads to start from another car – instant short-term fix
- Get a push start – a last resort

2 **Does the engine refuse to turn over at all?**

YES

It may be a flat battery or a jammed starter motor

SOLUTIONS

- Check step 1 above
- Rock the car back and forth until the starter unjams

3 **If the engine still turns at usual speed, is the weather damp or has the engine been washed?**

YES

You may have a damp ignition system which won't fire correctly

SOLUTIONS

- Spray water repellent over the ignition system
- Take off the distributor cap and dry it out with a cloth

4 **Is the ignition system completely dry, and the starter turning over the engine happily?**

YES

The problem is almost certainly another ignition system or fuel system fault

SOLUTIONS

- Check that there is a spark at the spark plugs
- Check that there are signs of fuel getting through to the engine

CHECKING BATTERY CONNECTIONS

Battery connections tend to suffer from corrosion over a period of time, which makes it more difficult for the high electric current needed to start the car to pass through. A simple clean-up could cure your problems.

1 Remove any covers over the two battery terminals, then unscrew each terminal. Clean up all the surfaces which make contact with a wire brush, file or abrasive paper until you get something of a shine.

2 Liberally smear petroleum jelly over these surfaces. This helps prevent further corrosion without affecting the conductivity of the joint. Tighten the connections and replace the covers.

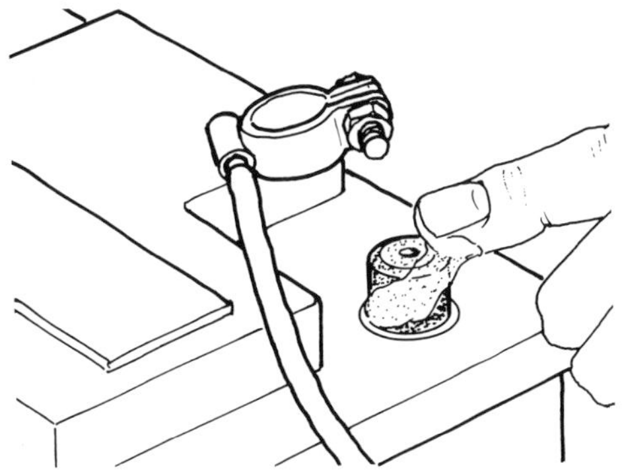

THINGS YOU NEED

- **Screwdriver**
- **Spanners**
- **Rag *or***
- **File *or***
- **Wire brush**
- **Coarse wet-and-dry abrasive paper**
- **Petroleum jelly**

RECHARGING THE BATTERY

1 Remove any covers over the two battery terminals before unscrewing them. In some cases you may find it more convenient to remove the battery from the car.

2 Some batteries have one, two or six removable covers. If these lift off readily, remove them while charging. Look into each cell – add *distilled* water to any where the fluid is not covering the plates.

3 Connect the crocodile clips from the charger to the battery terminals, making sure that positive is connected to positive, negative to negative (red to red and black to black).

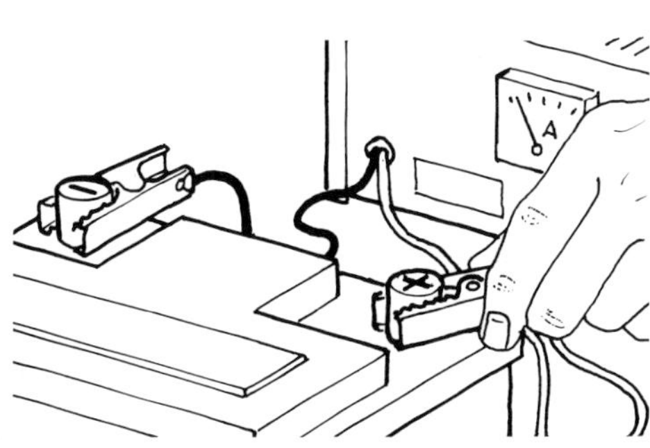

4 Plug the charger into the mains. Most have an instrument on the front which indicates that the battery is charging – if the needle doesn't move, check out that the connections are sound. To recharge a common size of car battery from flat can take up to 12 hours, but even after two or three hours you may have enough power to start the car. Commercial 'booster' chargers used by garages can get you going in half an hour or so, though a slow charge after that will still be beneficial.

5 During charging the battery gives off an explosive gas, so it's particularly important to avoid any sparks by following the correct procedure. Always unplug at the mains before unclipping the crocodile clips at the battery. Finally reconnect the battery terminals. Always recharge a battery in a well ventilated place.

Unless your car has been standing unused for a month or more, a battery which repeatedly goes flat points to the need for an imminent replacement or to a fault in the charging system

THINGS YOU NEED

- **Battery charger**
- **Screwdriver**
- **Spanners**
- **Distilled water**

USING JUMP LEADS

If the only reason your car won't start is a flat battery, you'll get it going instantly by 'jump-starting' it from another car battery

THINGS YOU NEED

- **Pair of battery jump leads**
- **Another car with the healthy battery**

As long as you cover ten miles or more immediately after getting going, the alternator should recharge the battery enough to ensure the car starts next time.

1 Park the car with the healthy battery next to the stranded one, close enough for the jump leads to reach from battery to battery, but not so the cars are touching.

2 The sequence in which you connect the leads is very important: if you get it wrong there will be a great flash of light as you make the final connection, possibly causing the battery to explode and probably damaging the electrical system. Neither engine should be running at this stage.

3 First, connect positive terminals on the two batteries using the red jump lead. Next, attach the black jump lead to the negative terminal on the healthy battery. Finally, connect the other end of the black jump lead to a suitable earthing point on the car with the flat battery. This earth point should be as far away as possible from the flat battery, and will most likely need to be the engine block or a screw connection into the engine. Ensure that no lead can foul on rotating parts under the bonnet.

4 Run the engine of the car with the healthy battery at a moderately high speed. Start the engine of the vehicle with the flat battery and let both cars run for a couple of minutes before disconnecting the leads.

5 Remove the jump leads in reverse sequence.

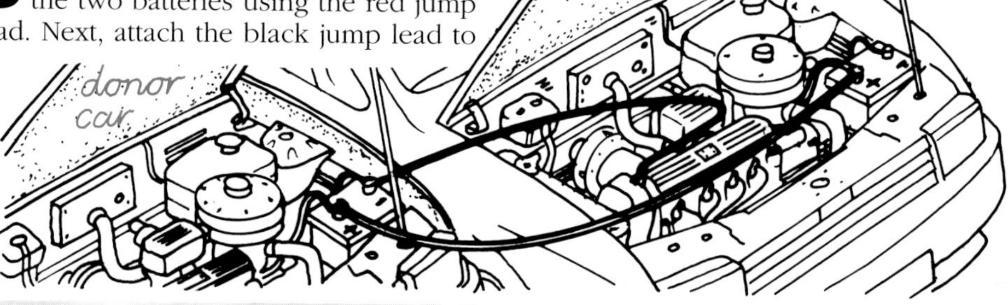

PUSH-STARTING

As a last, somewhat desperate, resort, push-starting will often get a car with a flat battery going

The disadvantage of a push-start is that if it doesn't work you might end up having to abandon the car in a less convenient place than you started from. You cannot push-start a car with an automatic gearbox. Nor should you push-start a car with a catalytic converter (all new cars since 1991 and some earlier – see car handbook) as the catalyst could be irreparably damaged.

1 Position the car, ideally facing down an incline or on level ground.

2 The driver should sit at the wheel, belted up, ignition switch on, choke out (if there is one and the engine is cold), clutch pedal pushed down and lever in second gear. The pushers should get the car moving along at a brisk walking pace (release the handbrake!) and the driver should then lift his or her foot off the clutch pedal quite sharply. If the engine starts, keep it revving while at the same time immediately depressing the clutch again. Brake to a halt, and put on the handbrake.

3 If you fail the first time, give it a couple more tries. Once the engine is running, don't stall it until you have driven a few miles, by which time a bit of life will have been put back into the battery.

JAMMED STARTER MOTOR

1 To be sure your problem is a jammed starter try the following test. First check that the headlights come on with their normal brightness. If they don't, you have a flat battery. If they are of normal brightness, switch them off and turn the ignition key. If the engine turns over, albeit very slowly, the starter isn't jammed – the battery needs recharging. But if you just hear a click when you turn the starter, the motor is almost certainly jammed.

2 To free it the car should be on more-or-less level ground. With the ignition switched off, move the lever into third gear and release the handbrake. Get out of the car, grab hold of the pillar behind the driver's door, and rock the car backwards and forwards a few times. When you hear a loud 'clunk' the starter has unjammed. This method will work in all but the most severe cases.

Occasionally the starter motor jams, which gives similar symptoms to a flat battery. Again this fix doesn't work on cars with automatic transmissions

DAMP ENGINE

1 Water-repellent sprays, available from all car accessory shops, are a very quick and effective way of dealing with all but the worst excesses of moisture. Just point the aerosol at the major components in the ignition system – coil, distributor and HT leads – and spray liberally. With luck the water should be driven off and the engine will start.

2 In more severe cases you may need to dry out the system with a cloth. At the same time, lift the distributor cap. Wipe around the inside with a clean dry cloth to remove all traces of moisture. Replace the cap – you'll find notches on the cap which ensure that it will fit in only one position.

Moisture can totally upset the ignition system in your car – older cars are the most prone. Luckily there is a quick easy solution which seems to work most of the time

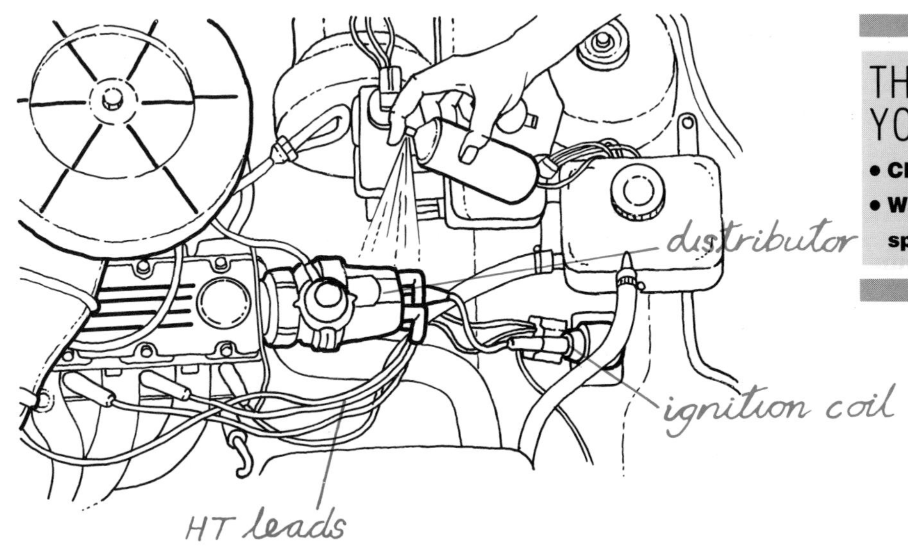

THINGS YOU NEED

- **Clean, dry cloth**
- **Water-repellent spray**

IGNITION SYSTEM

Unless you get a spark at the spark plugs, you're never going to get the engine running

THINGS YOU NEED

- **A helping hand**
- **Spark plug spanner**

Dealing with the root cause of an ignition problem is outside the scope of this book, but you can at least check whether this is where the problems lies.

1 First, check the vehicle's fuses (see page 185).

2 Remove one of the spark plugs (see page 199). Once removed, fit the lead back on to the plug.

3 Get your helper to sit in the car. Wedge or rest the spark plug so that the metal end is touching a major unpainted metal part of the engine. The helper should (with the gear lever in neutral) try to start the engine. Do not touch either the metal part of the spark plug or the lead as there is a risk of electric shock while the engine is running.

4 If the ignition system is reasonably healthy, a spark will be seen between the spark plug electrodes. If there is no spark there is likely to be a fault within the ignition system.

FUEL SYSTEM

Problems with the fuel system on an engine can be pretty complicated, but you can at least check whether fuel is getting through to the engine

THINGS YOU NEED

- **Spark plug spanner**

1 First, and most obviously, check your fuel gauge to make sure you haven't run out of petrol. Also check the vehicle's fuses (see page 185).

2 Remove one of the spark plugs using the spark plug spanner (see page 199).

3 If the end of the plug appears damp, and you can smell petrol from the plug hole, you know at the very least that fuel is getting through to the engine.

4 If that is the case, the problem could be that you have 'flooded' the engine – by pulling the choke out too far, or by pumping the accelerator pedal. This means that so much fuel has got into the engine that the spark cannot ignite it. After replacing the plug and reconnecting the lead, try to start it once more with the choke (if one is fitted) pushed right in and the accelerator pushed, and kept, on the floor until the engine splutters into life. If this final attempt fails, you are probably going to need the assistance of an experienced mechanic.

FIXING YOUR

EXHAUST

Excessive noise from an exhaust pipe demands immediate attention. Exhaust fumes can kill if they get into the car

SIMPLE REPAIRS

1 Park the car on level ground and position the ramps up against the rear wheels. With great care, and the guidance of an assistant, reverse the car up to the top of the ramp. Stop the engine, pull the handbrake firmly on, and then get out and place the chocks both in front of and behind the front wheels. Alternatively, axle stands can be used to support the car. Never rely on a vehicle jack alone to support a car while attempting to work underneath it.

2 Start the engine again and then crawl under the car to find the location of the leak in the exhaust. It could be that the noise is coming from a joint between two sections. If that is the case, you might cure the problem merely by tightening the clamp a bit further – stop the engine first.

3 For leaking joints which can't be cured like this, and for very minor holes elsewhere, apply an exhaust repair paste. First remove loose rust with a wire brush (wear safety goggles). Then smear the paste over the affected area and work in well. The paste may take a while to harden, but will cure much more quickly if you apply it to a warm exhaust pipe and then run the engine at idle for five minutes.

4 To fix larger holes, though never more than temporarily, use an exhaust repair kit. First, clean around the hole with a wire brush and tidy the edges of the hole. Warm the exhaust for a couple of minutes and turn off the engine. Wrap the metal foil supplied with the kit around the hole and then wrap with the repair bandage. Finally make the repair secure by tying with the wire provided. Run the engine gently to cure the exhaust repair bandage.

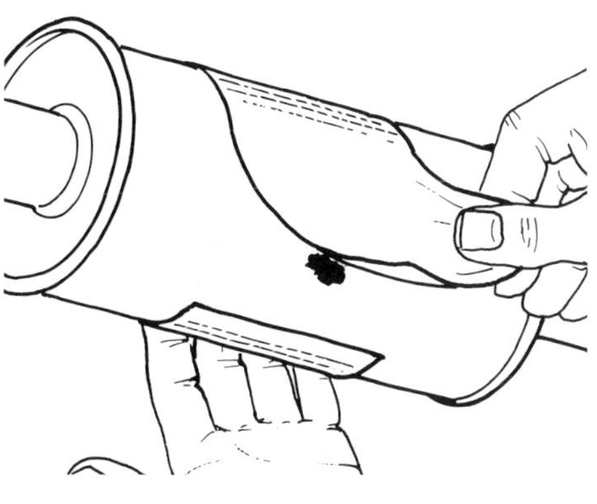

Wrap foil around a larger hole

In the long run it's rare that a simple repair will prove effective, but they are cheap and relatively easy to do

THINGS YOU NEED

- **Exhaust repair paste**
- **Exhaust repair kit**
- **Ramps or axle stands**
- **Wooden or brick chocks**
- **Wire brush**
- **Open-ended spanners**
- **Pliers**
- **Safety goggles**

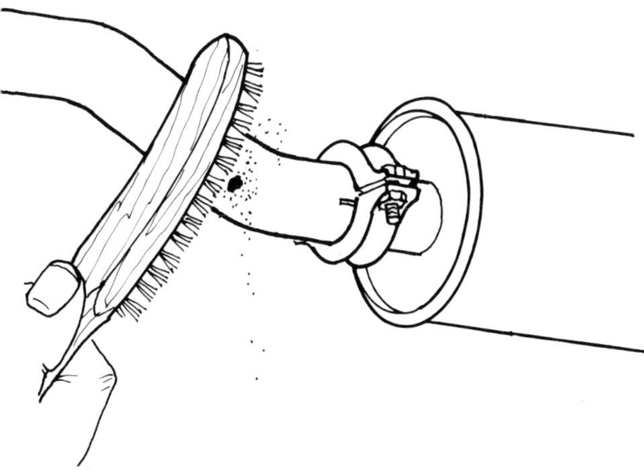

Remove loose rust before applying paste

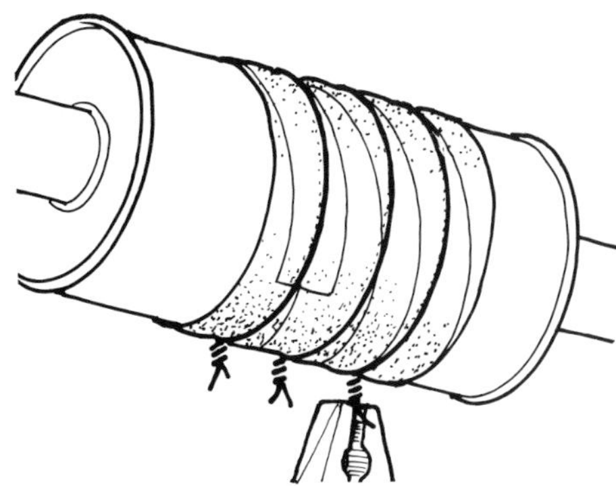

Bandage the foil and secure it with wire

FIXING YOUR

FAN BELT

A broken fan belt (or auxiliary drive belt) is thankfully less common these days. Failure means a loss of engine cooling and no power to charge the battery

CHECKING AND REPLACING

Although the car won't stop immediately, rapid attention is called for

THINGS YOU NEED

- **Replacement drive belt**
- **Open-ended spanners**
- **Lever**

1 The fan belt (or auxiliary drive belt) is situated at the front of the engine, just behind the radiator, or at the side. It runs around several pulleys and should be tight enough so that there is about half an inch (12mm) of waggle either way on the longest run. An over-tight belt can damage bearings in the alternator. The exact tension is dependent on the make and model of car; check with a garage for the correct tension.

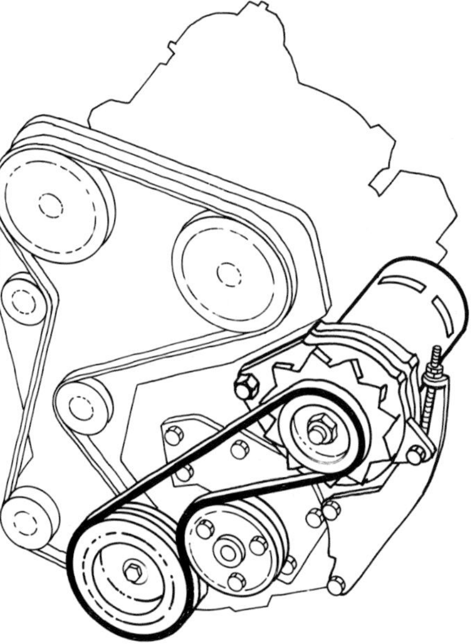

2 If the belt is missing – there's often a sudden noise from under the bonnet when a belt breaks – you'll need to effect a cure as soon as possible. Though a pair of tights has long been held as the ideal solution, their durability is suspect.

3 The alternator, which sends power to charge the battery, is usually hinged to allow for fitting the fan belt and adjusting the tension. Loosen all the securing nuts and/or adjuster if fitted, and swing the alternator towards the engine. Loop the belt over all the pulleys. Never use a sharp instrument to lever the belt on – instead rotate one of the pulleys to help wind it on.

4 Half-tighten the securing screws and nuts, and if necessary lever the alternator gently away from the engine until the belt is tensioned as described in step 3. Alternatively, if an adjuster is fitted, adjust the tension to the desired level. Retighten all the securing screws and nuts and recheck the tension.

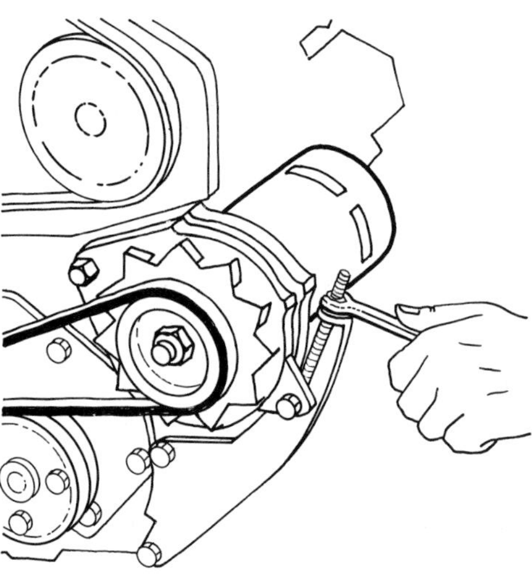

5 Occasional checking of the fan-belt tension is a sensible precaution; a high-pitched squealing is a common sign that it is loose. If necessary, tighten it using the above procedure.

LONG-TERM

MAINTENANCE

Some of the jobs a garage carries out in a service can be done easily at home for far less money

SPARK PLUGS

1 Mark each of the spark plug leads with tape so that you know which way they go when reconnecting.

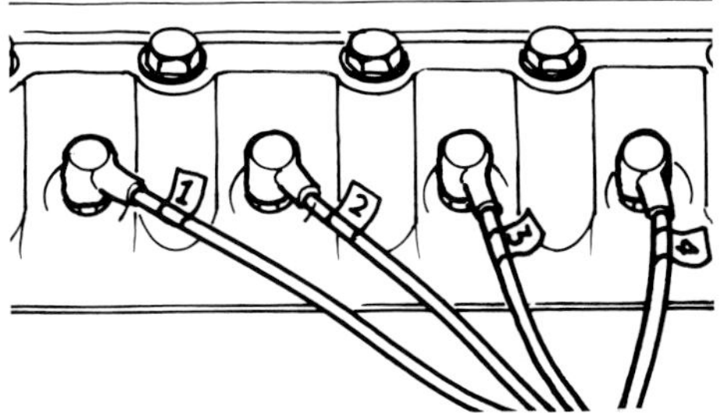

2 Remove the lead from each plug by gripping the connector as close to the plug as possible and pulling upwards. Don't pull on the lead itself as this may separate the lead from the connector. Using a special spark plug spanner, unscrew each plug from the cylinder head. Take care: if you don't keep the spanner square on the plug you may break the plug's ceramic top.

3 Whether you intend to clean up these spark plugs or fit new ones, they'll have to be 'gapped'. This is adjusting the distance between the side electrode and centre electrode (new plugs are usually pre-gapped to the most common setting, but it's worth checking them). Find out the correct gap from your handbook or manual or by checking with your dealer. Check this with the feeler gauge. If the gap is incorrect, adjust it by bending the side electrode with the spark plug gapping tool, then re-check.

4 Before replacing the spark plugs, make sure that the area around the location in the cylinder head is clean and free from dirt. If there is dirt, carefully clean the area around the hole where the plug goes, if this is possible. If not, be careful that none of the dirt falls down into the hole.

5 Put a touch of oil on the thread of each spark plug then screw it gently into its location until you feel resistance.

6 On spark plugs with flat seats and a gasket, give the plug another quarter to half turn to seal the joint. On plugs with a tapered seat, merely nip the plug down to seal – by just $\frac{1}{16}$ of a turn.

Spark plugs are pretty reliable so attention will usually be confined to changing them at the intervals noted in the handbook

THINGS YOU NEED

- **Spark plug spanner**
- **Feeler gauge**
- **Spark plug gapping tool**
- **Spark plugs**

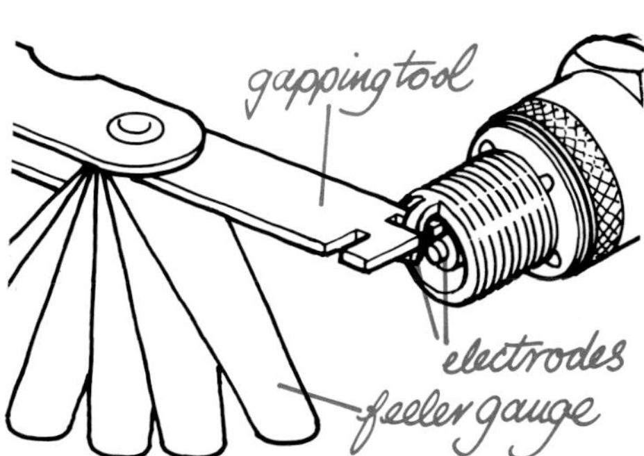

A feeler gauge has 'fingers' of different widths for checking the gap

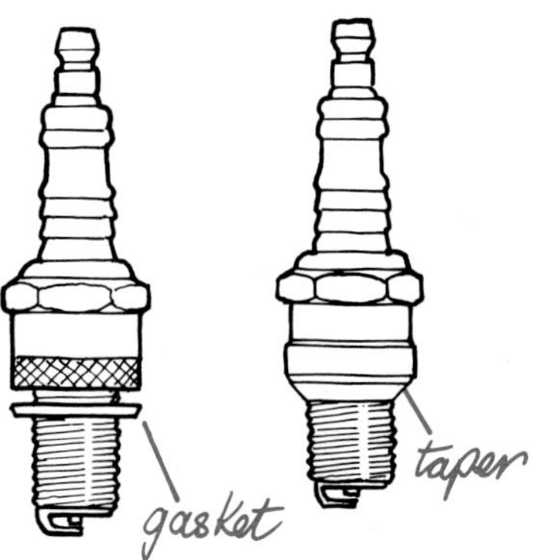

7 Reconnect all the spark plug leads in the correct order, pushing each one down until it clicks into place.

OIL CHANGE

Don't economise on the regularity of the oil changes: an oil change doesn't cost a great deal, and it will help maximise the life of your engine

THINGS YOU NEED

- **Can of fresh engine oil (see page 176 for choosing an oil)**
- **Oil filter cartridge**
- **Sump-plug sealing ring**
- **Lint-free rags**
- **Screwdriver**
- **Ring spanners**
- **Sump-oil drainer can**
- **Oil-filter wrench**

1 Park the car on level ground and apply the handbrake. Warm up the engine so that all the particles and deposits it contains are suspended in the oil and can be flushed away.

2 Undo the oil filler cap on the top of the engine. Clean around the sump drain plug with a rag. Put the sump-oil drainer can ready underneath it, and start to loosen it cautiously. Making sure the drain can is in place as the nut comes free, withdraw the nut and allow the warm oil to drain into the can – this takes two or three minutes.

3 Clean up the sump plug with a rag and replace the sealing ring. Once the oil has finished draining from the sump, clean up around the face of the plug hole with a rag and then reinsert and tighten the plug.

4 Now replace the oil filter – see right.

5 Now refill the engine with oil, taking great care not to overfill past the maximum mark on the dipstick. Run the engine at idle for a few minutes, then check for any leaks. These can usually be cured by an extra twist on the filter cartridge. Check again after you have made your first journey.

6 Dispose of used engine oil at approved collection points, as found at local authority refuse disposal sites.

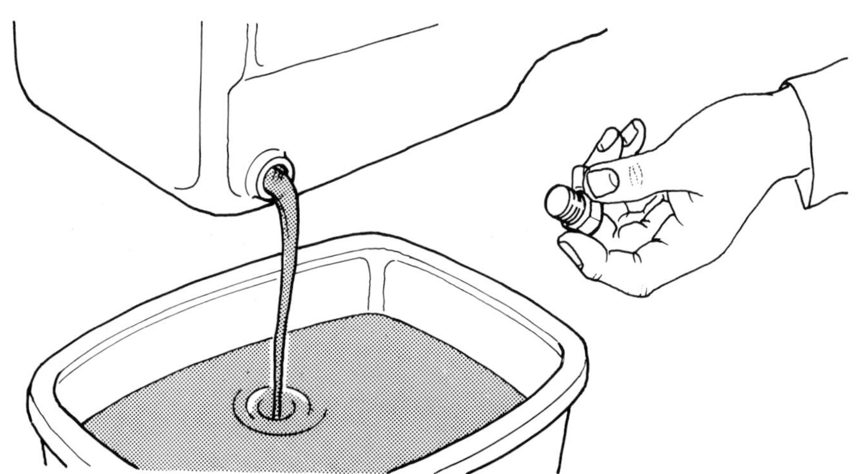

OIL FILTER

1 Modern cars have cartridge-type oil filters which just unscrew. If the filter is too tight to shift you can buy special tools to give you more leverage. Alternatively, you can drive an old screwdriver through the cartridge to act as a lever. Be sure to have your drain can underneath to catch the oil spills.

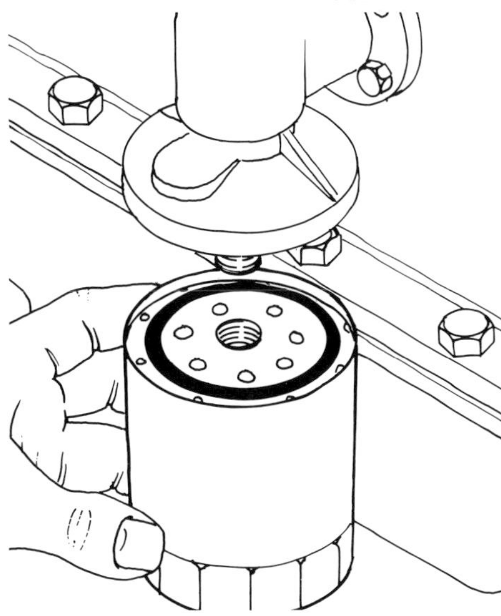

2 Clean the face of the plate to which the cartridge fits with a rag. Take the new cartridge, smear some clean engine oil on the rubber sealing ring at the top, and screw it into place. Once you can feel the sealing ring pressing against the sealing face, turn it no further than half to three-quarters of a turn more.

AIR FILTER

1 Locate the air filter box – usually made of black plastic and found either on the top or at the side of the engine, connected to it by ducting. Unclip the spring clips or screws holding the top on. If necessary, disconnect fixing screws and ducting carrying air to and from the filter box.

2 Remove the air filter element and carefully clean the inside of the box and lid. Fit the replacement element and refit the filter box lid, taking care not to dislodge the filter. Refit the clips and screws retaining the lid, and any ducting that was disconnected. Be careful not to drop anything such as screws into the engine while changing the element, as these could cause damage when the engine is started.

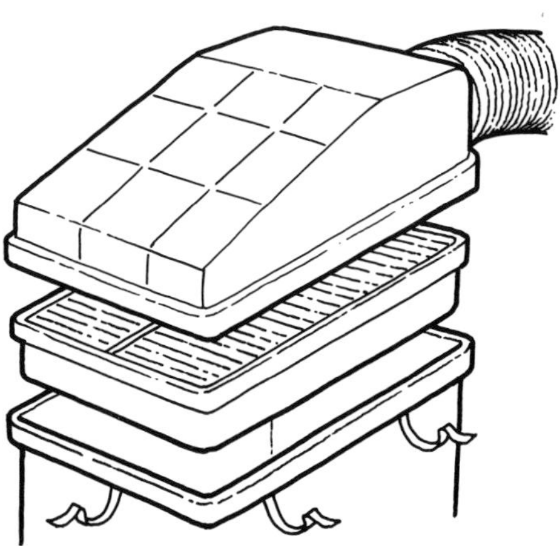

Replace the air filter element as recommended by the vehicle manufacturer. If it becomes clogged with dust or dirt this will affect engine performance and increase fuel consumption

THINGS YOU NEED

- **Air filter element**
- **Lint-free rags**
- **Screwdriver**

REFERENCE SECTION

USING

MANUALS & HANDBOOKS

If you are undertaking complex repair jobs, having access to a reference manual or handbook will make life a lot easier

When you buy a domestic appliance, a d-i-y or garden power tool, home entertainment equipment, a bike or even a car, you usually get some literature from the manufacturer (or from the UK distributor for imported items). This may range from a single sheet of paper telling you how to switch on an appliance to the glossy owner's handbook produced by most car manufacturers nowadays.

This literature may give you vital facts about product safety, general maintenance, availability of servicing, a checklist of spare parts and so on, but it is unlikely to include the sort of detailed technical information you may need to carry out your own repair work. For this you need either a specialist repair manual produced by an independent publisher (cars are very well served in this respect, and there are also d-i-y manuals available to help with a wide range of other repair jobs) or else the manufacturer's own service manual. While the former are freely available through bookshops, the latter can be very difficult for the general public to obtain.

With some types of equipment – hi-tech appliances such as televisions and video recorders, for example – this is quite understandable. Manufacturers either want to protect the interests of their own repair agencies or, more justifiably, want to prevent unqualified people from attempting repair work beyond their capabilities and perhaps making the item concerned unsafe to use as a result.

The best advice is to write to the manufacturer or distributor concerned and ask whether manuals or other technical literature are available; they can only say yes or no. To back up your case, there are two points worth mentioning in your letter. The first is whether what you want to repair is out of guarantee; if it is, the manufacturer may be less reluctant to part with a service manual for it. The second is to stress any particular talents you have that make you more suitable than the average person to tackle the repair – a relevant qualification or experience of similar work.

If this approach fails, it is worth looking for advertisements in general or specialist trade and hobbyist magazines offering manuals and other technical literature. Alternatively, approach local repair firms, who may be prepared to loan you their own copies of technical literature in return for your custom in buying spare parts through them.

WARNING

Even if you are able to obtain the manuals or guides you need, do not attempt any repairs unless you are confident that you know how to carry them out properly, that you have the necessary tools and equipment, and above all that whatever you repair will be completely safe for you and others to use afterwards. Remember that professional repairers do not take kindly to having to undo d-i-y bodges before they can tackle the original fault.

GETTING HOLD OF

SPARE PARTS

Spare parts are essential for many repair jobs. For some goods you have a choice, for others you need persistence and patience

It has always been easy to buy whatever you need for many household repair jobs, and car spares are also widely available, but the story has until recently been very different for domestic appliances and d-i-y or garden power tools.

APPLIANCE REPAIRS

Manufacturers and distributors – especially those without a chain of authorised local dealerships – have at last accepted the need to make spare parts available, both to the individual and to the growing number of independent appliance repair firms.

The result has been a welcome growth in the availability of spare parts, both through local 'spares and repairs' dealers and also via mail-order companies. Parts may be 'genuine' – in other words, supplied by the manufacturer direct or through an authorised agent, perhaps via an approved manufacturing sub-contractor – or 'patterned'. This latter term means that the parts are copies of genuine parts, perhaps supplied by the original component maker to the wholesale-retail chain. They are often marked 'suitable for...' or 'to fit...' and are generally considerably cheaper than the equivalent genuine parts. They are also often easier to obtain quickly, especially if 'genuine' parts have to be ordered from the manufacturer rather than through a local parts stockist.

When ordering spare parts for appliances, it is vital to have details of the make, model and serial number of the appliance concerned. Note the part number too if you were given a parts list when you bought the appliance. If you cannot find a local supplier, many manufacturers have a telephone number listed in phone directories for ordering spare parts.

If you can find a local supplier, it is wise to take the failed part with you so you can compare it with the replacement you are offered and make sure that it is identical in type, size, configuration, rating and performance. If it looks slightly different, it may still be suitable for the job, but double-check with the supplier.

OBSOLETE PARTS

Spare parts may no longer be available for older appliances. The Association of Manufacturers of Domestic and Electrical Appliances (AMDEA) has guidelines for its members on how long they should keep spares.

For small appliances, such as toasters and kettles, functional parts should be kept for five to eight years. For bigger appliances, such as fridges and washing machines, functional parts should be kept for eight to ten years. Parts like pieces of trim, which do not affect the appliance's operation, should be kept for a minimum of four years.

PARTS FOR OTHER JOBS

Equipment for household d-i-y tasks, plumbing and wiring can be found in large d-i-y stores or local hardware stores. A range of electronic parts is available in high-street hobby stores, but many more components can be purchased mail-order. Suppliers for car parts are easily found and you will rarely need to go to a dealership garage. A good bicycle shop should have anything you need in stock – buy parts of a standard and price to match your bike.

INDEX

INDEX

INDEX